Black Employment and the Law

Black Employment and the Law

ALFRED W. BLUMROSEN

RUTGERS UNIVERSITY PRESS

NEW BRUNSWICK, NEW JERSEY

Permission to reprint the following material is gratefully acknowledged:

George Washington Law Review: *Administrative Creativity: The First Year of the Equal Employment Opportunity Commission*, 38 GEO. WASH. L. REV. 695 (1970)

American Arbitration Association: *Labor Arbitration, EEOC Conciliation, and Discrimination in Employment*, 24 ARB. J. 88 (1969)

Rutgers Law Review: *Seniority and Equal Employment Opportunity: A Glimmer of Hope*, 23 RUTGERS L. REV. 268 (1969); *The Duty of Fair Recruitment under the Civil Rights Act of 1694*, 22 RUTGERS L. REV. 465 (1968)

University of Illinois Law Forum: *The Newport News Agreement: One Brief Shining Moment in the Enforcement of Equal Employment Opportunity*, U. ILL. L. F. 269 (1968)

Industrial Relations Research Association: *A Survey of Remedies for Discrimination in the Union and on the Job*, PROC. 21ST ANNUAL WINTER MEETING, 283 (1968)

This book is for Ruth, Steve, and Alex,
For Mr. Marion Reynolds of Birmingham, Alabama,
And for all men and women who seek justice in the work-
place.

Preface

The issue to which these essays are addressed is whether we can rid our society of patterns of racial discrimination in employment. Because our laws about discrimination were unenforced for a quarter century, the courts were not required to distinguish proper from illegal conduct and are only now beginning to do so. A substantial part of this book is, therefore, devoted to defining illegal discrimination in recruitment, hiring, promotions, and in the construction industry.

This question of definition is of fundamental social importance. If discrimination is narrowly defined, for example, by requiring an evil intent to injure minorities, then it will be difficult to find that it exists. If it does not exist, then the plight of racial and ethnic minorities must be attributable to some more generalized failures in society, in the fields of basic education, housing, family relations, and the like. The search for efforts to improve the condition of minorities must then focus in these general and difficult areas, and the answers can come only gradually as basic institutions, attitudes, customs, and practices are changed. We thus would have before us generations of time before the effects of subjugation of minorities are dissipated.

But if discrimination is broadly defined, as, for example, by including all conduct which adversely affects minority group employment opportunities—and this is the basic thrust of these essays—then the prospects for rapid improvement in minority employment opportunities are greatly increased. Industrial relations systems are flexible; they are in the control of defined individuals and institutions; they can be altered either by negotiation or by law. If discrimination exists within these institutions, the solution lies within our immediate grasp. It is not embedded in the complications of fundamental sociology but can be sharply influenced by intelligent, effective, and aggressive legal action.

This is the optimistic view of the racial problem in our nation. This view finds discrimination at every turn where minorities are adversely affected by institutional decisions, which are subject to legal regulation. In this view, we are in control of our own history. The destruction of our society over the race question is not inevitable.

This optimistic view has some support in the history of our efforts to civilize the workplace. Half a century ago the workplace was a dictatorship of the boss and the foreman. Contracts of employment were "at will," said the law, which meant at the will of the employer. Wages were the least that the employer could get by with paying, working conditions were those which were cheapest for him, hours were without limit.

All of this has changed. The employer has surrendered his ultimate power over the workplace without a revolution. Today, under collective contracts, men are not fired without "just cause." Wages are set with reference to the maximum influence that workers can bring to bear on the market, not the minimum influence. Even in areas which a few years ago were sacrosanct—professional workers, public employees, and agricultural workers—the winds of change are bringing unionization. We may bemoan the loss of idealism in the labor movement, but we need not belittle these accomplishments. The tyranny of the boss is less and different today, and, to that extent, the worker has achieved a greater measure of his manhood.

In winning this measure of dignity through collective bargaining, the worker has found himself confronted on occasion, not only by the boss, but by his union as well; and the question of the extent to which his new-found dignity must also be recognized by his union is unsettled.

The struggle over this question has been waged largely in the courts and the law reviews, and I have not burdened this book with an examination of the problem.* Yet at the heart of the concern over the problems of race discrimination in employment lies the question of individual rights in the employment relationship.

---

* The reader may wish to examine my article, *The Worker and Three Phases of Unionism: Administration and Judicial Control of the Worker-Union Relationship*, 61 Mich. L. Rev. 1435, 1963; and Vaca v. Sipes, 386, U.S. 171 (1967).

I believe that the problems of race discrimination in America are solvable! We need not make a lifework of ending discrimination and bringing civilization to this phase of American life. In two years we could break the back of racial discrimination in employment in this country. We have civilization within our grasp; but we have not reached for it in any systematic way.

Our system of industrial relations is more resilient and flexible than we tend to recognize. Those who suggest that a given industrial relations system would collapse instantly if it were tampered with are wrong. And yet it is hard to forge an effective institution, be it a union, a corporation, a government agency, or a university; and the guardians of such institutions must, of necessity, scrutinize proposals for change carefully. For the world beyond the institution is merciless and tough, and a false move can destroy the work of many. This fact creates conservatives.

Another aspect of these essays concerns the administrative process. Most antidiscrimination agencies are ineffective most of the time despite the efforts of men who struggle to make them function on behalf of the people. The pressures in the administrative process to soften the efforts of good men are powerful. Men who refuse to bow to these pressures are sometimes fired or their power destroyed. And so most men bow a little, hoping to salvage their strength for tomorrow's fight. Thus many government men focus on the internal struggles within the bureaucracy because they dare not face the fact that their administration has failed to change the world, failed to accomplish their statutory or presidential purpose. Effective administration is indispensable in this area, for the case-by-use approach will simply not reach the ramifications of the problem. While recognizing how indispensable effective administration is, I nevertheless conclude that the individual right to sue to eliminate employment discrimination in federal court is indispensable if we are to solve our problems. The availability of an individual suit not subject to administrative or political control gives the only reasonable likelihood of the vindication of the dignity of man in the workplace.

At some time toward the end of a proceeding to end employment discrimination, whether before a court or an agency, comes the question of remedy. The development of an effective remedy is the objective of the entire effort, and it is often the point of failure. My primary task with the EEOC between 1965 and 1967 was to shape practical, work-able, and effective remedies to end employment discrimination. Several of these essays discuss remedies for various kinds of discrimination, and the Newport News chapter discusses a whole package of remedies. My experience in negotiating remedies for discrimination reinforces the conviction that we can solve the problem of employment discrimi-nation.

There is an immediacy about most ordinary legal remedies. Once legal rights are declared, the remedy attaches at once. The insurance company held liable in a negligence suit does not have "all deliberate speed" to come up with the cash to pay the widow. The prompt recog-nition of rights is a hallmark of their existence. If there is a credibility gap or other manifestation of distrust of the formal institutions of our society, it is in part due to our failure to recognize and implement this concept of the immediate effectuation of rights.

These essays call for the imposition of "law and order" in the field of employment discrimination. As Tocqueville noted a century ago, we do use law more than most societies to solve our basic social problems. The challenge to legal institutions posed by the need to ameliorate the effects of discrimination becomes more pressing with the passage of time. The leisurely pace we have adopted up to now is no longer suffi-cient to prevent a crisis of confidence in governmental process which could shatter the fundamental assumptions on which we have con-structed our lives and institutions. Prompt and effective changes in the economic conditions of the lives of our minority citizens are essential to the preservation of our basic social system. These essays suggest that such changes may be achieved through practical and tough-minded implementation of existing laws.

Chapter 3 is an official report of the Equal Employment Opportunity Commission, prepared under the supervision of Mr. Charles Markham, then Director of Research for EEOC. It contains the first carefully reasoned analysis of the implications of the racial and ethnic distribu-tion of the work force. This analysis demolishes the popular idea that education and training will solve the problems of minority employment, and thus makes clear the necessity for effective law enforcement pro-grams to end discrimination.

Most of the other chapters have appeared in legal journals in slightly different form. I have included some supporting material which had developed by the fall of 1969 and an occasional reference to developments in early 1970. The area is changing too rapidly to identify a single date against which to measure the material.

Most of the thinking and writing was done between 1967 and 1969 with the help of my wife Ruth, whose experience in litigation under equal housing laws and administration of equal employment laws has contributed immeasurably to my understanding of this field.

Contents

Part I

THE STRUCTURE AND FUNCTION

OF FEDERAL EQUAL EMPLOYMENT

OPPORTUNITY LAWS

1 Equal Employment Opportunity Through Law, Administration, and Negotiation

The persistence of racial and ethnic discrimination in employment is the central fact of American urban life in our time. The social tension, atrocious housing, and inadequate schools which are characteristic of the cities are intimately related to this discrimination. The civil unrest generated by these conditions threatens a vast network of human values and challenges the assumption that social change can be carried out under law. At the very moment when our affluent society appeared to be assimilating the proletariat, racial conflict revived and sharpened class distinction. The key to this conflict is the fact that black unemployment rates have been at least double those of whites for the last quarter century.[1] During this period, massive state and federal efforts to enforce laws against racial discrimination in employment have been undertaken.[2] These efforts have failed. The expectations of fair treatment which they generated have not been realized. The laws have neither been enforced nor obeyed. Thus the violence in the streets embraces the ancient demand that the laws be faithfully executed.

The distortions in our social system which are traceable to and reflected by employment discrimination are not inevitable. The problems are not so difficult as to defy solution. The existing legal structure, cen-

---

[1] See Report of the National Advisory Commission on Civil Disorders (1968), ch. 6, Appendix I (E). Extracts from this report and other official documents describing either the historic or current condition of Negro employment in the United States appear as appendixes to ch. 6 *infra*.

[2] See SOVERN, LEGAL RESTRAINTS ON RACIAL DISCRIMINATION IN EMPLOYMENT [hereafter cited as Sovern] (1966); Hill, *Twenty Years of State Fair Employment Practice Commissions: A Critical Analysis with Recommendations*, 14 BUFFALO L. REV. 22 (1964); Bonefield, *The Origin and Development of American Fair Employment Legislation*, 52 IOWA L. REV. 1043 (1967); Blumrosen, *Antidiscrimination Laws in Action in New Jersey: A Law-Sociology Study*, 19 RUTGERS L. REV. 187 (1965); NATHAN, JOBS AND CIVIL RIGHTS (1969).

tering around Title VII of the Civil Rights Act of 1964,[3] if properly utilized, is capable of reducing employment discrimination. Title VII has made possible, for the first time in history, an effective working relationship between civil rights interests, labor, and management; between the courts and administrative agencies, and the network of lawyers and personnel officers involved in labor relations.

The crucial innovation in the 1964 Civil Rights Act was the enlargement of the role of the individual right to sue in the federal courts, rather than the enhancement of administrative agency powers. Victims of discrimination were given the right to sue in the federal courts if informal adminstrative efforts did not settle their claims.[4] The decision to prefer the courts over the administrative process was sensible, in light of the quarter century of failures by state and federal administrative agencies. This right to sue means that the civil rights interests can no longer be ignored or subordinated in low visibility decisions by administrative officials. The individual right to sue is frequently exercised as a group right, expressing the group interest in elimination of discrimination.[5] Under the statute as administered, the group interest of minorities is an equal with labor and management at the negotiating table and in the courtroom.

The decision to establish an individual right to sue rather than to expand the role of administrative agencies was a political compromise between "liberals" who wished to create an all-powerful administrative agency and "conservatives" who objected to the creation of such a bureaucracy.[6] The compromise, which the liberals considered a defeat, may have created the most effective possible arrangement for reducing employment discrimination. This arrangement places primary reliance on the federal courts, whose powers may be invoked either by individual suit or by the Attorney General.[7]

---

[3] Civil Rights Act of 1964, 78 Stat. 253, 42 U.S.C. 2000e (1964). Hereafter, citations will be to the sections of the official version only.

[4] See Title VII, Civil Rights Act of 1964, §706(a), (e), (g); §707.

[5] Blumrosen, *The Individual Rights to Eliminate Employment Discrimination by Litigation,* in INDUSTRIAL RELATIONS RESEARCH ASS'N, PROCEEDINGS OF THE 19TH ANNUAL WINTER MEETING 99 (1966).

[6] The history of the legislative compromises leading up to the passage of Title VII is well reported in Berg, *Equal Employment Opportunity under the Civil Rights Act of 1964,* 3 BROOKLYN L. REV. 62 (1964); BUREAU OF NATIONAL AFFAIRS OPERATIONS MANUAL, THE CIVIL RIGHTS ACT OF 1964, ch. 3 (1964); *Jenkins v. United Gas Corp.,* 400 F2d 28 (5th Cir. 1968).

[7] The individual may sue after invoking the processes of the EEOC under

At the same time, the judicial process has its inherent limitations. Courts do not engage in general regulatory activity. Congress recognized this by creating and maintaining administrative agencies with sufficient powers to complement the judicial process. These administrative agencies include the Equal Employment Opportunity Commission (EEOC), the Office of Federal Contract Compliance (OFCC), and various state and local agencies. They can investigate and conciliate. Some can hold hearings and issue orders enforceable in courts.[8] Thus they can dispose of those matters which can be settled without the necessity of suit. They can initiate proceeding without individual complaint, and thus strike at patterns of discrimination which would not be reached through *any* complaint process. And the Attorney General may sue to remedy discriminatory practices without awaiting individual complaints. The agencies can conduct general regulatory activity through research, public relations, advice, rule making, reporting requirements, and periodic inspections. All of these functions lie beyond the capacity of the judiciary.

With administrative agencies performing these functions, the judicial process is competent to define and enforce the antidiscrimination obligation. In the matters which have thus far come before the courts under Title VII, the judges have demonstrated a willingness to implement the statute which is more impressive than the record of the "powerful" administrative agencies in this field.

Many of the proponents of civil rights legislation consider the present legal structure inadequate. They desire a "powerful" administrative agency, modeled after state agencies and the National Labor Relations Board (NLRB).[9] This agency could investigate, hold hearings

---

§706(a) and (e). The Attorney General may sue under §707 whenever he has reasonable cause to believe the conditions for suit under the section exist. The Attorney General suit is not conditioned upon prior exhaustion of administrative remedies before the EEOC.

[8] The EEOC may only investigate, decide that reasonable cause exists to believe there is discrimination and attempt to conciliate; §706(a), (e). The Office of Federal Contracts Compliance may, in addition, hold hearings looking to suspension or cancellation of government contracts, under Exec. Order No. 11246. Most state agencies may investigate, decide if cause exists, attempt to conciliate, hold hearings and issue orders; see Sovern, ch. 3.

[9] Liberal bills introduced in the years after the passage of Title VII took this form. See, for example, S. 2029, 91st Cong. 1st Sess. 1969, S. 1308, 90th Cong. 2d Sess., reported by the Senate Labor Committee on May 8, 1968. See S. REP. No. 1111, 90th Cong. 2d Sess. 1968. The "liberal" attitude toward such legislation was so strong that the first EEOC Chairman, Franklin D. Roosevelt, Jr., testified in sup-

and issue orders which would be enforceable in the courts. Their desire
for this regulatory agency reflects policy decisions made by civil rights
leaders a quarter century ago. At the end of World War II, administrative agencies called Fair Employment Practice Commissions were
introduced, first in New York and then elsewhere. These laws were
modeled after the NLRB, which was the show piece of New Deal
regulatory administration. Impetus for the spread of these laws was
given by the 1947 report of the Truman Civil Rights Committee.[10]

This post-World War II ideal of an effective administrative agency
vigorously enforcing the laws persists in the minds of many. This vision
has not been informed—or at least not changed—by the dismal history
of these agencies. The history is one of timidity in investigation, vacilla-
tion in decisionmaking, and soft settlements which failed to aid the
victims of discrimination and did not remedy the broader social problems.[11] These failures are highlighted by two crucial facts: A quarter

---

port of this legislation during the summer of 1965 before the EEOC had begun to
function, and before there could possibly be experience under the statute.

[10] PRESIDENT'S COMMITTEE ON CIVIL RIGHTS, TO SECURE THESE RIGHTS (1947),
pp. 166–67:

> V. To strengthen the right to equality of opportunity, the President's Committee
> recommends: . . . . 2. For Employment:
>> The enactment of a federal Fair Employment Practice Act prohibiting all
>> forms of discrimination in private employment, based on race, color, creed,
>> or national origin.
> A federal Fair Employment Practice Act prohibiting discrimination in private
> employment should provide both educational machinery and legal sanctions for
> enforcement purposes. The administration of the act should be placed in the
> hands of a commission with power to receive complaints, hold hearings, issue
> cease-and-desist orders and seek court aid in enforcing these orders. The Act
> should contain definite fines for violation of its procedural provisions. In order
> to allow time for voluntary adjustment or employment practices to the new
> law, and to permit the establishment of effective enforcement machinery, it is
> recommended that the sanction provisions of the law not become operative
> until one year after the enactment of the law.
>> The federal act should apply to labor unions and trade and professional
> associations, as well as to employers, insofar as the policies and practices of
> these organizations affect the employment status of workers.

It is perhaps ironic that when Congress acted in 1964 to adopt a fair employment law, it adopted the recommendation of 1947 for the one year moratorium on
enforcement. See §716(a).

[11] Documentation of these failures is becoming more common as scholars manage to get inside the administrative process of the state agencies. The results of
my initial examination of state agency processes in this field, conducted as consultant to the New Jersey Civil Rights Commission, are reported in Blumrosen,
Antidiscrimination Laws in Action in New Jersey: A Law-Sociology Study, 19
RUTGERS L. REV. 187 (1965). Two years later, Professor Arthur Frakt, who had

century of administrative effort has failed to produce a body of law which defines discrimination and has failed to alter the basic social fact of 1940, 1947, 1964, and 1967: that minority unemployment rates were —and are—double those of the white majority.[12] The pure administrative process has proved incapable of coping with employment discrimination. The search for the ideal form of governmental action in this area should not blind us to these conclusions.

The modern judicial process is, under today's conditions, adequate to the task of law enforcement in this area. The principle of comprehensive construction of social legislation is well established, particularly in the area of employment relations. The availability of declaratory judgments and class actions permits judicial resolution of problems involving many individuals. Judicial remedies are sufficiently flexible to cope with complex problems arising out of discriminatory recruitment and seniority systems.[13] The judicial predilection for settlement is supported by administrative conciliation efforts, which include a staff with technical skill at proposing and negotiating solutions acceptable to all parties. The administrators may assist the court in efforts to obtain set-

---

participated in my study, conducted his own, and found that the situation had not substantially improved; Frakt, *Administrative Enforcement of Equal Opportunity Legislation in New Jersey*, 21 RUTGERS L. REV. 442 (1967).

Studies of other agencies have tended to reveal the same type of shortcomings as described in Sovern, ch. 3.

[12] See, *e.g.*, PRESIDENT'S COMMITTEE ON CIVIL RIGHTS, TO SECURE THESE RIGHTS, 53 (1947); H. REP. No. 914, pt. 2, 88th Cong. 1st Sess. (1963); S. REP. No. 867, 88th Cong, 2d Sess. 6–8 (1964); U.S. BUREAU OF LABOR STATISTICS, DEP'T OF LABOR, REP'T No. 332, SOCIAL AND ECONOMIC CONDITIONS OF NEGROES IN THE UNITED STATES at 29–42 (1967); REPORT OF THE NATIONAL ADVISORY COMMISSION ON CIVIL DISORDERS, ch. 7 (1968); S. REP. No. 1111, 90th Cong., 2d Sess. (1968). Relevant excerpts from each of the above are quoted in the appendixes to ch. 6, *infra*.

[13] See, for example, Vaca v. Sipes, 386 U.S. 171 (1967) for a discussion of the flexibility available in shaping remedies in labor relations matters. In connection with remedies for discrimination in employment, see the orders issued in Quarles v. Philip Morris, 279 F. Supp. 505 (D.C. Va. 1968), United States v. Local 53, Asbestos Workers, 407 F.2d 1047 (5th Cir. 1969), United States v. Local 189 United Paper Makers and Paper Workers, 416 F.2d 980 (5th Cir. 1969), Hicks v. Crown Zellerbach Corp. 58 Lab. Cas. ¶9145 (E.D. La. 1968), United States v. Local 73, United Association, Plumbing and Pipefitting, 61 Lab. Cas. ¶9329 (D.C. S.D. Ind. 1969), United States v. Local 36, Sheet Metal Workers, 416 F.2d 123 (8th Cir. 1969), Bowe v. Colgate-Palmolive Co., 416 F.2d 711 (7th Cir. 1969). See the discussion of class actions and related remedial problems in Oatis v. Crown Zellerbach Corp., 398 F.2d 496 (5th Cir. 1968) and the disposition of the mootness contention in Jenkins v. United Gas Corp. 400 F.2d 28 (5th Cir. 1968).

tlements, in proposing and evaluating judicial decrees, and in monitoring compliance with agreements and decrees.

The fundamental nature of the judicial process—the adjudication of concrete rights and obligations—provides a basic antidote to the malaise of the administrative agencies. As the courts decide cases and flesh out the law, their presence and performance may supply reason and courage to administrators who can begin to carry out the law enforcement function they have so long avoided.

I support the present legal structure because I believe that it is more likely to reduce discrimination than is the pure administrative process. The federal courts are more sensitive to the civil rights interests than the administrative agencies have been. Experience thus far under the existing legal structure has been better, in three short years, than the experience with two decades of the pure administrative process.[14] The existing legal structure allows individuals and civil rights groups such as the NAACP, the Legal Defense Fund, and CORE, (Congress of Racial Equality) as well as the Attorney General, to shape the course of litigation and settlement of discrimination problems. Where the pure administrative process operates, the course of decision is influenced by forces which reflect the interests of labor and management more than they do the civil rights community. At this time, therefore, I support the combination of administrative and judicial responsibilities, including the individual right to sue, which exists in the present legal structure.

Under the present legal structure, sound administration can (1) engage in systematic self-initiated enforcement activities in the area where the complaint process does not function effectively, (2) investigate, evaluate, and settle those complaints which are amenable to presuit settlement, (3) assist the courts in resolving disputes before them by shaping issues and offering views on the law and on appropriate remedies, and (4) engage in research, reporting, public relations and other regulatory functions. The judiciary can resolve those disputes which cannot be otherwise settled, and develop a body of law which will reenforce and channel the efforts of administrators to secure settlements. The body of law will also inform the judgments of attorneys and others as to the requirements of the statute and the wisdom of settlement. The settlements which the administrators secure can serve as useful guides to the judiciary in framing decrees which require modifica-

---

14 See cases cited in note 13, *supra*.

tion of industrial relations systems. I would propose one change in the existing structure. I would allow the continuation of government contracts to be influenced more heavily by individual law suits. This could be done by executive action changing procedures which have led the courts to hold that individual employees are not entitled to enforce the antidiscrimination obligation under government contracts in private litigation.[15]

I. The Emergence and Decline of the Administrative Process

Antidiscrimination laws at the state and federal level have a long history which has been documented by Professor Bonefield, and discussed extensively by other scholars.[16] It is agreed that these laws in effect prior to 1945 were not effective. The reasons for ineffectiveness varied with the nature of the regulatory mechanism.

A. *Criminal and Civil Actions Failed*

Some states adopted criminal statutes. These were ineffective because prosecutors would not prosecute. Judges would instruct on the presumption of innocence and would narrowly construe the statutes,

---

15 Farkas v. Texas Instrument, Inc. 375 F.2d 629 (5th Cir. 1967); Farmer v. Philadelphia Electric Co., 329 F.2d 3 (3rd Cir. 1964). In its initial interpretation of Sec. 706(a) of the Civil Rights Act of 1964, the EEOC adopted the policy that it would not settle a case unless the complainants signed a settlement agreement. In the absence of such a signed settlement agreement, the EEOC would issue a notice which enabled the complainants to sue. This decision which departed from the traditional parens patria view of most antidiscrimination agencies is the key to individual and group participation in Title VII processes, including litigation. Had the EEOC construed the statute so that it made a judgment as to whether there had been "voluntary compliance" independent of the question of whether the charging party was willing to sign a settlement agreement, an unsatisfied charging party who wished to sue a respondent would have had to sue the Commission as well to compel issuance of a notice of right to sue the respondent. This would have seriously hampered the course of litigation under Title VII and subordinated the views of the charging parties and the groups which they represented to the views of the administrative agency. The position taken by the EEOC was confirmed in Cox v. United States Gypsum Co., 284 F. Supp. 74 (D. ND Ind. 1968), aff'd, 409 F.2d 289 (7th Cir. 1969).

16 Bonefield, *The Origin and Development of American Fair Employment Practice Legislation,* 52 Iowa L. Rev. 1043 (1967), Sovern, ch. 3 (1966).

juries would not convict, and a slight fine or prison sentence would not protect the injured party or change the illegal practice.[17] My impression is that few complaints were filed under these laws and that such complaints as were filed rarely went beyond the prosecutor's desk. He decided not to proceed and thus foreclosed questions of interpretation, jury instruction, or penalty.

The criminal law approach floundered because it depended on prosecutors' discretion. Why did the prosecutors not prosecute? One reason, I suspect, was the view—which I share—that the criminal law is inappropriate in the context of social legislation. Confirming this was a conversation I had with the Assistant Attorney General of a New England state while I was with the EEOC. I advised him that the EEOC would not defer to his state because its antidiscrimination law contained only criminal penalties.[18] He agreed with the Commission's conclusion, stating "The criminal law is no way to handle this problem." I suspect that this is the lawyer's judgment about most phases of social legislation.

Another, and perhaps more fundamental, reason for the failure to prosecute was the absence of effective social and political pressure on the prosecutor. In the pre-1945 period, the civil rights movement was not organized to generate day-in, day-out political pressures at the local and state level.[19] The electoral power of minorities was not developed. Effectuation of the civil rights interest depended on the goodwill of individual officials. Such good will, while essential, is no substitute for the stern law of political necessity. Thus, the criminal law approach failed completely.

Other jurisdictions adopted statutes providing a civil action for the victim of employment discrimination. This approach was ineffective also, because of the social realities on which its enforcement depended.

---

[17] Bonefield, *ibid.* at 1048.

[18] The EEOC interpreted §706(c) as not requiring deference to state or local governments with criminal statutes prohibiting discrimination. The relevant statutory language requires deference for a period of time to a state or political subdivision thereof "which has a state or local law prohibiting the practice alleged and establishing or authorizing a state or local authority to grant or seek relief from such practice or to institute criminal proceedings with respect thereto upon receiving notice thereof, . . ." In light of references in §709(d) and 716(c), which suggest that Congress was referring to the typical state FEP agency with administrative powers and not to the local prosecutor; and of the undesirability of the use of criminal sanctions in this field, the EEOC concluded that the quoted language of §706(c) applied to traditional FEPC, to agencies which were part of state cabinet level departments, but not to prosecuting attorneys.

[19] See ROCHE, THE QUEST FOR THE DREAM (1963), p. 237.

There was no organization to exercise the rights which the law gave. The potential plaintiffs were lonely, isolated, ill-informed, ill-financed individuals, poorly organized, and without counsel. They would be unlikely to know of their rights or to complain if they believed their rights had been violated. They did not press for litigation or persevere to its conclusion. This system simply never functioned at all.[20]

B. *Organizational Weakness in Civil Rights Movement*

The failure of both the civil action and the criminal sanction may be traced back to weakness of organization in the minority community. It was not equipped politically to press upon elected and appointed officials for criminal prosecutions, or legally, to provide counsel and resources to carry forward the complexities of a civil action. In addition, both procedures depended on individual complaints which were infrequent.

One important consequence of the failure of these systems is that virtually no case law was made under these statutes. There was no judicially evolved definition of discrimination. The courts were not called upon to elaborate upon the general statutory texts, nor to give concrete guidance to the bar. Attorneys seeking to shape the conduct of clients had no authoritative guides beyond the bare words of the statute. The elaborate system of communications and commentary which has developed, for example, in the labor law and in the taxation field, had no counterpart in the field of employment discrimination. The new era of the administrative process which began in 1945 did not change this situation.

C. *Agency Action Inadequate*

The cure for the failure of the civil and criminal process was sought in the administrative agency with powers to investigate, conciliate, conduct hearings, render decisions, and issue orders which were enforceable in court. The post-World War II generation of civil rights supporters pinned their hopes on this regulatory device.[21] It was modeled after the

---

20 See Bonefield, *op. cit. supra,* note 16.
21 See note 10 *supra.*

National Labor Relations Board. The model state statutes, adopted first in New York in 1945, spread across the non-Southern part of the country. The liberal drive to create these agencies was based on the idea that they would be strong at precisely the points where the criminal and civil statutes were weak.

This analysis seemed sound. The administrative approach avoided the weakness of criminal process with its prosecutor's discretion, heavy burden of proof, narrow construction of the statute, jury trial, and inappropriate remedies. It focused the problem in a single-mission agency to assure singleness of purpose. It avoided the weaknesses in the civil action by relieving the complainant of the burden of moving his case forward. The agency would act "in loco parentis," as guardian of the interests of the victims of discrimination, investigating and framing the issues, and making informal settlement efforts. If this was unsuccessful, the agency itself would hold a hearing, thus assuring a friendly forum for resolution of fact questions and for initial interpretation of statutes. This avoided the cost, delay, and adverse attitudes associated with the courts. The expertise of the agency would assure the shaping of effective remedial orders. Judicial review would rest at the minimum level necessary to convince the judges of the constitutionality of the statute.

Finally—this concept may have evolved somewhat later—the agency would not be restricted to actions based upon individual complaints. It could seek out and eliminate patterns of discrimination. The agency would become an inspector general of industrial practices of discrimination. This function has been articulated more fully by the federal administrative agency enforcing the prohibition on employment discrimination by government contractors, now known as the Office of Federal Contract Compliance. Routinized and regularized "compliance reviews" are scheduled to review the practices of the contractors.

This general model of an administrative regulatory process did correct the *formal* defects of the earlier system of civil and criminal proceedings. The older systems had failed, however, not because of their form but because of underlying weakness and disorganization in the minority community. These defects could not be cured by a change in the form of the regulatory device, unless the change was tailored to overcome them.

The history of these post-1945 regulatory agencies provides a vivid demonstration that a change in legal form which is not tailored to the social realities will not change legal results.[22] The creation of an administrative agency solved the formal problems of the prior systems, but it consolidated the informal and institutional weaknesses which had been responsible for the earlier failures.

For example, the prosecuting function was vested in a single mission agency. This identified responsibility for carrying out the statute. But this function was performed by the administrators with no greater vigor than it had been performed by his predecessor in title, the prosecuting attorney.[23] One primary reason for the failure of administrators to press

[22] Legal institutions have been woefully deficient in the field of "research and development" in connection with legal programs or institutions. See Ass'n of American Law Schools, Report of Committee on Research, 65 (1967); Cowan, *Postulates for Experimental Jurisprudence*, 9 Rutgers L. Rev. 404 (1954).

The defects in the administrative process in connection with industrial accidents are well known and documented. See Somers & Somers, Workmen's Compensation (1954). In that field, too, the administrative process has fallen far short of the expectations held for it by its supporters.

[23] Statistics of agency performance are only approximations. Nevertheless, the figures published by various committees concerning the activities of state agencies from 1945 to 1961 are instructive, as is the fact that as of this writing the federal agency enforcing the antidiscrimination clauses in government contracts has *never* concluded a formal hearing on cancelations, and has actually suspended future contracting fewer than five times. None of these suspensions was for a lengthy period.

The table appears in S Report No. 867, 88th Cong., 2d Sess., p. 7 (1964), with accompanying text:

. . . Figures submitted to the committee based on a survey made in 12 states from the date of enactment of the state law to the end of the calendar

Comparative Complaint Experience under
State Fair Employment Practice Laws
[From date of law until Dec. 31, 1961]

State	Cases	Hearings	Cease and desist orders	Court actions
California	1,014	2	2	2
Colorado	251	4	3	1
Connecticut	900	4	3	3
Massachusetts	3,559	2	2	0
Michigan	1,459	8	6	4
Minnesota	184	1	1	1
Missouri	45	0	0	0
New Jersey	1,735	2	2	2
New York	7,497	18	6	5
Ohio	985	2	1	0
Oregon	286	0	0	0
Pennsylvania	1,238	19	0	0
Rhode Island	286	0	0	0
TOTAL	19,439	62	26	18

for enforcement of the fair employment practice laws was the absence of that daily lobbying-litigating-pressuring function on the part of the civil rights movement. The administrators were pressed by business and labor, the regulated groups. These pressures were not counted on a day-to-day basis by the civil rights interests. This failure of organized pressure had contributed to the failures of the older forms of remedy; the civil action and the criminal statute.

The new regulatory agencies became another challenge to business and labor by threatening their independence of action. They responded at all levels to minimize the possibility that administrative action would interfere with their substantial interests. Business and labor participated in the shaping of state legislation, in the selection of policy making and administrative personnel, in the development of agency policies, and in the decisions as to agency budget. In this conflict between the regulated groups and the less organized and articulate civil rights interests to shape, influence, and control the direction of the administrative process, the outcome was foredoomed. Budgets were restricted. Men were appointed to positions of power and influence whose view was that they were to "educate" rather than enforce the law.[24] Operating policies of the agencies were shaped around a concept of "voluntarism" and away from enforcement activities. A formula for ineffectiveness was evolved under the label, "education, not enforcement."

D. *The Effect of the "Education Versus Enforcement" Dialogue*

This formula immobilized the agencies. The idea was that the law should not be enforced because it dealt with basic human motivations and attitudes. These attitudes could be corrected only by "education." But education was then defined to exclude enforcement of the law, despite a long history which has justified much law on the grounds of its deterrence or educational function.

This "education not enforcement" idea required modification of the traditional views of the nature of legal rights. Traditionally, legal rights,

---

year 1961 established that somewhat more than 19,000 cases were opened during this period resulting in 62 hearings and 26 cease and desist orders.

[24] See Blumrosen, *op. cit. supra,* note 11, 191–96; Bonefield, *An Institutional Analysis of the Agencies Administering Fair Employment Practices Laws,* 42 N.Y.U.L. Rev. 823, 875–78 (1967).

once established through proper procedures, are entitled to immediate recognition. Under the education concept, "rights" under antidiscrimination laws were reduced to little more than advice to the wrongdoer and the hope that having received this advice, he would go and discriminate no more.

This concept flowered in Arizona, where the statute actually gives the discriminator a free first bite—a privilege which the common law never gave the dog owner.[25] Under Arizona law, respondent has a right to one adjudication that he is a discriminator without suffering any penalty. Only after a second formal finding of discrimination, is he obliged to obey the law. This provision is a clear illustration of an intention not to enforce the law.

Similarly, New Jersey adopted a strong law, then placed it under the jurisdiction of the Commissioner of Education rather than the Attorney General, so that the educator's rather than the lawyer's perspective would permeate the enforment process.[26]

By immobilizing the administrator in terms of personnel, philosophy, and budget, the regulated groups continued their relative immunity from enforcement of the statutes.[27] Many administrators believed the "education not enforcement" distinction, to the point that the decision to hold an enforcement hearing was considered an agencywide disaster. These men struggled manfully but ineffectively with problems far beyond their reach. For years, the field was full of "people of goodwill" who tried to implement the law as they saw it. Some stayed to suffer unending frustrations. I recall vividly one incident which reflected these frustrations. While serving as Chief of Liaison with State Agencies for the EEOC, I was involved in discussions as to whether the EEOC should defer more extensively to the state commissions. Several of these commissions had urged broader deference. One high state administrative officer took me aside and said: "Don't let the EEOC give

---

25 On discriminator's liability, see 41 Ariz. Rev. Stat. 1401; on dog owner's liability, see PROSSER, TORTS 516, 3d ed. (1964).

26 See Blumrosen, *op. cit., supra,* note 11, 191–96, 220, 274.

27 Blumrosen, *ibid.,* at 221, recounts one of the few times an agency has been publicly restrained by highest political authority from further investigation of employment discrimination. Governor Hughes of New Jersey publicly called off an investigation of discrimination in the construction trades after complaints from the unions. This type of activity is usually conducted in private, and frequently through quiet governmental shifts called reorganizations. See the illuminating description of the elimination of an aggressive enforcement unit in the Department of Defense by Congressman Ryan in 114 Cong. Rec. H 1536 (daily ed., Feb. 29, 1968).

us more power. The state chamber of commerce wants us to have it because they know they can tell us what to do."

E. *The Abuse and Use of the Concept of Voluntarism*

The logic of the argument which contrasts "education" and "enforcement" of the law is not clear. It implies that education will induce "voluntary compliance," whereas "enforcement" will engender resistance. The argument is thus based on the desirability of voluntarism. But when the theory was put into action, it did not generate meaningful settlements. Rather, it permitted discrimination to continue. Discriminators were not faced with clear-cut choices of voluntary compliance on the one hand or the imposition of sanctions on the other. They did not have to face the question of whether they were prepared to change their policies and practices. Of course, it is true that voluntary compliance is essential if these laws, or any laws, are to be enforced. But it is either naive or misleading to restrict the term voluntary to describe only actions which result when government promises in advance not to use any sanctions. The concept of voluntarism in American law includes choices made with awareness of the consequences; it is not confined to the situations where there will be no consequences.

In any event, the "education not enforcement" argument shows more concern for the sensibilities of respondents than with changing their behavior. More interest in providing practical opportunities for minorities might have produced a different agency approach, once the failure of the "educational" approach became apparent.

The development of this "education not enforcement" philosophy was a manifestation of the influence of the regulated groups in the administrative process. This is most vividly illustrated by the development of "Plans for Progress," an organization of blue-chip employers who promised "voluntary compliance" during the early years of the Kennedy administration as the price for minimal enforcement of the antidiscrimination clause in government contracts. Minimal enforcement was granted, but it was accompanied by minimal compliance.[28] Had the

---

[28] See Rep. Ryan's Comment, *op. cit. supra*, note 27, Equal Employment Opportunity Commission, Discrimination in White Collar Employment 593 (1968); Blumrosen, ch. 6 *infra*.

civil rights influence been greater, the philosophical mood of the agencies might have been less toward understanding the problems of respondents and more toward achieving results for complainants. Professor Bonefield's analysis of the sources of recruitment of state commissioners supports this conclusion.[29] Certainly the hollow distinction between education and enforcement and the abuse of the concept of voluntarism did not contribute to a solution of the problems of discrimination.

The important truth about the concept of voluntarism is that those in charge of the day-to-day functioning of industry and labor must cooperate if discrimination is to be eliminated from industrial relations systems. Government cannot station police behind every personnel officer or every union official. Nor is such action consistent with our traditions. Our basic philosophy assumes that substantial compliance with the law will follow once its obligations are made clear. Massive resistance to laws in our country leaves government nearly helpless, whether it comes from white Southerners refusing for fifteen years to integrate schools, or black Northerners taking over city after city in riotous manner. On a practical level, government lacks the skilled manpower to effectively police complex industrial relations systems. If there is stern resistance to the antidiscrimination obligation, the pace will be slow and results hard to achieve. On the other hand, cooperation by management and labor can produce spectacular results.

This was demonstrated by the Newport News Shipbuilding and Dry Dock Company conciliation agreement. This agreement, negotiated in 1966 while the government was asserting maximum pressure, provided in detailed and extensive ways for the elimination of discrimination in the 22,000-man establishment. After the agreement was reached, the company went to work with a will to carry it out. After a few months, the company was pressing the government to come down and finish the administration of the agreement. Without this kind of cooperation, the results of the agreement would have been far less significant.[30]

These considerations do not mean that business must be coddled by government, or that no pressure should be generated to achieve a change in corporate direction. Extensive pressures were organized by

---

[29] Bonefield, *op. cit. supra*, note 24.

[30] The agreement appears in BUREAU OF NATIONAL AFFAIRS, FAIR EMPLOYMENT PRACTICES, 431:55. See ch. 8 *infra*.

the government in the Newport News situation, including a finding of cause by the Commission, suspension of government contracting, and the imminence of a suit by the Attorney General. In addition, a private suit had been instituted with the support of the Legal Defense and Education Fund. These interlocking and mutually supporting pressures made it possible to negotiate a workmanlike practical arrangement for the elimination of discrimination. Without these pressures there would have been no such massive system change. Once the company decided to settle rather than litigate, they proceeded in a good faith manner to implement the agreement. Their choice—conciliate or litigate—was not coerced improperly. Having excellent counsel, they could have tied the government up in litigation, as subsequent litigation by others has shown. But they chose to settle. This was voluntary in the practical every-day sense in which lawyers normally use the term. The company freely chose between relatively clear alternatives.

Voluntary decisions are not necessarily easy. I believe that the anti-discrimination laws should be vigorously enforced so that management and labor will be compelled to make these hard decisions to change systems and end discrimination. Once enforcement programs have set the stage, reasonably intelligent negotiations in most cases will result in agreement to change systems and eliminate discrimination. Without major enforcement efforts, business and labor will continue to avoid the issues and carry on business as usual.

The significance of this conclusion is only now becoming apparent. In an exhaustive study, the EEOC has concluded that, at most, educational deficiencies explain about one third of the depressed condition of the nation's minorities. This finding is so crucial to an understanding of this field that the EEOC analysis is included as chapter 3. This finding means that education alone *cannot* end the depressed condition of minorities.[31] Education without the enforced revision of industrial relations systems to eliminate discrimination will leave the problem only slightly moderated. And, of course, education is far more costly to the government than law enforcement efforts. Thus the "education not enforcement" concept requires major government expenditures to deal with a minor part of the problem, while leaving the major part of the problem virtually untouched.

Vigorous enforcement activity will set the stage for meaningful set-

---

[31] See Thurow, Poverty and Discrimination (1969).

tlements. Working out these settlements, and then administering the
settlement agreement will require good faith efforts and participation
of all interested parties. There is sufficient flexibility and dynamism in
most situations that consensual settlements are possible which meet the
basic needs of all parties.

But the history of the last quarter century has demonstrated that
meaningful solutions will be approached only if the government is prepared for full-scale enforcement of the law. Enforcement is the civil
rights equivalent of labor's ability to strike in collective bargaining. If
enforcement does not generate solutions, then the civil rights interest
may continue to be expressed through massive waves of civil unrest.
Enforcement activity thus becomes a substitute, in our time, for demonstrations and civil unrest. Enforcement activities have the added advantage that they may lead to genuine improvement in the condition of
minorities. Whether civil unrest has this potentiality is as yet unclear.

F. *The Hallmarks of the Ineffective Agencies*

There are at least three outstanding measures of the ineffectiveness
of the administrative agencies. As of 1964, there was no substantial
group of professional personnel trained and competent to enforce the
antidiscrimination obligation; there were no adequate procedures; and
there was *still* no substantial body of law defining discrimination.

The first of these observations—about the lack of competent professionals—is no reflection on the dedication and the competence of many
individuals in the field.

The second hallmark of the ineffective agency is the absence of rig-
orous procedures in connection with their activities. The informal
efforts often secured general statements of intent to follow the law.[32]
The investigation efforts often failed to develop the facts before attempting a settlement. The result was that the agency did not have an
adequate factual foundation on which to shape its settlement demands.
The consequence was ineffective generality. It remains true that one
effective means of hobbling government effort is to divert it from a
factual inquiry into a premature discussion of broad policy.

The third weakness—the failure to develop a body of law—is a mat-

[32] Sovern, ch. 3; Blumrosen, *op. cit. supra,* note 11, pp. 237–246.

ter of record, and can be verified in the library. Just as the earlier regulatory institutions of civil and criminal failed to develop a body of interpretive law, the administrative agencies failed also. These failures meant that there was no steady, informed, and effective pressure on business and labor to cease discriminating. Such pressure could not develop without authoritative determinations of what constituted discrimination and a group of men and women competent to identify it and shape remedies to correct it.

G. The "Law Effectuation System" Was Not Invoked

The nature of law enforcement in our "new industrial state" requires a complex system to translate law from statute to behavior. This "law effectuation system" has been little studied. It includes the lawmakers, the administrators, the law transmitters, the law appliers, and the law executors. In this field, the lawmakers have acted, but matters have proceeded but little further. The administrators did not press for specific enforcement. Therefore, prior to 1965, there was no detailed body of decisional law and rules which could be made available to the interested public through the specialized publications such as those of the Bureau of National Affairs and Commerce Clearing House. These law transmitters only began to function with the advent of Title VII. They deliver information on what the law requires to attorneys, and to personnel officials who make general judgments as to what must be done in the circumstances in which their clients operate. Finally, these judgments are executed by lower-level supervision in corporations, and by local labor union officials. This entire system, elaborately developed in connection with labor relations in general, was not activated in the employment discrimination field before 1965, in part because there was no body of law on which it could function. This minimized the impact of the law.[33]

The absence of a detailed body of decisional law has been critical. The answers to many questions concerning discrimination are not self-evident. For example, it is sometimes assumed that racial discrimination requires "evil" intent. This is the *mens rea* idea imported from the

---

[33] See Lasswell, *Toward Continuing Appraisal of the Impact of Law on Society,* 21 RUTGERS L. REV. 645 (1967).

criminal law. This idea means that the statute will be narrowly applied because evil intent is hard to prove. Furthermore, this view leads generally to a narrow construction of the antidiscrimination law. Decisions holding that discrimination is a civil wrong, and that the statute will be comprehensively construed, will resolve these matters and provide a foundation for the broad interpretation and application of the statute by both the regulators and the regulated.

On the question of the "state of mind" requisite for discrimination, it seems that the supporters of such legislation have not always understood the nature of civil liability.[34] "Intent" in torts and in employment relations law means, as the Supreme Court has stated, the doing of an act with awareness (or assumed awareness) of the results substantially certain to follow.[35] With this elementary tort principle and a few other tools of liberal construction, the judiciary can quickly clear up the hiatus in law enforcement created during the era of the feeble administrative agencies. The evolution of a body of decisional law is critical. One court decision is worth ten written conciliation agreements and one hundred annual reports of administrative agencies.

At any rate, during the administrative era the agencies floundered, while issuing reports of progress. These reports simply did not correlate with income and employment statistics of Negroes. These statistics, which are conservative at best, established the persistence of the double unemployment rate for Negroes.[36] The most that could be claimed was that the presence of the agencies prevented a bad situation from getting worse, but even that is not clear. By some measures, the bad problem did get worse during the era of administration. This created some embarrassment at the ceremonial changing of the guard when an administrator moved on or a new agency was added to the field. It was somewhat awkward to both praise excellent work of the past and bemoan the fact that the problem had become worse during the prior administration.[37] One mark of agency ineffectiveness was the failure to

---

34 See Sovern, *op. cit., supra,* note 32, at 71, and Bonefield, *The Substance of American Fair Employment Practices Legislation I: Employers,* 61 Nw. U.L. Rev. 907, 956 (1967), for a narrow view of intent. For a broader view, see chapters 5, 6, and 8 *infra;* Blumrosen, *op. cit., supra,* note 11 at 234–37; Blumrosen, Book Reviews, 14 U.C.L.A.L. Rev. 721 (1967).

35 See Blumrosen, ch. 6 *infra.*

36 See appendixes to ch. 6 *infra.*

37 The problem was solved with adroitness by Vice-President Humphrey in his

hold hearings and issue orders or suspend government contracts. At one time it was fashionable for agencies to point with pride to the fact that they held so few formal hearings. Few were needed, it was said, because of the success of the agency in securing informal settlements. Recent scholarship has demonstrated that such successes often consisted of soft agreements in principle which neither aided the complainant nor eliminated patterns of discrimination.[38] In the New Jersey study, such "successful" adjustments of complaints were found to consist of a respondent's loosely worded statement that in the future he would obey the law. Success, if you call it that, was purchased at too

---

remarks before the White House Conference on Equal Employment Opportunity, Aug. 19, 1965, as follows:

The unemployment rate among non-whites is twice as high as among whites. Thirty-five years ago it was about equal. In fact non-whites still experience the crisis conditions of the great depression.

The unemployment rate for non-white teen-age boys is 23 per cent as against 13 per cent for unemployed whites. In 1948 it was actually lower for non-white youth.

Today, because of poor job opportunities, the median income of non-white families compared to whites is lower than it was a decade ago. It is, in fact, only half as large.

Moreover, the latest figures on unemployment give little cause for optimism. In July, one of the best months in the history of our nation's economy, the unemployment rate fell to 4.5 per cent. Less than 4 per cent of the white working force was out of a job. But for adult non-whites, the unemployment rate actually *increased*.

It is no exaggeration to say that non-whites, principally Negroes, are on the verge of a major economic crisis. For the gap is widening between Negro education and training on the one hand, and the requirements of the labor market on the other.

. . . .

On the federal level, the efforts of the President's Committee on Equal Employment Opportunity and its Executive Vice Chairman, Hobart Taylor, Jr., have helped end discriminatory practices by government contractors, on federally assisted construction projects, and within the government itself. We owe a debt of gratitude, too, to the Secretary of Commerce, Secretary of Labor, and other heads of federal departments and agencies for the work they have done.

But we must frankly acknowledge that these and other efforts represent only the first step towards solving the national employment problem which plagues Negroes and other minority groups—a problem which, as I have indicated, is becoming more severe.

. . . .

While we have made encouraging headway in many fields, I doubt whether anyone—and this includes the federal government, the business community, and the labor movement—can bring an unblemished record to this conference.

Let us, therefore, acknowledge the fact that we have often fallen short of our goals.

And let's get down to work without delay to improve this record.

[38] Sovern, pp. 46–53; Blumrosen, *op. cit. supra*, note 11, pp. 197–99.

high a price. In accepting such settlements, the agencies made themselves irrelevant to the solution of minority group employment problems. The argument that lack of enforcement activity reflects the success of the agencies has not been heard in recent times.

H. *Measurement of Success—Influence on the Unemployment Ratio*

For reasons not entirely clear to me, some legal scholars have much more difficulty in criticizing administrative actions than judicial decisions. This may in part be due to the greater difficulty in substituting one's judgment for a course of hundreds of administrative decisions which are not well understood, than in differing with a judge on a question of principle or its application in a particular context. Framing criteria for judgment about the administrative process may be more difficult than assessing the appropriateness of judicial decisions.

Berger, in *Equality by Statute*, discusses extensively his criterion for evaluation of the New York State Commission Against Discrimination. First he notes that it is difficult to separate the effect of the statute from the effect of general economic conditions which may influence employment of minorities. He then attempts to separate conclusions about the effect of the New York *statute* from conclusions about the effectiveness of the New York *commission*. He discusses several criteria for evaluation of agency performance and concludes: "The best measure is the degree to which members of minority groups, through action by the Commission, are admitted to jobs and into industries from which they were previously barred." [39]

This measure includes the number of persons who obtained jobs and the number of types of jobs opened up through administrative action.

At this stage of history, and for the purpose of the assessment of the overall effectiveness of such an agency, the distinction between the effect of "the law" and the effect of "the administrative agency" is artificial. As Justice Frankfurter wrote, "Administration is more than a means of regulation; administration is regulation." [40]

---

[39] M. BERGER, EQUALITY BY STATUTE: LEGAL CONTROLS OVER GROUP DISCRIMINATION (revised 1967) at 163.

[40] *San Diego Buildings Trades Council v. Garmon*, 359 U.S. 236 (1959):
But the unifying consideration of our decisions (giving the NLRB exclusive

It is appropriate to credit the agency with those general improvements in conditions of minorities, which are arguably related to regulatory activities, regardless of the particular mechanics which lead to the result. Pending the conduct of empirical studies, the meaningful way to measure the effect of general economic and social conditions would be with a control group against which the administrative and legal sanctions were not applied. Until this is done, only speculation is possible. But existing evidence does suggest that general improvement in levels of economic activity will not end discrimination or solve the social problem. Discriminatory patterns will assure that the improved economic conditions continue to benefit the majority more than the minority. Relative deprivation will continue. Improving economic conditions facilitate change and may be a necessary condition for ending discrimination. But there is no assurance that better economic conditions lead to less discrimination. Our post-1960 prosperity, with its continued high minority unemployment rates, demonstrates that improved economic conditions *alone* do not resolve problems of discrimination. Therefore, governmental action may *also* be a necessary factor in moderating discrimination.

My basic objection to the standard proposed by Berger is that he compares *past* minority employment opportunity with *present* minority opportunity. Percentage of improvement figures, measuring the "degree to which members of minority groups are admitted to jobs," can be badly misleading. As the Plans-for-Progress watchers know, to increase from one to two Negroes is to increase by 100 percent. The fundamental difficulty with Berger's proposed standard is that he compares past and present minority status, but does not compare the minority employment opportunity with that of the white majority.

My proposal is more direct. I would focus on the ratio of minority unemployment to white unemployment in all crucial job categories. As long as this ratio remains significantly different, it means that minorities are low earners, and are bearing a heavier share than whites of the

---

jurisdiction over certain labor matters and thereby preempting state court jurisdiction) has been regard to the fact that Congress has entrusted administration of the labor policy for the Nation to a centralized administrative agency, armed with its own procedures, and equipped with its specialized knowledge and cumulative experience. . . .

Administration is more than a means of regulation; administration is regulation. We have been concerned with conflict in its broadest sense; conflict with a complex and interrelated federal scheme of law, remedy and administration.

vicissitudes of the economic system. This ratio signifies inferior economic status, poorer jobs, more rapid layoff, poorer education, poorer housing—the whole sweep of grievances and concerns that the minority community now feels and sometimes expresses in violent ways.

This unemployment ratio is the reality behind much of the antidiscrimination legislation. It is the reality of the Truman Report in 1947, of the legislative debates in 1963, of the Labor Department Statistical Report of 1967, and of the President's Riot Commission Report.[41] Black unemployment rates have by and large been double those of whites. In addition, black employment is heavily skewed in the direction of lesser-skilled blue collar jobs which will be the next victims of automation. As long as these facts are true, there is no need for more sophisticated measures of agency effectiveness. The statutes today are well named; they are "equal opportunity laws." The absence of opportunity is demonstrated by the statistics. Maximum governmental pressure must be asserted to bring minority and majority unemployment rates into line. Once they have lost the sharpness of contrast, more subtleties may be the order of the day. Maximum regulatory effort in all fields is required until the minority unemployment rate is brought more into line with the white unemployment rate. Thus my measurement of success of any equal opportunity enforcement system is the reduction of the difference between white and minority unemployment rates in all relevant categories.

The Presidential Riot Commission moved in this direction, but placed heavier emphasis on upgrading employed Negroes than on influencing the unemployment ratio. My view is based on (a) the greater practicality involved in government programs to expand initial employment, and (b) on a healthy skepticism as to the capability of government-initiated programs concerning upgrading. In the upgrading area, the problems of seniority and ability are difficult and require individualized treatment. Recruitment systems, on the other hand, can be influenced on a mass basis. Furthermore, the individual self-interest of the employed minority will lead him to take initiative by complaint in a greater proportion of situations than is the case with the unemployed.

There is some debate in administrative circles as to whether the strategy with the maximum payoff would focus on recruiting or on the problem of promotion of incumbent employees. I believe that both ap-

---

[41] See ch. 3 and appendixes to ch. 6, *infra.*

proaches should be developed so that the more effective one may be used. During a period of increasing *unemployment*, it may be more desirable to focus on promotion; and during a period of rising employment, on the recruitment aspect. The crucial factor is the development of legal standards and administrative enforcement programs to cover both situations, for without these two elements, the dialogue will be an exercise in futility.

The criterion for success is not mere numbers of increased minority jobs. Rather it is the elimination of racial differences in the unemployment rate so that Negroes and whites share the same relative burdens of unemployment and benefits of our economy. As long as the burdens and benefits are unevenly distributed, there will remain the sense of unfairness and the seeds of civil unrest.

Within this framework, the question of whether a commission, "the law" or "economic conditions" is the "cause" of improvement in the situation is not crucial. If unemployment rates are brought into line, then there will be enough credit to go around.

This question of "credit" or "cause" for improved social-economic conditions also arises with respect to the National Labor Relations Board. Its "success" as a regulatory body may be due to a variety of social, economic, and political factors beyond its influence, and in particular cases the Board may "fail." Nevertheless, it symbolizes an equality of interests which were once unequal. So too, if the incidence of discrimination is reduced, the presence of a governmental agency will symbolize that this was desired by the lawmakers. These questions of cause and effect and of the relationship between regulatory agency and regulated institution are of the utmost significance. They go to the crucial questions of how society functions under law. But at this juncture, the debate does not seem likely to provide insights into how to do a better job of eliminating discrimination. Our experience thus far has vividly demonstrated that all "nonenforcement" approaches of these agencies have failed. A tough-minded and vigorous enforcement program is the only untried experiment.

Once the multiple minority unemployment rate has been reduced to insignificance, we can debate which programs or forces are entitled to credit. Until this is done, there should be no rest from maximum enforcement of the antidiscrimination obligation. When the unemployment ratios have evened out, the nature of our industrial society and the distribution of minorities within it will necessarily be substantially different. Blacks and other minorities will be better employed; the path to upward mobility will be trod by the many rather than the few; the youth will see that there are substantial numbers ahead of him who are making it. We will have passed through the current crisis. For the here and now of the practical world, I submit that the agencies administering the antidiscrimination obligation must pass the harsh test of the marketplace. The fruit of their work will be the cold statistics which reflect either the achievement of equality or our failure to implement our stated policies.

Program development takes time. A year from now, programs to reduce the differential in unemployment ratios should be in operation. Suspension of judgment for the moment is appropriate. But the moment is brief. By the test of whether such program development is underway, the EEOC is doing well. It has established the data base for programs through its requirement that employers report on the racial composition of the work force. The Commission has made good use of the opportunity to collect data, and now has sufficient information on which to mount a program to reduce the minority unemployment ratio. Not only that, but the Commission is undertaking research and development efforts to determine the most effective method of reducing this ratio.[42]

And, finally, the Commission is developing its body of interpretive law of Title VII in the direction of establishing a "duty of fair recruitment" which will induce employers to hire a higher percentage of minorities where they have shirked their social responsibilities in the past.

The criterion for success then is the difficult one of the marketplace, but it is the test on which we ultimately must rely if we wish effective government of action in this area.

II. The Attempt to Shift Focus: The Moynihan Report

In 1965 Assistant Secretary of Labor Daniel Moynihan prepared for limited government circulation a report entitled "The Negro Family:

---

[42] See ch. 2 for a discussion of the development of the reporting system. See REPORT OF THE NATIONAL ADVISORY COMMISSION ON CIVIL DISORDERS 233–35 (1968) for recommendations of the President's Riot Commission, particularly recommendations (c), (d).

The Case for National Action." [43] In this report he pulled together the brutal and familiar statistics concerning employment, the impact of urbanization of minorities, illegitimacy rates, and the like. His conclusion was that our society was destroying the Negro family structure—a structure which had played such a vital role in the successful assimilation of other minority groups. He proposed, as a test for development of meaningful national programs, the following:

> The policy of the United States is to bring the Negro American to full and equal sharing in the responsibilities and rewards of citizenship. To this end, the programs of the Federal Government bearing on this objective shall be designed to have the effect, directly or indirectly, of enhancing the stability and resources of the Negro American family.

Programatically, little new was offered in the Moynihan report. He emphasized employment, housing, and the civilizing of the welfare programs. Moynihan has been quoted by the Presidential Riot Commission as believing that employment opportunites are the crucial factor in improving the opportunities of Negroes.[44] One of his most interesting correlations is between the increase in unemployment rates for Negroes and the following year's increase in rates of separation of husbands and wives.

A. *The Focus on the Family*

The focus on the family suggested by the Moynihan report as a central element in the problems of Black America was reviewed and rejected by the civil rights community after nearly a year of discussion.

Yet, its impact is clearly discernible in the report of the Presidential Riot Commission.

Why the Moynihan report? Why the attempt to define the problem of minorities through the sociological focus of the impact on the Negro family? I submit that Moynihan may have been motivated by the same considerations which have led me to participate in this field: a concern

---

[43] The report, the President's Howard University speech, and other relevant materials are gathered in RAINWATER & YANCEY, THE MOYNIHAN REPORT AND THE POLITICS OF CONTROVERSY (1967).

[44] REPORT OF THE NATIONAL ADVISORY COMMISSION ON CIVIL DISORDERS 124 (1968), Blumrosen, ch. 6 *infra*.

with the failure of governmental processes to ameliorate the effects of discrimination. This concern has caused me to examine the processes and the reasons for failure as a legal scholar, consultant, and administrator. Mr. Moynihan was in a different situation by both training and circumstance. By training a sociologist, he was prepared to accept the conclusion that the legal process for eliminating discrimination was likely to be ineffective. Sociologists generally have not been impressed with the capability of the legal system to facilitate social change. In his position as Assistant Secretary of Labor, Mr. Moynihan probably was fed information which supported his predisposition. This information implied that the law had been enforced vigorously but had been inadequate to cope with the problem.[45] The federal law enforcement effort at that time was directed by the President's Committee on Equal Employment Opportunity (PCEEO) dealing with government contractors. The PCEEO held, but did not use, the big stick of economic power. If the legal system could work at all, the PCEEO should have succeeded. Moynihan might have concluded that the political pressures and staff inadequacies were themselves an integral part of the operation of the legal system and inhibited the use of law enforcement mechanisms. From this perspective, tinkering with the legal system might simply not have been worthwhile.

Under these circumstances, he could not attack the failure of the law without challenging the validity of his information concerning federal law enforcement efforts and impugning the capability of the officials who had supervision of the administration of these programs. Moynihan may have assumed that the legal system had failed, or at any rate was exhausted as an avenue of change. His strategy was to redefine the problem so that further progress could be made without appearing to repudiate the efforts of the past. In this redefinition, he focused on the effects on the Negro family. The civil rights groups viewed his approach as leading to a reduced emphasis on enforcement programs, providing additional emphasis on welfare and other paternalistic programs, and suggesting that the responsibility for the condition of the Negro rested with the Negroes, rather than with society. The prospect of such continued welfare paternalism collided with the concept of

---

[45] This was the view stated by Vice-President Humphrey at the White House conference during the same period (see note 37 *supra*) and may be taken to represent the administration view.

black equality. This was more than the civil rights interests could stand. They buried the report and what they thought it stood for.

The administration de-emphasized the focus on the Negro family. But there remained the necessity to cope with the very problem which Moynihan faced: the failure of the law to ameliorate the harsh conditions of the Negro. This was done by a tour de force of definition. The condition of the Negro, went the new explanation, was due neither to the deficiencies in the Negro family, nor to discrimination. It was the result of "cultural disadvantage." The Negro problem was simply part of the problem of the poor. Discrimination had in fact been ended. The remaining problem was to correct the disadvantaged condition of the Negro and of others. This became the official rationale to explain the problems dealt with by Moynihan. The Moynihan report, with its focus on the sociological impact of our failures, will continue to provide useful insights. Its demise as a formal premise for governmental action reflects, I believe, its lack of focus on the administration of the law. The law is the crucial link between programs of social reform and the institutions to be reformed. If that link is weak, the reforms will go astray. Those who deny this and think that reforms can be purchased should watch the manner in which the reform programs are rather easily warped to the benefit of the haves rather than the have-nots.

B. *The New "Disadvantage Not Discrimination" Rhetoric Examined*

In this decade, the "education rather than enforcement" analysis has lost favor. The current vogue is to speak more clearly of the need for affirmative enforcement of the antidiscriminaton obligation.[46] This is an improvement over the rhetoric of the past. However, as we have seen, another analysis has arisen to replace the old "education not enforcement" distinction. This new analysis says that employment difficulties of minorities stem from "disadvantage" rather than from "discrimination." Poverty, poor education, inadequate housing are said to be responsible for the limited skills, abilities, experiences, and opportunities

---

[46] See, for example, the "Philadelphia Plan" developed by the Department of Labor and upheld in Contractors Ass'n of Eastern Pennsylvania v. Shultz, 62 Lab. Cas. ¶9421 (D.C. E.D. Pa. 1970), Office of Federal Contract Compliance Order No. 4, 41 CFR Part 60–2, EEOC program developed by Peter Robertson, Director, State and Local Affairs, EEOC News Releases, Aug. 13, 1968, July 13, 1969.

of minority group members. The social and cultural context in which minority group members are raised and in which they function are the responsible agents. The implication which some have drawn from this analysis is that government should attack the "social problems" rather than address itself to discrimination. In this analysis, regulation of discriminatory practices is less important than the search for a more general solution of the social problems of minorities. "Discrimination" is defined out of existence. The difficulties of minorities are traced to vague sources "in society," rather than to the employer, the employment agency, and the union. Thus the "disadvantage not discrimination" analysis has the same effect as the "education not enforcement" concept. They both distract attention from attempts to define discriminatory conduct and to regulate it.

There is an element of truth in the "disadvantage not discrimination" analysis. The bars to employment and promotion of minorities are, in many cases, related to these other failures in the social system. Educational attainments of Negroes are lower, in general, than those of whites. Thus where educational standards are established as entry level qualification, the effect is to exclude a higher proportion of Negroes than of whites. For example, in Newark, New Jersey, 33 percent of white and 58 percent of the Negro labor force in the prime age group of 25-54 have gone no further than the eighth grade.[47] The Labor Department reports that as of 1966, 73 percent of the white males in the prime 20-29 age bracket had high school diplomas, while only 53 percent of the Negro males in the same age bracket had completed high school.[48] Thus the institution of a high-school-education requirement automatically skews the available labor supply to exclude a much higher proportion of Negroes than of whites.

The manner in which cultural deprivation is translated into restrictions in employment is vividly demonstrated by an EEOC case involving a new plant opened in the South to produce frozen food dinners on an automated basis. The employer in this case was sensitive to the equal opportunity problem and contacted Negro organizations in a genuine effort to recruit Negroes. The population in the area of the

---

[47] See CHERNICK, INDIK, & STERNLIEB, NEWARK, NEW JERSEY: POPULATION AND LABOR FORCE, SPRING 1967 (1967).

[48] U.S. DEP'T OF LABOR, SOCIAL AND ECONOMIC CONDITIONS OF NEGROES IN THE UNITED STATES, at 43–46 (1967); Blumrosen, ch. 6 *infra*.

plant was 20 percent Negro. After drumming up Negro applicants, the employer imposed entry-level requirements of an eighth-grade education and achievement of a certain score on the Wonderlic test. The result was that most Negro applicants were excluded, and the plant had an almost all-white labor force. Was this "discrimination" or "disadvantage"? The EEOC called it discrimination. The Commission held:

> Seldom will there be independent evidence that respondent intended its educational and testing requirements to eliminate a disproportionate number of Negro job applicants, but it is elementary that a person must be held to intend the normal and foreseeable consequences of his actions. If respondent did not anticipate the results of its screening procedures, it is certainly aware of them now. This is not to suggest that in all circumstances it is improper for an employer to utilize selection devices which may incidentally reject a disproportionate number of Negro applicants, but where, as here, the educational and testing criteria have the effect of discriminating and are not related to job performance, there is reasonable cause to believe that respondent, by utilizing such devices, thereby violates Title VII.[49]

The raising of qualification standards at the time when formal racial bars are dropped and it appears likely that minority individuals will have to be employed or promoted has been a common device of employers and construction unions. This is illustrated by a decision of the EEOC involving a papermill and converter plant which, in 1964, began to administer tests before it would allow transfers from "dead-end" jobs, largely held by Negroes, to jobs in lines of promotion. Employees, largely white, already in lines of promotion were not required to take tests to keep their jobs or move up the job ladder. The Commission said:

> Since 1964, 94 white employees and 17 Negro employees have taken the transfer tests. Of these, 58 whites (58%) and one Negro (6%) passed. The one Negro who passed was outbid for the job he was seeking by a higher-seniority white.
> It is significant that until 1963, shortly before the transfer tests were instituted, Respondent maintained segregated jobs and lines of progression, so that Negroes were categorically excluded on the basis of their race from the more skilled and better paying jobs which were reserved for "whites only." While the bars are no longer expressly in terms of race, it is plain that Respondent's testing procedures have had the effect of con-

---

[49] CCH Employment Practices ¶17,304.55 (1966).

tinuing the restriction on the entrance of Negro employees into "white" line of progression jobs.

We stated in our *Guidelines:* "If the facts indicate that an employer has discriminated in the past on the basis of race . . . the use of tests in such circumstances will be scrutinized carefully by the Commission." Accordingly, where, as here, the employer has a history of excluding Negroes from employment and from the better jobs because of their race, and where, as here, the employer now utilizes employment tests which function to exclude Negroes from employment opportunities, it is incumbent upon the employer to show affirmatively that the tests themselves and the method of their application are nondiscriminatory within the meaning of Title VII.[50]

The "disadvantages" to which the distinction applies are not distributed uniformly in our society. Minorities contain a higher proportion of the disadvantage because of their status as members of the minority group—because, in short, of discrimination. The "disadvantage" thus rests on a foundation of discrimination. The distinction between "disadvantage" and "discrimination" exists only if one ignores the reasons for the disadvantaged condition.[51]

In addition, the "disadvantage not discrimination" analysis makes it impossible to identify responsible parties and hence impossible to deal with the problem in a systematic, lawyerlike way. One cannot hail a "social system" before a court and demand that it stop engaging in "cultural deprivation." Social systems are sociological categories, not legal ones. Cultural deprivation is an abstraction, not a definition of behavior which may be regulated.

---

[50] *Ibid.* ¶17,304.53 (1966).

[51] The second Chairman of the EEOC, Steven Shulman, incorporated the concept of cultural disadvantage into his concept of discrimination before the Philadelphia Chamber of Commerce, June 8, 1967, as follows:

A failure to recognize—and thus to eliminate—discrimination may result from a misunderstanding of what discrimination is. The law's prohibition against discrimination is often viewed as a prohibition against doing something to harm someone, against taking an action which adversely affects a particular person, an individual Negro. We tend to think of discrimination as an act—a finite incident that can be pinpointed and discussed. When discrimination is so defined, nondiscrimination becomes easy—it means refraining from doing such an act. In fact, the true situation today is that discrimination is often not a specific incident, but a way of life. Discrimination is the result of a system, not the result of any one specific act. No single individual or action may be identifiable as the discriminator. Nondiscrimination in these terms means the difficult process and hard work of challenging the system, of undoing its discriminatory effects, of reforming or, perhaps, replacing it.

The workaday world with which we are concerned consists of employers and unions, corporations and associations, which engage in specific acts of recruiting, hiring, and directing the labor force. These are subject, in their actions, to concrete and specific legal regulation and control. The effect of the "disadvantage rather than discrimination" distinction is that this workaday world is ignored in the quest for some broader solution to an abstractly defined problem. This means ignoring or downgrading efforts to regulate specific conduct in the labor market where acts of discrimination take place.

The distinction between "disadvantage and discrimination" provides a basis for the argument that the employer has no legal responsibility to address himself to the effects of discrimination in education, housing, and the general culture. Under this view he may take the labor market as he finds it, and the resulting unemployment of minorities flows from disadvantage not discrimination. But this raises the central question of defining the responsibility of employers and others with respect to the complex of social problems arising out of the conditions of minorities. Whether employers are entitled to insulate themselves from the failures of the social system with respect to minorities is the issue at the heart of the passage of the Civil Rights Act. The fundamental message of that statute is that such employer irresponsibility must end. The implications of this fundamental policy should be openly examined, analyzed, evaluated, and resolved. A policy of employer irresponsibility should not be concealed in a semantic thicket and smuggled into the law under the slogan of "disadvantage not discrimination."

In the late 1960's a new form of the argument against a strong law enforcement program emerged. This argument suggested that manpower training should be the prime focus of government programs for the minorities. Compliance and enforcement would be de-emphasized in favor of carefully organized training programs which would culminate in employment opportunities. This was a more sophisticated version of the "education not enforcement" approach. It had all of the defects inherent in that approach, plus one more. To the extent that the government awarded a training contract to a company which had a pattern of discrimination in its industrial relations structure, the government, perhaps unintentionally, appeared to validate that structure. Thus a Manpower Development and Training Act (MDTA) contract became the practical equivalent of a certification that the contractor afforded equal employment opportunity. This conclusion lacked both logic and administrative support. Logically, one could justify awarding a training contract to a discriminating employer as a part of his program of correction of his industrial relations system. Training is necessary in many cases to permit employees to move into areas from which they have been historically excluded. Thus a MDTA training program may be an integral and indispensible part of a comprehensive program to eliminate the effects of discrimination. But as a matter of administrative practice, there was no "clearance" required before a MDTA contract was awarded to determine that the contractor was in compliance with the law, or had adopted a program by which he would come into compliance. Thus the conclusion that the MDTA award represented government certification was incorrect. Yet at the administrative and judicial discretionary levels, such a conclusion was frequently drawn, and enforcement activities were not emphasized against those who had obtained major training contracts.

This approach, which substituted training contracts for reform of industrial relations systems, afforded opportunity to new entrants to the labor force at the expense of those already there. It is, I believe, doomed to ineffectiveness. It seems unlikely that minority trainees can function effectively in a setting in which their older brothers are the victims of discrimination. The evidences of the present effects of past discrimination are bound to discourage young people who are inclined to view such a training program as a "buy-out" of the white man's conscience, rather than a realistic start on a road which can be traveled as far as ability, luck, and fortitude can take one.

Second, analysis has shown that educational deficiencies account at most, for one third of the explanation of the depressed conditions of minorites.[52] Thus total success in training will leave unremedied discrimination which will perpetuate the subordinate status of minorities until it is corrected. Thus the MDTA programs *cannot* be a substitute for an antidiscrimination program; and, in fact, training without enforcement may create situations of heightened racial tension.

---

[52] See ch. 3, *infra*; THUROW, POVERTY AND DISCRIMINATION (1969).

III. The Civil Rights Interest and Contemporary Administrative and Judicial Activity

A. *NLRB Distinguished by Different Capabilities of Labor and Civil Rights Movement*

The NLRB is a favorite analogy of senior liberals who cling to the notion that the administrative process which has failed in the race discrimination field must be perpetuated because it succeeded in labor relations. The Board came into being in 1935, some ten years before the passage of the first state antidiscrimination laws. The state antidiscrimination agencies which were created in the 1940's and early 1950's were clustered in the Northeast and along the West Coast. The federal antidiscrimination agency dealing with government contractors, reached "maturity" in 1961 in the PCEEO. Thus any comparison with the NLRB must be qualified. But even so, the differences are striking. The field of labor relations has spawned a massive set of institutions. The network of trained personnel of the Board; the extensive output of decisions, both of courts and agencies; the evolution of a "labor bar" with its official meeting ground in the section of labor relations law of the American Bar Association; the large group of labor-law teachers and scholars; the extensive list of distinguished public men who have participated in labor relations as teachers, arbitrators, conciliators, and administrators; the network of labor and industrial relations personnel who relate to the lawyers and other professionals; the public and private case- and data-reporting services supporting this massive manpower—this entire complex supports and often supplants the federal administrative agency and the courts. Labor arbitration has become a massive institution and has received a broad charter from the Supreme Court. In both administrative and arbitration phases, the institutions of labor law are majestic, compared with the puny developments at the level of state FEP agencies and with the unused power of the Office of Federal Contract Compliance.

This demonstrates that the enforcement of social policy in the employment field is not a simple or easy thing. One cannot wave a wand, albeit one called Plans for Progress, blessed with the presidential seal—

and get results—without the supporting structure which the NLRB helped to evolve. This "law effectuation system" simply does not exist in the employment discrimination field.

The NLRB is the formal vehicle by which the interests of the labor movement have been pressed against employers. But the labor movement has never relied on the NLRB alone to protect its interests, even when the Board was prolabor. It always preserved the right to strike even over matters within the jurisdiction of the Board. In addition, the labor movement has spawned an extensive network of political, legal, and technical personnel to press its positions before the Board and the courts. It has shared in developing the arbitration process as an alternative to the courts and sometimes to the Board. The Board is one of many institutions through which the labor movement works. And the labor movement has not confined its legal activities to the NLRB. It was labor which expanded the right to sue under section 301 of Taft-Hartley and secured legal sanction for the labor arbitration process.[53]

B. *The Staying Power of Labor*

One of the basic contrasts between the labor movement and the civil rights movement is the persistence and staying power of the labor movement at all levels of lobbying, pressuring, and influencing activity, backed by financial resources which have become stable and significant in recent years. The labor movement is not as skilled or persistent in the techniques of managing regulatory agencies as is business. But, in comparison with the civil rights movement, the labor movement is sophisticated and consistent.[54] It has a theory, albeit a simple-minded one which may have reached a dead end. It has qualified and dedicated technical and professional personnel including attorneys. It has political know-how, both in the lobbying and in the vote getting fields. This is all related to its "presence"—its day-in and day-out connection with myriad minute decisions, as well as the big ones by which life in the

---

[53] *Textile Workers v. Lincoln Mills*, 353 U.S. 448 (1957); United Steel Workers of America v. Warrior and Gulf Navigation Co., 363 U.S. 574 (1960); United Steel Workers of America v. American Manufacturing Co., 363 U.S. 564 (1960); United Steel Workers of America v. Enterprise Wheel and Car Corp., 363 U.S. 593 (1960).

[54] See, in general, *Industrial Conflict and Race Conflict: Parallels Between the 1930's and the 1960's*, in INDUSTRIAL RELATIONS RESEARCH ASS'N PROC. OF 1967 ANNUAL SPRING MEETING (1967).

law, in government, and in labor relations is carried on. This "presence" is felt at all levels, from the foreman who thinks twice before disciplining an employee because he knows he must deal with the grievance committee to the administrator who hesitates before taking an action which may be viewed as antilabor and the Congressman who must always consider his prospects for reelection.

In the civil rights field, after a short exposure to Don Slaiman, the AFL-CIO Civil Rights Director, any administrator automatically asks himself, "how will Slaiman react to this?" Slaiman is regularly on the job, has a few assistants, and is in the information network concerning the acts of the government which affect unions.

The contrast is that the NAACP lobbyist *for all purposes* in Washington is Clarence Mitchell. He is spread so thin that he can barely manage a visit or two a year to the Commission. By this I do not intend to either compliment Slaiman or disparage Mitchell. They are both excellent, competent men in their jobs. Slaiman's job is more manageable (he would say less unmanageable) than Mitchell's. But this itself is one test of the capacity and maturity of social-economic institutions. Business, by contrast with both civil rights and labor, maintains a staff of half a dozen men whose administrative costs are paid by the government (Plans for Progress) who assure that its views on matters of employment discrimination are expressed in government circles.

The civil rights movement is virtually without theory—or has an embarrassment of them—and lacks staying power. It has been dazed by cross-currents which are a reflection of the complexity of its problem and of the inability to come to grips with its elements. It rouses itself as a sleeping giant and takes a symbolic step—a march on Washington, a riot in a large city—and then falls back to be further disheartened when nothing happens. Its staying power is low. Its complement of men with expertise is limited.

On a day-in, day-out basis, the civil rights movement is not in the same ball game as the labor movement, and not in the same league as the business community. Yet, the administrative process pits these interests against each other at this very point. Success in the administrative process goes to the vigilant, the persistent, the technically adept, and the politically potent. Faltering at any point can be fatal. Thus the analogy between the labor movement and the civil rights movement breaks down because the labor movement and the civil rights movement are not similarly organized and do not function alike. Their roots in the social and economic structure are different, and their history is different. A regulatory structure based on the premise that they are alike will flounder. This is one lesson of the last quarter century in the field of employment discrimination regulation.

C. *Capacity of Civil Rights Movement to Litigate*

The same comparative weakness of the civil rights movement does not exist with respect to attorneys and the capacity to litigate. Therein lies, for the moment at least, the saving opportunity. By contrast with twenty years ago, the legal sector of the civil rights movement is far more stable and vigorous. The NAACP, the Inc. Fund (Legal Defense and Education Fund), and CORE compete in litigation as in other areas. A cadre of successful organizers and lawyers has developed. All of the resources of the movement had to be marshaled (no pun intended) for years, to participate in *Brown v. Board of Education.* Today, by contrast, the legal resources, including lawyers, "friendly" law professors, student research help, and institutional support are sufficient to support legal action on many fronts. Many of the lawyers who are sympathetic to the civil rights movement are themselves labor lawyers who help sustain the civil rights-labor coalition.

Thus one of the fundamental weaknesses which beset the civil action in the administrative law era is no more. The individual is not alone and afraid, unfriended and unfunded. His complaint is a group complaint. More than likely in a race case, it is succored by the NAACP or the Inc. Fund. In a sex case, female complainants band together, present themselves to the local attorney, who upon viewing the potential clients becomes an instant expert in employment discrimination, and assists in the securing of their rights. Thus litigation—although not administration as yet—has become a practical vehicle for the expression of the group interest in the elimination of employment discrimination.[55]

---

[55] On this concept, see Cowan, *Group Interests*, 44 VA. L. REV. 331 (1958); Blumrosen, *Group Interests in Labor Law*, 13 RUTGERS L. REV. 432 (1959); Symposium, *Group Interests and the Law*, 13 RUTGERS L. REV. 429 (1959). The crucial nature of the group interest in the context under discussion is central to the decision in NAACP v. Alabama, 360 U.S. 240 (1959). The concept has evolved since this decision in Brotherhood of Railroad Trainmen v. Virginia, 377 U.S. 1 (1964).

The fundamental social weakness of the individual right to sue has been cured by placing the individual in the context of "his organization," which is capable of competing and combating with other interests.[56] But if the administrative solution is adopted, the civil rights movement will lose its present position because it does not have adequate political muscle and staying power. The political process embodied in administration is simply against it. At the present state of development, the civil rights movement can compete with management and labor in court, but not in the administrative areas.

One reason why the legislators of the 1930's turned to the administrative process was that the courts had been unsympathetic to the needs of organized labor. The same cannot be said of the courts and the problems of discrimination. In the last decade, the institution in the United States most favorable to the civil rights movement and its interests has been the federal judiciary. Nevertheless, the courts were given expanded power in the field of employment discrimination in the Civil Rights Act of 1964 by conservatives. The primary spokesman for this position was Senator Dirksen, never specially identified with liberal causes. I suggest that his approach reflected a national mood of the business community (a mood which I felt in hundreds of contacts at various levels in my two years in government) that is interested in getting rid of the problem of discrimination. If the problem cannot be buried, let it be solved. But let us not have it drag on forever, perpetuated by less than competent administrative practices. The mood is "let's resolve it." For this, the judicial process is appropriate. It is the only governmental process which is self limiting and self liquidating. Judges do not seek expansion of their jurisdiction, nor do they need to keep a specific problem alive to justify their existence.

Administrators are the opposite. They cannot solve the problem which brought them into being without destroying themselves. Therefore, they routinize the problem. This is tolerable up to a point. But we will no longer tolerate it in the field of employment discrimination be-

---

[56] Once the group has become potent in protecting its members and the beneficiaries of its power, it also acquires the opportunity to injure them by denying their just claims. See Blumrosen, *The Workers and Three Phases of Unionism: Administrative and Judicial Control of the Worker-Union Relationship*, 61 Mich. L. Rev. 1435 at 1455 (1963). This calls for regulation of the relationship as in Vaca v. Sipes, 386 U.S. 171 (1967); but this should not blind us to the fact that, but for the group, there would be no relationship to protect.

cause other interests are too seriously jeopardized. Therefore, our response is to take the matter to another forum, take it away from the administrators and turn it over to the judges.

The Congress of 1964 was aware of the liberal views of the judges on questions of race relations. Yet it placed the issues in the hands of the judiciary rather than the administrative process. Congress thus assured that the problem would be dealt with by civil-rights-minded judges who decided cases, rather than perpetuated by administrators who did not.

In hindsight, it is hard to see why this decision was characterized as conservative or anticivil rights, unless one defines the issues in terms of the *form* of the legal process, rather than the *results* obtained by that process. The courts have been the leaders in elimination of inequality, beginning with *Steele v. Louisville &N. Ry.* in 1944,[57] *Brown v. Board of Education* in 1954,[58] and continuing through *Jones v. Mayer* in 1968.[59] The tendency of the courts to provide for equal opportunity through constitutional and statutory provisions designed for other purposes could certainly be expected to expand under a statute intended to achieve these results. As I write this the federal courts are the best forum for the civil rights interests.[60]

D. *Comparison of Strength of OFCC and EEOC*

Those who urge an all-powerful administrative agency confuse the form of power with the substantive ability to exercise it. There already exists in this field an "all-powerful" agency which is impotent. That is the agency administering the government contracts prohibition on employment discrimination. This agency, in its present incarnation, is the

---

[57] Steele v. Louisville & N. Ry., 323 U.S. 192 (1944).

[58] Brown v. Board of Education, 347 U.S. 483 (1954).

[59] Jones v. Alfred H. Mayer Co., 392 U.S. 409 (1968).

[60] This tendency is confirmed in the recent case under Title II of the Civil Rights Act of 1964, Newman v. Piggie Park Enterprises, Inc., 390 U.S. 400 (1968), holding that prevailing plaintiffs are to recover attorney fees as a matter of course in litigation with respect to discrimination in public accommodations. The same rationale is applicable under Title VII, in light of the similarity of statutory language, legislative history, and purpose. See also Jenkins v. United Gas Co., 400 F.2d 28 (5th Cir. 1968), and Oatis v. Crown Zellerbach Corp., 58 Lab. Cas. ¶9140 (5th Cir. 1968).

Office of Federal Contract Compliance of the Department of Labor.[61] It has all the trappings of the most potent power imaginable, the ability to either cancel government contracts or, more potent because less subject to judicial scrutiny, the power to suspend from future government contracts an employer who fails to meet the requirement that he take "affirmative action" to insure equal employment opportunity. The contract power is more potent than the power to issue cease and desist and specific performance orders, because it can affect the basic economic future of the establishment or company.

This power has been used in a meaningful manner only once, in the long history of the agency wielding it. The results were spectacular.[62] Why the restraints on the use of this power? For the reason that the political pressures against its use brought by industry and labor have been enormous. One manifestation was the creation of Plans for Progress. This was an association of large industry to "voluntarily" improve employment opportunity. The program was apparently a shield to protect large employers who did little, rather than a sword to end discrimination. An EEOC study of 100 large corporations based in New York concluded that "While there were individual exceptions, those companies (46) within the 100 which are signatories of a 'Plan for Progress'— a public posture of affirmative action in minority employment, utilized minorities in 1966 at a substantially lower rate as a group than the 54 companies not party to a comparable public pledge. For example, while nonmembers had 1.2 percent Negroes in positions as officials and managers, Plan members had only 0.3 percent in these jobs." [63]

The pressures have been so great that persons at high levels have lost their jobs, so powerful that a courageous director of contract compliance of a major government agency was "reorganized" out of existence, and the function of his office subordinated to those whose priority was the mission of the agency rather than the elimination of discrimination. [64] These are the big leagues of power politics in the bureaucracy. The penalty for a single slip is oblivion within a matter of months. As a result, there is little professional expertise available anywhere within

---

[61] See Sovern, ch. 5; NATHAN, JOBS AND CIVIL RIGHTS (1969).

[62] Ch. 8 *infra*.

[63] EEOC, HEARINGS ON DISCRIMINATION IN WHITE COLLAR EMPLOYMENT (1968), p. 598. In 1969, Plans for Progress was absorbed into the National Alliance of Businessmen (NAB). The focus of NAB is the "hard core" unemployed.

[64] See note 27 *supra*.

the OFCC-PIA (Predominant Interest Agency) complex, which embrace hundreds of men organized in a loose hierarchy. The power cannot be exercised for political reasons; hence there is no cadre of personnel skilled at its exercise, and attempts by the OFCC are sometimes clumsy.[65] The administrators of this agency have had to tread most cautiously, and have heretofore not exercised its extensive power. Power which cannot be exercised will not solve the difficulties of race relations in employment.

In 1969, a new Assistant Secretary of Labor, Mr. Arthur Fletcher, attempted to flex the muscles of the OFCC, and immediately was enmeshed in the internal and external constraints which are inherent in the administrative process. A program aimed at employment discrimination in the construction trades was developed for Philadelphia. This program required specific numbers of minorities in specific trades on each government-financed construction job. The Comptroller General declared the program illegal under Title VII, thereby precipitating a constitutional crisis as to whether he or the Attorney General had the power to interpret federal substantive law. This effectively delayed the expansion of the Philadelphia plan. Then the OFCC held hearings in Chicago, and actually temporarily suspended the contracts of seventeen building contractors. These hearings featured a recommendation by the Department of Housing and Urban Development for vigorous enforcement action. Almost immediately after the close of the hearings the Department of Labor announced its preference for "home town" solutions, rather than those imposed by the government. As of this writing, it is not clear whether such a preference means (1) lip service to the idea of local control, while actually requiring important corrective action to end discrimination, (2) participation at the local level to the extent that federal equal opportunity standards are met, or (3) leaving the civil rights groups to whatever their leverage is in the home town, without protection for their rights under federal statutes and executive orders.

E. *The EEOC*

Contrast the lowly Equal Employment Opportunity Commission. It has no power. Yet its success rate in conciliations is substantial and

---

[65] See Crown Zellerbach Corp. v. Wirtz, 281 F. Supp. 337 (1968).

meaningful. It is like the proverbial bumble bee. It seems to fly in defiance of the laws governing its operation. The answer is that because it lacks power, conciliation can consist of "helping" the respondent company or union avoid an uncertain but certainly unpleasant prospect of litigation conducted by private persons whom the government does not control, or a possible action by other government agencies. Commission personnel can take the posture that they are only "humble civil servants" who try to help achieve the national purpose in a difficult situation. In deciding that it would not consider a settlement as successful if the charging parties were not satisfied, the Commission forced respondents to deal with representatives of the civil rights interests. If conciliation fails, the adverse action will be taken, not by the Commission, but by some other public or private individual or institution. The availability of the individual right to sue means that pressures on the agency cannot terminate proceedings. This process of nonpower turns out to be of greater influence than the formal existence of much power. Its "notice of right to sue" and its decision on the issue of reasonable cause to believe there is discrimination lays a practical predicate for litigation which may be most persuasive in inducing settlement.[66]

F. *Emphasis on Formal Procedures at EEOC Has Led to Influential Written Decisions*

One of the manifestations of the nonenforcement approach taken by administrative agencies has been the failure to develop and utilize formal procedures for the handling of discrimination complaints. Upon receipt of a complaint, an agency would send out a man to take care of the matter. The agencies rarely distinguished the function of investigation, finding of reasonable cause, and attempts to conciliate, although state statutes so required. Rather, they would begin efforts to settle without first establishing that there was anything to settle. The result frequently was that the respondent was willing to enter into a symbolic settlement to get rid of the problem so long as it did not interfere with his operations. These symbolic settlements, which did not require the

---

[66] I have described the standard opening statement of conciliators in *The Individual Right to Eliminate Employment Discrimination by Litigation*, INDUSTRIAL RELATIONS RESEARCH ASS'N PROCEDURE OF 19TH ANNUAL WINTER MEETING 90–92 (1966).

assent of the charging party, were deemed "successful" by the agencies involved. Thus the "soft settlements" reached by the agencies are, in my view, directly traceable to the weakness of the agency when it went to talk settlement. It had not developed its case, had little bargaining strength to secure a meaningful settlement, and therefore secured weak settlements. The informality and absence of regular procedures tailored to achieve the agency objective is a hallmark of most of the agencies in this field.[67] In our time, a degree of formality is necessary for enforcement.

The EEOC took the view that, since it lacked power, it would follow the statutory procedure rigorously and elevate its only decisional process into a major function. The finding of "reasonable cause" became a major function of the commissioners and their staffs. Thus the Commission distinguished investigation (which was admininistrative fact finding only), decisionmaking (the reasonable cause decision was a formal document outlining the charge, the findings of fact, and the decision), and conciliation, which involved settlement efforts. These efforts are based on the factual premise set forth in the reasonable cause finding. The predicate for conciliation is the set of facts found by the Commission along with its conclusion that these facts established "reasonable cause" to believe there was discrimination. The same finding (of cause) at the New Jersey Division on Civil Rights is made by a low-level field employee, with little supervision.[68] The context of the conciliation discussions is that, in light of the reasonable cause decision, conciliation is an alternative to litigation by the aggrieved party or group.[69] The conciliator is to help solve the problem as thus defined. He is both an advocate for the charging parties, because the Commission has found them entitled to relief, and a "neutral" trying to solve the problem. The lurking right to sue if conciliation fails provides the one motivating force leading to settlement. This is strengthened by the Commission requirement that complainants agree if a settlement is to be considered a successful conciliation.[70]

---

[67] See note 32 *supra.*

[68] Frakt, *op. cit. supra,* note 11 at 442.

[69] See note 66 *supra.*

[70] The nature of this "low visibility" decision to treat the charging party as essential to a successful conciliation was one of the more creative acts of the Commission. Under the statute, §703(e), the Commission could have decided that it would exercise its own judgment as to what was "compliance with Title VII," and accept conciliation agreements regardless of the wishes of the charging parties.

The decision to focus on the reasonable cause finding has led to the production of many hundred written decisions on the question of what constitutes discrimination. These decisions constitute the largest reservoir of decisional matter on this question in the history of the nation. Without the formal distinction between investigation and conciliation, these decisions would not have been written, and the issues which they raise perhaps not poised as sharply or clearly for the administrators, the parties, and the courts. In the actual fabric of life, the influential nature of the decisions is attested by the relatively high rate of meaningful settlements which the Commission has achieved. That these are not taken settlements is itself attested to by the Commission practice of requiring the signature of the complainant on a conciliation agreement. Between the Commission and the respondent, there are no soft settlements of which the charging party is later advised.

G. *Power Defined*

Thus while the Commission lacked the power to make final decisions, it did have the power to make tentative ones. And these could be based on a less substantial record than would be necessary if the decision was to be definitive. An administrative investigation can be concluded with a total man-hour allocation of two weeks. A trial-type hearing would take many more man hours. A reasonable cause finding can be written in a far shorter time than would be necessary to review the record of a trial-type hearing. None of these shortcuts would be possible if the decision of the Commission were accorded administrative finality. Yet the cause findings have been highly influential in inducing

---

Under those circumstances, the Commission would not have issued a notice of right to sue and the charging party, if he were unhappy with the settlement, would have been forced to sue the Commission to issue the notice, rather than go directly against the respondent as he may now. In addition, under the alternative procedure, he might have been faced with a weighty administrative decision that the company was in compliance with the statute. Under existing procedures, no such decisions are issued. The theory of the Commission is that the rights under the statute are personal to the charging party and are not waivable by the Commission. Thus the Commission rejected the "paternalistic" approach to the administration of the laws which had been followed in many predecessor agencies. This theory has been confirmed by the federal district court in Cox v. United States Gypsum Co., 284 F. Supp. 74 (D.C. N.D. Ind. 1968), *aff'd,* 409 F.2d 289 (7th Cir. 1969).

meaningful settlements, and are likely to be influential with the courts in the interpretation of the statute. Is all of this activity the exercise of "power"? A negative answer is possible only if one looks at the law on the books and not at the law in action. If power is the ability to influence behavior in desired directions, then the Commission has exercised much power in its short life, precisely because it lacks the formal trappings of power. Contrast the muscle bound OFCC-PIA complex, which contains the most awesome arsenal of unusable power in the field.

From this perspective, the EEOC under Title VII exercises more power than that actually exercised by the Office of Federal Contract Compliance.

IV. The Importance of the Individual Right to Sue

The failures of the administrative processes at both the federal and state levels have been demonstrated. But what evidence is there of success of the existing combination of powers and procedures? I would concede it is sketchy, but it does exist. In three years since Title VII went into effect, the following significant results have been achieved.

1. Important decisions have been rendered on what constitutes discrimination in seniority systems and what remedies are required under Title VII. Significant decisions on remedies required in the case of discriminatory referral and membership activities of a construction union have been handed down.[71] Many of the cases in which these decisions were rendered were initiated by private parties operating within the framework of organized groups such as the NAACP and CORE. In some the government participated either as a party or amicus.

2. The single most significant settlement of a case involving a pattern of discrimination in the history of the field, the Newport News Shipbuilding and Drydock Company agreement, was negotiated. In this case, the EEOC informal conciliation efforts had failed, and a suit, again sponsored by the Legal Defense Fund, had been initiated in federal court. Only after this suit was initiated did the administrative process of the Office of Federal Contract Compliance and the Attorney General focus on the Newport News matter. The settlement agreement negotiated by the government became the vehicle for settlement of the

---

[71] See note 13 *supra*.

private suit, and this also meant that the complainants and those in interest with them participated in the settlement process, and were signatories to it, rather than having a decision imposed on them.[72]

3. The development and dissemination of information on the racial and ethnic composition of the labor force of employers has been achieved by the administrative agencies. It lays a foundation for planned governmental enforcement activities in the area where the individual suit is not likely to work for want of a complainant—in particular in the important sector of recruitment and hiring.[73]

4. Hundreds of cases of discrimination have been settled on terms satisfactory to the complainants and the respondents. The development of a body of informal decisional law on what constitutes discrimination is also underway.

V. Rejection of the Paternalistic Approach in the Pluralist Society

There is one further analysis which is relevant to the failure of the administrative process in this field. The administrative agency action was to act in loco parentis for the victims of discrimination. It was to process their cases and determine their remedies. This paternalism failed to protect the intended beneficiaries. The decision to treat minorities as wards of the administrative process subordinated their own interests to the judgment of the administrator. His judgment was shaped by the realities of his power position, which in turn was influenced by the position of the regulated groups. The result was nonenforcement.

Paternalism as a theory of governmental action has not worked in America. Our welfare administration is a shambles; our juvenile courts, intended to be paternalistic guardians of wayward children, got so bad that the Supreme Court finally had to scrap the entire process in the name of the constitutional rights of children;[74] the injustices perpetrated on the Indians under the guise of paternalism are monstrous. At every turn, when we have erected legal structures based on the principal of paternalism, the intended beneficiaries have become the legalized victims of the stronger interests. In the field of employment discrimina-

---

[72] See ch. 8 *infra*.

[73] See EEOC, Hearings on White Collar Discrimination (1968), for an illustration of analytical use of the reports on racial composition of the work force.

[74] *In Re* Gault, 387 U.S. 1 (1967).

tion, the political, social, and economic situation now suggests that the paternalstic era is at an end. The civil rights interests are demanding equal standing in the American society. I believe the existing regulatory structure more clearly provides for such equality than does the paternalistic administrative process.

VI. A Viable Alternative to Administrative Paternalism—Multi-interest Bargaining

Title VII, as administered, requires negotiation between the labor, management, and civil rights interests to adjust their disputes. A failure of these negotiations leave the civil rights interests free to press their position in court, and to seek pressure for administrative action. Without the freedom to go to court, this bargaining would not work, because the labor and management interests will probably continue to dominate within the administrative process. Thus the right to sue under Title VII, which in theory inures to individuals, in fact is exercised frequently by the civil rights interests. This right is transmuted, through the efforts of the Commission, into a duty to bargain with the civil rights interests, with the government's weight tipped on the side of the civil rights interest through the reasonable cause decision. Without the right to sue, the informal duty to bargain would not exist, because of the expectations of labor and management that they could manage the administrative process. They have no such expectations with respect to the courts. This combination of right to litigate with three interest negotiation which has been stimulated by the administration of Title VII holds promise of securing compliance with the equal employment opportunity obligation.

For when we finally reach the substance of issues in particular cases, we face difficult problems of both labor relations and human relations. Decent resolution of these problems requires careful negotiation within the framework of law.

Multi-interest bargaining, within a carefully established legal framework, is a process by which complex adjustments to socially required changes in relationships can be achieved. It is not easy to negotiate with three, four, or five groups which have conflicting and overlapping interests. Yet, in the typical seniority discrimination case, there are at least three interests—labor, management, and minorities—and often each of these is further fragmented. This type of multiparty "bargaining," building on our experience in two-party collective bargaining, is already a feature of modern urban life, and will become increasingly important as time goes on.[75] It has already proved its utility in the field of employment discrimination.[76] Once administration and the courts have identified the legal rules and policies applicable to various types of racial discrimination cases in employment, the process of multi-interest bargaining should be able to achieve decent results which are within the range of acceptability of all parties. But this process is difficult and requires skilled negotiations and analysts.

A decade ago, Dean Shulman sought to keep the law, but not lawyers, out of labor relations.[77] To solve the complex labor-civil rights problems of our time, we need both the law and the lawyers.

---

[75] The school dispute in New York City in the fall of 1968 involved at least a three-way conflict between the teachers' union, a local school district, and the city board of education. To cope with such situations, the Am. Arbitration Ass'n has recently expanded its horizons and established a new unit.

[76] See ch. 8 *infra* and the settlement of the seniority issue between the International Paper Co. and several unions described in a Dep't of Labor, News Release of Aug. 5, 1968; CCH EMPLOYMENT PRACTICES, NEW DEVELOPMENTS ¶8004 (1968).

[77] Shulman, *Reason, Contract, and Law in Labor Relations*, 68 HARV. L. REV. 999 (1955).

2   Administrative Creativity: The First Year
of the Equal Employment Opportunity Commission

There is a tide in the affairs of men,
Which, taken at the flood, leads on to fortune;
Omitted, all the voyage of their life
Is bound in shallows, and in miseries.
On such a full sea are we now afloat;
And we must take the current when it serves,
Or lose our ventures.

—*William Shakespeare,* from Julius Caesar

When faced with a problem of statutory
construction, this Court shows great
deference to the interpretation given the
statute by the officers or agency charged
with its administration . . . Particularly
is this respect due when the administrative
practice at stake "involves a contemporaneous
construction of a statute by the men charged
with the responsibility of setting its
machinery in motion, of making the parts work
efficiently and smoothly while they are
yet untried and new."

—*Chief Justice Earl Warren*

A new administrative agency has vast opportunities to demonstrate creative intelligence in its initial decisions. These decisions, made by a handful of men and women who comprise the initial staff, reverberate through time and space in a tidal wave of consequences for both procedure and substance. They translate legislation into concrete programs to bring the law to bear on social or economic activities of men in society. The administrators grapple with problems which were not addressed by the legislature, where ideological, theoretical, and even practical implications are not clear. Their decisions are often taken in an atmosphere where the choice is free, where judgment is unencumbered by immediate political pressure or judicial precedent, where administrators can either be creative or cautious, and where the larger forces of the bureaucracy and the courts will support their decisions, whatever they may be.

The potential scope of administrative creativity in a new agency makes it important to understand these "low visibility" decisions which shape the agency, the law, and the social problem which brought the agency into being. The EEOC, a five-member body created by Title VII of the Civil Rights Act of 1964, struggles with discrimination in employment because of race, color, religion, national origin, and sex. It may investigate, determine if reasonable cause exists to believe there is discrimination, and attempt to conciliate. If conciliation fails, the aggrieved individual may sue. The Attorney General may also sue to end patterns of discrimination. The EEOC was established to deal with the central aspect of the major domestic social problem of our time in a context where there had been many prior laws and prior administrative efforts, all of which had failed. The act represents the first modern federal civil rights legislation against racial discrimination in employment.

My purpose here is to convey the sense of openness, the opportunity for creative and constructive decisionmaking which the administrative process affords. I hope these illustrations of administrative creativity at the EEOC will stimulate attention to this process, and suggest to students who are struck by the negativism of their legal education that the creative and constructive role of law in grappling with important social questions is limited only by the imagination and opportunity of the lawyer. For example, the EEOC minimized the formal requirements for invoking Title VII, streamlined possibly complex federal-state relations, imposed a national reporting system in the face of seemingly restrictive statutory language, developed a compliance procedure protective of individual rights, laid a foundation for multilateral negotiation between labor, management, and civil rights groups, adopted "guidelines" since it had no power to engage in substantive rulemaking, and coordinated all of the federal government's power in a massive settlement with the Newport News Shipbuilding Company.[1]

Creative administration converted a powerless agency operating under an apparently weak statute into a major force for the elimination of employment discrimination. It is important to understand the opportunities for administrative creativity in the public and private institutions of our society. Our success in coping with the major problems of our time may be influenced by the degree of creativity shown and maintained by administrators. Legal education produces many men who become influential in the administrative process. But it rarely deals with the affirmative aspects of administration. Rather, the law schools provide elaborate intellectual equipment to *restrict* the efforts of administrators. Constitutional law and administrative law courses are still largely concerned with what government may not do, rather than with how it should decide what it may do. Students impatient with the negativism of present legal education would be better equipped as lawyers if they would focus sharply on the question of "how we can best fulfill the purposes which brought our agency into being" rather than on the question of "whether the courts will sustain this course of action." The latter question is, of course, important. Administrative processes must be confined to the channels marked by due process and legislative intent. These channels are often wide, though the lawyer's trained myopia tends to make him view them narrowly. Creative administration requires a view of alternatives as wide as legal limits permit and judgments between alternatives which are fitted to the task before the agency.

My first direct involvement with administrative decisionmaking in the field of racial discrimination came in 1963, when I became a consultant to the New Jersey Civil Rights Commission. The chairman, Mr. Sidney Reitman, was critical of the work of the Division on Civil Rights, which enforced the antidiscrimination laws of the state. Utilizing my Rutgers Law School class in social legislation, I conducted a comprehensive study of the Division on Civil Rights. The Division typified administrative caution and ineptness at every turn; its procedures were incredibly sloppy; it narrowly construed a statute which the courts were prepared to construe broadly; it did not secure relief for the com-

---

[1] See ch. 8 *infra*.

plainants, or for the general class of victims of discrimination. It was a failure.[2]

In order to reach these conclusions, I developed a method to evaluate the performance of the agency. I developed a mental image, a model of how the state agency *should* operate in order to have maximum impact on the problems of discrimination. Into this model went the policy of maximum enforcement, the "liberal construction" of the substantive provisions of the law, and the adoption of procedures which would be likely to implement this policy.

Applying this analysis, which is related to program planning and systems analysis but with a lawyer's bent,[3] I concluded that the New Jersey agency should have broadly construed its powers and then utilized them in a tough-minded, effective enforcement program. Many of my criticisms scored a lack of administrative energy and inventiveness. The Division refused to construe the statute broadly to achieve legislative objectives, and insisted on a series of legislative amendments instead. Thus the problems of discrimination remained focused in the legislative rather than in the administrative stage. This had been the pattern for a quarter of a century. It did not achieve social change. As long as the administration could pass the buck back to the legislature, the laws were not enforced. Civil rights groups accepted the premise that the statute required amendment and trouped with frustrating regularity to the state legislative halls for amendments to achieve the same results that aggressive administration could have accomplished. The administrators, meanwhile had an excuse for nonperformance.

The New Jersey study convinced me of the futility of this game, and of the importance of energetic administration. In a sense, the New Jersey Supreme Court had been calling for this kind of administration, but there was no response from the agency. Rather, the administrator took a defensive attitude toward my work and sought to have it suppressed or modified. Several years later, during the "black power" days of 1968, this administrator was toppled by pressures from the black community.

The study was made public, along with recommendations for vigorous enforcement of the existing law and the use of creative administra-

---

[2] The report was the basis for my article, *Anti-Discrimination Laws in Action in New Jersey: A Law-Sociology Study*, 19 RUTGERS L. REV. 187 (1965).

[3] See report of Committee on Research, Association of American Law Schools, II Proc. A.A.L.S. 65 (1967).

tion of its provisions. The study came to the attention of Tom Powers, then Executive Assistant to the Secretary of Labor, when he came to Newark to consult concerning racial discrimination problems incident to the construction of the new Rutgers Law School. He invited me to spend part of my forthcoming sabbatical year helping to set up the EEOC, of which he was to be the first Executive Director. I decided to spend six months with the Commission and the rest of the year writing on a Caribbean Island. I spent two years in Washington, which left me with a lingering case of Potomac fever. I never had my sabbatical in the sun, but I did have the opportunity to apply myself, through the EEOC, to the most pressing domestic problem of our time.

When I arrived in Washington to deal with the federal-state relations of EEOC, I found total confusion. The act had been signed on July 2, 1964, with a one-year moratorium on its substantive provisions. This year of grace was to allow "voluntary compliance" and to allow for the organization of its principle agency, the EEOC. But President Johnson confounded this objective by taking a full eleven months of that year before he appointed the commissioners. They in turn had to find a staff and be ready for business in one month. As a result, the initial interpretations of Title VII were done quickly and informally. In those early days, before major bureaucratic organization developed, the staff worked very closely with the individual commissioners. The initial commissioners were:

Franklin D. Roosevelt, Jr., Democrat, chairman. When he paid attention to the business of the commission, he was the best chairman of the four men who have held the job. He was knowledgeable, sophisticated, and had good judgment. But he was forever chasing the will-o'-the-wisp of political office. The office songwriter took the tune of the Navy "Fight Song" and wrote a parody beginning, "Franklin's away, my boys, ..."

Vice-Chairman Luther Holcolmb, Democrat from Texas. Dr. Holcolmb was not interested in the details of administration of the statute; he was interested in politics and in protecting the President. As chairmen appeared, promising to stay and solve the problem of discrimination, only to leave a short time after in pursuit of their own interests, Dr. Holcolmb held the commission together and is responsible for such continuity in administration as it has shown.

Aileen Hernandez, Democrat from California, attractive, articulate, and aggressive. She claimed to have been picked by a computer because of the many interest groups who could be said to be represented by her appointment. She was a Negro woman from Brooklyn who had worked in the labor movement and in the California FEPC, and she had a Spanish-sounding married name. She believed in creative administration and was one strong rallying point for those of us who sought to shape the actions of the Commission to achieve the social objective for which it was created. But she was deeply frustrated by the difficulties of accomplishing her objectives and by the neglect of the Commission by the President. She resigned in midterm.

Samuel Jackson, black lawyer, former Judge Advocate General captain, had practiced in Kansas, was a leader of the left wing of the NAACP and a Republican. He, too, understood how the administrative process could be shaped to achieve social results, and was busy from the first day attempting to influence and control the direction of the Commission. His efforts brought him into conflict with every chairman and staff director. He did good work in shaping the law, in insisting on procedures whch protected complainants, and in conducting hearings on discrimination in the textile industry in the Carolinas. He was not reappointed. In 1969, he was appointed assistant secretary of the Department of Housing and Urban Development.

Richard Graham, Republican businessman from Wisconsin who had been with the Peace Corps in Africa. Dick was called the "unguided missile" behind his back, because he was far more interested in outcomes than in the process which led to them. He considered sex discrimination a major problem. He was outspoken and independent. His appointment lapsed, and he was not reappointed.

These five people, assisted by Tom Powers as Executive Director, had to put together an agency in a month. Later, Herman Edelsberg became Executive Director and presided over many of the decisions taken during that year.

I. Creative Administration and Legislative Intent

After the commissioners were sworn in, a White House aide came up to Sam Jackson, the aggressive Negro commissioner, and said, "Well, you're the only lawyer on the Commission, aside from the Chairman. You better start preparing rules and regulations because the law goes into effect next month."

This set off a flurry of activity among a task force composed of half a dozen borrowed lawyers who met nearly every afternoon for two weeks and developed many of the procedures and initial substantive law interpretations. I joined the task force initially to deal with the federal-state relations problems under Title VII, but rapidly broadened my involvement to cover all aspects of the work of the task force. The task force attorneys had different backgrounds and brought different attitudes to the conference table. One view was based on personal knowledge of the legislative debates and cloak-room conversations which had surrounded the passage of the Civil Rights Act. Richard Berg, who would become Deputy General Counsel, had been in the Justice Department and acted as advisor to Senator Humphrey during the debates in the Senate. He saw the statutory language in the context of its original informal setting (or, more precisely, what he understood to be the original informal setting). He had a clear and personal understanding of the legislative intent. He knew of the compromises which were actually made in the process of putting together the Civil Rights Act of 1964. The proposals he made, and his reactions to the proposal of others, were influenced by his concern with keeping the bargain which he understood had been struck in the legislature. The statute was a compromise, and Mr. Berg intended to be reasonably faithful to this compromise. As he saw it, legislative intent was, not a standard for review of administrative action, but a reality to be observed. His view of many of the problems was explained in an article in the *Brooklyn Law Review*.[4]

Berg's view was but a special case of a generally held conception that Title VII had been a "defeat" for the civil rights movement. This conclusion was based on two items; first, the Congress had deleted the hearing and cease and desist powers which the liberals had wanted for the EEOC, and left enforcement to the courts. Second, a series of amendments designed to allay the fears of the conservatives over the scope of the statute had been agreed to by the Democratic "leadership conference" as a part of the decisional process which broke a long filibuster and secured passage of the bill. But neither of these

---

[4] Berg, *Equal Employment Opportunity under the Civil Rights Act of 1964,* 31 BKLYN L. REV. 62 (1965).

episodes warranted the negative conclusion drawn from them. It turned out that the agency was far stronger because it did *not* have hearing and decision powers than it would have been otherwise, and that fair interpretation of the various Dirksen amendments would deprive them of any crippling effect. This defeatist view of Title VII was not warranted. After all, it was the first federal legislation in the employment discrimination field, its substantive provisions were written in broad language, and it provided for extensive federal court jurisdiction for enforcement purposes.

In the New Jersey study, I developed some basic attitudes toward the enforcement of antidiscrimination laws. I read them as charters of equality, to be broadly construed, with the administration carrying the initial interpretation of the laws as broadly as possible, subject to judicial restraint. I applied this view to Title VII. I read all the statutory language against the postulate that it had been difficult to achieve any civil rights legislation, and that the statue was a political compromise which recognized the need for federal action to end employment discrimination. Therefore, it should be liberally construed, and procedures should be shaped to the needs of the minorities for whom the statute had been adopted. The objective was to maximize the effect of the statute on employment discrimination without going back to the Congress for more substantive legislation.

The legislative history set limits beyond which administrators could not go in carrying out the statutory mandate, but it did not dictate the course of administration. One of the major functions of written legislative history is to force the legislators to operate in the open. Informal cloak-room deals not embodied in statutory language, reports, or debates are simply not limiting factors shaping administrative interpretations. This view of legislative history requires the administrator to develop ideas, policies, and procedures which derive from an informed understanding of the dynamics of the social problem and the role of government in its resolution. The statute and its history both set the goal and define the limits available to the agency to reach that goal. But within these confines, the agency is free to shape its own destiny with respect to the problem it is required to solve.

As an administrator for EEOC, I attempted to bring my model of an aggressive and effective agency into reality. The fact that I had a model gave me a great advantage in the early days at EEOC. The

model gave me a basis to propose and evaluate substantive and procedural decisions which would shape the agency. In addition, my study of
the New Jersey agency made me conscious of certain pitfalls to be
avoided. Of course one should not confuse energy with wisdom, and
during my time with EEOC I was sometimes comforted to know that
the agency's word was not final, that the courts were available to prevent serious errors. However, I felt that most of the problems confronting the EEOC could be solved by creative interpretation of Title VII
which would be upheld by the courts, partly out of deference to the
administrators.

When I went to Washington, I shared the liberal view that the
Commission was too weak, because it had no power to enforce the law.
(We called it a toothless tiger). As time went on, I realized that there
are many sources of power, and the weakness of the Commission might,
itself, become a strong point in the solution of employment discrimination problems. After a year with the Commission, in which I learned
more about how the statute works and how government works in our
pluralistic society, I came to the conclusion that it would not help—but
would positively harm—the drive to end employment discrimination if
the Commission were given that additional statutory power which the
liberals believed so important in 1965. I believed a *more powerful*
Commission would become a captive of those interests which were to
be regulated, while the existing weak institution enabled civil rights
groups to use the federal courts which are favorable to their demands.

II. Developing Procedures

The source materials which we had to work with in developing procedures in those early days were minimal. The Bureau of National
Affairs (BNA) and the Commerce Clearing House (CCH) had each
published excerpts from the legislative history[5] and the various changes
in statutory language which had been made as the legislation had
worked its way through the Congress. Berg had published his article.
There was nothing else. The initial interpretations were made almost

---

[5] Bureau of National Affairs Operations Manual, the Civil Rights Act
of 1964; Commerce Clearing House, Civil Rights Act of 1964 with explanation (1964).

exclusively by the judgment of the individual lawyers involved, supported by arguments made from these limited materials. Thus the interpretations were basically the product of the experiences of the various attorneys, shaped minimally by extrinsic aids, and leavened by the policy orientations of the commissioners.

The first set of administrative rules was rushed through in two weeks to be ready on July 2, 1965. Those rules have been slightly modified, but they have stood up rather well, considering the haste with which they were drawn.[6] The form of the rules was importantly the work of NLRB Trial Examiner Bruce Hunt, who was lent to the Commission by the Labor Board and whose experience in race relations stretched back to the original President's Committee of the early 1940's.

Those of us who believe that the procedures should be shaped for maximum enforcement had certain objectives with respect to the rules. They should be simple. They should leave the heaviest burden on the Commission, rather than on the complainant. They should protect the complainant from risks of retaliation. They should facilitate, rather than impede, the carrying out of the investigative, finding, and conciliation efforts of the Commission. Some of these objectives turned out to be internally inconsistent as applied to situations which emerged as the Commission developed. For example, a totally informal procedure would have speeded the handling of cases; but this was incompatible with the desire to get decent settlements, which required a high degree of formality in proceeding.

With mixed feelings overshadowed by questions as to why the President delayed to the last minute in making the appointments to the Commission, the voyage of the Commission was launched by the staff. Despite this air of overall pessimism, the challenge of the work was sharp and clear, and the camaraderie between the small group of staff members who were putting the agency together was high. It was an exciting adventure in a good cause.

A. *Avoiding the "In Writing and Under Oath" Requirements*

When we sat around the table in Commissioner Jackson's anteroom, one of the first questions was posed by the opening language of Section

---

[6] 29 C.F.R. 1600. et seq.

706 (a) of the Title. It began: "Whenever it is charged in writing under oath by a person claiming to be aggrieved . . ." the Commission should investigate, determine if there is reasonable cause, and then attempt to conciliate. Failing conciliation, the individual could sue, and the Commission could recommend that the Attorney General sue in the name of the United States.

The first draft of proposed regulations required that a "complaint" be in writing and notarized. Some of us objected vigorously to embodying these requirements into the procedural rules. Our experience in race relations, and sociological studies of Negro attitudes toward law, had demonstrated that it was difficult enough to get any minority group members in significant numbers to file any complaints.[7] If the Commission were to return complaints which were not sworn, or tell people who made oral complaints to submit one in writing under oath, the clientele of the agency would consider themselves rebuffed, and would reject the Commission as they had rejected other agencies. In addition, in some parts of the South, it was difficult for a Negro to get a document notarized. One instance of coercion induced by a notary was reported.

Thus we proposed that the Commission act on an informal statement regardless of whether or not it was in writing or notarized, stopping to comply with these requirements when appropriate. We proposed putting the burden of writing and notarizing on the Commission, not the complainant. The majority of the draftsmen rejected this approach. They felt either that Congress intended that it be difficult to invoke the Commission processes or that these procedural provisions would be complied with without difficulty. But some of us persisted. We changed the language of our proposal so that it was relevant to whatever subject was currently before the group. (One afternoon, when I had raised the issue for about the fourth time, Commissioner Hernandez happened to be sitting in our meeting. "I like that idea," she said. It was embodied in the draft proposal on the spot.) When the rules were finished, we took them before the entire Commission and explained them paragraph by paragraph. At that time, the concept of informal complaints was raised to one of the first statements in the rules. The present Rule 1601.5 provides:

---

[7] Zeitz, *Survey of Negro Attitudes Toward Law*, 19 RUTGERS L. REV. 288 (1965).

The Commission will receive information concerning alleged violations of this title from any person. Where the information discloses that a person is entitled to file a charge with the Commission, the appropriate office will render his assistance in the filing of a charge . . .

This "victory" for a pro-enforcement policy plunged the Commission into further problems, but the rule has remained Commission policy and has now been vindicated by judicial decision.[8] For example, once it was decided to accept unsworn charges, the questions of the timeliness of charges arose. If an unsworn charge was submitted within the ninety-day statute of limitations, but was not "perfected" by the oath until after the ninety days, was the charge timely filed? This difficulty created a distinction between perfected and unperfected charges which perplexed us for months until the General Counsel ruled that the date of receipt was the date filed, whether sworn to or not. This cutting of the Gordian knot thus finally relegated the oath to a formal requirement. The Commission then authorized its own personnel to administer the oath. This allowed the investigator to satisfy the statutory requirement of a sworn complaint at the time he commenced his investigation even though the investigation was ordered on the basis of an unsworn letter sent to the Commission.

We were worried about possible retaliation against Negroes who filed charges with EEOC. The charges were many and the Commission staff few. We knew that the bulk of our first year's work would be in the South because Congress required the EEOC to defer to the state agencies when we received complaints, and the South had no such agencies. We feared that retaliation might take place before the Commission representative appeared on the scene. Thus the decision was made that investigators would serve the charge on the respondent at the time they made their first investigative contact. Thus the respondent would not have a pre-investigative opportunity to harass the charging party. This policy, while not literally at odds with the Commission's written rules, was inconsistent with the concept of prompt service of the charge.[9] Many investigations would not be undertaken for months because of

---

[8] See 29 C.F.R. 1601.11, *King v. Georgia Power Co.*, 58 Lab. Cas. ¶9150 (D.C. N.D. Ga. 1968).

[9] "Upon the filing of a charge on the amendment of a charge, the Commission shall furnish the respondent with a copy thereof by certified mail or in person." 29 C.F.R. 1601.13.

shortage of manpower. This policy aroused resentment.[10] Large corporations and unions were accustomed to notice from the PCEEO (a predecessor agency) before an investigation took place. With advance notice they could examine the situation, marshal the evidence, perhaps remedy a problem if they believed that it existed, or prepare to demonstrate that there was no problem.

The Commission's approach meant that company and union respondents either were represented in the investigation by local personnel who lacked the sophistication of home office personnel, or that the local personnel had to take an uncooperative stance and refuse to discuss the case until the home office had given advice.

The resulting embarrassment led companies and unions to pressure the Commission to serve the charges by mail. There was no practical problem with respect to sworn charges, but with respect to unsworn charges there were obvious difficulties. These difficulties were compounded by the fact that the Commission entered into many "notice" agreements. The Commission agreed to notify the home office of certain corporations when a charge was served against a local office; to notify the Construction Industry Joint Council if a charge was filed in the Construction industry, to notify the AFL CIO if the charge involved a local of an international affiliated with it, and so on. If the charges were sworn to and served by the field investigator, then he had the burden of seeing that the various notice obligations were complied with. In this there was considerable slippage which caused further embarrassments and claims that the Commission was not living up to its obligations.

Finally, the underlying rationale for the "no advance notice" rule proved not to be valid. Of the thousands of situations in the South which came to the attention of the Commission, probably less than a dozen, as of April, 1967, had generated anything which might be called retaliatory coercion. The respect for federal law ran deeper than we knew. This problem simply was not worth the travail that the Commission procedure caused. This was my view as I left in mid-1967. The Commission was then moving toward a change in its procedure. But one measure of the difference between the Commission as I came to it and as I left, was the great difficulty in introducing anything new or in

---

[10] *Local 5, IBEW v. EEOC* 58 Lab. Cas. ¶9143 (3d Cir. 1968) *cert. denied* 59 Lab Cas. ¶9190 (1969).

changing any existing procedure. Certainly, with regionalization and two years experience, the rationale for lack of quick service on respondent, aside from the oath problem, does not exist. The Commission did gather some facts by virtue of surprise which might have been concealed or explained differently if advance notice had been given, but I do not consider this a justification for the policy.

B. *Streamlining Deference Procedures*

Once the formula of aiding the complainant to invoke the statute had been accepted, it was used to solve other problems. For example, the statute required that where a state fair employment practice existed, charges could not be filed with the Commission until after sixty days from the time when the complainant had filed with the state agency. A literal reading of the statute would have required the Commission to return the charge to the complainant, and tell him that he had to file the charge with the state agency first but could again ask the EEOC for help more than sixty days after he had filed with the state, provided he asked within 210 days of the act of discrimination.[11]

---

[11] Deference procedures are set out in §706(b) and (c) as follows:

(b) In the case of an alleged unlawful employment practice occurring in a State, or political subdivision of a State, which has a State or local law prohibiting the unlawful employment practice alleged and establishing or authorizing a State or local authority to grant or seek relief from such practice or to institute criminal proceedings with respect thereto upon receiving notice thereof, no charge may be filed under subsection (a) by the person aggrieved before the expiration of sixty days after proceedings have been commenced under the State or local law, unless such proceedings have been earlier terminated, provided that such sixty-day period shall be extended to one hundred and twenty days during the first year after the effective date of such State or local law. If any requirement for the commencement of such proceedings is imposed by a State or local authority other than a requirement of the filing of a written and signed statement of the facts upon which the proceeding is based, the proceeding shall be deemed to have been commenced for the purposes of this subsection at the time such statement is sent by registered mail to the appropriate State or local authority.

(c) In the case of any charge filed by a member of the Commission alleging an unlawful employment practice occurring in a State or political subdivision of a State, which has a State or local law prohibiting the practice alleged and establishing or authorizing a State or local authority to grant or seek relief from such practice or to institute criminal proceedings with respect thereto upon receiving notice thereof, the Commission shall, before taking any action with respect to such charge, notify the appropriate State or local officials and, upon request, afford them a reasonable time, but not less than sixty days (provided

But this procedure would run afoul of the known difficulties in establishing relations between the charging parties and the government. The complexities in the various time limits would discourage all but the hardiest complainants, and many claims would simply get lost in the statutory maze of time limits. So we decided that the Commission, rather than the complainant, would operate the deference procedure. When a complaint came to the Commission which required deference, the Commission would send it directly to the state agency and attempt to get the state agency to treat the charge as coming to it—i.e., filed— from the charging party. The rule was written as follows: ". . . the Commission may not accept the charge for filing, but shall assist the aggrieved person in complying with Section 706(b)."

This language both complied with the statute and facilitated the processing of cases. Although there were bugs in this procedure, it worked reasonably well, and did not become a major stumbling block in the administration of the act. At the end of the sixty-day period, the Commission would write the complainant and ask if he wished it to take jurisdiction. His affirmative statement would be taken as the filing contemplated by the statute.

These two examples of the initial procedural decisions of EEOC illustrate the difficulties confronting administrators. These decisions do not now appear controversial. I am sure many would say that there were no real alternatives. Where a judgment seems sound in retrospect, no great credit seems to flow from the making of it. Yet these judgments were not preordained. They turned on the attitudes of those present during their formulation and on the network of informal relations and alliances formed in the small group concerned with the problem. Either of these two judgments could have gone the other way within the statutory framework, and could have produced and reflected a radically different kind of commission, a commission which *also* followed the statute, but with less concern for the beneficiaries of the law. The choices left open to the Commission by Congress were genuine.

For example, if both of these decisions had gone the other way, the EEOC would have rejected literally thousands of complaint letters dur-

---

that such sixty-day period shall be extended to one hundred and twenty days during the first year after the effective day of such State or local law), unless a shorter period is requested, to act under such State or local law to remedy the practice alleged.

ing the first two years, explaining that it could not process the charge because it lacked notarization or because it had not been processed through the state agency. Many of these complaints would have been dropped at that point by the writers of these letters. The resentment which gave rise to the letter in the first place would continue, but the focus would not be on the processes of law. At the same time, the backlog of cases at the Commission would have been much lower, and the EEOC could claim a much more impressive success record and speed record. This approach would be equally consistent with the statutory language and legislative history as the one actually adopted, and probably would have been confirmed by the courts.[12] Yet the nature of the agency and its relationship to the social problem, to the clientele, and to the regulated groups would have been drastically different from what it is today. The choices here were not dictated by statutory language, or by legislative history. They were the product of the judgment of the original commissioners acting in response to views developed by this small group of lawyers. These men, in turn, had developed a conception of the function of the agency along the lines described above, based on their view of the proper role of law and administration in coping with the problems of employment discrimination.

This does not mean that there were no constraints. There were constraints in terms of political realities, of statutory language, and in terms of the quality and quantity of manpower available.

III. The National Reporting System

My study of the New Jersey Civil Rights Division established that that agency was not effectively handling its own complaint load, but, more importantly, that the complaint load had little relation to patterns of employment discrimination in New Jersey. The Negro commu-

---

[12] The deferral procedure described in the text was disapproved in Love v. Pullman Co., 61 CCH Lab. Cas. ¶9324 (10th Cir. 1969) (rehearing held Mar. 9, 1970. See Note, 37 U. CHI. L. REV. 181 (1969). See International Chemical Workers v. Planters Mfg. Co., 54 Lab. Cas. ¶9025 (N.D. Miss. 1966). This case reflects judicial support for another exercise in administrative creativity, in which the Commission held that a labor union could be an "aggrieved party" under Title VII although in the legislative debates, the authority to file complaints "on behalf of" aggrieved parties, had been deleted. Mr. Berg was responsible for the development of the Commission position on this point.

nity simply did not utilize *any* legal processes with respect to problems of discrimination. Our sociological study of Negro attitudes toward law made clear that the Negro community did not act like white middle-class bourgeoisie and go to agencies of government to complain if they believed their rights were violated. In addition, there were many areas of discrimination where the facts were unknown to the black community, as in the case of an employer of "whites only," whose existence was unknown because he filled his jobs through an informal employee referral system which perpetuated segregation. It was clear, then, that the government would have to use its own initiative with employers who engaged in discrimination if discrimination was to be effectively countered.[13]

The objections to this approach which had been raised by administrators during the New Jersey study were the lack of authority, money, and manpower. In meeting these arguments, I had urged the New Jersey Division on Civil Rights to undertake a program first, and to use it to justify additional financing. Theodore Roosevelt is said to have secured additional funds from Congress by sending the fleet halfway around the world without funds to bring it back, and then demanding an additional appropriation. These arguments about a policy of agency initiation effectively concealed from my thinking the question how such a program would be implemented. Professor Sovern, who was writing his book on employment discrimination at about the same time, came out in favor of spot-check investigations by state agencies to identify discrimination where no complaint was filed.[14] I probably would have taken that view also had it not been for an extraordinary event which took place shortly after I arrived in Washington.

The new EEOC staff was housed temporarily in the Labor Department offices which also housed the President's Committee on Equal Employment Opportunity, the handful of men who administered the antidiscrimination clause in government contracts. The PCEEO was a jerry-built organization which attempted to move contract officers in various operating agencies to enforce an obligation toward which their

---

[13] Blumrosen, note 2, *supra*, especially 234–37. Some years later, I was still persuing this idea. See ch. 6 *infra*.

[14] SOVERN, LEGAL RESTRAINTS ON RACIAL DISCRIMINATION IN EMPLOYMENT (1966) at 56. He was not as clear about the EEOC, *id.* at 90, but did note the relationship between reports and compliance reviews of government contractors, *id.* at 125.

agencies were lukewarm at best and for which there was little specific guidance. The failure of PCEEO to ameliorate discrimination, although it had the mighty contract power, was one of the reasons for the passage of Title VII. I got to know these administrators fairly well in a short time. One day I had a problem concerning the EEOC, the PCEEO, and state agencies with respect to reporting and record-keeping requirements. I went down the hall to talk to the people in the reports sections of the PCEEO.

A. *Sociological Radar*

There I discovered the gold mine. The offices were not large, and bales of Form 40 reports lined the walls. These reports had been filed by government contractors. They indicated the racial and ethnic composition of the work force of most of the contractors doing business with the government. The reports had been analyzed by computers, and there were several books of print-outs listing employers who had no Negro employees—so-called zero lists—lists of employers with low percentages of Negroes in blue- and white-collar occupations—so-called underutilization lists. The figures were being manipulated by a group of frustrated administrators because there was no program in connection with their use.

I saw this as perhaps the most important tool in any program to eliminate employment discrimination. Here were lists of major employers excluding minorities in a massive way which outraged any reader of the statistics. And here were target lists of employers whose practices should be probed to determine whether the low—or zero—utilization of minorities was a result of discrimination. Here at last was a basis for government-initiated programs which were not based on complaints and which could focus on possible potential discriminators effectively. In explaining this potential of the reporting system, I conceived this analogy: Without radar Britain might have lost the air war with Germany in World War II—because she did not have enough planes to intercept the German bombers. With radar, those few planes could be sent to the crucial interception points to defeat the *Luftwaffe*. The parallel with the problem of employment discrimination was clear. There was a perennial shortage of manpower and money in antidiscrimination programs. If government could focus, through the reporting system, on those employers where underutilization was sharpest, there was a possibility of success fully combatting discrimination. And so the reporting system became sociological radar, directing the government energies to places of underutilization of minorities. This view I formulated rather quickly.[15]

However, there were a number of practical obstacles to putting this view into practice. The first was noncooperation from the PCEEO. Because I was new to administration, I did not understand this resistance.

A new agency, the EEOC, had been set up to encroach on PCEEO's jurisdiction, and the PCEEO personnel could not help but act defensively. In fact, they had a lot to be defensive about. They had no program for the use of the Form 40 data, and the compliance reviews were not effective. Thus when it came to the sharing of the Form 40 data or working out joint plans for its use, there was little cooperation.

This was true although the Executive Director of the Commission was formerly the Executive Assistant to the Secretary of Labor and Special Counsel to the PCEEO itself. Matters were so snarled that it was ultimately necessary for Tom Powers to get an opinion from the Office of Legal Counsel in the Justice Department that the PCEEO could give access to the Form 40 data to the EEOC.

B. *The Wilderness of Statutory Construction*

After I had seen the zero lists and realized their significance, I understood how crucial it was to develop a useful national statistical reporting system to deal with employment discrimination. The importance of a system for EEOC was underscored by the refusal of the President's Committee to share its data with us. As a result, I wandered for two weeks in the wilderness of statutory construction. I had heard about the problems of statutory interpretation dealing with the report-

---

15 In preparing a part of the report on the White House Conference on Equal Employment Opportunity, which was held in August 1965, I managed to insert the concept as follows, at 10:

The possible ways in which the Federal government might initiate proceedings were discussed. These included . . . . the use of employer reports of the racial composition of the work force as a sociological "radar net" to determine the existence of patterns of discrimination.

ing system when I arrived in Washington but had not realized their significance until I focused on the reporting system as a foundation for an enforcement program.

The problem was this: section 709(c) of Title VII gave the EEOC power to require reports on the racial, ethnic, religious, and sex of employees from every covered employer. The next section said that this power did not exist in states which themselves had fair employment practice laws.[16] Since almost all states outside the South had such laws,

---

[16] Sections 709(c) and (d) read as follows:

(c) Except as provided in subsection (d), every employer, employment agency, and labor organization subject to this title shall (1) make and keep such records relevant to the determinations of whether unlawful employment practices have been or are being committed, (2) preserve such records for such periods, and (3) to make such reports therefrom, as the Commission shall prescribe by regulation or order, after public hearing, as reasonable, necessary, or appropriate for the enforcement of this title or the regulations or orders thereunder. The Commission shall, by regulation, require each employer, labor organization, and joint labor-management committee subject to this title which controls an apprenticeship or other training program to maintain such records as are reasonably necessary to carry out the purpose of this title, including, but not limited to, a list of applicants who wish to participate in such program, including the chronological order in which such applications were received, and shall furnish to the Commission, upon request, a detailed description of the manner in which persons are selected to participate in the apprenticeship or other training program. Any employer, employment agency, labor organization, or joint labor-management committee which believes that the application to it of any regulation or order issued under this section would result in undue hardship may (1) apply to the Commission for an exemption from the application of such regulation or order, or (2) bring a civil action in the United States district court for the district where such records are kept. If the Commission or the court, as the case may be, finds that the application of the regulation or order to the employer, employment agency, or labor organization in question would impose an undue hardship, the Commission or the court, as the case may be, may grant appropriate relief.

(d) The provisions of subsection (c) shall not apply to any employer, employment agency, labor organization, or joint labor-management committee with respect to matters occurring in any State or political subdivision thereof which has a fair employment practice law during any period in which such employer, employment agency, labor organization, or joint labor-management committee is subject to such law, except that the Commission may require such notations on records which such employer, employment agency, labor organization, or joint labor-management committee keeps or is required to keep as are necessary because of differences in coverage or methods of enforcement between the State or local law and the provisions of this title. Where an employer is required by Executive Order 10925, issued March 6, 1961, or by any other Executive Order prescribing fair employment practices for Government contractors and subcontractors, or by rules or regulations issued thereunder, to file reports relating to his employment practices with any Federal agency or committee, and he is substantially in compliance with such requirements, the Commission shall not require him to file additional reports pursuant to subsection (c) of this section.

the two sections taken together seemed to permit the Commission to require reports only in the South. But, because of the difference in patterns of discrimination in the South and elsewhere, it was more important to have a reporting system outside the South. In the South, the typical pattern of discrimination involved the employment of many Negroes in lower-paid jobs. The problems involved promotional opportunities. In this situation, the complaint process worked to some degree, and the reporting system was not as necessary. Outside the South, the basic pattern of discrimination involved exclusion of minorities from employment. There the reporting system was most important to identify those employers, and the complaint process did not function. Thus the statute seemed to permit reporting requirements where they were less needed, and to deny them where they were more important.

When I arrived in Washington, the staff and the Commission had accepted this interpretation,[17] and were considering whether there was any way to get a national reporting system within the confines of the statute as they understood it. They were thinking of a bureaucratic monstrosity in which the EEOC lured state agencies to adopt a reporting system by rule or amendment to state law, and then to use the EEOC as a central clearing house for these reports. Fresh from my experiences with the New Jersey situation, I was horrified by the prospect of trying to get twenty-five state agencies or legislatures to adopt a reporting system. This seemed to promise years of futility.

After two weeks I produced what now seems the obvious answer. Congress did not intend the curious result described above. Rather, Congress was trying to protect employers against duplication of reporting requirements between the state and federal agencies. Thus, if a state required reporting, the Commission could not. This principle of nonduplication was expressly adopted in the last sentence of Section 709(d) with respect to government contractors. They did not have to report separately to the EEOC and the agency administrating the anti-

---

17 This was Berg's view of the sections. See Berg, *op. cit.*, note 4 *supra* at 89. Professor Sovern, too, thought that §709(d) precluded any reporting system in FEP states; Sovern, *op. cit.*, note 14 at 88:

This provision does not, as some may have thought, merely except from the federal record-keeping and report-filing requirements those subject to similar state requirements. The exception is much broader, exempting all those covered by a state fair employment practices law, without regard to whether that law contains record-keeping provisions.

discrimination clause in government contracts. It thus seemed reasonable to read the entire section in light of nonduplication. Under this analysis the Commission could require reports in all states unless a state agency required reports. Since no state required reports, the EEOC could require reports on a nationwide basis. The analysis has the merit of simplicity, and of achieving the policy of securing a national reporting system. It had the additional advantage of being a sensible construction of section 709(d); and it had some support in the written legislative history.[18]

It also had some failings. One was that it required a reading of the statute contrary to the plain meaning. The second was that, in the last sentence dealing with government contractors, the draftsmen demonstrated that they knew how to spell out the principle of nonduplication. Hence, it could be argued that Congress would have used similar language with respect to the state-EEOC relations had that been its intention. A third difficulty was the view of Mr. Berg, that, in fact, the legislative bargain had been that there would be no reporting system in states which had FEP laws—that is, that the curious result had, in fact, been intended. It was a part of the leadership compromise with Senator Dirksen. Berg had expressed this view in his law review article.[19]

But the importance of the matter required that it be pressed. Mr. Charles Markham, who later became Director of Research and Reports,

---

[18] Senator Humphrey's explanation of the compromise bill (EEOC, LEGISLATIVE HISTORY OF TITLE VII AND XI OF THE CIVIL RIGHTS ACT OF 1964, p. 3004) was as follows:

> This authority (in Sec. 709(c)), to required record keeping and reporting has been limited, in the substitute, to prevent duplication of record keeping requirements. Where the employer, agency, organization, or committee is also subject to a state fair employment practice law, the Commission may not prescribe general record keeping requirements.

Long after the decisions described in the text were taken, while preparing this material in the spring of 1969, I discovered a bit of legislative history which confirmed the nonduplication thesis. Senator Dirksen's proposed amendment No. 509, EEOC, LEGISLATIVE HISTORY at 3269, was close to the language of §709(d) finally adopted. The explanation: "This amendment is necessary to prevent the superimposition of different record-keeping requirements by the various State and Federal agencies dealing with discrimination in employment." This information was not available at the time the initial decisions described in the text were taken.

[19] Berg, *op. cit. supra.* In his Preface, written after the interpretation had been announced, Professor Sovern stated that the EEOC has "gone further than I believed possible in requiring the filing of reports by employers in states with their own fair employment practices law." Sovern, *op. cit. supra,* note 14, at viii.

and I prepared memoranda and argued in support of my reading of the statute. Mr. Berg went back to the Justice Department and checked his recollection with other attorneys. They were not so sure that there had been any legislative bargain on the question. So, it was suggested, why not go see Senator Dirksen?

A trip was arranged to Senator Dirksen's office. When the visitors returned, they reported that the Senator seemed unconcerned about the proposed construction, and had not made major objections. Thus it was decided to go ahead with the broad reading of the section. Thus was the national reporting system born.

Since that time, three years of reports have been filed by literally hundreds of thousands of employers, masses of information have been developed and are being analyzed, and the entire approach to the solution of the problems of employment discrimination is being heavily influenced by the existence of the statistical information contained in the reports.[20] At the EEOC white-collar hearings in New York in early 1968, numbers of employers voluntarily disclosed to the public their own statistics. Because of the existence of the reporting system and the analysis of its product, statistical analysis of the racial and ethnic composition of the work force has become a common and, I believe, a fruitful way of evaluating progress in the elimination of employment discrimination. But my purpose in pressing for a national reporting system was not to spread information about the racial composition of the work force. In fact, I probably underestimated the importance of the pure flow of information as a method of achieving social change. Rather, I wanted to lay a foundation for enforcement programs based on the data, to deal with employers who were underutilizers of minority workers.

But I had great difficulty in selling the idea of an enforcement approach based on analysis of the figures. There were a number of reasons for the difficulty. First there was the unanswered question of whether such an approach was likely to be more effective than a softer approach seeking voluntary compliance. Second there was the political difficulty involved in government initiation of action as distinct from government response to the filing of an individual complaint. Third there was the

---

[20] United States EEOC, HEARINGS ON DISCRIMINATION IN WHITE COLLAR EMPLOYMENT (1968). Chapter 3 consists of the EEOC analysis of the first year's reports filed by employers under Title VII.

heavy backlog of individual complaints and the lack of money and manpower to process them. And, finally, there was the lack of any precise program to deal with employers if it was decided to go ahead with such a plan. There were no standard procedures and basic operational manuals to establish and administer a program.

As I look back, I realize that my analogy comparing the reporting system to radar at the battle of Britain had at least one flaw. At the start of World War II, Britain had the finest fighter aircraft in the world in the Spitfire. Once the targets had been located through radar, the British had an effective program for the elimination of the enemy aircraft. But in the field of race relations in employment, even when the target was identified, the government had not developed an equivalent program of action to eliminate discrimination. Two years were to pass before serious effort would be put into the development of such programs. I finally engaged in this research and development in 1967–68 when I returned to Rutgers.

C. *The Weekend of July 9, 1965*

My emphasis on the reporting system as enforcement tool nearly led to my expulsion from Washington during July 1965. During the latter part of June, as I was working on the statutory construction problems of the reporting system, my sense of outrage that the government had not made significant use of the EEO-1 reports continued to mount. In early July I thought I could further the use of this material. Commissioner Graham pressed for EEOC action on the problems of the Negroes in Bogalusa, Louisiana. Chairman Roosevelt summoned from all branches of the executive those who were familiar with Bogalusa and its employment problems and began questioning them. At that time unfamiliar with the bureaucracy, I failed to appreciate the extraordinary feat involved in calling together officials from ten agencies on one day's notice. As one representative began to discuss the seniority problem at one of the plants in Bogalusa, it became clear to me that either he didn't know what he was talking about, or he was being evasive. (I now think it was a combination.) The evasiveness troubled me.

The basic attitude of an academic is openness, an attempt to communicate at all times and all levels. But a common attitude of administrators is secretiveness, of limiting information lest it be used in ways the administrator cannot control—hence evasiveness. This new agency was treading on the jurisdiction of the older and more established agencies, and they were trying to keep EEOC from disrupting their operations.

Since that time I have attended many meetings with the objective in mind of (1) seeing that someone else's hair-brained idea did not succeed in getting anywhere; (2) not exposing my own position unnecessarily while destroying the other fellow's; and (3) in the event that something was going to be done about this hair-brained idea, that it would not be done by me and my staff unless (4) I decided that I wanted to control its direction, in which case I would allow myself to be maneuvered into the position of taking on the task. This is a fairly basic part of any durable administrator's equipment, and I now realize that I should not have been surprised by the responses that we received.

Chairman Roosevelt wanted to do something in Bogalusa. But there was turmoil in Bogalusa at the time, and he didn't want to appear to be headline hunting. Therefore he thought the Commission should not focus *only* on Bogalusa. I seized this as an occasion to utilize the lists of underutilizing employers. (Later Roosevelt did try his hand at settling the Crown Zellerbach dispute in Bogalusa. His efforts came to naught, as did subsequent efforts of the Labor Department. Finally, the federal court in New Orleans, abolished the discriminatory seniority system.)[21]

I explain to Roosevelt briefly about the zero lists—with which he was totally unfamiliar—and promised him a list of worthwhile targets the following day. I had visions at that point of the Commission commencing its operations in grand style.

The next step was to get a copy of the zero and low-utilization lists. Commissioner Jackson asked a man on the PCEEO staff who was hoping for a position with the EEOC for a copy of the materials. This man walked in with a set of the print-outs under his arm and gave them to Commissioner Jackson. Again, I was new in Washington and did not realize that this was an act of disloyalty. It seemed to me simple common-sense, interagency cooperation. I had not learned that control of information is control of everything, and that administrators handle in-

---

[21] See United States v. Local 189A, United Paper Makers, 416 F.2d 980 (5th Cir. 1969) *Cert. Denied* 62 Lab. Cas. ¶9406.

formation with the tender loving care which most of us reserve for rare paintings or beautiful women.

As I worked with the list, my sense of outrage grew. Many of the industrial giants of the nation, many of them members of the much-vaunted Plans for Progress, were on either the zero list or the low-utilization list. The abdication of decency and social responsibility, the implication of discriminatory practices of these blue-chip organizations, and the shabby failure of even minimum enforcement of the executive order tumbled through my mind. The sense of outrage thus struck high in the establishment. Lyndon Johnson, while Vice-President, had been in charge of the PCEEO. A strengthened PCEEO had been one of the early acts of the Kennedy administration. I learned later that Johnson himself had chosen a soft rather than a tough enforcement policy by backing Hobart Taylor, the Executive Vice-Chairman, over the more aggressive John Feild.[22]

As I worked through the zero lists, I contrasted the stark failure reflected in the figures before me with the plush PCEEO party in Philadelphia which I had attended before I came to Washington. For all I could see, the government had sold out its obligations for a mess of hors d'oeuvres.

By the end of the day, I had culled a selection of employers from the massive list. I took the selection to Roosevelt, who scanned it in disbelief. He asked what could be done about it.

I decided to push my luck. At the Labor Department, a jerry-built training program was grinding to its conclusion for a group of investigators detailed to the Commission from various government agencies. These men would investigate cases until the Commission could develop its own staff. This was the first week of the operation of the Commission, and only a few complaints had trickled in. Most of the investigators, their training finished, would be returned to their agencies until called by the Commission. There were some sixty uncommitted investigators, most of whom had had some experience in either race relations or labor relations. The manpower situation at that moment was unique to the history of race relations law. I suggested to Roosevelt that we develop a special training program over the weekend, and conduct it the following Monday. By the middle of that week, the investigators

---

[22] EVANS AND NOVAK, Lyndon B. Johnson: The Exercise of Power (1966) (Signet ed. 1968), at 335–37.

could be at work on the implication of discrimination that the list suggested.

He said, "All right, we will do it."

I said, "How many of the investigators can I have?"

"Take them all."

"Are you serious?"

"Yes, I'm serious. Use them all."

That was an incredible moment. The Commission was in support of what Roosevelt was doing. The training program was concluding, and the trainees were ready to return to their duty stations until called by the Commission. Roosevelt delivered the closing remarks of the training session. He described the information available, asked those who could to remain. I discussed details of the proposed investigations of patterns of discrimination which were to begin the following Monday.

Roosevelt flew to his farm in Poughkeepsie. I began pulling people together for a dinner to decide the strategy for the program. We needed the cooperation of the PCEEO because it had access to compliance files concerning each of the companies with which we intended to deal. Ultimately, we arranged a dinner at the Mayflower Hotel, with representatives from the Commission, including Commissioner Jackson, and representatives from the PCEEO. The dinner was a disaster.

The PCEEO officials made it very clear in many ways that (1) they were not authorized to let us see the Form 40 data, (2) they would not participate in the development of the plans for the crash program, and (3) they thought the entire effort ill advised. These objections were raised in many forms. Some ill will developed at that meeting which would take a long time to dissipate. Charles Markham suggested that the Commission staff go ahead and work up the program. One group worked on the training program, and I headed a small group which refined the list of target employers.

On Saturday we wanted to advise Roosevelt of the reaction of the PCEEO staff but could not reach him. By Sunday he had been reached from a level higher than ours. He told us he would have to meet with Hobart Taylor on Monday. Mr. Charles Markham and I prepared a legal memorandum on the right of PCEEO to let us use the Form 40 data.

Monday the training program was underway. Some thirty of the investigators had stayed. The revised target list was completed, and we were ready to take the next steps. Monday afternoon Roosevelt met with Taylor. Tuesday morning, the Commission called me into their meeting and ordered me to cancel the proposed operation because, officially, there was a program underway concerning the zero list employers and a duplication of effort was not desirable—and, unofficially, because of the intense anger of some people at the whole state of affairs.

I went before this group of investigators, all of whom were more worldly wise in the ways of government than I, and told them of the decision: "I don't know whether this casts a shadow over the future of the Commission or not. I hope not." I thanked them, and told them that the Commission would call them when they were needed.

Thus ended the chapter. A unique opportunity for administrative creativity had been bypassed. The Commission thus lost its initiative during the first week it was in operation. In this one episode of weakness, programs to end employment discrimination lost at least three years. I momentarily thought of resigning or dropping the lists at the office of newspaper. When, a month later, a question of my appointment as a staff member arose, the weekend of July 9 was still reverberating. At a garden party I had to take a dressing down for my role in it from a high administration official. After that, resistance to my appointment ceased, and I was named Chief of Liaison with Federal and State Agencies, and later, Chief of Conciliation for the Commission.

That was the first of the compromises which were the price I paid for what influence I have had on the course of events in this field. Was the price too steep? I cannot tell.

I was useful to the Commission, and hence able to influence its actions for several reasons. I was more knowledgeable in labor and race relations law than most of the initial staff, from both academic and practical perspectives. I could visualize alternative solutions to some kinds of problems easily. I have a faith that there is more flexibility in most situations than is usually admitted, and that the art is to find it. I feel deeply about the central nature of employment discrimination for the fundamental problem of our time—the individual in an industrial society—and the role of law in dealing with that problem. Finally I had tenure at Rutgers and ten years of living in an environment of academic freedom. I was not conditioned to the subordinate ways of even high-level bureaucrats. I had developed independent habits of thought and action, and could back them with indications of willingness to leave if necessary.[23]

And so I stayed, and we moved on to other matters. Occasionally I wonder what might have happened in the nation if we had been allowed to proceed on the weekend of July 9. We might have accelerated the elimination of employment discrimination by several years, and influenced the entire sorry picture of race relation which has unfolded since then. Two years later, when I left the Commission, I did develop procedures for investigation of companies on low-utilization lists, and a year after that these procedures were put into effect in state and local agencies through the EEOC state grant program.

IV. Federal-State Relationships

The field of federal-state relationships provided further insight into the operation of the administrative process and into the open-ended quality of the initial administrative decisionmaking under a statute such as the Title VII.

A. Deference Provisions and the Need for Simplicity

One of the first problems was to design procedures to implement the deference provisions of the statute. These provisions required the Commission to defer cases to state agencies for sixty days in states with fair employment practice commissions. I found three law student summer interns, and devised a form on which for them to compare, section by section, the provisions of the state statute with the new provisions of Title VII.

---

[23] The academic freedom of a professor in government service has been noted by ROGER HILLSMAN, TO MOVE A NATION (1967) (Delta ed., 1968), p. 354:

When Averill Harriman had been promoted to Under Secretary and I to his old post as Assistant Secretary, Sidney Hyman, the writer and authority on the presidency, expressing his pleasure, had said that Harriman's wealth and my alternative career as a professor gave us something particularly precious in government service—the freedom to speak up, to stand on principle. "You are both free men," Hyman said, "and in my opinion free men is what these two hot jobs most need."

When these elaborate forms came in, I realized that my plan was unworkable. The Commission would receive a general letter of complaint from a state with a FEP law. To use my forms, someone would have to decide which provisions of Title VII were at issue, whether the state law had comparable provisions which were interpreted by the state in the manner in which the Commission intended to interpret Title VII. Only then could the decision on deferral be made. This would require a preliminary investigation of the case. It threatened to make a major issue of a minor one, and to dilute limited energies. The initial decision on deference should be simple enough to be made by a clerk who could compare a letter of complaint with a simple list of states. I scrapped my initial approach and worked out a simple plan. The Commission adopted the principle of complete deference to the states, unless the complaint fell into an area where the state agency had no subject matter jurisdiction. For example, some state laws did not cover sex discrimination. In that case, the clerk would be advised not to defer a sex complaint in such a state. Some states had no jurisdiction over public employment agencies; again, the clerk could be simply instructed not to defer that type of case.[24] Otherwise, there was to be deference. Check-lists were prepared indicating the areas of subject matter jurisdiction. Some aspects of government-administered programs must be simple, because of the character and quantity of the manpower available to perform them.

B. *The States with Criminal Statutes*

The next problem involved a conflict between desirable policy and the language of the statute. The statute required deference to any state

---

[24] The deference procedures have, in the main, worked satisfactorily, although there have been a few problems. See EEOC policy on deferral to state FEP agencies, CCH EMPLOYMENT PRACTICES ¶16,905. One court has required deference to a state in a sex case because the state had an "equal pay law" enforceable by the Labor Department; EEOC v. Union Bank, 58 Lab. Cas. ¶9157 (9th Cir. 1968). This decision fails to take account of the need for administrative simplicity achieved by focusing only on the state antidiscrimination laws. Posing a similar problem is Edwards v. North American Rockwell Corp., 58 Lab. Cas. ¶9153 (N.D. Cal. 1968), where a complaint alleging race and sex discrimination was not deferred because state law did not proscribe sex discrimination. The district court held EEOC and itself to be without jurisdiction over the race discrimination aspect. This problem could easily be avoided by administrative practice of total deferral if any part of the case is under the jurisdiction of a state FEP agency.

which "has a state . . . law prohibiting the unlawful employment practice and *establishing* or *authorizing* a state or local authority to grant or seek relief from such practice or to *institute criminal proceedings* with respect thereto. . . ." [25]

This language applied to three types of state statutes. First was the traditional FEP law under which a complaint would be investigated, and, if it could not be settled, would go to a hearing before the agency which could issue an order to cease and desist from the practice and take affirmative action to correct the situation. Deference to such agencies was clearly required. The second type of agency was the "good neighbor council" variety, which had no enforcement powers. No deference was required here because this agency was without power. Some five states fell into a third category. They had criminal laws prohibiting employment discrimination, enforceable by complaint to the local prosecuting attorney.

Did the EEOC have to defer to this type of state legal structure? There were two reasons of policy against deferring to state criminal laws. The first was the fundamental principle that the criminal law is not well suited to enforce social legislation, especially in the area of social tension and change. The norms of the criminal law require a narrow construction of the law, proof of intent, and proof of facts beyond a reasonable doubt. Prosecutors won't prosecute, juries won't convict, and the law is unenforced. Far better a civil or administrative remedy which requires conformity to a broadly construed code of social legislation rather than the inapposite and cumbersome process of the criminal law.

Second, if there was deference by EEOC to the criminal law, some states could keep the Commission processes at bay and thus delay the day of reckoning when the individual sued in the federal courts. For both of these reasons, it was desirable to discourage the use of the criminal laws prohibiting employment discrimination. Thus the Commission should not defer to states with criminal statutes. The problem was to construe the statutory language as not requiring deference to such laws. I finally produced a theory. It was that the words "state or local authority" in the statute referred to a specialized FEP agency or a cabinet department of a state, but not to the prosecutor's office. Under this interpretation, the ordinary criminal law enforcement mechanism

---

[25] Section 706(b).

would not qualify. In two other places in the statute, Congress had clearly referred to fair employment practice agencies.[26] Hence it was reasonable to conclude that this was what had been intended.

My interpretation was received with some incredulity by the other lawyers, who were getting accustomed to what they considered my free and easy ways with statutory construction. The office wit suggested that I was working on a textbook on Title VII entitled "Blumrosen on Loopholes." The forum in which the issue was finally hammered out—as far as the Commission was concerned—was the Chairman's office the morning that Roosevelt was to testify before one of the House committees.

C. *Policymaking in Testimony*

We put both sides of the argument to Roosevelt, my side and the view which said that the statute was explicit and the Commission could not abort its "plain meaning." Roosevelt listened to the arguments for a time, then said, "The criminal law won't get a man a job." That earthy wisdom carried the day for my interpretation. We went along with him while he explained how the Commission was getting started and how it had decided not to defer to states with criminal laws.[27] Outside, reporters asked Roosevelt to name the states, and I provided the information. Executive Director Tom Powers then gave me another lesson in federal-state relations. "Well, aren't you going to call the Attorney General in each of those states so he won't read in the morning paper that the federal government will not defer to him?" I agreed.

D. *The Value of Information*

When the phone calls were finished, I had learned several things. The first was an awareness of the gratitude which comes when an official is consulted before something happens in his arena of operations. There is a mystique that the good administrator is at all times on top of

---

[26] Section 709(d) and 716.
[27] EEOC Legal Interpretations, July 2, 1965, to Oct. 8, 1965, ¶34; CCH EMPLOYMENT PRACTICES ¶17,252.

all developments in his jurisdiction. This is simply nonsense. A top-level or middle-level administrator cannot possibly have up-to-the-minute information on all of the activities of his staff unless he diverts most of his energy to supplying that information. Nevertheless, the concept that the administrator "controls" and hence must have "knowledge" persists.

The assistant attorney generals with whom I talked would brief their bosses, and, if necessary, their bosses would tell inquiring newsmen the next day that there had been discussions with the federal government, and perhaps hint that the state had participated in the decision, or else that the state had protested against this bureaucratic decision. In either event, the information provided a freedom of action to the state attorney general in his own affairs, for which he was appropriately grateful.

Furthermore, most of the officials of the states agreed with me that the criminal law was not an effective device for dealing with employment discrimination. Thus they were sympathetic with the underlying reasoning which had led to the Commission decision.

V. The Compliance Process

During late summer and early fall of 1965, as Chief of Liaison, I dealt with a myriad of details concerning the development of the compliance procedures of the Commission. I will not detail here the hundreds of experiences, the meetings which gradually crystalized my ideas about the compliance process in the field of employment discrimination. The thinking began with my study of the New Jersey Division on Civil Rights. I had been shocked by the inadequacies of the settlements which the Division had reached, and concluded that this was at least in part due to the inadequate procedures followed by the Division.[28] One basic inadequacy consisted of failure to separate the investigation function from the conciliation function. A Division representative would go out on a complaint and try to settle the case on the spot. This usually involved taking the settlement which the respondent offered. Usually this consisted of a paper promise to obey the law, and rarely did it entail any relief for the complainant. I concluded that one reason for this situation was that the Division representative was told to talk set-

---

[28] Blumrosen, *op. cit.*, *supra*, note 2 at 223.

tlement before there had been any finding that there was anything to settle. Thus the respondent could say, "Okay, I deny there is any discrimination at all, but I'm willing to make some gesture to get rid of this case." And the Division representative, interested in a good record for himself, and empowered to reach a "satisfactory adjustment," would proceed to take the settlement.

I was determined that the Commission should avoid these errors. Thus I found myself, for the first time in my academic life in the law, stressing the importance of procedure. The statute provided for the filing of a charge, an investigation, and a finding of reasonable cause to believe the charge to be true, and then efforts at conciliation. The Commission adopted the principle of separation of these functions. As a result, the procedures for conciliation are separate from those for investigation, and the personnel who conciliate are different from those who investigate. Between the two processes is the written decision that there is "reasonable cause" to believe the statute has been violated, which is, in turn, a predicate for conciliation. Because of my New Jersey experience, I was quite doctrinaire on this subject of separation of functions and of the need for a written decision on cause to believe there was discrimination.

There were errors made in maintaining such a position—a position which would have been quickly eroded if exceptions had been made. There was really a Catch-22 quality about the decision to be doctrinaire. If the EEOC was doctrinaire, there would be mistakes arising from failure to evaluate each situation in light of its own facts. But if one evaluated each situation in light of its facts, the inevitable push would have been in the direction of informal settlements which were high on words and low on content.

A. *The Reasonable Cause Concept*

In building the compliance program we took the innocuous clause in the statute which said that the Commission could conciliate after making a finding of reasonable cause and elevated the reasonable cause decision to a high policy level. The reasonable cause decision was initially written by a commissioner's assistant, and circulated to the Commission; it was a Commission decision. In some state agencies, the reasonable cause decision is made informally on the scene by an investigator. In the Commission procedure, the decision is still made in Washington by the Commission.

Those of us who "upgraded" or "dignified" the Commission decision had several objectives in mind:

First, to assist in making a body of law as to what constitutes a discrimination. The incredible laxity of state fair employment practice agencies and their failure for nearly a quarter of a century to act as law enforcement agencies meant that there was no detailed body of law as to what constitutes discrimination; therefore, no firm guidance was given to employers, unions, and government officials as to what situations had to be corrected. Under Title VII, the federal courts would interpret the act, but it seemed likely that busy federal judges would pay considerable attention to the concept of discrimination developed by the Commission through the decisional process. The reasonable cause finding thus became a vehicle for development of the law with respect to discrimination.

Second, after I became Chief of Conciliation in October 1965, I became intensely aware of the function of the reasonable cause decision in laying a foundation for conciliation. The conciliators could use the cause finding as their factual premise and concentrate the discussion on remedies. For this purpose, the decision should appear to be a lawyer-like document, not a rambling exploration of issues. I drafted the model format for the reasonable cause finding with this in mind. Had I pressed the principle of the importance of lawmaking, I might have stressed what lawyers like to call the "reasoning" in the cause finding, that is, the written demonstration of the connection between the facts, the law, and the result in the case.

Yet, in this early stage of the Commission process, the important thing was judgment, not reasoning. So I deliberately left the reasoning step out of the decision format. The decision format is (a) summary of charge, (b) summary of facts found, and (c) conclusion of the reasonable cause issue.[29] This was a conscious choice not to bog down the EEOC in its own precedents so early in the game. I think this was wise at the time, but it, too, had its price. The wisdom lay in not opening the question of the Commission's own precedents early in the administra-

---

[29] A typical reasonable cause decision can be found in Jenkins v. United Gas Corp., 58 Lab. Cas. ¶9154 (5th Cir. 1968), note 45.

tion of the act. The difficulty lay in the fact that, in the absence of expressed reasoning processes, it was very difficult for Commission personnel to operate. Investigators didn't know what facts to look for; decision writers didn't know what to write. The only cure for this was some explication of Commission reasoning which, once done, would involve the Commission deeply in the precedentmaking and interpreting process. Two years later, as I was leaving the Commission, I spent several months with the thousands of Commission decisions, and worked them into a 250-page manual which attempted to supply some of the links of reasoning so that one original purpose of the elevation of the reasonable cause decision could be achieved. But by this time the federal courts were beginning to render decisions, and the entire chain of reasoning was in jeopardy because the Commission staff only had four or five lawyers and they could not regularly file briefs amicus on behalf of the Commission in these various cases. Thus the theory of development of law through Commission decision, which was one prime reason for the elevation of the Commission decision, floundered during the administrative phase of the act.

A third reason for having the reasonable cause decision written by the Commission was to maintain for the Commission and for headquarters staff some control over the field activities of the agency. If the Commission did not decide what constituted discrimination, then each regional office, and perhaps each staff member, would formulate his own definition. Any hope of application of a uniform national policy would be lost; persons' rights would be subjected to the vagaries of the personal feelings of staff members; and these staff members themselves would be placed under a variety of psychological pressures which they might be helped to withstand if they had Commission guidance and decision.

Finally, the Commission's decision was to interrupt the flow of Commission activity from the investigation to conciliation. With the decisionwriting steps in the hands of the Commission, it was easier to develop the concept of separate functions of investigation and conciliation. After some struggles the distinction was established. Investigators were to investigate, not try to settle cases; and after the decision was rendered, the conciliators would try to conciliate. No conciliation would be attempted during investigation.

This was one of the hardest positions to maintain. It was challenged from several perspectives:

1. Economy of Effort. The agency was understaffed and underfunded. If one person could do both the investigation and conciliation on one trip, then it was an unnecessary expenditure of funds and allocation of manpower to send in two men on separate occasions, with much paperwork in between.

2. Undesirable Position. If an employer or union wanted to settle the case when the investigator arrived, what sense did it make to tell him: "No, you have to wait until the Commission's procedures make it appropriate to talk settlement"?

3. The NLRB Combined Functions. Some of the people in a position to influence the course of Commission decisions had had experience with the NLRB. Under NLRB procedure, the field representative has wide latitude to secure a settlement at the earliest stages of the proceeding, before any formal papers are filed. In fact, most of the work of the NLRB is done at this stage. NLRB-trained persons thought that the NLRB procedure was the appropriate model to use for the Commission.

I answered these questions and variations on them again and again and again. Experience had demonstrated that there was no economy of effort except at the expense of inadequate settlements, that the investigator could not conciliate change in the system of discrimination because he did not have a firm factual foundation on which to operate, and did not have any official way of communicating Commission policy to the respondent. A possible buy-out of the claim of the charging party might be possible at the instance of the investigator, but he could not induce a change in discriminatory systems; and without change in system, there was no true economy of effort because each individual victim of discrimination would then have to come to the Commission separately. This would require repeated instances of Commission involvement.

The occasions on which a respondent would in fact say to an investigator, "Okay, I'm discriminating, what do you want me to do?" were rare. Usually no offer would be made by the respondent; and if he did make any overture toward settlement, it was usually to see how little he could get away with. Obviously all respondents preferred settlement discussions before there was finding of reasonable cause, because they could settle for less than when there was an official finding against them. However, if the objective was to maximize the effect of Commission involvement to eliminate discrimination, there was no advantage in negotiations under conditions favorable to respondent.

Furthermore, as a matter of statutory language, the Commission had no business suggesting conciliation until it had found reasonable cause. I pressed for the literal interpretation of this section of the statute because I believed it to be a wise position. It was comforting to be on the side of the "plain meaning" of the statute in at least this one instance. Once in a while a respondent would manage to slip into settlement discussions, usually disguised as an effort to "learn what facts the Commission had," which really turned out to be an effort to avoid a reasonable cause finding. In one case, a construction union settled the case in the investigative stage by taking in a Negro as a journeyman. The Commission, nevertheless, found cause. An effort to conciliate those circumstances was bound to be futile and somewhat embarrassing. It would have been better to take a withdrawal of the charge from the satisfied complainant. Of course, the story of that episode was magnified by the construction union representatives as an argument for noncooperation in later situations.

But the basic response to those who wanted an informal procedure was simply that so few respondents came forward offering to settle that it was not appropriate to design a basic procedure on the assumption that this would be the case. Such a procedure would make it inevitable that investigators would encourage settlement discussions which would lead to the endless cycle of discussions and weak settlements.

The answer to the NLRB admirers was that experience in state agencies with the type of informal merger of investigation and conciliation had been a dismal failure. In addition, the reason for failure in the race area and success in the NLRB area involved the difference in structure and function of the union movement and the civil rights movement. In many cases of NLRB involvement, the union movement was on the scene daily pressing its position. The civil rights organizations do not have the day-to-day staying power of the union movement, but rather muster up great amounts of effort for a big push and then fall back exhausted. Thus there is not the regular pressure on the government investigator in the race relations area which the union puts forth to assure that its interests are protected by labor board personnel. In the absence of this pressure, the counterpressures from the respondents have the inevitable effect of producing weak settlements. The parallel of NLRB and race relations experience is inaccurate as a matter of sociological fact.

B. *The Concept of Conciliation*

Finally, the entire conciliation concept was built around the reasonable cause finding. The concept that the Commission would seek a change in the system of discrimination rather than a buy-out of the charging party was based on the use of the reasonable cause finding as an indictment of company practices in general, not only as a foundation for protecting an individual complainant. For this purpose a written document from the Commission level was absolutely indispensable. Without such a document, the Commission staff was reduced to pitting its judgment against that of management or union officials. With such a document, the staff was in a better negotiating posture because it had an official—though nonadversary—finding of discrimination as a predicate for conciliation discussions.

This theory of the Commission procedures prevailed.[30] Investigations were undertaken, reasonable cause findings were made, and, in September 1965, the Commission suddenly found that it was time to begin conciliating. Relatively few people on the Commission staff had practical experience in negotiation, conciliation, arbitration, or any other informal procedure. With my labor arbitration experience and my experience in advising Rutgers in the handling of its race relations problems, I was prepared for conciliation at a time when no concept of what constituted conciliation existed. Conciliation obviously entails informal settlement short of litigation. But this leaves open a wide range of matters. What issues should be settled, on what terms, and under what conditions? There was no body of experience in this area, because the state agencies and the federal government contracts enforcement program up to that time had been failures. Particularly there was no expe-

---

[30] It was modified by the Commission in 1970. See 35 Fed. Reg. 3163.

rience under the formal procedures with a written reasonable cause decision because, as I have suggested; the use of such formal procedures was novel to the field.

Stated another way: We can envision two models of conciliation of a race discrimination case. In one model, traditional, the conciliator would attempt to cool off the situation by the minimum steps necessary. He would inevitably try to push the weaker party toward the stronger to achieve at least a temporary settlement. He would have nothing to do with litigation.

A second model would find the conciliator as the settling lawyer in a process which could lead to a formal decision on the complainant's rights. In this view, the conciliator was operating at the stage prior to suit but after a preliminary determination of plaintiff's rights (i.e., the reasonable cause finding) had been made. Conciliation was, in this view, a preliminary part of a full-blown litigation process designed by Congress. This latter view was the one I adopted. In implementing this view, as Chief of Conciliations, I prepared a memorandum on the nature of Title VII conciliation which included the following:

> The nature of the conciliation process under Title VII must be explored in light of [the] statutory mandate. Conciliation, while highly developed in specialized fields of human endeavor, has no single fixed meaning. Its essentials vary depending on the circumstances to which it is applied, the attitudes of the parties toward the process, and the legal context within which it takes place. The minister who talks privately to his parishioners in the Southern town about the end of discrimination, the marriage counselor, trying to save a family, the representative from the Federal Mediation and Conciliation Service trying to avoid a strike, the constant scurryings of diplomats attempting to avoid international conflict, and the constant dealing of thousands of lawyers and others trying to settle problems without formal proceedings, all involve "conciliation." The urge to conciliate to avoid formal proceedings is almost as fundamental as the drive to establish such formal procedures in the first place. One might suggest that as soon as a program for formal settlement of disputes is established, those subject to it promptly decide to avoid it and to settle matters informally in terms and under conditions which may be more to their liking.
>
> Since conciliation has no fixed meaning, the Commission must shape the concept of conciliation under Title VII. To assist in this process it may be useful to distinguish Title VII conciliation from two other related types of conciliation, conciliation under state fair employment practices laws, and under the National Labor Relations Act.

1. Conciliation under the Labor Laws

Conciliation under Title VII must necessarily differ in several respects from conciliations under the National Labor Relations Act. The legal context is sharply different. The objective of national labor policy is industrial peace within the context of collective bargaining. The objective of labor conciliation is to bring the parties (who usually have relatively equal bargaining power) to an agreement which is acceptable for the limited duration of their contract. National labor policy seeks a solution acceptable to the parties, and little more. In fact, the original understanding under the Wagner Act was that the government was not to be concerned at all about the content of the collective bargain. In this legal context, conciliation consists of techniques by which the clearly expressed demands of the parties can be accommodated. The nature of the bargain struck by the parties is not the concern of the conciliator or the government.

Conciliation under Title VII proceeds under a different legal mandate. It is aimed not only at satisfying the immediate demands of the parties, but at achieving compliance with the law. It therefore requires attention to the detailed terms of the solution, which is not necessary under the National Labor Relations Act.

2. Conciliation under some state FEP laws.

Under most state FEP laws, the aggrieved party has no individual right to litigate. If settlement is not achieved through conciliation, the state agency may hold a public hearing and may, after finding discrimination, issue a cease and desist order which is then judicially enforceable. In some jurisdictions, the settlement agreements reached through conciliation have focused more on the general behavior of the respondent than on the specific rights of the complainant. While this may appear to be desirable, its consequence has been in some cases the acceptance of "letters of intent" to comply with the law as a "satisfactory adjustment of individual grievances. This approach has led to the proposed remedy of the "next available job" rather than immediate employment in refusal to hire or discharge cases, and to limited use of back pay or other monetary relief.

The legal context of a Title VII conciliation requires concentration on the rights of complainants, for the right to litigate rests with them. No settlement can bind them unless they are a party to it. Therefore, the settlement agreement, in addition to facing general problems which the respondent may have, must meet the legitimate needs of complainants for present recognition of his legal rights. Title VII conciliation must provide present, visible, and genuine protection for charging parties if it is to both secure their rights and protect respondents from the risks of suit. The outcome of a Title VII conciliation should be an agreement which is legally sufficient to achieve these results.

3. Conciliation and Title VII

The nature of the legal, social, and economic context thus shapes the concept of conciliation under Title VII. One can visualize two models of conciliation. One is the "hat in hand" approach, urging the respondent to sin no more, to go out and do good. The other is the more matter of fact and mundane approach which suggests that, in order to avoid a lawsuit, the respondent must take certain specific steps which will solve his problem. It is this latter approach which is suggested for conciliation under Title VII. Our experience supports this approach. Respondents need no preaching. They know that Title VII is the law of the land. They are not certain what acts constitute a violation of Title VII and are not certain what must be done to comply with it. The primary tasks of the conciliator is to focus on the latter point, and to persuade the respondent to take such "affirmative action" as will constitute "voluntary compliance" with the statute by recognizing the rights of complainants and the interests of the minority group members in being free from future discrimination and having genuinely equal employment opportunity.

The first two cases ready for conciliation were in Birmingham and Memphis. I chose Birmingham, the symbolic center of the South to the civil rights movement and to organized labor and industry. Most particularly, it is the home of United States Steel and the steel workers in the South.

1. THE FIRST EEOC CASE

My first experience in Birmingham was with a small plant which employed some forty workers in a continuous-flow process of manufacturing sewer pipe. The day I arrived in Birmingham I was met by investigator John Hennigan, a devoted and intelligent representative who was on loan to the Commission from the Navy Department. (He was later to become Deputy Director of the EEOC Atlanta office, and then to open the Birmingham office of the Commission. After that, he was side-tracked and ultimately left the EEOC.) John had been working in the field for several years; I was new. He was genuinely helpful. He helped me through the first of many midnight sessions with the charging parties, at an attorney's house on the west side of Birmingham surrounded by a high fence and floodlights because of a bomb episode of the previous year. He helped me through the period of hostility and uncertainty as we gained the confidence of the charging parties so that I would have a full grasp of their problem when I went to see the company and union the next day.

One thing that John did not warn me about. Despite all these years of disappointment, the faith of the Negroes in the government ran high. Their will to believe was so strong that they wished for assurances of help from the government representative. Later, if he was unable to solve their problem, they blamed him. The feeling of dependence may be nice for the ego of the government representative, but it is a luxury in which he cannot indulge for it is unfair to build expectations when delivery is uncertain. As a result of one such experience, I directed the conciliators to make very clear to the charging parties that there was no certainty that conciliation would work and that the alternative was litigation.

The next morning we visited the plant to talk to the company representative and the union leaders. The plant manager was a Californian, new to the South, not sympathetic (then) to the position of the white employees but unable to see any alternative. The problems in this little plant were, in microcosm, the problems of the South. Some 30 per cent of the labor force were Negro—nine employees. They were all confined to the shipping and finishing department, and were not allowed into the white production department. The entry-level jobs in the white department paid at least forty cents per hour higher than the top rate in the Negro department but were no more difficult. Newly hired white employees had seniority in the production department, which the Negroes did not. The union and company were willing to let the Negro employees begin to move into the white department as vacancies developed, but their seniority would be less than the junior whites who had recently been hired. In addition, there were segregated toilet, locker, and shower facilities.

I began discussions by advising the manager of his alternatives: if conciliation failed, a private suit might be filed or the Attorney General might be asked to file suit, and the Office of Federal Contract Compliance might be asked to suspend further contracting. I said I was not there to review the facts of discrimination; this had been established in the reasonable cause finding of the Commission. I was there to help eliminate the system of discrimination if possible. This became the standard opening statement of Commission conciliators.[31]

An international vice-president of the union "happened" to be in town and attended part of our session with several of the employees.

---

[31] The conciliation process is more fully described in ch. 4 *infra*.

The manager seemed willing but could think of nothing to offer except allowing the Negroes to move into white jobs as vacancies developed. Turnover was low; therefore, this offer appeared to have little substance. As the day of discussion wore on, someone mentioned that the men were working seven days a week. I did a double take. This was virtually unheard of in modern American industry.

The men explained that two years previously they had won in arbitration the right to work seven days a week. By now, they were tired. I saw a solution to the problem. I suggested that if the men went to a five- or six-day week, this would immediately create openings in the production department to which several Negroes could be transferred without delay.

All of the difficult legal problems involving discrimination seniority systems and remedies for discrimination evaporated. The union was willing, on behalf of the whites, to amend the contract. The company was pleased, because they acquired more flexibility in scheduling, and three Negro employees received immediate promotions. The men were willing to have the segregating wall removed from the locker-shower facilities.

I must try to describe my feelings of that moment. I felt elated and whole, as if, after days thrashing around futilely, I had gotten a grip with my feet and ripped away the cobwebs which bind most of life. It was a soaring feeling, akin to watching a Boeing 727 lift sharply from an airstrip. I had a brief glimpse of a future when men would shed the "tyranny over the mind" which prevented them seeing and acting in ways to improve conditions of life.

2. The significance of a signature

While the union and the company amended the collective agreement to move to the five-six-day week, I drafted the first written conciliation agreement in the history of the Commission. It took the form of a settlement agreement between the charging parties and the respondent. I started with some statutory language, and followed it with the details of the settlement, including a drawing of the changes which were to be made in the facilities. I discussed details over the phone with corporate counsel in New England and gave a copy to the attorney for the charging parties. The principle on which I operated was that the agreement had to be signed by the charging parties to be valid. This seemed to be of the essence of any settlement under Title VII, because the statute gave the complainants the right to sue. Hence, I reasoned, they had the right to settle, and the Commission could not and should not settle their case for them. I viewed the statute as creating individual rights which were not within the authority of the Commission to destroy. Without a great deal of theorizing—that was to come later—I implicitly rejected the paternalistic idea that the government—that is to say, the conciliator—could decide for the Negro employees if the settlement was adequate. By requiring their signatures, we opened a new chapter in the history of race relations. (At the time I did what seemed normal. I had not thought through what a radical change I was making in the usual processes of government.) The traditional view had been that the government had the power to make settlements and to determine what constituted a satisfactory adjustment. In theory this was because of the weakness of the victim of discrimination and the necessity for having the government protect these victims of injustice. In practice, deals made between representatives of the government and respondents often had little relevance to the charging parties. Professor Sovern describes one horrible example of action by the New York Commission in which a complainant filed a charge, and the next thing he knew he was told it had been satisfactorily adjusted, all intervening steps being taken without his knowledge and the ultimate adjustment not benefiting him at all.[32]

I rebelled at this paternalism. Our experience is that when government acts in a paternal way, it deprives its beneficiaries of any chance of decent treatment. Our treatment of Indians and of juvenile offenders, as well as our handling of race relations, demonstrates the inhumanity of government when it operates in *parens patriae*.

3. MULTILATERAL BARGAINING

And so the theory emerged that the conciliation agreement had to be signed by the complainant, that there could be no ending of the case without that, and that the alternative to dealing in conciliation with the charging parties was a lawsuit. This principle aggravated the large employers and unions, who were used to doing business with government

---

[32] Sovern, at 49.

representatives; time and again they objected to our view that a settlement had to be acceptable to the complainants or it was no settlement. Since many complainants were represented by the NAACP and the Legal Defense Fund, the effect of our view was to require companies and unions to sit down and negotiate with the sophisticated representatives of Negro employees. Thus emerged three-interest bargaining, between labor, management, and civil rights interests.

Time and again I was pressed by a company or union to accept a solution on behalf of the government regardless of the views of the charging parties. After all, we were the administrators of the law, we were told. It was up to us to decide what constituted "voluntary compliance" with the statute, rather than allow the charging parties or their organizations to frustrate settlement. At one time, one of the largest corporations and largest unions brought their top personnel to Washington to press this view. After sitting before them for a full day, I decided to take the matter to the Commission with a recommendation that the proposal made by them be rejected. The Commission accepted this recommendation. Three months later, the company and the union began to negotiate with the representatives of the Legal Defense Fund.

The theory which emerged and which was implemented through conciliation was that individual rights under Title VII were inalienable, at least as far as the Commission was concerned. This meant that if respondents wished to avoid suit, they might have to sit down with representatives of the charging parties, such as civil rights organizations. Thus the civil rights organizations were given standing and status to negotiate, a standing and status they did not have if only the government and the respondent decided what the result should be. Further, the civil rights organizations were given a seat at the bargaining table, which they had never had before. Respondents could no longer ignore the civil rights interest; they had to listen and respond.

The simple act of asserting that a Title VII settlement required the signature of the complainants had the effect of converting Title VII into a rough "duty to bargain" on the part of labor and management. If they wished a settlement, they had to negotiate with the representatives of the civil rights interests. If they refused to negotiate, or if no settlement could be reached, the civil rights interests could take the matters to the courts.

At this time in our history, the courts were friendly to the civil rights interests, and were developing a line of decisions liberally construing the antidiscrimination laws. Thus it was in the interests of labor and management to work out solutions to the problems which were posed in these Title VII negotiations. In addition, the risk of long and sometimes public involvement with the agency enforcing the antidiscrimination clause in government contracts, and the possibilities of a suit by the Attorney General, added impetus for settlement to these cases. In creating this duty to bargain, we introduced into this field the concept of multilateral negotiations, a vastly expanded version of collective bargaining in which multiple interests are in fact represented.

Multilateral bargaining is quite possibly one of the ways of the future in resolving the increasingly more complex disputes within our society. It is a logical extension of pluralism. If collective bargaining represented the process by which the interests of labor were recognized in the employment scene, then multilateral bargaining represents the method by which the interests of still further organized groups can be taken into account in the informal processes by which the business of life is carried on. As we expand the scope and activities of organized groups in society, they will come to need such channels for articulation and implementation of their interests. The experience under Title VII may illuminate this way.

Thus our decision to require the signatures of the charging party constituted at once an act of faith in the principles of individualism, a denial of the concept of paternalism which had infused the antidiscrimination laws in the past, and an introduction to multilateral bargaining between labor, management, and the civil rights movement. (This is quite a burden for that single afternoon in a small plant in Birmingham. Yet, in retrospect, that afternoon was the crossroads where these concepts were born.)

This entire thesis required that the charging parties—and hence the civil rights interest—would themselves determine if conciliation was successful. If we had once recognized that the government could determine what constituted "voluntary compliance" with the statute, there would have been a totally different kind of process and outcome. For example, one could read the provisions of sections 706(a) and 706(e) as providing that if the Commission thought that a conciliation proposal was acceptable and constituted voluntary compliance with Title VII,[33] it would never issue a notice of right to sue. This would have been fully compatible with past administrative practice in this field. The charging party would never have his day in court against the respondent; he would have to sue the Commission for arbitrarily refusing to give him the notice. In such a suit the issue would not have been "did the respondent violate the statute," but "did the Commission behave

---

[33] The sections read as follows:

Sec. 706. (a) Whenever it is charged in writing under oath by a person claiming to be aggrieved, or a written charge has been filed by a member of the Commission where he has reasonable cause to believe a violation of this title has occurred (and such charge sets forth the facts upon which it is based) that an employer, employment agency, or labor organization has engaged in an unlawful employment practice, the Commission shall furnish such employer, employment agency, or labor organization (hereinafter referred to as the "respondent") with a copy of such charge and shall make an investigation of such charge, provided that such charge shall not be made public by the Commission. If the Commission shall determine, after such investigation, that there is reasonable cause to believe that the charge is true, the Commission shall endeavor to eliminate any such alleged unlawful employment practice by informal methods of conference, concilation, and persuasion. Nothing said or done during and as a part of such endeavors may be made public by the Commission without the written consent of the parties, or used as evidence in a subsequent proceeding. Any officer or employee of the Commission, who shall make public in any manner whatever any information in violation of this subsection shall be deemed guilty of a misdemeanor and upon conviction thereof shall be fined not more than $1,000 or imprisoned not more than one year.

     ◦ ◦ ◦

(e) If within thirty days after a charge is filed with the Commission or within thirty days after expiration of any period of reference under subsection (c) (except that in either case such period may be extended to not more than sixty days upon a determination by the Commission that further efforts to secure voluntary compliance are warranted), the Commission has been unable to obtain voluntary compliance with this title, the Commission shall so notify the person aggrieved and a civil action may, within thirty days thereafter, be brought against the respondent named in the charge (1) by the person claiming to be aggrieved, or (2) if such charge was filed by a member of the Commission, by any person whom the charge alleges was aggrieved by the alleged unlawful employment practice. Upon application by the complainant and in such circumstances as the court may deem just, the court may appoint an attorney for such complainant and may authorize the commencement of the action without the payment of fees, costs, or security. Upon timely application, the court may, in its discretion, permit the Attorney General to intervene in such civil action if he certifies that the case is of general public importance. Upon request, the court may, in its discretion, stay further proceedings for not more than sixty days pending the termination of State or local proceedings described in subsection (b) or the efforts of the Commission to obtain voluntary compliance.

arbitrarily in accepting the settlement?" In that event there would be few suits under Title VII and fewer meaningful settlements.

This decision was the most important of the free choices available to the administrators of Title VII. The language of the statute lent itself equally well to either interpretation;[34] the legislative history is confused because it was not addressed to this issue,[35] and the historic practices of administrative agencies in this field have been to downgrade the role of the individual by the adoption of a paternalistic reading of the same statutory language.[36]

In one sense, a decade of work in the area of individual rights in our industrial society came to fruition that afternoon in Birmingham. By that I do not imply that any single-handed effort achieved the present complex processes of the EEOC. At least a dozen, perhaps twenty, people were, in the early days, involved in the myriad of decisions which established the EEOC procedure. By now, literally hundreds of persons have learned these procedures and adopted them as basic premises from which to reason about newly emerging problems. But in the beginning, there was only the Commission and a small group of staff members to assist in the making of these free choices.

In evolving this concept of conciliation, which emerged through the crucible of the first year's experience with the EEOC, the work of Kenneth Holbert, then my deputy and later Chief of Conciliations for the Commission, was indispensable. Holbert had practiced law with a top Negro law firm in Dallas and had come to work in the labyrinth of the Labor Department in 1961. His shrewd insights into the operation of the administrative process, his trial lawyer's sense of timing and empha-

---

[34] Professor Sovern, writing at about the same time these initial decisions were being made in the EEOC, was not at all clear on the question of whether the Commission could conclude the rights of the charging party. Sovern, note 14 at 82–83.

[35] The primary discussion can be found in EEOC, LEGISLATIVE HISTORY at 3301–12. The focus of the discussion was whether a commissioner should be able to file a charge. In explaining why this power did not involve a combining of prosecuting and judicial functions, proponents of the bill focused on the fact that the EEOC had no power of decision, and that the charging parties could secure de novo review in the court. Opponents of the power of the commissioner to file a charge maintained that the Commission held "the key to the court house door" in its reasonable cause determination and, therefore, its decision was at least "quasi judicial."

[36] Sovern, *op. cit., supra,* note 14 at 48–53; Blumrosen, *op. cit., supra,* note 2 at 237–43.

sis in negotiation, and his dedication to the preservation of individual rights to combat employment discrimination, made us an effective working team then and afterward, when he served as Acting Director of Compliance and Acting General Counsel for EEOC.

The work of conciliations that first year was done largely by Holbert, myself, and four other men who contributed in their daily work to the development of many of the concepts discussed here. Jules Gordon brought expert technical legal knowledge from the NLRB to bear on our problems; Andrew Muse brought an ability to draw out respondents toward his solution and a sense of judgment about individuals; Chris Roggerson brought insight and the incredibly patient negotiating skills necessary to solve the first of the complex sex discrimination cases in the meat packing industry; and Herb Belkin brought youthful energy, enthusiasm, and intelligence in conciliating a great volume of cases.

My first year with the Commission saw the negotiation of the Newport News Agreement, at the end of March 1966, as the high point. In reaching that agreement the EEOC, the Justice Department, the OFCC, and the Defense Department cooperated as they never had before or have since. To negotiate with the contract compliance officer on one side and a representative from the Attorney General on the other was an exhilarating experience. The agreement and its administration demonstrate the potentiality in the administrative process for breaking the back of the problem of employment discrimination in the country. This potential has not been realized. I have written separately in chapter 8 about the Newport News Agreement because of its importance in pointing out how it is possible to solve rather than perpetuate the problem of discrimination. It is one of my deepest frustrations that the concept of unified governmental action to achieve carefully tailored changes in industrial relations systems to correct discrimination has not been adopted by the government.

In April or May 1966, shortly before he left, Chairman Roosevelt asked me to stay on for another year. I debated long and hard in an utterly inconclusive way. I was growing tired of the bureaucracy and was spending more time on less important matters as the administrative process unfolded. My decision was crystallized on one of my many trips to Birmingham. The Negro employee who had brought the charges involved in my first conciliation conference had been fired under apparently discriminatory circumstances. I went to Birmingham to unscramble the matter, and ultimately got him his job back.[37] He symbolized for me the courage of all minorities who were challenging their oppressed conditions and seeking justice in the work place. I decided to stay for a second year.

---

[37] See ch. 5, pt. 1 *infra.*

3   The Many Faces of Job Discrimination

A Report by the EEOC on Job Patterns for Minorities and Women in Private Industry—1966

Discrimination against persons because of their race, color, religion, sex, or national origin is based on emotion rather than reason. It is often a mental reflex rather than a conscious conviction. It cannot be isolated, quantified, and neutralized in the same manner in which a scientist deals with an undesirable chemical or a malignant tumor.

Like other diseases, however, bias has predictable and precise symptoms and, regardless of the underlying causes, these manifestations of discrimination can be identified and measured. *Equal Employment Report No. 1* marks the first attempt by the Equal Employment Opportunity Commission to measure the impact of discrimination in employment on minority groups and women.

This study is limited to that one aspect of discrimination; however, in another sense it deals with all aspects of minority group problems because the lack of meaningful, purposeful jobs that provide adequate earnings is one of the basic reasons for the tragic plight of minority groups in America.

The statistics presented in the report, the Commission believes, show that job discrimination is one of the major reasons why minorities generally have lower incomes than those fortunate enough to be born into the majority group, and therefore they have less to spend on food, housing, education, clothing, travel, and recreation—the goods and services needed to sustain and enrich life in the computer age.

Because of the controversy surrounding this subject, it is important to state what is not included in this report.

There are no polls of public opinion. The figures are derived from reports submitted by employers. No attempt has been made to measure the secondary impact of job discrimination—the economic, social other effects on the *majority* group itself, although some general state ments on this subject are contained in the concluding paragraphs of the text.

No studies by sociologists or psychologists are included, although the abundance of statistics should be very useful for those trying to gauge the psychological, emotional, and social damage caused by discrimination in employment.

No sweeping solutions are offered, although the numerical patterns in some cases may strongly suggest the sectors that need attention.

The statistics themselves tell the story, without eloquence perhaps, but also without ambiguity.

The findings are based on a 1966 nationwide survey of 43,000 employers covering 26 million workers, and on statistical analyses by EEOC economists and other specialists and independent authorities. The survey is required by law and is conducted by means of Employer Information Report EEO-1 (Standard Form 100). The 1966 data and the accompanying analyses comprise the most comprehensive work attempted in this field.[1] Except for specific references to the Bureau of the Census or other sources, all of the material in these volumes was developed by the Commission or by academic authorities working under Commission sponsorship.

To most Americans, the primary conclusion will not come as a surprise. It corroborates the opinion long held by most authorities on employment and population:

Discrimination in employment is widespread and takes many forms; it can be found in almost every area, occupational group, and industry; and it has a crushing impact. In short, it is a profound condition, national in scope, and it constitutes a continuing violation of the American ideal of fair play in the private enterprise system.

President Johnson and the Congress recognized the urgent need for a nationwide attack against job discrimination in establishing the Commission in Title VII of the Civil Rights Act of 1964.

---

[1] A full description of the survey is found in the report's Editorial and Technical Notes and Acknowledgments, at page vii. That section also describes the limitations of the data and serves as a guide for their interpretation. The survey includes employment of Negroes in all areas of the United States; Orientals, American Indians, and Spanish-surnamed Americans are covered in those areas where they constitute an identifiable factor in the labor market.

Almost all Americans now recognize that a problem exists, but many of them probably have only a vague notion of its magnitude. Thus far, only a relatively small part of the nation's scientific resources has been devoted to this long-standing, deeply rooted element which seems to permeate the American scene.

In an address to the 1967 convention of the American Psychological Association, Dr. Martin Luther King, Jr., said, "If the Negro needs social science for direction and for self-understanding, the white society is in even more urgent need. White America needs to understand that it is poisoned to its soul by racism, and the understanding needs to be carefully documented and consequently more difficult to reject."

Lest anyone forget that millions of Americans are economically suppressed, there is a sober reminder every month in the employment statistics; they always show a significantly higher percentage of unemployment among Negroes and other nonwhites than among workers of the majority group. Figures on total unemployment and labor force participation have been compiled for years, and they indicate widespread discrimination in hiring and firing. This aspect of job discrimination is well known, and it is not treated here in great detail.

But that is only the tip of the iceberg. In addition to simple employment and unemployment, this report deals with that part of the story which has been largely submerged: underemployment caused by discrimination.

Some may think of the underemployed as part-time workers or those who receive wages or salaries below a certain level. In this study, the term "underemployment" describes the status of men and women who perform work which does not fully utilize their education, skills, and talents. A low wage does not necessarily mean that a worker is underemployed; perhaps he is not capable of performing higher-paying tasks.

A skilled machinist working as a janitor or a teacher working as a waitress are historic examples of underemployment. If underemployment is caused by discrimination, it represents the capricious—and sometimes malicious—underutilization of our most precious resource.

Obviously, underemployment and unemployment are closely linked, and both must be considered in any attempt to determine how equal job opportunities can be provided in the nation as a whole, or in a given sector of the economy. For example, an employer cannot claim that he provides equal employment opportunity by merely pointing to the number of Spanish-surnamed persons on his payroll, or the percentage of his employees who have black skins, or the large number of women workers in his typing pool. The problem goes much deeper. How many of those employees rise above the lowest occupational levels? How many have skills that are going to waste? How many of them are given a chance to participate in apprenticeship and training programs? Underemployment is emphasized in this report because it represents a largely unexplored dimension of job discrimination.

I. The Significant Findings

The general conclusion is that discrimination strongly influences personnel practices in virtually every sector of the United States economy.

But it is the less general findings—the statistics on specific occupations, industries, and areas—that represent the true worth of this study as a document on discrimination. These data contain the raw material for a renewed, better-planned, and better-coordinated antidiscrimination campaign by the Commission, by other governmental authorities, and most important of all, by employers, unions, and others who have the power to determine which man or woman will be hired, trained, or promoted. Moreover, minority group workers, must be kept informed about those doors which have begun to open for them.

The survey of employers serves the Commission both as an aid in considering specific complaints and as a useful guide in determining how best to mobilize its facilities to combat patterns of discrimination in occupations, industries, and geographical areas. The statistical analysis, summarized here, should alert all Americans to the compelling need for a day-in, day-out effort to make sure that every jobseeker in this free society gets a fair chance at a position commensurate with his abilities.

Here are some of the significant findings based, among other sources, on a study made by Princeton University for the Commission.

1. With very few exceptions, minority group workers are found primarily in the lower-paying occupations, and they are underrepresented in the higher-paying occupations.

a) A rating system based on the number of each race in each occupational grouping reveals a significant gap between male Negroes, Spanish-surnamed Americans, and American Indians and males in the majority group; females in these three minority groups also rate significantly lower than majority group females. For example, Negro men average only three fourths as much earning power as do majority group men.

b) Among the nine major occupational groupings, Negro, American Indian, and Spanish-surnamed males are underrepresented in the six highest-paying categories. For example, all four minority groups covered in this report—Negroes, Spanish-surnamed Americans, American Indians, and Orientals—have relatively few representatives in the managerial class—the level where hiring, promotion, and firing decisions are made.

2. Women workers of all groups are underrepresented in the highest-paying occupations; and Negro, Spanish-surnamed, and American Indian women are heavily concentrated in the low-paying laborer and service-worker class.

3. The lower educational level of some minority groups is a factor in their lower occupational status, but statistical analyses using two different approaches show that it accounts for only about one third of the difference in occupational ranking between Negro men and majority group men; the inevitable conclusion is that the other two thirds must be attributed to discrimination, deliberate or inadvertent.

4. The study of 41 industries—in which educational attainment is taken as a variable—indicates that relatively few industries offer truly equal opportunity throughout the occupational range, although the pattern varies greatly from industry to industry.

5. Negro and Spanish-surnamed American men and women are clustered in the low-paying industries, and they are underrepresented in the highest-paying industries; for example, an analysis of 41 industries shows that the percentage of Spanish-surnamed men employed in the five lowest-paying industries is 3½ times the proportion in the 5 top-paying industries.

6. One of the exceptions to the minority group pattern is the high occupational ranking of Orientals; however, as noted above, relatively few Orientals are promoted to managerial jobs even though a large

proportion of them have attained the high-paying professional and technician occupations.

The following findings relate to Negroes, the largest and most widely dispersed minority group.

7. Only 1 out of every 7 Negroes is in a white collar job compared to a proportion of 3 out of 7 for the population as a whole.

8. As far as Negro men are concerned, discrimination is apparently strongest in the skilled trades; for Negro women, in the clerical category.

9. One seventh of all workers are skilled craftsmen but only 1 out of every 14 Negroes is in that category.

10. Four out of 5 Negroes are employed in semiskilled and unskilled blue collar jobs; for the population as a whole, the proportion is about 2 out of 5.

11. While 28 percent of Negro women are employed in white collar jobs, the proportion is only 7 percent for Negro men. By contrast, for the population as a whole, 57 percent of women workers and 37 percent of men workers hold white collar jobs.

Perhaps the most telling conclusions—and, in a sense, the most discouraging—regarding underemployment are those which show that certain characteristics are associated with unequal opportunity. For example, this set of conclusions indicates that education of minority groups is not a panacea; its lack is only one factor in the lower occupational status of minority groups.

This analysis shows that job discrimination is strongest against Negro men in those industries which:

• have a high proportion of Negro employees;

• have Negro and white employees with high average educational levels;

• have a high proportion of well-paying positions;

• have a high proportion of their operations in the South.

Thus, there are some built-in discrimination factors which would seem to place ceilings on Negro achievement—and they probably apply to other minority groups as well.

In other words, it would seem that greater progress for Negroes brings forth progressively stronger discrimination against them. The statistical conclusions above could well be stated this way:

If a large number of Negroes succeed in getting jobs in an industry, relatively fewer of them can expect promotions.

If large numbers of Negroes in an industry have high educational attainment, the bias against them will be stronger.

If an industry has many well-paying jobs, a relatively higher proportion of those jobs will be restricted to majority group employees.

And finally, there emerges the well-known story of lower employment status for Negroes in the South.

The study offers no evidence to substantiate the outmoded theory that inherent racial factors account for the lower employment status of minority groups. Proponents would have to believe, for example, that in the skilled crafts the inherent racial factors are four times as strong among Negroes in the Southeast as compared to West Coast Negroes— although both groups obviously have the same racial heritage. In the majority group, the percentage of skilled craftsmen is approximately the same in all nine Bureau of the Census geographical regions, ranging from 13.1 to 15.9; but among Negroes the percentages range from 5.6 in the three Southern regions to 21.4 on the West Coast.

Obviously, some of the conclusions were not derived by merely calculating the percentages of the respective minority groups in certain sectors and making comparisons with the majority group; the statistical processes used range from the simple to the fairly complex. A more detailed explanation of the statistical analysis is available in the Commission's library.

II. Three Broad Occupational Categories

The plight of minorities can be illustrated by using Negroes as a representative group since they comprise a large proportion of all minorities and are widely dispersed geographically. Herbert Hammerman, Chief of Reports for the EEOC, employed this traditional method in a preliminary research report on EEO-1 data.

All of the twenty-six million workers covered in the employers' reports were classified as (1) white collar, (2) skilled craftsmen, and (3) semiskilled or unskilled. In general, white collar workers rank higher in earnings than craftsmen, who, in turn, draw higher paychecks than the semiskilled or unskilled employees. Although there are some cases in which highly skilled craftsmen receive higher pay than some white collar workers, these three broad categories generally reflect workers' economic status.

Negroes comprised slightly more than 8 percent of all covered employees, and if they were distributed among these three occupational categories in proportion to their total, one would expect to find the same percentage in each category. The data show unmistakably that Negroes are not distributed evenly by occupations. They held only 2.5 percent of the white collar jobs and 4.1 percent of the craftsman jobs.

Hammerman's figures indicate the relatively few upgradings which would be required to produce a significant improvement in the occupational standing of minority group workers. For every 40 white collar jobs, 1 is held by a Negro; obviously, the number of Negro white collar workers could double—and Negroes would still be outnumbered by 20 to 1. If the number tripled, Negroes would hold 7.5 percent of white collar jobs—a figure which would be fairly close to the 8 percent which Negroes should be expected to hold on the basis of their representation in the overall workforce.

Thus, a relatively small change in the total white collar employment structure would result in an enormous improvement in the occuptional status of the Negro race.

For all workers, majority and minority groups, male and female, 43 out of every 100 wore white collars; 14 were craftsmen, and 43 were classed as semiskilled or unskilled blue collar workers. But for every 100 Negroes, only 14 were in the white collar occupations, 7 performed skilled craft work, and 79 were in the low-paying blue collar and service jobs.

Thus, 4 out of 5 Negroes are classed as semiskilled or unskilled workers. For all workers, the proportion is about 2 out of 5.

About 1 out of every 7 Negro workers held a white collar job compared to 3 out of 7 for all employees; only 1 out of 14 Negroes was classed as a skilled craftsman compared to a ratio of 1 out of 7 for all workers.

III. Regional Employment Patterns

The procedure of grouping employees by three broad categories also was used by Hammerman to illustrate the significant differences in hiring patterns among geographical regions. The finding of an extremely low occupational status for Negroes in the South does not come as a surprise, but there are significant variations among other regions as well.

In the three Southern regions, which contain 41 percent of Negro employees, approximately 9 out of 10 Negroes work at semiskilled or unskilled jobs. For the Southern working population as a whole, the proportion ranges from 40 to 53 percent.

Outside the South, the percentage of Negroes employed in the lowest classification ranges from 58 percent for the five states which have Pacific Ocean borders to 82 percent in the East North Central area (Wisconsin, Michigan, Illinois, Indiana, and Ohio). For all workers outside the South, the percentages range from 34 to 47.

The proportion of all workers classified by their employers as skilled is about the same in all regions—13 to 16 percent. By comparison, the proportion of Negroes in this category ranges from 4.8 to 7.6 percent in eight of the nine regions. The ninth region, the Pacific Coast, represents a sharp reversal of the pattern: more than 21 percent of Negro workers are employed in the skilled trades, a significantly higher proportion than the 14 percent for the workforce as a whole.

The demand for white collar workers in the South is lower than in other areas, but it does not account for the extreme underutilization of Negroes in office jobs in that area. For example, in the West South Central region (Texas, Arkansas, Oklahoma, and Louisiana), the percentage of the total white collar jobs is about the same as the national average (43 percent), but only 7 percent of Negroes in the region are classified as white collar workers.

IV. Spanish-Surnamed American Employment Patterns

The following analysis relates to Spanish-surnamed Americans, who accounted for 2.5 percent of the 26 million workers reported in the 1966 employment survey.

1. Spanish-surnamed Americans held only 1.2 percent of all white collar jobs, 2.0 percent of the craftsmen jobs and 2.0 percent of all other blue collar and service occupations.

2. Only 2 out of every 7 Spanish-surnamed Americans were in white collar jobs, compared to 3 out of 7 for the population as a whole.

3. While one seventh of all workers were skilled craftsmen, only one tenth of the reported Spanish-surnamed American workers were in these skilled jobs.

4. For the unskilled, semiskilled, and service occupations, 43 percent of all workers and 68 percent of the Spanish-surnamed Americans were in these jobs.

The findings show a heavy concentration of Spanish-surnamed workers in five of the nine Bureau of the Census geographical regions (Middle Atlantic, East North Central, West South Central, Mountain, and Pacific). These five regions accounted for 93 percent of the 643,679 Spanish-surnamed workers employed in 1966.

The West South Central region (Texas, Oklahoma, Louisiana, and Arkansas) with 17 percent of reported Spanish-surnamed American employment reported 67 percent of the Spanish-surnamed workers in semiskilled or unskilled jobs, compared to 40 percent for all employees in the region.

The concentration of Spanish-surnamed Americans in the lower-paying jobs is reflected even further in the West (Mountain and Pacific regions). This area accounts for 42 percent of Spanish-surnamed Americans employed. In the Mountain region, 7 out of 10 Spanish-surnamed Americans are semiskilled or unskilled workers, compared to about 4 out of 10 for all employees reported. The Pacific region reflects the same patterns, with 65 percent of the Spanish-surnamed Americans in the less-skilled blue collar categories, compared to only 34 percent for all employees. California accounts for one third of all Spanish-surnamed workers and 96 percent of those reported in the Pacific region.

In the Middle Atlantic region approximately 6 percent of the Spanish-surnamed Americans are in the less-skilled blue collar jobs, while 38 percent of all employees in the region are in these jobs.

The proportion of all workers in the five regions classified as craftsmen ranges from 13 to 16 percent. By comparison, the proportion of Spanish-surnamed Americans in this category ranges from about 8 to 13 percent.

Among all employees in the five regions, those classified as white collar workers ranged from 39 to 51 percent. For the Spanish-surnamed Americans the range was 11 to 27 percent.

V. Women Workers

Although women account for more than 40 percent of all white collar workers, sex discrimination continues to prevent them from reaching jobs at the managerial and professional levels. EEO-1 data for 1966 indicate that only 1 out of every 10 management positions and 1 out of every 7 professional jobs are filled by women. In contrast, of the 4.5 million women working in white collar jobs, 3 million are clerical workers, filling nearly three fourths of all clerical positions.

While over half of the 8 million women in the employment survey are in white collar jobs, a significant number, 2.5 million, are blue collar workers. Most of these women work as operatives, but they account for less than 30 percent of the total operative jobs.

Women service workers, the lowest paid category for women, number less than one million. However, it is important to note that while women represent only one of every three workers in the total labor force, they fill nearly 45 percent of all service jobs.

The occupational distribution of women in the top twenty industries, which employ 80 percent of the women in the employment survey, shows there is a sharp variation in the utilization of women from industry to industry. While only 2.4 percent of all women employed are in official and managerial positions, nearly 9 percent of the women in the communications industry are in this occupational group. In contrast, only 0.5 percent of the women working in the electrical machinery, textile mill products, and transportation equipment industries are employed as managers. Although less than 3 percent of women workers

are professionals, the percentage of women working in professional occupations ranges from about 21 percent in educational services to only
0.1 percent in the apparel, textile mill products, and leather products
industries and food stores.

Geographically, eight states, including New York, California, Illinois, Pennsylvania, Ohio, Texas, Michigan, and Massachusetts, account
for almost 60 percent of all white collar employment of women.

VI. Measuring the Differences in Dollars

In a study conducted by Princeton University under the joint sponsorship of the EEOC and the Manpower Administration of the United
States Department of Labor,[2] the EEO-1 survey which classified employees in the majority group and four minority groups into nine Bureau of the Census occupational categories was used to construct an
index to show the relative standing of each racial group based on how
many were employed in low- or high-paying occupations. Obviously,
this was a much broader and more complex study than the preliminary
analysis described in the preceding sections.

The use of an index system to present data in a simplified form is
not a new concept; the innovative element is the application of the
concept to figures on racial employment. A great variety of indexes
have been used by specialists for many years, and most laymen are
familiar with the United States Department of Labor's Consumer Price
Index.

A detailed explanation is presented here for the benefit of laymen
who are interested in the steps involved in constructing an index. For
illustrative purposes, let us assume there are 10 men in group A and 10
in group B. In group A, three men earn $15,000, four $10,000, and three
$5,000; in group B, one man earns $15,000, four $10,000, and five
$5,000. In group A, the earnings total comes to $100,000, or a simple
arithmetical average of $10,000 per man; in group B, the earnings total
is $80,000, or an average of $8,000.

---

[2] ORLEY ASHENFELTER, MINORITY EMPLOYMENT PATTERNS, 1966. Several technical appendixes may be examined at the library of the Commission. This study
does not necessarily represent the official position or policy of the United States
Government.

Group B obviously has earnings 80 percent as large as group A. In the index, group A is used as a base of 100, and group B is expressed as 80. The main purpose is to show the gap between the two groups, which in this case is 20 points, or 20 percent. If a third group which has average earnings of $7,500 enters the picture, its index would be 75. Thus, the new group's standing also would be expressed as a percentage of group A.

It should be emphasized that the indexes used in this report are not based on actual earnings because the EEO-1 data do not include information on earnings. The earnings figure used for each employee is based on his occupational classification. In each of nine job categories, the average earnings reported in the 1960 Census are used in computing the index.

This means that every professional, regardless of race, is assumed to have the same earnings as all others in the professional class, each skilled craftsman is assumed to have the same earnings as all other skilled craftsmen, etc. The result is that the differences among the races undoubtedly are understated in the indexes. *The indexes may be described as a measurement of the earnings potential of each group based on occupational standing—the actual earnings differences between the majority and minority groups are probably greater in most cases.*

Following are the nine occupational categories, ranked according to median male earnings for each category reported in the 1960 Census:

1. managerial,
2. professional,
3. technical,
4. craftsman (skilled),
5. sales,
6. clerical,
7. operative (semiskilled),
8. service, and
9. laborer (unskilled).

Another set of indexes was constructed for females based on their median earnings in each occupational category. The ranking of the occupations according to female earnings is substantially different from the male ranking:

1. professional,
2. managerial,
3. technical,
4. clerical,
5. craftsman,
6. operative,
7. laborer,
8. sales, and
9. service.

Based on occupational standing, the average figure for men in the majority group is $5,016 compared with $3,883 for Negro men, or a difference of $1,133. Both of these figures would be substantially larger if the computation were based on current earnings; the 1960 Census reported 1959 income, and earnings of workers in private industry have advanced sharply in the strong and uninterrupted economic expansion of the 1960's. Nevertheless, these figures are considered reliable as a measure of the *differences* in earnings among occupational groups, and the *relative* standings of the various occupational groups is the key factor in the index.

As indicated above, when these figures were used in computing an index for Negro men, the result was an average earnings figure of $3,883 per year. For Anglo men,[3] the figure was $5,016. The figure for Negro males was 77.4 percent of the Anglo figure; thus Table 1 shows the Negro male index as 77.4 and the Anglo index as 100. *Based on occupational status alone,* the average Negro male worker earns $77.40 for every $100 earned by the average Anglo male worker.

The table also shows that the occupational status of Spanish-surnamed and American Indian males is significantly lower than that of Anglo males. The index for Spanish-surnamed males was 83.1 percent of the Anglo figure and American Indian males 89.2 percent of the Anglo figure.

The indexes for females show a somewhat different, but nevertheless significant, pattern of underutilization of minority group workers as far as these three groups are concerned.

Orientals of both sexes represent an outstanding exception to this pattern of apparent discrimination. Their top ranking—even higher

---

[3] "Anglo," as used in this report, means majority group. It is a residual derived by deducting minority group employees from the total.

TABLE 1 Indexes of Occupational Position, United States and Regions, 1966

	U.S.	North		South		West	
	Percent*	Percent*	Ratio†	Percent*	Ratio†	Percent*	Ratio†
Male							
Negro	77.4	80.6	1.04	73.9	.95	77.9	1.04
Oriental	101.3	113.6	1.12	112.4	1.11	94.1	.96
American Indian	89.2	90.5	1.01	92.5	1.04	82.7	.96
Spanish-surnamed American	83.1	82.2	.98	84.6	1.02	81.1	1.01
Anglo	100.0	100.0	.99	100.0	1.00	100.0	1.03
Female							
Negro	84.7	87.2	1.03	80.4	.94	87.2	1.05
Oriental	105.0	114.4	1.09	111.4	1.05	99.1	.97
American Indian	89.4	85.2	.96	94.5	1.05	88.4	1.01
Spanish-surnamed American	90.8	92.3	1.02	88.9	.97	89.2	1.00
Anglo	100.0	100.0	1.00	100.0	.99	100.0	1.02

* Percentage of the Anglo index
† Ratio of Regional to United States index

than the Anglo group—can be attributed almost entirely to the relatively large number of Orientals who have achieved entry into the professional and technical occupations.

The index system provides a broad-gauge formula for measuring underemployment of minority group workers, and it yields interesting esults when applied to geographical areas and industries. It also proves invaluable in analyzing the effect of the education factor on minority group employment. These applications of the index system are described in other sections. The section immediately following gives further details on how well minority groups fare in the various occupational categories, and it outlines some of the reasons for the results shown in the indexes.

VII. Details on Nine Job Categories

In the process of preparing the indexes, the workers reported in the EEO-1 survey were arranged according to occupation, race, and sex in the manner described above. This is an enlargement of the Hammerman analysis which showed only three major job categories and compared only one race, Negroes, with the working population as a whole.

The data used by the Princeton researchers in computing the basic indexes are presented in Table 2. The pattern of lower occupational status for minority groups becomes clearly evident in these numbers. In almost every case, minority group workers are clustered in the lower-paying occupations, and relatively few of them are employed in the higher-paying categories.

For example, 12.0 percent of Anglo men are classified as officials and managers; but for Negro men, the figure is slightly less than 1 percent. For Spanish-surnamed Americans, it is 2.5 percent; for Orientals 7.0 percent; and for American Indians 6.5 percent.

This one category illustrates an important part of the pattern. A male Oriental has a little better than half as good a chance of becoming a manager or official as an Anglo; the American Indian's prospects are slightly lower than the Oriental's; the chances of a man with a Spanish surname are only one fifth as good as that of a member of the majority group; and for Negroes, the figure is one twelfth.

It is important to consider the actual numbers of workers involved

TABLE 2 Percentage Distribution of Anglo and Minority Group Employment in the United States by Occupation and Sex, 1966

Occupation	MALE					FEMALE				
	Negro	Oriental	Am. Ind.	SSA*	Anglo	Negro	Oriental	Am. Ind.	SSA*	Anglo
Managers, Officials, Proprietors	.97	6.95	6.49	2.54	12.01	.68	1.86	2.19	.80	2.64
Professional Workers	.85	21.50	3.38	2.38	9.03	1.55	9.48	2.28	1.10	3.03
Technical Workers	1.19	7.84	3.23	2.33	4.83	4.55	8.75	3.32	2.53	4.35
Sales Workers	1.25	4.80	4.74	3.00	7.35	3.95	5.92	12.50	6.92	9.25
Clerical Workers	2.70	8.31	3.89	5.14	7.13	17.52	41.05	21.67	24.05	40.77
Craftsmen	7.90	13.60	19.32	13.92	20.44	2.43	2.28	5.13	4.81	2.80
Operatives	37.22	14.01	29.94	32.08	25.49	24.93	11.39	24.18	29.81	21.67
Laborers	29.82	10.91	22.27	26.38	8.37	14.14	7.04	11.81	17.61	6.39
Service Workers	18.10	12.08	6.73	12.23	5.35	30.25	12.23	16.92	12.39	9.10
Total No. Employed	1,449,998	84,287	37,857	445,128	15,519,583	639,677	45,177	17,136	198,551	7,155,656
Percent of All Males/Females Employed	8.17	.48	.21	2.51	88.62	7.91	.56	.21	2.46	88.86

* Spanish-surnamed Americans

in this category—as well as percentages—because it is the persons at the top who hold the primary responsibility for hiring, firing, promoting, and training employees. The survey showed 1,917,000 male Anglos holding positions as officials or managers compared to 14,000 Negroes —a ratio of 137 to 1.

About 40 percent of male majority group workers are operatives, laborers, or service workers, but 85 percent of Negroes are in these three bottom classes. The opposite is true at the top of the occupational ladder: almost half of the male Anglos are in the four highest-paying occupations—managerial, professional, technical, and craft—but only 1 Negro male in 25 can claim such status.

The tables show clearly that the occupational pattern for Spanish-surnamed workers is similar to, but far less pronounced than, that of Negroes. Spanish-surnamed men also are heavily concentrated in the three lowest-paying occupations—70 percent compared to 85 for Negroes—but their chances of reaching the four top groups are six times greater than that of Negroes, primarily because of their much easier entry into the craftsman class.

The occupational standing of American Indian males is very similar to that of Spanish-surnamed males with two notable exceptions: their position in the managerial occupations is 2½ times stronger than that of Spanish-surnamed males and the proportion of American Indians in the craftsman occupation is only slightly below that of Anglos. The percentage of American Indians who work as craftsmen is 19.3 compared to 20.4 for Anglos, 13.9 for Spanish-surnamed, 13.6 for Orientals and 7.9 for Negroes.

Based on occupational standing alone, Orientals represent an outstanding exception to the pattern of underutilization described above. This can be attributed almost entirely to the high proportion of Oriental men (and women) in the professional and technical occupations. More than 1 out of every 4 Oriental men is a professional compared to 1 out of 11 among Anglos (and 1 out of 100 among Negroes) and, again in relative terms, the chances of an Oriental male being a technical worker are twice as high as the chances of an Anglo worker.

The indexes show that Oriental men and women have a slightly higher occupational standing than Anglos. Does this mean that job discrimination is a myth as far as Orientals are concerned? It should be noted that despite the large proportion of Oriental males in the professional group, only 6.5 percent of Oriental men have been able to move into the managerial occupations compared to 12.0 percent for the majority group. When the occupational standings are subdivided by geographical regions, significant discrimination against Orientals is apparent in the West.

For women workers, the distribution patterns are less obvious. The configuration of discrimination emerges once again although it is not as consistent nor as pronounced as it appeared in the male groupings. The percentage of majority group women in the professions is twice as high as that of Negro women, and the chances of an Anglo woman being a manager are about four times as high as those of her Negro counterpart. Almost 1 out of every 3 Negro women workers is employed in the lowly service occupations compared to 1 out of 11 Anglo women.

The exceptions are important. Negro women actually rate slightly higher in the technical category than Anglo women. The large number of Negro women in technical occupations is due primarily to the relatively large number who work at technical trades in medical services (for example, laboratory employees in hospitals).

The most important data are the figures on Anglo and Negro clerical workers. About two out of every five majority group women are employed in this class; for Negro women, the ratio is about one out of every six. These ratios are a convenient form, but one must return to the actual figures to illustrate how many jobs they represent: of the Anglo women covered in the survey, 2.9 million worked in clerical jobs; for Negroes, the figure is about 113,000.

The clerical occupation is one of the most important, in earnings and in number of employees, as far as women are concerned, and it is the sector in which discrimination against Negro women is most pervasive. For men, craftsman is one of the most important occupations, in earnings and in number of jobs, and it is the sector in which discrimination against Negro men is the most prevalent.

Oriental women, like the men of that race, actually have a higher occupational standing when compared to Anglos of the same sex. Again, this can be attributed in large degree to the comparatively large percentage of Orientals who work as professionals and technicians. Also, the percentage of Oriental women who work in the clerical occupations is almost identical to the proportion for majority group women.

Both Spanish-surnamed and American Indian women have attained higher employment status than Negro women, but their burden of discrimination is still plainly evident when comparisons are made with the majority group. While Negro women are heavily concentrated in service occupations, Spanish-surnamed women are employed primarily in the operative (semiskilled) class. Both Spanish-surnamed and American Indian women are somewhat better represented than Negro women in the clerical occupation, but there is less likelihood that they will be found in the technical class.

VIII. The Job Picture by Industries

Part of the system used in developing the national indexes in the Princeton report was applied to industries to determine how minority groups fare in various sectors of the economy.

This analysis:

1. Shows a wide variation in the percentage of minority group workers on payrolls of various industries.

2. Demonstrates that the occupational status of minority groups in relation to the majority group—the gap between minority groups and Anglos—varies greatly among industries.

3. Shows that, as might be expected, there are wide differences among industries in occupational standing of all workers.

4. Leads to the conclusion that Negroes, both male and female, are heavily concentrated in industries which have a relatively large number of low-paying occupations, and that a similar but less pronounced pattern, holds for Spanish-surnamed Americans.

The figures showing the proportion of jobs in each industry held by minority group workers are interesting, but they do not necessarily indicate whether an industry is doing well or poorly in providing job opportunities for minority groups. For example, an industry which has very few Orientals and Negroes among its employees may be located primarily in areas where these two groups comprise only a small segment of the population.

The results on underemployment are more significant. For example, they provide corroboration for earlier findings that minority groups generally have lower occupational standings.

Moreover, they provide the foundation for the analysis of the education factor in underemployment which is described in the next section.

The analysis of underemployment of minority groups in industries is limited to Negroes and Spanish-surnamed Americans; there is some doubt whether valid conclusions can be drawn in regard to Orientals and American Indians since they comprise such small fractions of total employment in many industries. The analysis is limited in another way. Out of the 79 industries covered by EEO-1 data, only about half were used in the computation (41 for males and 42 for females). A comparison of the figures for each industry with Census reports indicated that many of the industries may not have been adequately represented because of the limited coverage of the survey. However, the industries included in the analysis accounted for about 85 percent of all workers covered in the survey.

In determining whether an industry has a high- or low-paying occupational structure, the jobs held by Anglos were used as a yardstick since the majority group represents the bulk of employees. The average earnings for an industry, based on occupational structure, were calculated in the same way that earnings were computed in developing the nationwide industry indexes. An industry with a high percentage of white collar jobs, for example, would have a high average earnings figure.

The substantial differences in occupational structure which appear in the figures were not unexpected. The occupational requirements of a trucking firm, for example, obviously are vastly different from those of an investment company.

Some meaningful indicators emerge when the industries are ranked according to their occupational structure.

Negro workers, both male and female, are clustered in those industries which have the fewest jobs to offer in the top-paying occupations, and, to a lesser degree, the same is true of Spanish-surnamed employees.[4]

Negro men hold only 2.1 percent of the jobs in the five industries which have the highest ccupational ranking—insurance services, hold-

---

[4] Simple observation of the rankings strongly supports this statement; it was more definitely established by the use of more sophisticated statistical processes described in the Ashenfelter report. Copies are available in the library of the Commission.

ing and other investment companies, nonbank credit agencies, communications, and insurance carriers. At the other end of the scale, Negro males fill 9.6 percent of the jobs in those five industries which have the lowest occupational ranking—food trade, water transportation, motor freight and warehousing, furniture and fixtures manufacturing, and anthracite coal mining. Thus the percentage of Negro male employees in the bottom five industries is about 4½ times the percentage in the top five industries.

For the purpose of making the point absolutely clear, the pattern is exemplified by the two industries at the top and bottom of the male occupational ranking scale. In water transportation, which has average Anglo earnings (based on occupational status) of about $4,310 per year, some 22.7 percent of the male employees are Negroes; in insurance, where average Anglo earnings exceed $6,000, only about 1 per cent of the male employees are Negroes.

(*As noted in section VI, the earnings figures are based on 1960 Census data, and they undoubtedly are well below current earnings in those industries; however, relative figures are important to this analysis, and Census data are appropriate for this purpose.*)

Spanish-surnamed men represent only 0.9 percent of the employees in the top five industries, but the figure is 3.0 for the bottom five. Thus, the concentration is more than three times as great in the five low-ranking industries.

The findings for women are similar. For females, the top industries by occupational index are communications, insurance services, nonbank credit agencies, petroleum refining, and insurance carriers. Only 3.1 percent of the employees in those industries are Negro women. But, in the five lowest-rated industries—retail trade and general merchandise, air transportation, tobacco manufacturers, food manufacturers, and miscellaneous manufacturing industries—Negro women represent 9.5 percent of all employees.

The percentage of Spanish-surnamed women in the lower-rung industries is about twice the proportion reported in the higher-paying groups.

Thus the industries with the greatest proportion of high-paying jobs employ a lower percentage of Negroes and Spanish-surnamed workers. This is not a surprising result, but it raises questions which cannot be dismissed lightly.

Does it mean that Negroes and Spanish-surnamed Americans must move out of these industries if they hope to improve their occupational position? Again, no firm conclusions can be drawn, but it appears that members of these two groups face a double obstacle: first, they have lower occupational positions as was illustrated by the occupational indexes; and second, they are more likely to be employed in those industries in which all workers are given fewer chances for advancement.

For example, some minority group workers may have few chances of moving up to higher-paying occupations through employer-sponsored training programs because they are employed in industries where there are few top-paying jobs to fill, and therefore these industries are not interested in extensive training programs.

Some industries, regardless of how well intentioned, may be severely limited in trying to reduce underemployment among minority groups because of their occupational structure.

Also, it would appear that programs to reduce *unemployment* and *underemployment* of minority group workers should be directed in particular to those industries which have high occupational ratings. Obviously, they offer the greatest opportunities, and as demonstrated by the figures, they have fewer minority group employees.

IX. The Education Factor in Underemployment[5]

The indexes presented in section VI are general indicators of the magnitude of underemployment caused by racial discrimination. But they can be refined further if another major element, job qualification, is brought into the analysis.

The indexes developed at Princeton used the majority group as a base of 100; if a minority group had an index of 80, then its earnings potential based on its occupational standing was 20 points, or 20 percent, below that of the majority group. (As noted previously, this difference is computed solely on occupational standing; the actual gap undoubtedly is considerably greater because the indexes do not measure discrimination within an occupation.) But, if the minority group workers are not as well qualified as Anglo workers, then this gap,

---

[5] Data on educational attainment by industry are not available for Spanish-surnamed Americans.

or part of it, may be caused by differences in qualifications rather than unequal employment opportunities.

The analysis described below indicates that about one third of the gap between Negro males and Anglo males can be attributed to lower educational attainment on the part of Negro males; this leads to the conclusion that two thirds of the difference must be attributed to unequal employment opportunities. For women, the results are similar: only slightly more than one third of the gap between Anglos and Negroes can be attributed to educational differences.

From one viewpoint, the entire gap between Anglos and Negroes can be considered part of the pattern of discrimination because the lower educational level of Negroes, or at least part of it, merely reflects racial bias in educational institutions. But this aspect of racial prejudice generally falls outside the Commission's area of responsibility. Thus, discrimination in education or other sectors should not be confused with discrimination in employment.

The amount of formal education seems to be a logical measure of job qualification; it is unquestionably one of the major factors in economic success in this technical age, and it is the only element which can be measured in precise terms. Census data show that the amount of earnings is associated with the number of years of formal schooling.

Experience could be considered as another element in job qualification. But length of time served in a job does not necessarily reflect a person's fitness for that job. And, if discrimination exists, some technically well-qualified minority group workers might show little or no experience because of difficulty in gaining entrance to some types of jobs.

Analyzing the education factor involves the construction of indexes to show the occupational rank of both male and female Negroes (and other minority groups) in comparison to Anglos in about forty industries, and a comparison of these indexes with the educational attainment of both groups in each industry. The preliminary steps, constructing the indexes and arranging the educational data, are fairly simple and they are explained in detail below. But the two methods used in making the statistical comparisons in order to prove that a pattern exists are somewhat sophisticated. In effect, they involve measuring the differences in education against the differences in occupational status. The results are in the form of two sets of figures for both male and female Negroes: one set consists of indexes showing the occupational positions of Negroes in about forty industries; the other shows what the occupational positions of Negroes would be in these industries if their educational levels were equal to that of the majority group.

In the preceding section, average earnings were computed for Anglo men and women, based on the numbers in each occupation, for each of some forty industries. The same procedure can be used to find the average earnings in each industry for each of the four minority groups delineated in the EEO–1 data.

These figures for minority groups can be translated into indexes which measure the occupational standing of each minority group, men and women, in each industry. The earnings figure for a minority group in a given industry is divided by the figure for Anglos in that industry, and the result shows how high the minority group's earnings are in relation to those of the majority group.

For example, if male Anglo earnings in an industry average $5,000, and male Negro earnings in that industry average $4,000, the result is .80 or 80 percent. If Negro earnings were $5,500, the result would be 1.10 or 110 percent.

In effect, these percentage figures for the minority groups are indexes, with the Anglo group as a base of 100. The percentage figure for any industry may be compared to 100 to show a minority group's occupational standing in relation to the majority group in that industry.

The analysis of education is limited to Negroes—the only minority group considered by the Princeton researchers large enough to yield accurate statistical results.

The figures for all workers are used to represent Anglos since the latter comprise the bulk of all employees. In a given industry, the relationship between the two figures on educational attainment can be expressed as a percentage; thus, if the average level of schooling for all workers in that industry is ten years and the average level for Negroes is eight, then the educational level of Negroes is 80 percent as high as that of all workers. This, in effect, is an index of educational attainment and it can be compared to the index of occupational status or each industry. Conversely, there is a gap of 20 percentage points, and this difference can be measured against the gap in the occupational indexes of Negroes and Anglos for that industry.

The occupational indexes for Negro men for the 41 industries averages out to about 80. (This compares to an index of 77.4 for Negro men reported in section VI when all 79 industries were used.) When these indexes are recomputed to take into account the lower educational level of Negro men, the average is 85.93. Thus the total gap in earning power between Anglo and Negro men in these 41 industries is 20 percentage points and about 6 points, or one third of the gap, can be attributed to educational differences.

Thus, with the data used, Negro men would be predicted to have an index of 85.93, about 14 points below majority group men, when their educational level is set at a value equal to that of Anglo men. It is interesting to note that Negro men in one industry, leather manufacturing, have almost exactly the same educational attainment as all workers in that industry. One would expect the Negro employees in leather manufacturing to have an occupational index close to the 85.93 calculated above if the analysis is accurate. The actual index for Negro men in that industry is 85.9.

When the formula is applied to Negro women, their occupational index for 42 industries averages about 86 (about the same as the national index which includes all 79 industries),[6] and the index moves up to 91 when educational differences are taken into account. Thus, there is a 14 point gap in the potential earning power of Negro and majority group women, and only 5 points, or a little more than one third of it, is attributed to educational differences.

These findings strongly indicate that more education is only a partial solution to the Negroes' problem of low employment status because a lessening of the difference in years of schooling between Negroes and Anglos does not produce a proportional narrowing of the gap in employment status.

It should be made clear that education is almost always of tremendous value to an employee of any race. On the average, employees with higher levels of education earn more money. But the central point of these analyses cannot be ignored: *inequalities in employment opportunities do not disappear as soon as the Negro attains equal status in education.*

---

[6] A slightly different set of industries was used in calculating the indexes for Negro women because several of the industries which are important in analyzing workers of one sex do not have enough employees of the other sex to yield reliable results. For example, for women, anthracite coal mining was dropped and the apparel industry was added.

X. The Characteristics of Job Discrimination

Discrimination in employment does not fall evenly on all minority groups, geographical areas, occupations, or regions. Where is the invisible curtain most effective? And what determines its strength?

When the Princeton researchers examined the Negro occupational indexes by industries—which reflect the earning power of Negroes in comparison to that of the majority group—they found interesting data on some characteristics of industries which can be associated with inequality of opportunity in employment.

Statistical tests were run to see if four characteristics sometimes mentioned in connection with racial discrimination were associated with industries in which there are particularly large gaps in employment status between Anglos and Negroes.

In general terms, it was found that gaps in job status between Negro and Anglo men were greater:

• in those industries in which the educational levels of *all* workers are high

• in those industries which have a large proportion of high-paying jobs

• in those industries which employ a relatively high percentage of Negroes

• in those industries which have all or a major portion of their operations in the South.

No significant patterns could be established when the characteristics above were tested on Negro women. The analysis could not be applied with accuracy to the other, less numerous minority groups.

In each of the tests, a formula was applied to measure the statistical association between the given characteristic and those industries in which there are large gaps between Anglo and Negro occupational indexes.[7]

The first three findings are particularly important because they suggest that automatic brakes are applied when Negro men reach a certain

[7] Technical explanations and the regression equations employed in the Ashenfelter report.

level of achievement; their position improves—but the majority group moves ahead at a faster pace.

The analysis of educational level effects revealed that the occupational gap between Negro men and Anglo men would widen by about 5 percentage points for every two-year advancement in the *overall* educational level.

In the previous section, it was found that a narrowing of three percentage points in the education gap would produce only a 1 percent decrease in the difference in occupational status of the two groups.

The result of the educational level analysis can be illustrated by a simple example: assume that in an industry both Anglo and Negro employees have an average of ten years of schooling, and that the Negro male occupational status is 85 percent as high as the Anglo men's rating. If, in a second industry, the educational level of both groups is twelve years, the Negroes' relative occupational status would be 80 percent. On the average, the occupational gap grows by five points for every two years in the general educational level.

It should be emphasized that in the example above Negroes in the second industry undoubtedly would have higher earnings than the Negroes in the first industry because their average number of years of schooling was two years higher; but the difference in earnings between Negroes and Anglos would be greater in the second industry.

In summary, Negro men undoubtedly can increase their earnings by obtaining more education, but the rate of gain in earnings is significantly less than that of Anglos.

The second test poses the question: is it true that the occupational status of Negro men in relation to majority group men tends to be lower in those industries which have a large proportion of well-paying jobs?

The statistics give a positive response. Analysis shows that, on the average, the gap in the occupational indexes between Anglo and Negro males widens by 3.5 percentage points for every $500 increase in the Anglo index.

An illustration will help clarify this point. If Industry A has an Anglo occupational index (which represents the typical pattern) of $5,500 while Industry B's Anglo index is $5,000, the gap between Anglo and Negro men will be 3.5 percentage points greater in Industry A.

Does discrimination increase as the number of Negro workers increase? Again, statistical analysis shows that the difference between Anglo and Negro males is wider in those industries which have a higher percentage of Negro male workers. On the average, if the proportion of Negro men in the industry goes up by 5 percentage points, the gap between Negro and Anglo indexes will widen by 3.7 points.

A great deal of evidence has already been presented on discrimination in the South. Intensive investigation renders still more evidence: in industries which have all or a portion of their operations in the South, the gap between the occupational indexes of Anglo and Negro men is 11 points greater, on the average, than the gap in industries located entirely in the North and West.

As noted, the first three statistical analyses indicate that some unknown factor starts to work, or work more strongly, against Negro men when they become part of an economic group which has a high educational level, when they enter an industry in which there are many well-paying jobs, or when large numbers of them are employed in an industry. Is this factor discrimination? It is difficult not to assign it a major role.

XI. Detailed Studies of Specific Industries

If more detailed data become available, the technique of comparing occupational indexes, educational levels, and numbers of racial groups could be applied to companies and segments of companies to pinpoint the sectors in which there is significant underutilization of minority group labor. Even without using such devices as the occupational index, the pattern of racial discrimination in employment can be outlined for specific industries by intensive study. This section presents the major employment features of all or major parts of three industries: the rubber industry in Ohio, the textile industry in North and South Carolina, and drug manufacturing nationwide.

The Ohio rubber industry report was prepared by Professor Alan Batchelder of Kenyon College for the Ohio Civil Rights Commission under a grant from the EEOC.[8] The textile industry data represent the

---

[8] ALAN BATCHELDER, A NEARLY FREE MARKET FOR OHIO RUBBER MANUFAC-TURERS BUT NOT FOR OHIO NEGROES.

work of Dr. Phyllis Wallace of the EEOC Office of Research and Donald D. Osburn, then Assistant Professor of Economics at North Carolina State at Raleigh; and the studies of the drug industry were conducted by Dr. Wallace and other members of the EEOC research staff. All of the reports rely heavily on the information supplied by employers.

While all of these reports indicate significant and deep-seated prejudices in personnel practices, there are threads of optimism as well. The textile industry undoubtedly is now hiring a much larger proportion of minority group workers than in the past, and the most flagrant offenders in the rubber industry apparently have taken steps to remedy some of the serious imbalances in that sector.

The textile industry in particular can be used to illustrate how rapidly progress can be achieved if the racial obstacles to employment are removed.

One important reason for these progressive moves may have been the increasing attention which society has focused on minority group problems. It is significant that these deliberate, solid steps along the road toward equal opportunity in employment were taken after active antidiscrimination programs were put into operation by federal and state authorities.

Each of the three industries has distinctive characteristics:

The rubber industry employs large numbers of both skilled and unskilled workers, and it is particularly concentrated in Ohio—the area covered in the report.

Textile manufacturing is a labor-intensive industry which provides a great many jobs for semiskilled workers; a large part of the industry is located in the Carolinas, and the discussion here pertains to that area.

Drug manufacturing has most of its operations in about a dozen states; a majority of the employees are in the professional and technical occupational categories.

There were great disparities among the major rubber companies in the percentage of Negro workers they employed in the most desirable occupations even though all drew on the same pool of labor. These variations pertained to the largest four companies in Akron, which employ 93 percent of the city's rubber workers. The fact that some hired Negro workers in significant numbers in certain occupations while their nearby competitors hired only a few, or none at all, provides overwhelming evidence of racial bias in employment.

About 18 percent of the nation's rubber workers live in Summit County, where Akron is situated. Negroes comprise 8 percent of the county labor force and 15 percent of the labor force in the city. Yet, they constituted only 7.6 percent of total employees, less than 1 percent of white collar employees, and only 2.6 percent of the skilled craftsmen. Negro women in particular had difficulty in obtaining employment in the industry; only 2.2 percent of all female employees in the rubber industry were Negroes.

Negroes made up less than 2.5 percent of apprentices and on-the-job trainees for both white collar and production jobs.

Another interesting point: The rubber plants in Ohio with 500 or more employees had a significantly higher percentage of Negroes as compared to the plants with fewer employees. In the nine Akron plants with fewer than 500 employees, there were no Negroes among 439 white collar workers and only 1 Negro among 80 craftsmen, and no Negro white collar employees were found in plants with fewer than 200 white collar workers.

The textile industry in North and South Carolina accounts for about 45 percent of the manufacturing jobs in an area which has a large Negro population. Since a large percentage of the jobs do not require a high degree of technical training, the industry presents a significant potential opportunity for the many Negroes who have been displaced by farm mechanization in recent years.

Prior to the 1960's, few Negroes found employment in textile mills. The labor supply was large relative to demand, and even in periods of tighter labor markets many employers apparently preferred to hire white women for many jobs instead of Negroes of either sex. One reason, perhaps, was the desire to avoid racial friction; some employers apparently believed that they could not put Southern whites and Negroes on an equal employment footing without generating racial strife.

In 1960, Negroes represented 22 and 30 percent of the total labor forces in North and South Carolina, respectively, but they comprised only 3.9 and 5.2 percent of textile employment. An analysis of reports from more than 400 establishments showed the Negro textile employment in both states at 8.6 percent in 1966. Although these figures are not precisely comparable, the difference is highly significant.

Of even more importance was the acceleration of this trend toward hiring more Negroes between 1964 and 1965. An analysis of 103 North Carolina establishments showed that three fifths of the employees added to payrolls from 1964 to 1965 were Negroes; in one year, the number of Negro men employed in these textile mills increased 5 percent; and for Negro women, there was a jump of 312 percent. The number of units which had no Negro employees dropped from 78 to 36 from 1964 to 1965. Of the 81 units which reported higher Negro employment, 23 experienced a decline in the total number of workers and 2 reported no change.

For the thirty-three South Carolina plants which reported in both years, 38 percent of the new employees were Negroes and total Negro employment moved up 58 percent. The percentage increases by sex also were remarkably similar to the North Carolina figures—a 48 percent gain in the total number of Negro males and 311 percent in the total number of Negro women employees.

The number of South Carolina units which reported an all-white female workforce dropped from 24 to 4 in this one-year period. It should be noted that this remarkable progress was possible because there was so much room for improvement. Also, the labor market has changed substantially in the Carolinas. Many of the Anglo workers in textiles have been attracted to new, higher-paying manufacturing industries such as machinery and chemicals, which have moved into the area in recent years.

Even in 1966, Negro women represented only 3.7 percent of female textile employment, and Negroes of both sexes were heavily concentrated in the lower-paying job categories. Fourteen percent of all textile workers wore white collars in 1966, but the ratio was 1 out of 100 for Negroes. And 95 percent of the Negro blue collar workers were at the operative level (semiskilled) or lower. Among all textile employees, 8 percent and 12 percent in North and South Carolina, respectively, were laborers; for Negroes, 32 and 37 percent were in this unskilled class. Out of 10,211 officials and managers, only 11 were Negroes; of 2,104 technicians, only 13 were Negro; and no Negro was counted among the 526 sales workers.

In summary, the evidence strongly suggests that the textile industry has begun to utilize minority group labor in the Carolinas in significant numbers; but strong barriers must be broken down before minority groups gain access to the jobs above the laborer and semiskilled levels.

The drug industry contrasts sharply with textile manufacturing; it is growing faster, it expends a major portion of its resources on research and development, it employs an extraordinarily high proportion of white collar workers, and most of its facilities are located in large metropolitan areas outside the South.

There is also a marked difference between the drug and rubber industries in regard to minority group employment: the smaller establishments—those with less than 1,000 employees—utilize more Negro labor than those plants with 1,000 or more employees. One company of about 500 employees reported that 18 percent of its white collar workers were Negroes, and another firm of about 300 employees reported a figure of 25 percent.

The 398 drug manufacturing establishments reporting in the Employer Information Survey of 1966 showed that Negroes held only 1.8 percent of the white collar jobs even though the drug industry is heavily concentrated in metropolitan areas where the population is more than 12 percent Negro. The industry reported 133,000 total employees —5.3 percent of them Negroes and 2.1 percent Spanish-surnamed.

Negroes were underrepresented in every white collar category. For example, only 2.1 percent of the 15,893 official and clerical positions were held by Negroes. There were only 91 Negro salesmen, about one half of one percent of the total—not even enough to cover the nation's 9,000 Negro physicians and dentists if Negro salesmen were restricted to such clientele.

There were almost 10,000 foremen and craftsmen in the industry—but only 3.8 percent of these jobs were held by Negroes.

There appear to be a relatively large number of potential job opportunities in the drug industry for minority group workers who have not obtained a top-level education. A 1965 survey by the Pharmaceutical Manufacturers Association revealed that 41 percent of the 16,390 workers engaged in research and development had less than a bachelor's degree—and this sector of the industry is expected to continue to grow at a rapid rate.

The few Negro technicians in this industry are in sharp contrast to the unusually large representation of Negro technicians in another growing industry—medical services.

XII. Concluding Comments

The essence of a statement made at the beginning of this report should be repeated: job discrimination is a profound and pervasive condition in the American economy; it is a root cause of minority group problems because the lack of meaningful and purposeful employment that provides adequate earnings is one of the basic reasons for the tragic plight of minority groups in America.

None of the statements in this report should be interpreted as a blanket indictment of any region, industry, or occupation. There are bright spots of progress in any given sector regardless of what the figures show for that sector as a whole.

Thus despite the widespread inequities in employment set forth in this report, there are grounds for optimism. As mentioned earlier in this report, textile companies, for example, showed significant progress in the short run.

Information and education on the principle of equal opportunity are at least as important as organized community campaigns and the force of law. For example, minorities must know their rights before they can exercise them, they must be aware of opportunities before they can take advantage of them. Some evidence indicates strongly that, once rebuffed, minority groups do not persist in their efforts to gain entry to a company or occupation even though there may have been a genuine change of attitude. The rigid mores molded by centuries of practice persist on both sides.

Obviously, minority groups should be given an equal chance for education and training and equal consideration for job openings. But they must be given hope as well. The incentive factor must be considered because it is the moving power behind every man, and collectively the impetus behind our efficient and productive economy. It is the expectation of reward—the anticipation of productive labor, money, status, and social acceptance—which enables men to endure the apprenticeship of training, education, and experience.

The young minority group worker must see living, visible proof of those rewards; he must be assured that his skills and intellect will be utilized or he will not develop them. He is weary of waiting for the next generation.

Like every other person, the minority group worker has a responsibility to himself to obtain as much education and training as he can absorb. The member of a minority group who passes up opportunities for learning because he is afraid his knowledge will never be used is like a baseball player who refuses to learn to bat because some players are prejudiced. The rules of the game can be enforced.

Minority groups desperately need education. There should be no misunderstanding on this point. The analysis on the relationship between education and attainment of Negroes should not be misinterpreted. It showed that education is not a panacea, that it will not erase the disparities between Negroes and majority group workers. However, this finding is expressed in relative terms and it does not alter the fact that education is almost always a highly profitable investment for all workers. There is a great gulf between the educated and the uneducated Negro.

Formal credentials are particularly important to the worker who is likely to encounter job discrimination.

This report is couched in monetary terms, and on that basis alone, minority groups obviously could be given a tremendous uplift if job discrimination can be blunted. But what of the majority group? Is one man's gain another man's loss? Will the typical white American family have to sacrifice some of its high standard of living in order to accommodate the less fortunate minorities?

Economists have shown that many billions of dollars could be added to the nation's annual production of goods and services if minority group workers were fully utilized, and there is very little controversy on this point. And this type of analysis does not consider the savings that would result from reduced welfare payments, reduced crime, and reduced unemployment payments. Nor does it count the additional taxes that would be collected after unemployed or underemployed workers become fully productive.

The person who is hired or upgraded suddenly has more money to spend; this means more sales, more profits, and eventually the creation of more jobs. Everyone benefits.

The enlargement of markets tends to increase efficiency, thereby reducing pressure for higher prices.

From the businessman's viewpoint, the elimination of job discrimination increases the supply of labor.

For decades the federal government has recognized the need for conservation of our natural resources. But most people tend to think of these resources in terms of mineral wealth, wildlife, or beautiful scenery. Only relatively recently have we recognized officially that the most important and "natural" resource of all is human skill and intellect and creativity.

Replacements for minerals can be found and stored if there is no ready use for them. We can protect our wildlife and preserve our streams and woodlands but we cannot store or reclaim labor or time. If a man is unemployed or underemployed for a week or month, that much production is lost; it is gone forever.

4   Labor Arbitration, EEOC Conciliation, and Employment Discrimination

The drive for racial and ethnic equality in employment in the 1960's is as compelling and dynamic as the drive for union recognition during the 1930's.[1] Our response to the earlier challenge demonstrated that the American industrial relations system could accommodate a major organized movement for social change. We learned how to adapt industrial relations processes to the new situations created by an expanding labor movement supported by legal protection for collective bargaining. The civil rights movement, supported by laws against employment discrimination, is now pressing the industrial relations system to accommodate to its demands.

Labor history and labor law involve the elaboration of three basic concepts: recognition of the union as representative of the workers, negotiation of the basic relationship between union and management, and a dispute settlement mechanism to resolve problems arising out of the relationship thus established. These three concepts are applicable, albeit in altered form, to the problems of employment discrimination.

Recognition: Traditionally, neither labor nor management has recognized a representative for racial or ethnic minority employees as an organized force in a legitimate collective bargaining relationship.[2] Both have established Plans for Progress or minority group specialists to deal

---

[1] For a general survey of the dimensions of the problem, see SOVERN, LEGAL RESTRAINTS ON RACIAL DISCRIMINATION IN EMPLOYMENT (1966); R. MARSHALL, THE NEGRO AND ORGANIZED LABOR (1965); REPORT OF THE NATIONAL ADVISORY COMMITTEE ON CIVIL DISORDERS, ch. 7 (1968); ch. 9 *infra*.

[2] I exclude the "segregated local" from this discussion on the grounds that the device usually connoted an inferior status for minorities. Occasionally, the segregated local could be an effective force in protecting minority rights.

with some aspects of discrimination and to blunt the drive for an independent voice for minorities in employment problems. Unions take the view that all employees must be represented by the union which is the majority representative.[3] Thus the minority group view on issues of discrimination can arise only within the general union structure. Through the Civil Rights Department of the AFL-CIO, and comparable persons and institutions in various international unions, the views of the civil rights movement are expressed and disseminated, if not always fully supported. The Civil Rights Department of the AFL-CIO attempts, not only to express the civil rights viewpoint, but to interrelate it with the overall objectives of unionism. Thus it is not, and cannot be expected to be, singlemindedly in support of the minority positions in general.

Despite this, there is a form of recognition for the civil rights organizations. The EEOC considers that a complainant may represent the class of minority employees, and that he, or his association, is an indispensable party to any conciliation agreement.[4] This position compels employers and unions to negotiate with the civil rights representative in cases brought before the EEOC.[5]

Negotiation of the basic terms of the relationship between the civil rights movement and labor and management has largely taken place in the legislative arena. The result is the Civil Rights Act of 1964, and an assortment of executive orders, state statutes, and local ordinances prohibiting employment discrimination. Occasionally, a more specific code of conduct will be negotiated which looks much like a collective bargaining agreement. Amendments to collective bargaining agreements will be an ultimate form of solution.[6]

The *dispute settlement mechanism* consists today of a wide range of tribunals from informal mediation to more formal conciliation, to arbitration, and administration action and, finally, judicial proceedings.

---

[3] This view is, of course, confirmed by the Fair Representation doctrine arising from Steele v. Louisville & N. Ry., 323 U.S. 192 (1944).

[4] See Cox v. United States Gypsum Co., 284 F. Supp. 74 (N.D. Ind., 1968) *aff'd* 60 Lab. Cas. ¶9230 (7th Cir. 1969).

[5] See Blumrosen, *The Individual Right to Eliminate Employment Discrimination by Litigation,* INDUSTRIAL RELATIONS RESEARCH ASS'N, PROC. 19TH ANNUAL WINTER MEETING, 99 (1966).

[6] See, *e.g.,* The Agreement Between the EEOC and Newport News Shipbuilding and Dry Dock Co., CCH, EMPLOYMENT PRACTICES, NEW DEVELOPMENTS (1966) ¶8055; Hotel Employers Ass'n, 66–3 ARB ¶8935 (1966).

I. Labor Arbitration Faces the Issue of Racial Discrimination

By now we have some experiences with the manner in which labor arbitrators have dealt with the issue of racial discrimination when it has been raised in the ordinary course of arbitration proceedings.[7] When one surveys the reported arbitration opinions involving allegations of racial discrimination, a clear impression emerges. Where the arbitrators deal with the cases which are the grist for the arbitration process—the promotion denied, the layoff or discharge protested, the working conditions challenged—their opinions are respectable and workmanlike. The facts appear to be carefully reviewed, and the background of employer actions on the racial question, which is often so important in discrimination cases, is carefully taken into account.[8]

In several denial of promotion cases, the arbitrators have considered the generally good record of performance of the employer on the race question in reaching the conclusion that the denial was not the result of discrimination.[9] Yet where the facts indicated that Negro trainees or applicants were subjected to different standards of job assignment or testing, the arbitrators have so found, and ordered appropriate relief without regard to the subjective intent of the employer.[10] They have applied the concept of an implied condition of fair dealing to these cases.[11] In the more volatile area where personal feelings and sensibilities may have been uppermost in the minds of the parties, the arbitrators seem to have been at their best. For example, one arbitrator set

---

[7] See Platt, *The Relationship Between Arbitration and Title VII of the Civil Rights Act of 1964,* 3 GA. L. REV. 398 (1969); Gould, *Non-Governmental Remedies for Employment Discrimination,* A.B.A. Institute on Equal Employment Opportunity, March 29, 1969; and CCH EMPLOYMENT PRACTICES, ¶2501, 2525–2527.

[8] All these cases appear to involve a conflict between union and employer, with one side asserting the public policy claim within the framework of the contractual language. Under these circumstances, arbitrators generally handle public policy claims in an able manner. See Blumrosen, *Public Policy Considerations in Labor Arbitration Cases,* 14 RUTGERS L. REV. 217, 221–37 (1969). For an illustration of a settlement within the arbitration context, see ch. 5, pt. I *infra.*

[9] American Sugar Refining Co., 62–1 ARB. ¶8111 (Rohman, Arbitrator); Mobile Oil Co. 64–2 ARB. ¶8520 (Williams, Arbitrator).

[10] Tri-City Corp., 67–2 ARB. ¶8603 (Pigors, Arbitrator); Armco Steel Corp., 64–2 ¶8622 (Sherman, Arbitrator).

[11] McCall Corp., 67–2 ARB. ¶8498 (McIntosh, Arbitrator). The arbitrator shaped a remedy which was more meaningful than that provided by a state anti-discrimination agency.

aside the discharge of a Negro who had solicited dates with white married women[12] and, in perhaps the most sensitive of the decisions, another arbitrator upheld the company action in allowing its black employees to take off the day of Martin Luther King's funeral, against a claim that this action discriminated against the white employees.[13]

These cases, involving discharge, job assignments, promotions, and the like, require the application of the conventional concepts of the collective contract, such as just cause for discharge, to a situation where race may have been the motivation for the violation of the contractual norm by the employer. In these cases, arbitration seems to work to enforce the principle of fair dealing implied into the contract. In all of these cases, the arbitrators are enforcing the contract, and not the statutes prohibiting employment discrimination. Furthermore, the clauses in the contract which are usually applied in these cases are the *substantive provisions* governing promotion, layoff, and discharge, *not* the antidiscrimination clauses. To this extent, arbitration seems to work.[14]

But when arbitrators are asked to go beyond this point in the implementation of the antidiscrimination policies of the nation, they tend to beg off. If a seniority clause is weak, and leaves much to managerial discretion, the fact that a Negro is the victim of that discretion will not help him before the arbitrator.[15]

Perhaps the most impressive illustration of this limitation on labor arbitration is in the opinion of Arbitrator Lehoczky in the arbitration phase of the famous *Local 12, Rubber Workers'* case.[16] That case involved, in microcosm, many of the problems of employment discrimination in the South. From 1943 to 1962, the Goodyear Rubber Company, in Gadsden, Alabama, operated with segregated groups of jobs, white

---

[12] Milgram Food Stores, Inc., 68–2 ARB. ¶8655. An article anticipating arbitration problems arising from the hiring of "Hard Core" unemployed is, Seligson, *Minority Group Employees, Discipline and Arbitration,* 19 LABOR L.J. 544 (1968).

[13] Sligo, Inc., 50 L.A. 1203 (1968) (Dunsford, Arbitrator).

[14] See Platt, *op. cit. supra* note 7; Meltzer, *Ideology, Law and Labor Arbitration,* 34 U. OF CHI. L. REV. 545, 557 (1967); Blumrosen, *Public Policy Considerations in Labor Arbitration Cases,* 14 RUTGERS L. REV. 217 (1960).

[15] United States Plywood Corp., 65–1 ARB. ¶8377 (Marshall, Arbitrator). Similarly, with respect to sex discrimination, see Eaton Mfg. Co., 66–3 ARB. ¶9089 (Kates, Arbitrator); United Airlines, 67–1 ARB. ¶8207 (Kahn, Arbitrator).

[16] The case was before the Board, 150 NLRB 312 (1964). The Board ordered arbitration of some matters. The arbitrator's opinion appears *sub nom.* Goodyear Tire & Rubber Co., 45 LA 240 (1965) (Lehoczky, Arbitrator). The Board decision was later upheld, 386 F.2d 12 (5th Cir. 1966), *cert. denied* 389 U.S. 837 (1967).

and Negro, although the contract called for plantwide seniority. In 1962, under urging of the President's Committee on Equal Employment Opportunity, company and union entered into a verbal agreement to end some of the discriminatory practices. Negro employees then sought arbitration of certain questions, including back pay for denial of job opportunities.

The Union refused to take this and other questions to arbitration. The Negro employees then sought the aid of the National Labor Relations Board (NLRB). The Board held, in 1964, that it could enforce the Union's duty of fair representation, and that the Union had breached this duty in refusing to take certain matters to arbitration, and in not reducing the verbal agreement in writing. The Board ordered the Union to submit the questions to arbitration. The Board noted that the arbitrator would not be bound by the interpretation of the contract made by the Company and Union if it was discriminatory.[17] The Board's remedial order covered all of these points. The Union both appealed the decision and complied with the part of it which required the submission of questions of back pay under the seniority system to the arbitrator.

Board had invited the arbitrator to disregard the intention of the parties if he found it illegal. The arbitrator declined this invitation. In denying back pay on the merits to the Negro employees, he stressed that the question of retroactivity of the verbal agreement, which opened promotional opportunities for the Negro employees, was peculiarly one of the intention of the parties. Since they did not intend to make this provision retroactive, he concluded that it was not. Thus the question of a back pay remedy for discrimination was decided on the basis of the "intention" of the parties charged with discrimination.

The net effect of the Board decision was to remand the employees to a forum which (a) did not share the Board's view of the responsibilities of the arbitrator and (b) which protected the victims only to the extent "intended" by the perpetrators of discrimination. One gets a distinct impression of the buck passing back and forth between the Board and the arbitrator to the detriment of the Negro employees in Gadsden. If the contract provision in question was illegal, and it was within the jurisdiction of the Board to say so, then it should have so stated in the

---

[17] "Obviously, an arbitrator would not have been bound by the racially invalid interpretation and might have awarded back pay." 150 NLRB at 317 (1964).

remand to the arbitrator.[18] Instead, the Board urged the arbitrator to apply the federal statutes as well as, or instead of, the collective contract.

The arbitrator, mindful of the lesson that his award is valid only if it "draws its essence" [19] from the contract, declined the proffered commission as a junior grade EEOC. After the arbitration decision, the court of appeals decided the appeal from the Board decision, and upheld the Board in ringing tones. This decision, hailed by many civil rights enthusiasts, pales somewhat when it is realized that the remedial order referring the matter of arbitration had already been carried out, and had been futile. There is no mention in the court opinion of this fact, and I assume that the decision was based on the record as it had been made by the Board, without supplementation based on the arbitrator's opinion.[20]

My criticism is not of the decision of the NLRB on the merits in *Local 12*, but rather of the attempt by the Board to pass the problem to the arbitrator, who was not in a position to handle it. The arbitrator risked biting both hands that fed him if he had ruled against both Company and Union. In addition, he had no basis in arbitral experience for rejecting the decision on the nature of the collective bargaining relationship which had been made by the Company and Union. Arbitrators are "neutral" only as between company and union. When a third interest arises, the arbitrator will side with the company and union to promote collective bargaining relationships.

The instinct, self-interest, and the training of the arbitrator, as well as the body of law surrounding his work—all call out for him to accept that position which will secure the assent of both of union and management. Union and management want him to operate within the frame-

---

[18] Determinations of illegality of such systems are only now, in 1969, beginning to flow from the courts under Title VII of the Civil Rights Act of 1964. See Quarles v. Philip Morris, 271 F. Supp. 842 (E.D. Va. 1968); Local 189, Paper Makers v. United States, 416 F.2d 980 (5th Cir. 1969); ch. 5 *infra*.

[19] United Steel Workers v. Enterprise Wheel & Car Corp., 363 U.S. 593, 597 (1960); See Platt, note 7 *supra* at 401.

[20] The tendency to appeal abstract issues in this field seems irresistible. In Dent v. St. Louis & S.F. R.R. 59 Lab. Cas. ¶9189 (5th Cir. 1969), the court finally put to rest the heavily litigated question of whether an EEOC conciliation effort was a jurisdictional prerequisite to a suit under Title VII of the Civil Rights Act of 1964. In all of these cases, a prompt effort by EEOC at conciliation after the dismissal in the district court, followed by the reinstitution of suit would have advanced the trial on the merits by as much as two years.

work of contractual principles which *they* have established, rather than range over their relationship with a roving commission to implement federal legislative policy.[21]

Arbitrators are able, it seems to me, to implement public policies in the interstices of their decisions. I think they did that in the run-of-the-mill cases described earlier. But their charter and their institutional authority is limited, and they cannot bear the burden of institutional reform which the Board attempted to impose in the *Rubber Workers'* case.

Several implications flow from the analysis thus far. First, the typical discharge, promotion, or assignment case which involves discrimination may be expeditiously and fairly handled by arbitrators if the unions genuinely press the case. Secondly, challenges to the basic institutions structured by the collective bargaining agreement are not likely to be successful before the arbitrator whose own charter flows from that agreement. Where such a challenge is made, the evidence suggests that recourse to the arbitrator would be futile, and is, therefore, not required before relief is sought elsewhere.[22] Arbitrators are simply in no position to reform the institution which brought them into being.

The question arises, however, as to whether this flows from the inadequacy of representation of the civil rights viewpoint before the arbitrator. The classic tragedy of the unrepresented position is in the San Francisco *Hotel Employers Association* case.[23] The case deserves separate consideration because of its implications concerning the use of arbitration in discrimination matters.

II. The Civil Rights Interest as a Participant in the Labor Arbitration Process

In the *Hotel Employers Association* case, the employers' association had an industry-area-wide contract with the culinary workers which included an arbitration clause. In 1964, the Hotel Employers Association negotiated a Plans-for-Progress-type agreement with the NAACP

---

21 See Meltzer, *op. cit. supra* note 14.
22 Glover v. St. Louis & S.F. R.R., 393 U.S. 324 (1969).
23 Hotel Employers Ass'n, 66–3 ARB. ¶8395 (Burns, Arbitrator).

and CORE in San Francisco, to increase the proportion of racial and ethnic minority employees. This agreement expired in 1966, after which there were several months of picketing and demonstrations. This terminated when the Hotel Association negotiated another agreement with NAACP and CORE which also provided for dissemination of equal employment opportunity information, and set targets or goals of specific percentages of racial and ethnic minority employees expected to be developed by managerial activities "within the framework of the Collective Bargaining agreements. . . ." This agreement also included an arbitration clause, and designated the Human Rights Commission as the arbitration-appointing agency if the parties could not agree.

The Union then brought arbitration proceedings under the collective bargaining agreement to have the civil rights agreement set aside.

The arbitration panel, consisting of two employers, two employees, and one neutral member, wrote an opinion which set aside the civil rights agreement on numerous grounds. It was negotiated by a "labor organization," the civil rights groups, in derogation of the exclusive recognition rights of the Union; it provided for discrimination in reverse, it ignored vested seniority rights, it was inconsistent with the collective agreement, and it was induced by coercion, menace, and duress.

All of these issues were decided on the basis of evidence and argument marshaled by attorneys for the Union and the employers. The opinion reflects this representation. The agreement could easily have been construed as consistent with the collective contract. Inquiry could have been made as to whether the use of the Union referral arrangement was itself discriminatory. The efforts to increase minority employment might have been explored as appropriated remedial action in the face of a history of racial and ethnic exclusion.

These issues, which are apparent on the face of the opinion, might have been raised if *any* proponent of the 1966 agreement had been in the hearing room. But only the Union and the employers were represented. The case does have an aura which one associates with some of the less complimentary things Judge Hayes has had to say about the labor arbitration process.[24] (I assume that the four partisan arbitrators would have divided evenly and cancelled each other out. If not, the "tribunal" was not an arbitration panel, but a union-employer combina-

---

[24] HAYES, LABOR ARBITRATION: A DISSENTING VIEW (1966).

tion to void the civil rights agreement through a rigged award.) This use of arbitration to pull the Hotel Association's chestnuts from the civil rights fire raises some serious problems.

The inadequate representation of the third party's interest in this case would certainly have led the California Supreme Court to strike down the arbitrator's award on the grounds that it affected the interests of a third party, i.e., the civil rights groups, through a proceeding in which it was not a party and for which it did not have notice.[25] Such a proceeding denies due process in the view of California. While the United States Supreme Court's view of this question is at least clouded,[26] the Court has not yet had to face the question of whether such an arbitration is entitled to the deference normally shown by the Court. There are cases, however, in which the Supreme Court has indicated that its deference will be reserved for those institutions which give notice and opportunity for hearing, and make a good-faith effort to accommodate and adjust to a difficult situation,[27] and that this deference concept will not apply if the tribunal involved is hostile.[28]

Thus these cases raise the old question of the rights of third parties in connection with labor arbitration. Substantively, these questions have been explored many times. Procedurally, they have been examined carefully by Professor Jones, who suggests a form of arbitral interpleader, to provide the third parties with opportunities to participate in the arbitration process.[29] Certain considerations appear to flow from the raising of these questions in the racial relations context.

---

[25] Local 770, Retail Clerks v. Thrift Mart, Inc., 30 Cal. R. 12, 380 F.2d 652 (1963).

[26] Carey v. Westinghouse Electric Corp. 375 U.S. 261 (1964) *But see* Transportation-Communication Employees Union v. Union Pacific R.R., 385 U.S. 157 (1966).

[27] Humphrey v. Moore, 375 U.S. 335 (1964); Vaca v. Sipes, 386 U.S. 171 (1967); Steele v. Louisville & N. Ry. 323 U.S. 192 (1944). For a similar view under the United States Arbitration Act, see Commonwealth Coatings Corp. v. Continental Casualty Co., 393 U.S. 145 (1968).

[28] Glover v. St. Louis & S.F. R.R. *supra* note 22.

[29] Jones, *Autobiography of a Decision: The Function of Innovation in Labor Relations and The National Steel Orders of Joinder and Interpleader,* 10 U.C.L.A.L. Rev. 987 (1963); Jones, *An Arbitral Answer To a Judicial Dilemma: The Carey Decision and Trilateral Arbitration of Jurisdictional Disputes,* 11 U.C.L.A.L. Rev. 327 (1964); Jones, *A Sequel in The Evolution of Trilateral Arbitration of Jurisdictional Labor Disputes—The Supreme Court's Gift to Embattled Employers,* 15 U.C.L.A.L. Rev. 877 (1968).

First, the usual arbitration clause does not extend to the issues tendered in the *Employers Association Hotel* case. Whether the company was coerced into signing a contract other than the collective agreement is normally not for the arbitrator under the collective agreement, because it does not involve the interpretation or application of the collective contract. Similarly, the interpretation of the civil rights agreement in absence of a clear conflict with the collective contract seems a gratuitous undertaking by the arbitrator. Third, the arbitrator assumed the functions of the NLRB in deciding that the civil rights groups were labor organizations, and all but held the company in violation of section 8(a)(5) of the NLRA for negotiating with an entity other than the majority representative. The arbitrator then assumed the functions of the EEOC and the federal courts in ruling the various proposals to increase minority employment unlawful. The broad sweep of the arbitrator here is in sharp contrast to that of the arbitrator in *Rubber Workers*. The only thing these decisions have in common is their subordination of the civil rights interests to the position of labor and management.

In the social dynamics of race relations, the right to set aside the award under California law is small solace indeed. If the civil rights groups had prior notice of the hearing, they could have enjoined it, or sued to intervene. But an injunction against the hearing might have been denied on the grounds that no irreparable injury could be shown by the civil rights groups; and if they had been allowed to intervene, they might have been bound by the actions of a tribunal which was the servant of the very parties—employer association and union—which had created the alleged discriminatory situation. Thus neither alternative seems desirable.

However, it might have been desirable for the arbitrator to invite the civil rights groups into his hearing. This invitation could have been based on the concept of due process, or on an agreement from union and management. Once the invitation was extended, the civil rights groups could respond. This response could range from a suit to enjoin to an agreement to participate, perhaps before an altered tribunal, or to an agreement to be bound by the result. The important thing is that notification to the civil rights groups would have allowed them to participate in the decision, and have forced labor and management to consider their views. These certainly would include a challenge to the fairness of the arbitration panel which consisted of four representatives of the union and company and one "neutral."

It is clear that "neutrals," as defined in the labor-management context, are not neutral at all from the perspective of the civil rights interests. Rather they are the agents of those who are alleged to have discriminated. This is a most difficult point for labor arbitrators to accept, because they are used to thinking of themselves as neutral. Yet they are legally and, in substance, the handmaiden of the collective agreement. If this agreement or its operation is under attack, they must defend it. They are in fact and in law the agents of union and employer. If it is alleged that union and employer are discriminatory, their joint agent, the arbitrator, *cannot* be a neutral in such a proceeding. Thus the "futility exception" to the exhaustion requirement appears automatically applicable to them, and any concept of "deference" to the arbitral forum must be put aside.[30]

If the civil rights groups had been given notice and opportunity to participate, an entirely new dimension to the situation might have emerged. For all three parties—labor, management, and civil rights groups—might have agreed on the nature of a forum and on ground rules; or they might have agreed on how to integrate the collective agreement and the civil rights agreement. Inventive energies might have been unleashed.[31] This opportunity was foreclosed by the course which was followed.

The reluctance of the arbitrators in the *Hotel Employers Association* and the *Rubber Workers'* cases to apply the antidiscrimination policies, and to emphasize instead the policies of labor management cooperation, stems in part from the absence of decisional law concerning employment discrimination on which the arbitrators could rely. It is one thing to expect arbitrators to apply well-established legal standards, such as those relating to theft, but another to expect them to break new ground at the expense of their principals. Without some clear legal decisions, the arbitrators almost inevitably fall back on the concepts of contract and intention.

Given a body of clear background law, and some experience in mul-

---

30 Glover v. St. Louis & S.F. R.R., *supra* note 22.
31 This, I take it, is the heart of Prof. Jones's thesis. See the articles cited in note 29 *supra*, particularly his Sequel, 15 U.C.L.A.L. Rev. 877 (1968).

tilateral conciliation and arbitration, it is possible that situations such as the *Hotel Employers Association* case could develop workable solutions to some vexing problems of employment discrimination. But neither of these conditions existed in 1965 or 1966. They are only now coming into being. The courts are on the edge of major substantive decisions on discrimination. Such experience is beginning to accumulate in connection with efforts of the United States Equal Employment Opportunity Commission to enforce the antidiscriminatory provisions of the Civil Rights Act of 1964.

III. The Conciliation and Arbitration Functions of the EEOC Under Title VII

The Equal Employment Opportunity Commission administers Title VII of the Civil Rights Act of 1964.[32] The statute proscribes discrimination in employment opportunities because of race, color, religion, sex, or national origin. The Commission's powers are limited. It may investigate on complaint or on the motion of a commissioner. If it finds "reasonable cause to believe" that discrimination exists, it may seek voluntary compliance with its view of the statute's requirements through conciliation. If this fails, the complainant may sue on behalf of himself and others in the federal court, and the Attorney General may sue to remedy patterns of discrimination.

The EEOC early determined that it would conciliate only *after* it had found reasonable cause to believe that discrimination existed, and that a successful conciliation required the concurrence of the charging party, the respondent, and the Commission.[33] Both of these decisions were contrary to past administrative practice in the FEPC field. Prior to EEOC, most state agencies attempted to conciliate without finding discrimination,[34] and would take settlements regardless of the wishes of the complaining parties.[35] By adopting the position that the agreement of

---

[32] 78 Stat 253; 42 U.S.C. 2000 (e) (hereafter cited by official section number only).

[33] See ch. 2 *supra.*

[34] See Blumrosen, *Antidiscrimination Laws in Action in New Jersey: A Law-Sociology Study,* 19 RUTGERS L. REV. 187 (1965).

[35] See Sovern, *supra* note 1, at 48–53. This is illustrated in McCall Corp., 67–2 ARB. ¶8498 (McIntosh, Arbitrator), where the arbitrator went beyond such a "settlement."

the complainant was necessary for a settlement, the EEOC vindicated the individual rights under Title VII, and created the conditions for trilateral negotiation of cases of employment discrimination.

The effect of these EEOC decisions was to create an informal tripartite negotiation procedure in the conciliation process; and to lay the foundation for an arbitration process to resolve disputes arising under conciliation agreements.

A. *The Tripartite Negotiation Procedure*

By adopting the view that conciliation should come *after* a reasonable cause finding, the EEOC put its weight behind the position of the charging party and similarly situated persons in the settlement process. It followed up this approach by requiring its conciliators to consult with the charging party concerning the terms of the settlement to be proposed *prior to* discussions with the respondents. In this way, the views of the charging party would be influential in shaping the position of the conciliator in settlement discussions. After the conciliator talks to the charging party, he talks to the respondents. Both union and management will usually be involved in cases where there is a collective agreement. (The rest of this discussion will assume that the union and management are parties to the conciliation efforts.) The conciliator will frequently solicit and then produce a written proposal as the basis for settlement discussions. These discussions take on a three-part character, with union, employer, and charging party participating, usually in separate meetings with the conciliator. Since the charging party is often represented by a civil rights group, the effect of this procedure is to create a three-way bargaining situation between union, employer, and minority group of employees. While this situation runs counter to the usual view of labor unions concerning the exclusiveness of their right to represent the employees, they rarely refuse to participate in such negotiations. While a union would not permit a minority of its members to negotiate with management, they recognize that Title VII gives minorities a new status. Since many complaints are supported by groups such as the NAACP, this procedure in effect places the civil rights groups, the unions, and the company at the same bargaining table. A Commission determination of reasonable cause is thus transmuted into something like a duty to bargain with the civil rights groups on the part of labor and management. This bargaining process is complex and time-consuming, but it does work, as the many EEOC conciliation agreements attest.[36]

There remains a core of problems which must be resolved by the courts before meaningful bargaining can take place, particularly in the area of seniority; but the process for dispute settlement has been developed at the Commission. In this process, the conciliator functions as both an advocate for the charging party, after the EEOC has found cause in his case, and as a neutral interested in settlement. The reasonable cause decision which *precedes* conciliation places the weight of the government on the side of the complainant, and provides some protection against soft settlements. This process is strengthened by the theory of EEOC conciliation, which seeks to use the individual complainant as a basis for changing an entire system of industrial relations to eliminate its discriminatory character. Through this process, which is the informal administrative equivalent of a class action, the EEOC converts the individual complaint into a vehicle for a reform of industrial relations systems. Involved in the EEOC conciliation process, then, is constant checking with a multitude of parties, and, at the core, the development of a set of concrete remedial proposals, which will change the industrial relations system under review as well as providing relief for charging parties. A comprehensive EEOC conciliation agreement looks and reads much like a part of a collective bargaining agreement, with extensive provisions necessary to work the change in industrial relations practices.

If this tripartite negotiation fails, the alternative is litigation. But failure is not universal, and the outcome of a successful EEOC conciliation is an agreement between labor, management, and the civil rights organization which backed the complainants, approved by the EEOC.

---

[36] The process is described in Blumrosen, *op. cit. supra* note 5 and ch. 2, pt. V *supra.*

B. *Enforcing the Conciliation Agreement*

The conciliation agreement then becomes the code establishing the basic relation between the civil rights interests, labor, and management. The theory of the Commission is that these agreements constitute legally enforceable obligations on the employer. The charging party has waived his right to sue in consideration of the promises and undertakings contained in the agreement. This theory, which is contrary to the traditional administrative agency view of settlement agreements, has not yet been tested. The usual administrative view is that settlement agreements which are not complied with may be set aside, so that the agency may proceed on the underlying violation. But since the EEOC has no hearing powers, it has moved to the more sensible theory of implementing the settlement agreement.

Since the settlement agreement is viewed as creating binding legal obligations, the question of its enforcement then arises. The standard form of an EEOC conciliation agreement, subject to negotiation in specific cases, is as follows:

The heading indicates that it is between the EEOC, the complainant, and the respondent. It then recites that charges had been filed, reasonable cause found, and that the parties have settled the matter on the conditions which follow.

The first page of the agreement contains the preprinted "boiler plate" language in seven paragraphs:

1. The right of the Commission to review compliance with the agreement.
2. The agreement is not an admission of a violation of Title VII.
3. "The Charging Party hereby waives, releases, and covenants not to sue any Respondent with respect to any matters which were or might have been alleged as charges filed with the Equal Employment Opportunity Commission, subject to performance by the Respondent of the promises and representations contained herein. *The Commission shall determine whether the Respondent has complied with the terms of the agreement.*" (Emphasis added)
4. (5), and (6) are recitals of the statutory obligation not to discriminate in connection with employment, nor to retaliate against

any person because he opposed discrimination, filed charges with EEOC, or assisted the government in enforcing Title VII.

7. States an obligation to report on compliance.

On the following page, beginning with paragraph 8, are the specific provisions of the agreement, which provide relief for the charging party, and correct the systems found to be discriminatory. The agreement is signed by the charging party, the respondent, and then approved on behalf of the Commission.

It is, of course, the underlined sentence of paragraph 3 which is of concern here. This sentence was inserted into the form agreement in the early days of the administration of Title VII in a sex discrimination case. It was suggested by an attorney for a large Southern employer who was familiar with labor relations. He said that he did not want to run into the federal courts to deal with inevitable disputes which would arise under the conciliation agreement which we had just negotiated.

Needless to say, I was pleased with his concept, and incorporated it into the "boiler plate" page of the conciliation agreement. By now, it has been adopted in hundreds of conciliation agreements. However, it has come under the sharp focus of litigation in only one case, and that case is inconclusive at present.

If I may speculate, I believe that EEOC conciliation agreements will be held legally enforceable by either the complainant, the EEOC, or a third-party beneficiary. Suit by the complainant can be upheld on simple contract principles, by third-party beneficiaries on similar grounds, and by the Commission on the grounds that Commission supervision of conciliation agreements is a part of the conciliation process itself.[37] The Commission, in attempting to correct discriminatory practices, necessarily involves itself in the relation between unions and employers, or into management practices, which are part of the continuous relationship between the workers and an employer. Of necessity, the concept of conciliation must be adapted to this fundamental concept of a continuous relationship. The Commission having thus defined its conciliation function, the courts will, in all likelihood, sustain that definition. If further statutory authority be needed, the Commission is authorized to render "technical assistance" under the act,[38] and the inter-

---

[37] See §706(a).
[38] See §705(g)(3).

pretation of conciliation agreements could constitute such assistance. Finally, enforcement of conciliation agreements can be likened to enforcement powers with respect to court orders.[39]

The narrow question here, however, is whether the conciliation agreement's standard form language confers on EEOC the power to interpret the conciliation agreement which will be then upheld by the courts—and, if so, what is the extent of these powers? Here, I believe that the United States Arbitration Act is relevant on the interpretation of the agreement's language, and will lead to the conclusion that the EEOC has primary initial decisional authority with respect to questions of breach of conciliation agreements.[40] In addition, the doctrine of exhaustion of administrative remedies would normally lead a court to stay its hand in a Title VII action, pending the EEOC interpretation of the conciliation agreement.

In this view, the Commission becomes an arbitrator under a code of conduct which includes the conciliation agreement, Title VII itself, and, of course, the background federal legislation dealing with labor-management relations.

The next question is, how will the EEOC implement this arbitration provision? As of the time I left the Commission, there had been little development on this question. A few cases of alleged violation of the agreement had been disposed of informally and there was talk of a formal proceeding, but none had been held. The usual EEOC proceeding is an informal administrative investigation, without a trial-type hearing. The EEOC has had no experience with trial-type hearings of the administrative or arbitral nature. But the decision in the *Burrell* case may precipitate such a hearing if the court finds that the parties all agreed to it.[41] In such a hearing, the EEOC will be expected to listen to labor, management, and the complainant-civil rights interests and then decide the case. The EEOC will thus provide a forum for all parties,

---

[39] See §706(i).

[40] 9 U.S.C. 1–15.

[41] In Burrell v. Kaiser Aluminum, 58 Lab. Cas. ¶915 6(E.D. L.A. 1968) The court dismissed a Title VII complaint on the concurrent grounds that an EEOC conciliation had not been attempted and that the EEOC had not determined that a prior conciliation agreement had been violated. The court of appeals reversed and remanded because EEOC conciliation was not required, but did not deal with the issue of whether EEOC was obligated to determine if its conciliation agreement had been violated. 59 Lab. Cas. ¶9215 (5th Cir. 1969).

with notice and opportunity to participate. From this experience, we should learn much about multilateral arbitration.

Yet, at this point, administrative courage is in short supply, and I wonder whether the EEOC will be more courageous than was the NLRB in the *Rubber Workers'* case. The history of the failure of administrative agencies attempting to enforce antidiscrimination laws concerning employment is not encouraging. In the end, I believe that the courage of the administrators and of the arbitrators must come from the courts.

IV. When the Courts Speak, Administrators and Arbitrators Can Act

This chapter has been in one sense a study in nondecisionmaking. Administrative abdication and narrow arbitration interpretation seem the order of the day. At the root of this phenomenon lies the fact that there is only one institution in our society capable of the difficult tasks of articulating the meaning of modern antidiscriminatory statutes in the complex setting of labor relations. The courts must speak before the less formal processes can operate effectively. Once the courts speak forcefully and clearly on the substantive law, then the administrators and the arbitrators will have guidance, private counsel will be able to measure the results he seeks against what is possible, and the industrial relations community can work out detailed changes which the law requires. At that point, the administrative and arbitral processes will gain in importance, as part of the "law transmission system" which takes the basic ideas of the courts and Congress and converts them into social and economic reality. The techniques of negotiation, settlement, and informal decision will then be more valuable and effective than they have been in the past.

Part II

THE SUBSTANCE

OF EQUAL EMPLOYMENT

OPPORTUNITY

5   Seniority and Equal Employment Opportunity

The shaping of meaningful remedies for racial discrimination in seniority systems is difficult. Effective remedies may require that blacks or other minorities be afforded increased job opportunities at the expense of the white majority. But white employees seek to retain their expectations concerning those same job opportunities, and maintain that they have "vested rights" in the seniority system. Thus white and black employees contest for scarce job opportunities. This is the conventional analysis of the remedial problem. It pits white worker against black at the plant level. In addition, it pits the civil rights movement against the labor movement at the institutional level, and weakens the liberal-labor coalition which has been so influential at the political level.

This conventional analysis is inadequate in two respects: First, in focusing on the conflict among the employees, it ignores the legal responsibility of the employer. In the conventional analysis, the employer is the forgotten man, a spectator at the black-white struggle among his employees. This, of course, is an incorrect view of the legal consequences of a discriminatory seniority system. In virtually every such system, the employer is a wrongdoer who has discriminated by hiring minorities into subordinate positions and then confining them to a specific group of jobs through the operation of the seniority system.

Second, the conventional analysis, with its focus of specific relief, ignores the damage remedy. This remedy is capable of reallocating burdens and benefits where specific relief is unavailable. New attention to the damage remedy in seniority cases is now required because Title VII of the Civil Rights Act of 1964 creates a federal cause of action for employment discrimination. Under the Title, the federal courts may award all appropriate relief, including both specific performance and damages.

These ideas of employer responsibility and the damage remedy converge with the traditional ideas of reform of seniority systems to suggest a comprehensive remedy for discriminatory seniority arrangements. This remedy would include both reform of the system to increase minority employment opportunities and a species of damage remedy to cover those losses which may not appropriately be dealt with by specific performance.

The availability of the damage remedy against the employer should moderate the conflict between black and white worker and, in that sense, reduce the tensions between the civil rights and labor movement at the plant, institutional, and political levels. Once the availability of the damage remedy is recognized, it can be shaped and administered as part of an overall version of a discriminatory seniority system. This may involve the establishment, either through negotiation or by court order, of an "equal opportunity fund" as part of a remedy for discrimination in seniority systems. Such a fund, financed by the employer, would be analogous to the "automation fund" which has been developed through collective bargaining to meet problems of technological change.

I. The Background

Half a century ago, the employer ruled the workplace. His dominion was assured by common law rules providing that employment was "at will" [1] and that unions could not interfere with this relationship.[2] A state or federal legislature was powerless under the Fifth and Fourteenth Amendments to alter the common law.[3] Today, the constitutional rule has changed and the two common law principles have been

---

[1] Martin v. New York Ins. Co., 148 N.Y. 117 (1895), relying on Wood, Master and Servant, §134 (1877), which in turn relies on a series of cases which do not support his conclusion that, "[W]ith us (as distinct from the English) the rule is inflexible, that a general or indefinite hiring is *prima facie* a hiring at will, and if the servant seeks to make it out a yearly hiring, the burden is upon him to establish it by proof. . . ."

[2] Hitchman Coal & Coke Co. v. Mitchell, 245 U.S. 229 (1917).

[3] Adair v. United States, 208 U.S. 161 (1908); Coppage v. Kansas, 236 U.S. 1 (1915).

eroded by court decisions,[4] by statutes,[5] and by academic challenge.[6] But, in operation, they have been most seriously undercut by the emergence of collective bargaining. The collective bargaining process has, in turn, produced other principles which provide a meaningful measure of job security and promotional opportunity for the worker: seniority and the requirement of "just cause" for discharge and discipline.[7]

These two principles are usually implemented through grievance and arbitration procedures. They represent one of the major achievements of organized labor during the last half century. They *can* operate to civilize the work place for black as well as white.[8] For racial discrimination can exist where there is managerial freedom of action as well as where employment policies are set and administered through collective bargaining between labor and management. In fact, as this analysis will show, collectively bargained seniority systems generally discriminate by confirming and perpetuating racially discriminatory management decisions in the hiring process.

Not only may seniority and just cause protect minorities against discrimination, but the administration of these principles through the grievance and arbitration procedures may provide relief which is more timely and effective than the efforts of a distant bureaucracy or the

---

[4] Lincoln Fed. Labor Union v. Northwestern Iron & Metal Co., 335 U.S. 525 (1949).

[5] See the National Labor Relations Act, *as amended*, 49 Stat. 449, 29 U.S.C. 151; Universal Military Training and Service Act, 62 Stat. 604, 50 U.S.C. Appx. 451; Title VII, Civil Rights Act of 1964, 78 Stat. 253, 29 U.S.C. 2000(e); Title III, §304(a) Consumer Credit Protection Act, 82 Stat. 163.

[6] Blades, *Employment at Will vs. Individual Freedom: On Limiting the Abusive Exercise of Employer Power*, 67 COLUM. L. REV. 1404 (1967); Blumrosen, *Common Law Limitations on Employer Anti-union Conduct: Protection of Employee Interest in Union Activity by Tort Law*, 54 Nw. U.L. REV. 1 (1959); Blumrosen, *The Right to Seek Workmen's Compensation*, 15 RUTGERS L. REV. 491 (1961); *Discussion* in INDUSTRIAL RELATIONS RESEARCH ASS'N, PROCEEDINGS OF THE 19TH ANN. WINTER MEETING 99 at 104 (1966).

[7] The literature on seniority and just cause is voluminous. See, for example, SLICHTER, LIVERNASH, & HEALY, THE IMPACT OF COLLECTIIVE BARGAINING ON MANAGEMENT, ch. 5 (1959).

[8] In the conciliation agreement with the Newport News Shipbuilding & Dry Dock Co., the EEOC built in a system of filling vacancies based on length of service and ability, coupled with posting of notices of vacancies. This system was adopted by the company in the agreement, and later confirmed by the shipyard union. It was instituted to meet claims that Negro employees had been improperly denied promotions. Prior to the agreement there was no principle of seniority with respect to promotions. See ch. 8 *infra*.

lengthy processes of the judiciary. The foreman who finds the Negro- or Spanish-surname American to be insubordinate, or to lack "ability" may be reversed, not because he acted on the basis of race or national origin, but because he has transgressed the seniority or just cause principle. The company involved may face immediately the wrath of a shop steward, grievance committee, and international representatives who are concerned that, if the employer can unfairly punish a minority worker, he may later use the same principle on the majority.

This possibility was illustrated in the aftermath of my first conciliation effort for the Equal Employment Opportunity Commission under Title VII of the Civil Rights Act of 1964.[9] This case involved seniority problems in a small plant in Alabama. It was successfully concluded, and I was subsequently appointed Chief of Conciliations partly on the strength of that case. Six months later the company discharged the complaining party for urinating on the plant premises. This dismissal appeared to be intended to intimidate the charging party and other potential Negro complainants, to discredit efforts of the NAACP in Alabama, and to demonstrate the weakness of the federal government. We believed that the grounds for discharge had been selected because they would seem too embarrassing for the government to challenge. I persuaded all parties to submit the issue to arbitration under the Collective Bargaining Agreement. The charging party was reluctant to arbitrate because he believed that both union and company officials planned to get rid of him. I told him that the government would not be bound by the results of the arbitration and that he had little to lose. The company sent counsel from the home office in New England to conduct the arbitration in its behalf. I sat in the corner as an observer.

After the opening exchanges, the company put on its first witness, the foreman who had discharged the Negro employee. His direct testimony suggested that, at the least, the penalty of discharge had been too severe. There was no further testimony. In corridor discussions, I advised company counsel that the Commission would not be bound by an

---

[9] 78 Stat. 253, 29 U.S.C. 2000(e) [hereafter cited by official section number only]. The statute provides that the EEOC will investigate charges of discrimination, determine whether there is reasonable cause to believe the charges to be true, then attempt to conciliate. It the Commission is unable to settle the matter, the aggrieved party may litigate in federal court. See ch. 1 *supra;* SOVERN, LEGAL RESTRAINTS ON RACIAL DISCRIMINATION IN EMPLOYMENT (1966).

award against the complainant. This suggested that the company had little to gain by "winning" its arbitration. I also spoke with the grievance committee of the union. Listening to the foreman testify, the committee had become conscious that his power of discipline could be turned against them. And so they lent their honest weight to a settlement, as distinct from going through the motions. Charging party was back at work the following Monday.

If the issue arose today, it is possible that the Civil Rights Division of the Department of Justice could move quickly to enjoin the retaliatory discharge.[10] But it also is possible that the injunction would be denied pending hearing on the merits, that delay would result, and that the reason given for the discharge would make the case politically unacceptable as a basis for governmental action.[11] At any rate, in those early days of Title VII, it seemed desirable to galvanize the grievance and arbitration procedures and the union in support of the effectuation of Title VII of the Civil Rights Act of 1964.

This picture of union cooperation in resisting discrimination in specific cases is a part of the history of our era. It is not a large part, but it is important, both for its own sake, and because the government has limited ability to deal effectively with problems of discrimination without support from outside institutions. Government in a vacuum is not effective in this field. The labor movement does have a massive, if lethargic, institutional structure which can, and sometimes does, assist in the elimination of discrimination. The common interest of labor and the civil rights movement lies in restricting that managerial freedom of action which can injure workers unfairly, regardless of their color. Thus there is a deep and abiding basis for organized labor to support equal opportunity.

But the system has not always worked that way. Organized labor sometimes was the moving force (as in the construction industry) or the cooperating force (as in most Southern plants) in maintaining dis-

---

[10] The actions of the defendants arguably violated §704(a) of Title VII, and also constituted a "practice" denying the full enjoyment of Title VII rights entitling the Attorney General to sue under §707.

[11] Pettway v. American Cast Iron Pipe Company, 411 F.2d 998 (5th Cir. 1969) is the only reprisal case to reach the courts of appeal. The complainant was discharged on September 15, 1967. The court of appeals ordered his reinstatement on May 22, 1969.

crimination in employment.[12] This "Southern pattern" involved an agreement between union and employer that certain jobs or groups of jobs were reserved for whites only. Seniority rules were applied to make sure that minorities did not acquire opportunities with respect to the "white jobs," but were remitted to the "Negro jobs" reserved for them, which were less desirable, lower-paying. In such situations, seniority and "just cause" meant one thing for whites, another for Negroes. The institutional protection of trade unionism did not cover the Negro. It was this practice which created the sharp conflict between the civil rights movement and the union movement on the issue of seniority. In this context, the civil rights movement viewed seniority rights, not as a protection against arbitrary managerial action, but as an instrument of oppression, perpetuating the subordinate status of the Negro. Seniority assured that the white man who climbed to his present preferred position over the backs of blacks would forever stay on top. This aspect of seniority has been subject to challenge by the civil rights interests for a quarter century and has been condemned as illegal under our labor laws since 1944. In that year the Supreme Court held that racial and other invidious discrimination was illegal under the Railway Labor Act. Had the doctrine of *Steele v. Louisville & N.Ry. Co.*[13] been enforced and followed, the problem of seniority and discrimination would have been resolved long ago. But, in fact, the *Steele* doctrine was largely ignored by labor unions and by management.

From the perspective of the civil rights interests, management is a full participant in discriminatory seniority systems. Not only did management negotiate and administer such systems, but management, usually alone, engaged in the discriminatory hiring practices which lay the foundation for discrimination in seniority. These hiring practices placed Negro employees in the position of subordination. The seniority system kept them there. Thus the restriction on minority opportunities resulted from the conjunction of seniority systems supported by unions and racist hiring practices of employers. This explains why the civil rights movement does not discredit the seniority system as such, but opts for

---

[12] See, generally, MARSHALL, THE NEGRO AND ORGANIZED LABOR (1965); SOVERN, LEGAL RESTRAINTS ON RACIAL DISCRIMINATION IN EMPLOYMENT (1966); NORGREN & HILL, TOWARD FAIR EMPLOYMENT (1966).

[13] 323 U.S. 192 (1944).

the one which, in the circumstances, will provide the maximum rapid advancement and protection for Negroes. This means, at least in the South, a full elaboration of the principle of promotion from within to benefit those Negroes who have been victimized by the system.[14]

At higher levels, management states that it is willing to do what is needed to correct evils which "just growed." But at the operating levels, other managers are reluctant to disturb a situation which enables them to meet their production quotas.[15] Local managers often believe that because of the attitude of their white employees (attitudes protective of seniority, not necessarily anti-Negro) and the assumed limited abilities of Negro employees, nothing can be changed without adversely affecting production. Such managers may prefer to litigate and delay the change rather than meet the challenge directly.

I recall a conciliation effort in New York with the general counsel of a major manufacturing company. I discussed the changes in seniority needed in the plant and offered to organize a meeting with the NAACP Legal Defense Fund which had, through local counsel, instituted litigation. The company general counsel reviewed my proposals, and stated that, in principle, they were acceptable. With his agreement, I set up the meeting with the Legal Defense Fund. When I came back to the plush oak-paneled conference room, a new actor had appeared on our stage: the plant manager of the facility in question. General counsel indicated that he wanted me to review the proposals with the manager.

---

[14] See, *e.g.*, Jenkins, *Study of Federal Effort to End Job Bias; History, A Status Report, and a Prognosis*, 14 HOWARD L.J. 259 (1968); Gould, *Employment Security, Seniority and Race*, 13 How. L.J. 1 (1967).

This view has been adopted in numerous EEOC conciliation agreements. For example, one agreement provides: "Respondent company agrees to adopt a policy of promotion from within, whereby all openings will be filled from existing employees based on seniority and ability to do the job, before the Respondent will seek to hire from the outside."

[15] Mr. Leo Beebe, vice-president of Ford Motor Co. and director of the National Alliance of Businessmen, a group organized to develop minority employment opportunities, stated: "I used to sit in my office at Ford and receive memo after memo from Mr. Ford telling me I'd better hire some Negroes. . . . I kept throwing the memos away. Mr. Ford was dedicated to that approach, but I wasn't. I looked at it this way; I said I refuse to hire any man for a job on any other criteria than his competence to do the job. And I was right.

"But . . . I was stupid for the times. Hiring the most qualified man is a good philosophy—the right philosophy—so long as you give everybody the opportunity to become qualified. That simply has not been possible for many Negroes. . . ." [NEWSWEEK, July 1, 1968, at 22, col. 3.]

I did so. The manager rejected them out of hand. I turned to general counsel. He shrugged and said, "This is my client," referring to the plant manager. The deal fell through, then and there.

The point of the story is the deference that the general counsel paid to operating personnel. The plant manager was not the client of the general counsel. General counsel's function was to represent total corporate interests. The manager became the client only in a sense that general counsel made (or at least expressed) the judgment that the manager's view was to control. The corporate decision to sustain the manager's judgment was made, I believe, because he turned out the product. This was the dominant consideration. (The result of the failure of conciliation was litigation terminating in a court order revising the seniority system more drastically than my original proposals.)

Thus the problems of seniority involve us most deeply in the tripartite relationship of company, union, and civil rights interests. All tend to conflict at various points in the seniority complex. Conciliation and litigation in this field is difficult and time-consuming. However, there is no shortage of cases with which to examine the various aspects of the seniority problem. In contrast to discrimination in recruitment and hiring, where the complaint process does not generate many meaningful cases, discrimination in seniority has produced many complaints under the Civil Rights Act of 1964,[16] and under executive orders dealing with the antidiscrimination obligation of government contractors. Many of these cases are now arising in the South, where there have been no state agencies whose involvement may delay litigation under the Civil Rights Act of 1964, as in the North.

II. Establishing Discrimination

In the traditional southern industrial relations system, Negroes were hired into certain jobs or groups of jobs. They were confined to these jobs, and whites hired into the better jobs. Sometimes Negroes worked in connected groups of jobs, all of which were subordinated to the jobs

---

[16] Of the 3,732 respondents charged with race discrimination in complaints before the EEOC in fiscal 1967, 1,933 respondents were charged with discrimination concerning terms, conditions, and classification of employees, all of which relate to promotional opportunities, EEOC, 2d ANN. REP. 52 (1967).

available to white employees. The grouping of jobs available for Negroes took several forms: (a) identification of individual jobs as "Negro jobs," (b) the establishment of related groups of jobs (lines of progression) as "Negro lines of progression," (c) the establishment of certain Negro departments, or (d) sometimes the establishment of separate bargaining units for Negro employees.

The Negro employees were denied access to the jobs reserved for white employees. Thus, *later-hired* whites would be assigned initially into better jobs, and would be promoted up through such jobs, while the Negro employees remained confined by race to the jobs reserved for them.[17]

Seniority provides an order of priority for promotion and layoff based in part on length of service in some determined unit. Thus seniority confirmed the pattern of racial restriction in hiring by giving the Negro no rights at all with respect to jobs which were reserved for whites. Negro seniority rights did not extend above the top Negro job. This limitation was sometimes imposed overtly in collective agreements but, after World War II, it was increasingly applied through unwritten understandings. But, written or unwritten, these practices which restricted Negroes to lower-paying jobs were open and notorious. These practices continued into the early 1960's in the South, despite the fact that they had been declared illegal in 1944 in the case of *Steele v. Louisville & N. Ry.*[18] The *Steele* doctrine required unions and companies to treat all employers fairly and without discrimination on the grounds of race. The doctrine was flouted by both labor and management, who understood that contract rights which appeared to be fair were simply not available to Negroes. This understanding was confirmed in the day-to-day administration of the collective bargaining agreement, despite an occasional court decision holding that such practices were improper, and that the unions had the duty to negotiate away discrimination as well as to administer contracts without it.[19]

Sometime during the early 1960's, this southern pattern changed. The occasion for the change was governmental activity under the Kennedy executive order, Executive Order No. 10925, prohibiting discrim-

---

[17] See ch. 3 *supra* for the economic consequences of this pattern.

[18] 323 U.S. 192 (1944).

[19] Central of Georgia Ry. v. Jones, 229 F.2d 648 (5th Cir. 1956) *cert. denied* 352 U.S. 848 (1956); Richardson v. Texas and N. R.R., 242 F.2d 230 (5th Cir. 1957); Local 12, Rubber Workers v. NLRB, 368 F.2d 12 (5th Cir. 1966).

ination by government contractors.[20] This order produced a flurry of activity on the part of employers in the South. Many of them gave up the formal barriers to Negro advancement. Sometimes they erected a substitute barrier to continue the confinement of Negroes, but most frequently the normal operation of seniority could be relied upon to keep the Negro in his place. Thus, if Negroes had been confined to certain departments and the seniority system functioned on a departmental basis, company and union could be reasonably sure that few Negroes would sacrifice their job security in the Negro department to become the junior man in a white department, even if that privilege was made available, subject to being laid off first in the event of a cutback in employment. If the wage structure was such that the top Negro job paid more than the bottom white job, the principle that one enters seniority units at the bottom would add a barrier of loss of income to any possible transfer opportunities. Thus no special arrangements were necessary to discourage Negro employees from seeking to obtain white jobs under those conditions.

By refusing to give credit to the Negro for time spent in the Negro lines or jobs when he moved to the white lines or jobs, the seniority system meant that a Negro who could obtain a previously white job would be the junior man, lowest paid and the first to be bumped in the event of layoff. Under many systems, when a man has transferred to a new seniority unit, he has no "bump-back" rights and, if later laid off, cannot return to his previous unit. These factors prevented Negroes from moving into jobs from which they were previously excluded because of their race. Senior Negroes generally decline to move out of their Negro seniority units if in the process they would lose the very rights which seniority gives. The loss of job security on transfer or promotion plus the junior status in the white unit constituted the key elements making seniority systems discriminatory as to Negroes who were hired and assigned to jobs on the basis of race. When this was coupled with a cut in pay on transfer to a new line, and when the whole process was further encumbered with a battery of tests excluding a higher proportion of Negroes than whites, the entire pattern of restriction on Negro opportunity was revealed.

There were a number of cases in which Negro employees had sen-

---

[20] On the history and scope of these executive orders, see SOVERN, *supra* note 9 at 93–114.

iority rights written into contracts which they were simply not allowed to exercise because of race. When the formal racial barrier was dropped, employers and unions were faced with the alternatives of permitting Negroes to advance, of erecting other barriers not overtly based on race, or of downgrading Negro contract rights to prevent them from being promoted past white employees. Frequently aptitude tests and formal educational requirements also functioned as barriers to Negro advancement.[21]

During this period of the late 1950's and early 1960's, the seniority system allocated promotional opportunities to incumbent white employees ahead of Negroes and, because of these other barriers, new white employees continued to be hired into previously white jobs. In sum, the situation remained substantially as it had been during the period of open and notorious racist practices, except that opportunities were opened to some Negroes to take lower-paying, less-secure jobs, as they became available, which had previously been reserved for whites. Employers and unions were prepared to view long-time Negro employees as if they were newly hired whites, but refused to give seniority credit for time spent in Negro jobs. Under this system Negroes began slowly to trickle into the lower of the white jobs in some cases. This, in general, was the situation in much of southern industry when the Civil Rights Act of 1964 became effective on July 2, 1965.[22] Title VII prohibited discrimination in employment by both unions and employers.

The basic issue under Title VII is whether this form of opportunity satisfies the obligation imposed by the statute and, if not, what further remedies are required.

III. Past Discrimination Perpetuated

The first question is whether a seniority system which has openly discriminated in the past but now allows Negro incumbents to obtain

---

[21] On testing and discrimination, see Cooper & Sobel, *Seniority and Testing under Fair Employment Laws,* 82 HARV. L. REV. 1598 (1969). Note, *Legal Implications of the Use of Standardized Ability Tests in Employment and Education,* 68 COLUM. L. REV. 691 (1968); Blumrosen, ch. 7 *infra.*

[22] Factual situations illustrating this type of case were present in Quarles v. Philip Morris, 279 F. Supp. 505 (F.D. Va. 1968); Local 189, Paper Makers v. United States, 416 F.2d 980 (5th Cir. 1969); Griggs v. Duke Power Co., 420 F.2d 1225 (4th Cir. 1970).

jobs in previously white seniority units, but without seniority credit for time worked in Negro jobs, is illegal under Title VII. In other words, has such a system discriminated during the post-July 2, 1965, period, or did the discrimination cease when the formal barriers to promotion were lifted? It is clear that such seniority systems transmit into the present the discrimination of the past. The mechanism which transmits this discrimination into the present is twofold: (1) the refusal to give Negro employees seniority credits for time spent in Negro jobs when they compete with later-hired whites for "white jobs," and (2) the rule that one must "start at the bottom" of the white line.

All seniority systems classify. They create an enclave consisting of a group of jobs and give certain individuals priorities with respect to these jobs. This is the essence of "competitive status" seniority.[23] This is what is meant by the phrase that "all seniority systems discriminate." In truth, they all classify. Whether they discriminate is neither answered, nor addressed, by the fact that they classify.

Seniority systems function on the principle of first in, last out. They protect persons within each seniority unit at the expense of outsiders. Once seniority units are defined, a new entrant into the unit comes in at the bottom, both with respect to his tenure and his rate of pay. It is the subordinate status of the new employee in the unit which makes it risky for the Negro, now emancipated in theory by law, to take advantage of his new freedom by exchanging the insurance against layoff of his Negro seniority for the uncertain status of a new employee in the previously white units, even if he can hurdle the barriers of tests and possible loss of income.

In the South, virtually every seniority system which is more than a few years old has embraced a hiring pattern which confined Negroes to certain limited groups of jobs, and excluded them from white jobs. To the extent that this is the case, the classification process inherent in seniority tends to perpetuate the protections of those who are "in" at the expense of those who are "out." Where the ins and the outs are distinguished on racial grounds, because of history, Title VII is violated. As a technical matter, the employer under such a system violates the law because he "otherwise discriminates . . . with respect to terms, conditions, or privileges of employment . . ." under 703(a); and because his action does "limit, segregate, or classify" employees in

---

[23] SLICHTER, LIVERNASH, & HEALY, *supra,* note 7, ch. 5.

ways which "deprive or tend to deprive any individual of employment opportunities or otherwise adversely affect his status as an employee . . ." under 703(a)(2).

The union participant violates 703(c)(1) in that it discriminates in enforcing the agreement; it violates 703(c)(2) in that its actions constitute a limitation, segregation, or classification of its membership and of those whom it represents; and it violates 703(c)(3) in that it is insisting that the employer violate 703(a). Thus in the operation of typical seniority systems in the South today, both company and union are still classifying, segregating, limiting, and discriminating against Negro employees by acts which deprive or tend to deprive them of employment opportunities or "otherwise adversely affect their status as employees" because of their race.

The existing seniority systems do not credit time spent in Negro jobs, lines, or departments toward opportunities available in previously white lines, jobs or departments. This is the operative fact which carries the overt discrimination of the past into the present. If a Negro chooses to leave his "Negro seniority unit," he loses what job security that unit afforded him, in exchange for a less secure job as the "low man" in the white unit, often at reduced pay. Most Negro employees will not take such risks as the price of ending illegal discrimination against them. They remain in the Negro jobs and units. Whites continue to fill the previously white jobs. By refusing to allow a Negro to count his "Negro time" in seeking a white job in competition with a later-hired white, the seniority system uses the discrimination of the past to allocate this present opportunity to the white employee. Hence, it presently limits, classifies, discriminates, and segregates on the basis of race in allocating present opportunities.

These procedures tend to confine Negroes to the departments and units into which they were hired. This, of course, is a primary function of any seniority system from the perspective of management. The system is supposed to keep trained and skilled employees in jobs, units, and departments where their skills will be most effectively used in production. Such rules are intended to discourage major changes of job or role of the employee and to keep most men in the mainstream of their employment history. As applied to the case of discriminatory initial assignments, this normal operation of seniority does in fact inhibit Negro transfers, and thus adversely affects the opportunities of Negro employees. It is improper to require the victims of discrimination to give up what little job security they have as the price for an opportunity to which they were entitled all along.

Five considerations are often urged in opposition to this analysis. These considerations are asserted either to narrow the concept of discrimination or as matters of justification. These considerations include: (1) no intention to discriminate (2) present equality, (3) improvement of Negroes (4) statutory protection for "bona fide seniority systems," and (5) the doctrine of the *Whitfield* case. In the following paragraphs, these five arguments will be presented, along with the response to each argument. I believe that the responses effectively refute the thesis of each argument. Each argument and its response may be found to be intertwined with others in any specific legal context.

1. No intention to discriminate

THE ARGUMENT: Discrimination consists of conscious wrongdoing deliberately calculated to disadvantaged persons because of their race. To establish a violation of Title VII, it is necessary to prove that the defendant desired to adversely affect Negroes because of their race. This is not established merely by showing that a decision in the administration of a seniority system harmed a black person. All decisions in the administration of seniority arrangements harm at least as many persons as they benefit, because the function of seniority is to determine who is to be benefited and who is to suffer a particular loss.

The Southern pattern of traditional discrimination and segregation of Negroes in inferior jobs is admitted, but this period is over. Labor agreements and company policies have been reformed to eradicate racism. The period of hostile discrimination and evil intent to which the statute is addressed is no more. The importance of intent in finding discrimination is underscored by the legislative insertion of the requirement, both in the remedial section dealing with private litigation and in the section authorizing the Attorney General to litigate.[24] Intention of the type required by the law did exist in the now abandoned practices of restricting Negroes to lower-paying jobs. But this period has ended, and with it, the period in which the intention requisite for violation

---

[24] See §§706(g), 707.

could have been proved. Race relations have moved swiftly in the 1960's. The pattern of overt racial discrimination against which Congress legislated in 1964 had already been changed by the employers and unions and did not exist in significant measure by the time the Civil Rights Act came into effect in 1965.

THE RESPONSE: Title VII makes unlawful those actions which "adversely affect" employment opportunities of persons because of their race.[25] Thus Title VII establishes a standard of conduct to effectuate the public interest represented by the statute.[26] The body of law regulating in civil cases the relations of one person to another is called the law of tort. Thus Title VII establishes a body of "statutory tort law" regulating the relations of employers unions and employment agencies toward minority group persons. In traditional legal terms, the tort we are concerned with would be classified as an intentional tort. This "intention" has nothing to do with the evil motive (*mens rea*) of the criminal law. Rather, it involves awareness that the acts of the defendant would inflict harm on the plaintiff.[27] This awareness provides the element of "blameworthiness" which distinguishes the intentional from the negligent infliction of harm in modern tort law. The narrow concept of intent espoused by those who would restrict the application of Title VII and, strangely enough, by two commentators who otherwise seem friendly toward the objectives of Title VII,[28] has no place in the modern

---

[25] See §§703(a)–(c), 704(a)–(b).

[26] The Supreme Court has stated that the individual suing under Title II of the Civil Rights Act of 1964 with respect to discrimination in public accommodations is to be viewed as a "private Attorney General, vindicating a policy that Congress considered of the highest priority," Newman v. Piggie Park Enterprises, 390 U.S. 400, 402. The same view appears applicable to Title VII. See Jenkins v. United Gas Corp., 58 Lab. Cas. ¶9154, (5th Cir. 1968). This concept of paramount public interest suggests that there is substantial identity of issues and solutions in a class action brought under section 706 by employees to end discrimination. See Oatis v. Crown Zellerbach Corp., 58 Lab. Cas. ¶9140 (5th Cir. 1968) and a public action brought by the Attorney General under §707. This discussion will draw no distinction between the two forms of proceeding.

[27] Local 189, Paper Makers v. United States, 416 F.2d 980 (5th Cir. 1969). See PROSSER, TORTS, (3d ed. §8, 1964); RESTATEMENT OF TORTS, §13, comment *d* at 29 (1934); RESTATEMENT (SECOND) OF TORTS, §8A, comments *a*, *b* at 15 (1965); 86 C.J.S. *Torts* §20; Holmes, *Privilege, Malice and Intent*, 8 HARV. L. REV. 1 (1894). See ch. 6 for another application of this concept.

[28] SOVERN, *supra* note 9, at 70–73 (1966); Bonefield, *The Substance of American Fair Employment Practice Legislation I: Employers*, 61 NW. U.L. REV. 907, 956 (1967).

law of tort. Rather, if the defendant is aware that his action is reasonably certain to adversely affect persons because of their race, he has the intention required by the law of tort.

A similar rule with respect to the intent to discriminate on the basis of union membership or nonmembership has emerged under the National Labor Relations Act. There the Supreme Court has held that consequences reasonably certain to follow from a given action will be considered as intended.[29] In other words, once the effect of a given action is known in advance, the achieving of this effect is considered to be intended in the civil law, regardless of motive or desire on the part of the actor.

This concept of intent is compatible with the understanding of Title VII as a charter of equal employment opportunity, to be construed broadly to achieve the general objectives of the Congress which enacted it. The legislative history confirms the validity of this definition of intent.

The word "intent" was inserted into the remedial section of Title VII as a part of the Dirksen amendments which constituted the Senate-House compromise bill which was enacted into law.[30] Senator Humphrey called this addition "a clarifying change." He said:

> Since the Title bars only discrimination because of race, color, religion, sex, or national origin, it would seem already to require intent, and thus, the proposed change does not involve any substantive change in the Title. The express requirement of intent is designed to make it wholly clear that inadvertent or accidental discriminations will not violate the Title or result in the entry of court orders. It means simply that the respondent must have intended to discriminate.[31]

Senator Dirksen's explanation added nothing beyond restating the language which was agreed to in the leadership compromise.[32] However, Dirksen's perception of the significance of the insertion of the con-

---

[29] NLRB v. Fleetwood Trailer Co., 389 U.S. 375 (1967); NLRB v. Great Dane Trailers, Inc., 388 U.S. 26 (1967); NLRB v. Erie Resistor Corp., 373 U.S. 221 (1963); Radio Officers Union v. NLRB, 347 U.S. 17 (1954).

[30] On the process of adoption, see EEOC, LEGISLATIVE HISTORY OF TITLES VII AND XI OF THE CIVIL RIGHTS ACT OF 1964, pt. 1 (hereafter cited as LEGISLATIVE HISTORY); Berg, *Equal Employment Opportunity under the Civil Rights Act of 1964*, 31 BROOKLYN L. REV. 62, 64–67 (1964); BNA OPERATIONS MANUAL, THE CIVIL RIGHTS ACT OF 1964, ch. 3 (1964).

[31] LEGISLATIVE HISTORY 3006.

[32] *Id.* at 3019.

cept of intention may be gleaned from Amendment No. 507, which he
had proposed a month before the leadership compromise was adopted.
He had urged the insertion of the term "willfully" in the remedial section of the bill then before the Senate. Quoting Corpus Juris Secundum,
the Senator suggested that the term "willfully" means:

> nothing more than that the person, of whose actions or default the ex-
> pressions are used, knows what he is doing, intends what he is doing, and
> is a free agent; that is, that what has been done arises from the spon-
> taneous action of his will. Thus the terms imply a conscious act of the
> mind . . . and include the idea of a consciousness or knowledge, that is
> knowledge of all the circumstances. . . .
> The terms are also employed to denote an intentional act . . . as dis-
> tinguished from an accidental act, an act done by accident . . . or acci-
> dentally, or carelessly, thoughtlessly, heedlessly, or inadvertently, or
> otherwise beyond the control of the person charged. . . . In distinguish-
> ing in the use of the words in civil or criminal statutes it is stated on
> page 630 that, "the words willful and willfully are frequently used in a
> sense that does not imply any malice or wrong, or anything necessarily
> blamable or malevolent, and the words are generally used in this mild
> sense in civil cases. . . ." [33]

While Senator Dirksen's proposal was rejected, it is quite likely the
genesis of the idea for the insertion of the word "intentionally" in the
remedial portion of the statute during the leadership compromise. The
word "intentionally" seems a fitting compromise point which meets the
Senator's objections to the possibility of "accidental discrimination,"
without running the risks of narrow construction implicit in possible
interpretation of the word "willful" as imposing a more specific intent
requirement. The language of the Humphrey explanation for the insertion of the word "intentional" seems to echo the Dirksen memorandum.

Finally, Senator McClellan attempted to inject the word "solely"
into the statute, so that the operative sections prohibited discrimination
against any individual "solely" because of his race. Senator Case opposed the amendment stating:

> The difficulty with this amendment is that it would render Title VII
> totally nugatory. If anyone ever had an action that was motivated by a
> single cause, he is a different kind of animal from any I know of. But
> beyond that difficulty, this amendment would place upon persons at-

---

[33] *Id.* at 3268.

tempting to prove a violation of this section, no matter how clear the violation was, an obstacle so great as to make the Title completely worthless.[34]

Senator Magnuson concurred:

. . . The difficulty is that a legal interpretation or a court interpretation of the word "solely" would so limit this section as probably to negate the entire purpose of what we are trying to do.[35]

The amendment was defeated.[36]

This exchange makes clear that the Senate did not wish the issue of the motive of the defendant to prevent plaintiff from prevailing in a Title VII case. The compromise had been struck in the Dirksen amendment. The term "intentional," with its implication of knowledge of the circumstances in which the action takes place, was as far as the Senate was prepared to go on this issue. The Senate drew the line short of where Senator McClellan wished to take it.

I conclude that the intent requirement in Title VII is the intent requirement of a civil action in tort—that the defendant be aware of the consequences of his action which are reasonably certain to flow from his behavior. If he has this level of awareness, the law of tort is satisfied.

Application of this concept of intent to the seniority situation which we have previously described is not complicated. There are few inadvertent decisions made in the administration of a seniority system. The operation of the system is predictable, and the results of its operation are, therefore, intended. The refusal to credit Negro employees with time spent in Negro jobs when they compete with white employees necessarily means that they will either lose in competition with whites whose time in white jobs is counted, or that they will decline to compete in recognition that, if they are successful, they will lose their job security. The result is that incumbent Negro employees who were originally openly discriminated against continue in the job patterns established by the discrimination. These are intended consequences in the sense that intention has been defined above.

---

[34] *Id.* at 3124.

[35] *Id.* at 3125.

[36] A similar proposal had been defeated earlier during the debate in the House of Representatives, 110 CONG. REC. 2728 (1964).

2. Present Equality But Not Retroactivity

The Argument: Title VII is not retroactive. It does not require changes in seniority systems because of past discrimination so long as the system presently does not discriminate. This was guaranteed several times in the legislative debates. For example, Senator Clark responded to questions raised by Senator Dirksen on this issue as follows:

> Question: Normally, labor contracts call for "last hired, first fired." If the last hired are Negroes, is the employer discriminating if his contract requires that they be first fired and the remaining employees are white?
>
> Answer: Seniority rights are in no way affected by the bill. If under a "last hired, first fired" agreement a Negro happens to be the "last hired," he can still be "first fired" as long as it is done because of his status as "last hired" and not because of his race.
>
> Question: If an employer is directed to abolish his employment list because of discrimination, what happens to seniority?
>
> Answer: The bill is not retroactive, and it will not require an employer to change existing seniority lists.[37]

The same idea is expressed in that most important document, the Clark-Case Memorandum on Title VII:

> Title VII would have no effect on established seniority rights. Its effect is prospective and not retrospective. Thus, for example, if a business has been discriminating in the past and as a result has an all-white working force, when the Title comes into effect the employer's obligation would be simply to fill future vacancies on a non-discriminatory basis. He would not be obliged—or indeed, permitted—to fire whites in order to hire Negroes, or to prefer Negroes for future vacancies, or, once Negroes are hired, to give them special seniority rights at the expense of the white workers hired earlier. (However, where waiting lists for employment or training are, prior to the effective date of the Title, maintained on a discriminatory basis, the use of such lists after the Title takes effect may be held an unlawful subterfuge to accomplish discrimination.)[38]

Finally, a similar statement by the Department of Justice was introduced into the record early in the debates by Senator Clark:

---

[37] Legislative History at 3013.
[38] *Id.* at 3043.

First, it has been asserted that Title VII would undermine vested rights
of seniority. This is not correct. Title VII would have no effect on seniority
rights existing at the time it takes effect. If, for example, a collective
bargaining contract provides that in the event of layoffs, those who were
hired last must be laid off first, such a provision would not be affected in
the least by Title VII. This would be true even in the case where, owing
to discrimination prior to the effective date of the Title, white workers
had more seniority than Negroes. Title VII is directed at discrimination
based on race, color, religion, sex, or national origin. It is perfectly clear
that when a worker is laid off or denied a chance for promotion because
under established seniority rules he is "low man on the totem pole," he is
not being discriminated against because of his race. Of course, if the
seniority rule itself is discriminatory, it would be unlawful under Title
VII. If a rule were to state that all Negroes must be laid off before any
white man, such a rule could not serve as the basis for a discharge subsequent to the effective date of the Title. . . . But, in the ordinary case,
assuming that seniority rights were built up over a period of time during
which Negroes were not hired, these rights would not be set aside by
the taking effect of Title VII. Employers and labor organizations would
simply be under a duty not to discriminate against Negroes because of
their race. Any differences in treatment based on established seniority
rights would not be forbidden by the Title.[39]

All of these statements compel one conclusion: where seniority rights of
white employees are based on traditional practices in the plant, these
rights are not to be disturbed by Title VII, unless there is some new act
of discrimination, other than the carrying out of the pre-existing seniority system. The argument that these systems are discriminatory because
they perpetuate past discrimination misses the mark because this kind
of discrimination was specifically saved, under the above quoted legislative history, from being illegal under Title VII.

THE RESPONSE: This analysis of Title VII presents a more complex
challenge to the thesis that present perpetuation of past discrimination
violates Title VII. It is founded on two grounds: the term "retroactivity" and the above quoted legislative history.

The term "retroactivity" suggests at least two possible meanings in
the Title VII context. One is that the statute will not reach back to
make illegal that conduct which prior to the passage of the Act was
either legal or void under some other law. An associated meaning is

---

[39] *Id.* at 3244.

that the statute will not reach back to condemn conduct which took place beyond the period of the statute of limitations contained therein. This is the common understanding of the term. It is the understanding associated with the common phrase, "You can't turn back the clock," which is so often heard in this field.

But the second possible meaning attributed to the term retroactivity is the one which poses the more difficult problem. The argument is that Congress, in passing Title VII, intended not only to protect *acts* done prior to its date (or the applicable limitation period) but also to validate *systems of seniority* which were established prior to its date and were not discriminatory on their face. Thus if the system was established prior to Title VII effective dates, it could operate into the indefinite future without change, even though it continued to allocate job opportunities on a racial basis after July 2, 1965. In short, the argument is that Congress understood seniority as a system for allocating preferences for promotion and protection against layoff. Those preferences which the whites had on July 2, 1965, are not to be altered by the statute. This use of the term retroactivity purports to give a privilege to continue to discriminate in seniority systems after the effective date of Title VII as long as the discrimination started earlier.

Since this view will provide a privilege to engage in conduct which Congress otherwise clearly intended to proscribe, the Congressional intention to provide that privilege should be clearly articulated.[40]

When one turns to the legislative history, one finds a void on this question. That history simply is not addressed to the conflict between incumbent whites and earlier-hired Negroes, but rather to a possible conflict between incumbent whites and later-hired Negroes. The history does suggest that white employees would not be displaced to provide jobs for later-hired Negroes. It is virtually silent as to the relation between earlier-hired Negroes and later-hired whites.[41] The problem of earlier-hired Negroes and later-hired whites is mentioned once, with the clear implication that past discrimination may not be perpetuated. The parenthetical statement at the conclusion of the Clark-Case Memorandum refers to waiting lists for employment or training which were

---

[40] See Local 357, Teamsters v. NLRB, 365 U.S. 667 (1961) for an illustration of such a situation.

[41] See the quotations at notes 37–39 *supra;* SOVERN, *supra,* note 9 at 72–3.

compiled before the act on a discriminatory basis. After the act, the paragraph suggests, their use would be illegal as "an unlawful subterfuge to accomplish discrimination." [42]

With respect to promotions and layoffs, a seniority list is a waiting list. It determines the order in which benefits are conferred and detriments allocated. Pre-act discrimination in seniority means that the seniority lists, the waiting lists, are compiled on a discriminatory basis. Their post-act use, perpetuating the pre-act discrimination by bringing it into the time frame covered by the act, may, likewise, be "an unlawful subterfuge to accomplish discrimination."

This suggests that pre-act discrimination may not be carried forward and privileged under the statute. This view is confirmed in the earlier Justice Department memorandum where it states that ". . . if the seniority rule itself is discriminatory, it would be unlawful under Title VII. If a rule were to state that all Negroes must be laid off before any white man, such a rule could not serve as the basis for a discharge subsequent to the effective date of the Act. . . ." [43]

Discriminatory seniority systems often depend on the distinction between white and Negro jobs. Negroes receive no credit for time spent in Negro jobs in seeking and holding white jobs. Hence, if they are now allowed into the white units "at the bottom of the list," the effect is that all Negroes must be laid off from the white jobs before any incumbent whites. This is virtually the situation described as illegal in the Justice Department memorandum.

An examination of the legislative history leads to the following conclusions: (1) Most of the history assures earlier-hired whites that they will not be displaced by later-hired Negroes, and does not deal with the conflict between incumbents where the Negroes have equal or longer employment histories; (2) to the extent that the history does deal with this problem, it clearly implies that the present perpetuation of the subordinate status of Negroes is unlawful under the Title. The argument concerning "retroactivity," then, fails to refute the basic thesis that the perpetuation of pre-act discrimination through the administration of the seniority system is a violation of Title VII.[44]

---

[42] See text at note 38 *supra.*

[43] See text at note 39 *supra.*

[44] This is the view of Quarles v. Philip Morris, 279 F.2d 505, 516 (E.D. Va. 1968). "Congress did not intend to freeze an entire generation of Negro employees into discriminatory patterns that existed before the Act." *Accord,* Local 189, Paper

3. Improvement

The Argument: This is the argument for gradualism, with the appropriate standard of improvement being that actually afforded the Negro employees by the white employers and unions. Since the days of overt discrimination, some Negroes have moved into some white jobs. The extent of the movement, either by permanent assignment or temporary appointment, and the frequency of such assignments are matters frequently in dispute. But in virtually every establishment in the South, the solid color line has been breached to some extent. This fact will be asserted as demonstrating the "good faith" of the employer and union and suggesting that further improvement is likely if the parties are left to their own devices.

The Response: Such improvement as does exist came not by virtue of good-faith awareness of an indecent situation, but under pressure asserted by the government. Voluntarism without such pressure does exist, but it is a rarity. But, more importantly, the improvement agreement assumes that the standard for appropriate improvement is that which was *in fact* afforded Negro employees by the company and union. This exposes the fundamental issue of whether the white power structure which so long subjugated Negro employees may determine what improvement is "appropriate"—or on what terms Negroes are to be allowed equality. Whether equal opportunity is afforded in any given situation is a question of law. It cannot be delegated to the very parties—labor and management—who have imposed racist restraints on promotional opportunities in the past. Thus the standard for equality can never be the actual conduct of the parties in the situation, unless that conduct measures up to abstract and objectively imposed standards of the law.[45]

But what are these standards? To answer this question is to decide the appropriate remedy, and this will be discussed separately. This analysis makes clear that the discriminators are attempting, through the "improvement" argument, to control the scope of the remedy. The im-

---

Makers v. United States, 416 F.2d 980 (5th Cir. 1969) *Contra,* Griggs v. Duke Power Co., 58 Lab. Cas. ¶9163 (M.D. N.C. 1968).

[45] As Dean Prosser points out, in connection with the standard of the reasonable man in tort, "Even an entire industry, by adopting such careless methods to save time, effort, or money cannot be permitted to set its own uncontrolled standard." Prosser, Torts, §33 (3d ed. 1964).

provement argument attempts to substitute what the discriminators—union and employer—have, in fact, done for what ought to be done to correct the past discrimination, and to avoid the type of remedial discussion suggested here. But the rule of tort law has long been that neither business nor labor can establish its own standard of conduct. Yet this is the objective of the improvement argument. It must be rejected; the obligations and their extent must be determined by law, not by the combined actions of the defendants.

4. The "bona fide seniority system" exemption under Title VII

THE ARGUMENT: Section 703(j) of Title VII includes a proviso holding exempt from illegality any "bona fide seniority or merit system" if the differences resulting from the system are not themselves "the result of an intention to discriminate. . . ." The argument has been made that this section, and particularly the term "bona fide," saves from illegality any seniority system which was not gerrymandered to exclude Negroes or other minorities because of their race. Thus if the system of seniority in operation in a given establishment is common, the system is "bona fide" and its operation is insulated from Title VII.

THE RESPONSE: There is no single seniority system. Rather, there are infinite varieties of systems. Negotiation and administration produce unique variations on the basic themes of seniority—the boundary of its units, the weight given to length of service versus ability, the manner of exercise of rights, the adjustment of conflicts in administration. The technology in which the system operates, as well as the personal views of strong leaders in labor and management, influences the course of development of any seniority system. Almost any combination of seniority elements can be found in any industry if one looks long enough. Seniority serves multiple values, and the systems vary accordingly. Thus almost any racially oriented system will have its counterpart in a nondiscriminatory context.

The traditional pattern of discrimination through seniority in the South has infrequently involved a special racial gerrymander of seniority units.[46] Most frequently, perfectly legitimate departmental or line of

---

[46] The classic case of gerrymandered units has not yet been resolved. This involves the labeling of Negro employees on passenger trains as porters and white

progression distinctions were administered by confining Negroes to certain jobs and departments. The nondiscriminatory counterpart system is readily available, with the one exception that its jobs were not filled through racist hiring practices. The "deliberate racial gerrymander" theory of section 703(j) would insulate this most common form of seniority discrimination from the operation of the statute. Thus the exception would swallow up the rule.

Yet the exception is itself limited in that it does not apply if the system is "designed, intended, or used" to discriminate. Thus it is clear that the Congress intended the courts to focus on the particular operation of the system before it.

The issue under Title VII with respect to any seniority system is the manner in which that system allocates work opportunities. The test for discrimination is whether each system allocates such opportunities on the basis of race. To interpret the "bona fide seniority system" proviso as creating an immunity for "types of seniority systems" would require an abstract search for a "comparable" seniority system which does not discriminate. Title VII does not mandate such sterile judicial research. There is nothing in the statute suggesting that the evidence in a Title VII suit should range over the fifty-seven varieties of seniority in a given industry in disregard of the day-to-day operation of the particular system before the court. If *that* system discriminates, then it is not protected by the "bona fide" proviso. The fact that a similar system might operate in a nondiscriminatory manner is no defense. In most cases in the South, the fundamental reason why a seniority system discriminates will relate to the racist hiring and assignment practices which underly it. Where those racist practices are absent, almost any system can pass muster under Title VII. Thus the hunt for "neutral principles of seniority" generated by this concept of "bona fide seniority systems" must be

---

employees performing similar work on freight trains as brakemen. This situation was the subject of a decision of the Supreme Court in 1952. Brotherhood of R.R. Trainmen v. Howard, 343 U.S. 768 (1952). Mr. Howard did not get the relief of merger of jobs, however, and was rebuffed by the Eighth Circuit in subsequent efforts in 1966. Howard v. St. Louis-S.F. Ry., 215 F.2d 690 (8th Cir. 1954); 361 F.2d 905 (8th Cir. 1966). He filed a complaint with the EEOC, which found cause in his case. His patience has not been rewarded as yet, and it is possible that the abandonment of passenger service plus attrition due to death by old age will end the plight of the Negro porters before the law in its majesty can be brought to bear. See Norman v. Missouri Pacific R.R., 414 F.2d 73 (8th Cir. 1969).

put aside in favor of a sharp look at the facts of the case before the court.[47]

This reading of the statute is sustained by a review of the history of the law concerning seniority and race.

The Supreme Court in 1944 held that the union and employer may not discriminate on grounds of race in negotiating and administering seniority provisions. This holding has been more honored in the statement than in compliance. Furthermore, most major employers are government contractors and, as such, have been subject to regulations against discrimination in employment systems, including the seniority system. And finally, in most of the non-Southern states, employment discrimination—including that in seniority systems—has been proscribed since the enactment of state FEP statutes which go back to 1945.

Thus the seniority systems of which we speak were illegal as early as 1944. They were illegal prior to July 2, 1965. Yet the effect of the adoption of the argument about "bona fide seniority systems" would be to treat those systems as if they had been lawful prior to the effective date of Title VII. Title VII is not the mockery that such a construction would make it.

The exception for "bona fide" seniority systems is itself limited by the proviso that the "differences" which result from the system are not "the result of an intention to discriminate. . . ." This phrase reintroduces all of the original problems of defining discrimination. It makes the entire exception meaningless unless the phrase "result of an intention to discriminate" is narrower than the "intention to discriminate" found in the combination of 703 and 706(e). Thus this provision, like the testing provision, has the symbolic value of calling close attention to the problem of seniority, but otherwise does not affect the course of decision under the Title.[48]

What of the legislative history here? It speaks only of a conflict between white employees and Negroes outside of employment; it makes clear that later-hired Negroes are not entitled to displace earlier-hired whites. If anything, this history supports remedies which protect incumbent employees—especially Negroes—against outside competition from whites because it adopts the idea of protecting incumbents in gen-

---

[47] Local 189, Paper Makers v. United States, 416 F.2d 980 (5th Cir. 1969).
[48] See ch. 7 *infra*.

eral. The history says little of the problem of earlier-hired Negroes competing with later-hired whites for the better "white" jobs after racial bars were let down. Whether this silence constituted artful dodging of a tough question, or reflected ignorance of the realities of the problem, is not now in point.

What is clear is that the crucial issues of the adjustment required, as between incumbent employees in discriminatory seniority systems, were left to the Commission and the courts. The provision in section 703(h) does not measurably affect this process, other than as a reflection of congressional recognition that this job ought to be done with great care as befitting the importance of the matter.

What, then, does the "bona fide seniority system" language mean? It is consistent with the foregoing analysis to conclude that the proviso crystalizes the concern of Congress to protect earlier-hired whites against later-hired Negroes. The proviso means only what it says: that it does not insulate seniority systems which operate in a discriminatory manner, and that it therefore has no impact on the determination of appropriate relationships between incumbent Negro and white employees.

It is sometimes claimed that seniority rights are vested and are not to be disturbed by Title VII. This argument is another version of the claim that systems of seniority established before Title VII are privileged to perpetuate discrimination. Such arguments seek to use the past as a shield for the present operation of seniority systems.

The vested rights argument is based on the concept that a collective bargaining agreement establishes certain relationships between employers, employees, and the union which cannot be arbitrarily changed. The legal doctrine which protects employees against improper modification of their seniority rights is the duty of fair representation. The facts of the case which enunciated the doctrine involved the destruction of pre-existing seniority rights of Negro employees. Many fair representation cases involve claims that seniority rights which had been recognized in the collective contract were diluted or destroyed.[49] In dealing with these cases, the courts have been careful not to freeze seniority rights beyond the possibility of negotiated changes. When an argument

---

[49] See Blumrosen, *The Worker and Three Phases of Unionism: Judicial and Administrative Control over the Worker-Union Relation*, 61 MICH. L. REV. 1435, 1476–82 (1963).

is made that seniority rights have been diluted through unfair representation, the courts state that the union has a wide range of discretion to modify seniority rights in order to adjust conflicts among groups of employees and to accommodate to changing needs of employers.[50] Seniority rights are not immutable; they are not vested in the sense of property rights which require formal condemnation with compensation for the loss. This rule, which is the corollary of the duty of fair representation, puts union lawyers in a seemingly inconsistent position. When confronted with claims that a union has disregarded individual rights under collective contracts, they argue that unions require flexibility in negotiating with management, and that individuals' rights cannot be allowed to freeze the relationship. The individuals' rights, they argue, are not vested but are the creature of the agreement and may be negotiated away for the common good.

On the other hand, when union lawyers are confronted with an attack on a seniority system as racially discriminatory, they may argue that it is a system of vested rights which cannot or should not be tampered with. This seeming inconsistency reflects the duty of representing the client. The union's interest is in being flexible when it wants flexibility—hence the rebuff to the individual claimant—and in protecting its gains against outside interference—hence its rebuff to those who would challenge the gains. The union's ultimate interest is in the maintenance of its discretion to pursue its own interests in negotiation with management. It wants flexibility to negotiate, and protection for the results of its negotiation.

This discussion should make it clear that the vested rights argument is a statement of a desired conclusion, rather than a reasoned analysis of a problem. Clearheaded decisionmaking in this important area requires analysis and evaluation of competing claims in light of public policies.[51]

In fact, interests do clash. The principle of collective bargaining thrusts toward union-employer freedom and discretion. The principle of elimination of discrimination requires an administrative and judicial check on that discretion. The boundaries of those principles must be worked out by careful analysis with heavy emphasis given to the anti-

---

[50] Humphrey v. Moore, 375 U.S. 335 (1964).

[51] See Blumrosen, *Seniority Rights and Industrial Change: The Case of Zdanok v. Glidden*, 47 MINN. L. REV., 505 (1963). *But see* Local 1251, U.A.W. v. Robertshaw Controls Co., 68 L.R.R.M. 2671 (1968).

discrimination principle. The label of vested rights does not serve the interest of wise decisionmaking.

5. THE DOCTRINE OF THE WHITFIELD CASE

THE ARGUMENT: *Whitfield v. United Steel Workers,*[52] dealt with the question of the steps which a company and a union were required to take to eliminate discriminatory seniority arrangements. The case arose in 1956 under the duty of fair representation. In this case, the company and union had abandoned formal segregation and provided that Negro employees could henceforth enter the previously all-white lines at the bottom of the lines. However, they could not carry forward their seniority rights acquired in the Negro line. In effect, they started as new employees. The court of appeals upheld this arrangement in 1959, fully recognizing that the decision was a question of *judicial judgment,* under the law which had been created by the Supreme Court requiring a union to fairly represent all employees.[53]

---

[52] 263 F.2d 546 (5th Cir. 1959).

[53] Whitfield v. United Steel Workers, 263 F.2d 546, 551 (5th Cir. 1959):

We think that Sheffield and the Union have acted well within the standards discussed in the Steele, Syres, and Ford Motor cases.

The problem before us is not unique. It is bound to come up every time a large company substitutes a program of equal job opportunity for previous discriminatory practices. In such case it is impossible to place negro [*sic*] incumbents holding certain jobs, especially unskilled jobs, on an absolutely equal footing with white incumbents in skilled jobs. In this situation time and tolerance, patience and forbearance, compromise and accommodation are needed in solving a problem rooted deeply in custom.

We attach particular importance to the good faith of the parties in working toward a fair solution. It seems to us that the Union and the Company, with candor and honesty, acknowledged that in the past negroes [*sic*] were treated unfairly in not having an opportunity to qualify for skilled jobs. They balanced the interests of negroes starting Line 1 jobs against the interests of employees who have worked previously in Line 1 jobs, in the light of fairness and efficient operation. After many months of negotiations, and having in mind their duty to all the employees and the need for proper management, they came up with the May 31 agreement, an honest attempt to solve a difficult problem. Courts, when called upon to eye such agreements, should not be quick to "substitute their judgment for that of the bargaining agency on the reasonableness of the modification". . . . The Union and the Company made a fresh start for the future. We might not agree with every provision, but they have a contract that *from now on* is free from any discrimination based on race. Angels could do no more.

It is undeniable that negroes [*sic*] in Line Number 2, ambitious to advance themselves to skilled jobs, are at disadvantage compared with white incumbents in Line Number 1. This is a product of the past. We cannot turn back the

Early in the administration of Title VII, the question was raised as to whether the Commission would accept the so-called *Whitfield* principle as valid under Title VII. The argument is based on an appeal to precedent and the reasoning in that precedent.

My first encounter as Chief of Conciliations for the EEOC, with an eminent union attorney in Birmingham, took place in his conference room in a large modern office building. After the introductory amenities, he said, "There is a case—*Whitfield* against *Steel Workers*. If we can agree that that case sets forth the law, then we will get along." My response was, "I'm familiar with the case. I don't agree that it states the law under Title VII, and I don't think that it states the law under *Steele*. [I referred him to an article I had written which criticized the case.[54]] But I hope we can get along anyhow."

As negotiations concerning important seniority matters proceeded, the *Whitfield* decision was not, at the end of my term with the commission, a central or even a persuasive element in the discussions. We had proceeded far beyond the point marked by that decision.

However, in the first major seniority litigation in Birmingham, Alabama, under Title VII brought by the Attorney General, the "*Whitfield* defense" was again raised.[55] It obviously must be disposed of by higher authority than that of the EEOC, the district courts, or the law reviews.

THE RESPONSE: The *Whitfield* doctrine represented judicial response to facts which took place in 1956, in light of the legal principle of fair representation. It represented the judgment of the court of appeals in 1959 that the company and union had done "enough" to remedy discrimination by the standards of 1956. Both Congress, in the Civil

---

clock. Unfair treatment to their detriment in the past gives the plaintiffs no claim now to be paid back by unfair treatment in their favor. We have to decide this case on the contract before us and its fairness to all.

Considering the contract from the standpoint of all the employees and recognizing the necessity for reasonable standards of operating efficiency, we find that there is no evidence of unfairness or discrimination on the ground of race.

The judgment is
Affirmed.

[54] Blumrosen, *Union-Management Agreements Which Harm Others*, 10 J. PUB. L. 345, 360–62 (1962).

[55] United States v. H. K. Porter Co., 296 F. Supp. 40 (N.D. Ala. 1968). Since I advised the Government in this case, I have refrained from commenting directly or relying on the decision of the district court.

Rights Act, and the Executive, in amendments to the executive order regulating discrimination by government contractors, have since recognized that the standards applied in 1959 were not an adequate governmental response to the problem. It would be ironic if those now discarded standards were to be imported into the situation in the late 1960's under the doctrine of *Whitfield*. We live today in a radically changed legal and social context from that which confronted the court of appeals in 1959. The law has changed so much in the last decade that the judgment of the court as to "all that angels could do" might well not meet minimum standards in 1969. Certainly, considering the change in view of the Fifth Circuit over the last decade on the question of "how much" is required to cure school segregation, it seems reasonable to expect that the court which decided *Whitfield* would not consider itself at all bound by that decision in the present context.[56]

Whitfield was decided under the judicially developed doctrine of fair representation. The issues today arise under the Civil Rights Act's specific provisions prohibiting actions which would "deprive or tend to deprive any individual of employment opportunities or otherwise adversely affect his status as an employee because of such individual's race, color, religion, sex, or national origin." To require that Negro employees remain subordinate to white employees because of historic discrimination would constitute a deprivation of employment opportunity and an adverse effect on employment status because of race, in violation of the statute. Thus, the language of Title VII suggests, if it does not compel, a rejection of *Whitfield*. In addition, Congress, in 1964, entrusted the preliminary decision on this question to a Commission composed of persons appointed by the President with the advice and consent of the Senate. The Commission's judgment, based on a full review of the situation, is itself entitled to considerable weight. The Commission's judgment is that *Whitfield* is not the law under Title VII.[57]

The fact of the matter is that times, standards, and judgments have changed in this field. Both the difficulty and the importance of prompt recognition of the rights of minorities are far clearer today than when

---

[56] The course of judicial decision in 1969 had clearly sapped the *Whitfield* doctrine of most of its vitality in the circuit in which it originated. See Local 189, Paper Makers v. United States, 416 F.2d 980 (5th Cir. 1969), and Local 53, Asbestos Workers v. Vogler, 407 F.2d 1047 (5th Cir. 1969).

[57] See EEOC 2d ANN. REP. 42–44 (1968), Quarles v. Philip Morris, 279 F. Supp. 505 at 519 (E.D. Va. 1968).

Whitfield was decided. The nation is living through a crisis in which the capacity of law to achieve social change is at issue. Its courts will not be tied in the 1970's to a doctrine announced in the fifties.

IV. Seniority Systems Examined

With this background, we now examine the manner in which some of the seniority systems discriminate:

1. Dead-end jobs. Jobs are established as Negro jobs. There is no line of promotion or advancement. Some or all white jobs are grouped within lines or departments or plants for advancement purposes. The act of classification of these jobs as dead end is the discriminatory act, because it restricts promotional opportunities for Negroes disproportionately. Those white jobs which are dead-ended tend to be the higher-paid craftsmen's jobs which are careers in themselves, whereas the Negro dead-end jobs tend to be less skilled and hence not comparable. Dead-end jobs do not provide any promotional opportunity. When filled on a racial basis, they violate Title VII.

2. Job or occupatonal seniority. A line of promotion (or progression) is hypothetically drawn between jobs, and the employees are expected to be promoted through each of these jobs. The jobs are supposed to be related in that experience on the lower job is relevant to performance of the higher job. The higher jobs invariably pay more than the lower jobs, and may be more skilled. Employees climb the job ladder as follows: They enter the lowest job as the junior man. They remain in the lowest job, acquiring seniority in that job. When they become the senior man on that job, they are then in a position to promote to the next higher job, where they become the most junior man. They work up in that job, and follow the same sequence up through successive jobs. Under such a system, discrimination on the basis of race was simple. Negro employees were simply excluded from the entry-level jobs. If this happened after the passage of Title VII, the discrimination is obvious. However, the post-Title VII practice is to admit Negroes to these beginning jobs, which were previously reserved for whites, as vacancies develop. They become the junior men, subordinate to all the white employees who came in earlier, even though they may have had much more plant experience than the white employees. Thus,

job seniority restricts the Negro employee to promotion behind all of the white employees who acquired their job status under the discriminatory system. It, therefore, perpetuates the system of discrimination which had previously existed by maintaining preferential promotion rights for white employees over Negro employees based on the historic exclusion of Negro employees from the classification. It requires the present perpetuation of the system of past discrimination and is, therefore, discriminatory in the present.

This operation of job or occupational seniority is at war with Title VII and requires wholesale revision. This may not be true of other systems. But job seniority, by definition, protects the senior man and, in the southern context, almost by definition, perpetuates discrimination.

The incidence of job seniority is not clear. It is not the dominant pattern in either the paper or steel industry, which is where I encountered it. Its abrogation will not likely require unmanageable changes in seniority. This is the type of seniority held illegal by the federal court of appeals in the *Crown Zellerbach* case.[58]

3. Line of Progression seniority. A type of seniority which is common in heavy manufacturing, particularly the steel industry, is line of progression seniority. The various jobs in the relevant unit (which may be a plant or a department or, more likely, some smaller subunit) are tied together in a ladder of jobs for promotion and layoff purposes. When a vacancy develops in the line, then the most senior man *in the line* who wishes the job may have it, provided he has the requisite ability. He may leap over less senior men who may have acquired jobs which intervene between his job and the vacant job. (A variation on this system involves progression up the line job by job, but the man with the greatest line [not job] seniority gets the first vacancy in the next higher job.)

The administration of these lines of progression gives rise to serious problems under Title VII. The problem involves both transfer between lines and promotion within lines. In some instances, the lines were completely divided on the basis of race—that is, Negroes occupied some lines and whites other lines. In other instances, Negroes occupied lower jobs which were nominally within lines of progression which extended upward to white jobs, but they were not allowed to promote into the

---

[58] Local 189, United Paper Makers v. United States, 416 F.2d 980 (5th Cir. 1969); Hicks v. Crown Zellerbach Corp., 58 Lab. Cas. ¶9145 (E.D. La. 1968).

white jobs. Sometimes (often after government involvement) Negro lines were "tied" to the bottom of white lines, with Negroes advancing behind the whites. The two situations can be diagramed as follows:

	Situation 1 (Transfer)	Situation 2 (Promotion)
	W	W
	W	W
	W	W
N	W	W
N	W	W
N		N
N		N
N		N

Assuming that the allocation of jobs in these lines of progression was done on the basis of race, and assuming further that Negroes are now able to enter the bottom of the previously white lines by transfer when vacancies develop, where is the present discrimination? The answer requires an examination of the barriers to transfer, as in situation 1, and promotion, as in situation 2.

The barriers in situation 1 will usually include (1) loss of pay in moving to the bottom white job, (2) loss of seniority rights in the event of a reduction in force in the white line because the Negro will be the bottom man in the white line and will often not have the right to return to the Negro line in the event of layoff, and sometimes (3) the requirement of passage of tests.

These barriers in fact do discourage most Negroes from moving into the previously white lines of promotion. Thus they are the "practical equivalent" of the formal barriers which previously had prevented movement because of race. Thus they "adversely affect" the promotional opportunities of Negroes and perpetuate in the present the initial racially discriminatory assignments.

The barriers in situation 2 are similar. Negroes who now seek to enter the white line do so in the bottom job, and are subject to being bumped down by any white in the line because they are not allowed to count their time in the Negro line with respect to protection against layoffs. There may, also, be testing and other obstacles. Compared with a later-hired white, the earlier-hired Negro is perpetually behind if he promotes without credit for time spent in the Negro line. His efforts to transfer to other lines are circumscribed by the barriers described with respect to situation 1. In this situation, the past discrimination is perpetuated in that the Negro remains behind later-hired whites as future opportunities become available because he was slotted into jobs on a racist basis in the first instance. Thus the historic discrimination continues to have an "adverse effect" on his employment opportunities.

The extent to which the loss of seniority, possible reduction in pay, and other barriers have in fact deterred Negroes from breaking out of the segregated job category into previously white jobs is, of course, a question of fact in each case. Proof of this fact may involve four elements: (1) general projections of the probable effect on minorities of loss of seniority, cut in pay, and the like, such as those expressed in this article, based on general notionals of probable human behavior, or, in my own case, on numerous personal experiences with Negro workers in this situation; (2) specific testimony in each case that "I didn't transfer because I didn't want to lose my 'age' on the job"; (3) illustrations of individuals who had rejected transfer or promotion opportunities, or who had accepted them, usually from the personnel director; and (4) an analysis, often made with the assistance of the computer, showing in dollars and hours the extent to which Negroes had taken previously white jobs, compared to the dollars and hours spent in those jobs by later-hired whites. The results of such an analysis may be far more convincing proof of the actual effect of the barriers to promotion and transfer than the recitation of specific instances of Negro advance or refusal to advance. In most large modern industry, the employer has the essential information required for a computerized analysis stored in his computer for cost control and payroll purposes. Its availability in court is largely dependent on the skill of counsel in organizing the material for meaningful presentation.

Where Negro and white employees have been placed in separate lines of progression, there is often considerable talk about the need for a "functional relationship" between the lines. The purpose of such a requirement should be carefully analyzed. In accordance with the above analysis, it is not necessary to find such a relationship in order to find that there has been discrimination. The discrimination consists in the original racist assignment perpetuated by barriers to transfer out of the racially circumscribed group of jobs. Thus a functional relationship is not necessary for a finding of discrimination. It may be useful in shaping a remedy, however, because it can assist in outlining the specific linkages which should be established between the Negro and white jobs in developing integrated or merged lines of progression.

The theory of such a remedy embraces the concept that "but for" the discrimination against Negroes, Negro and white jobs might have been linked differently, but this should not be confused with the theory of liability which has been outlined. The functional relationship concept is slippery because much of industry does not operate on a production line concept, where the component product moves down an assembly line with one worker putting on a bolt and the man next to him turning it. Industrial operations are more complex and sophisticated. The men at one end of a paper machine have something in common with those at the other, but also have some differences. The crane operator has something in common with his hooker, i.e., they both work the crane. But the hooker also has something in common with those on the ground with whom he works. This leads to the conclusion that in many cases there is no single functional relationship because there are multiple relationships, all of which are functional. In the largest sense, all jobs in a plant are functionally related to the total production process in the plant. But the concept of functional relationship is not as broad as that. It goes to the rational relationship between groups of jobs and the productive process in terms of (1) working with the same productive process, (2) working under common supervision, (3) working with the same employees, and (4) working in the same geographic area.

One should not be led too far afield in the search for this functional relationship. It is no talisman. Its only function is to assist in determining whether the existing lines were discriminatorily inspired; and perhaps to suggest avenues for solution in the revision of the lines. The risk is that we may become bogged down in trying to define a functional relationship rather than focus on the ultimate questions of (1) was there discrimination, and (2) what is the appropriate remedy? Within that context, the exploration of a functional relationship may be meaningful and useful.

4. Departmental or other general unit seniority. Sometimes discrimination consists in hiring Negro employees into all-Negro units, such as janitors or maintenance men or general laborers. These units may have

specific job assignments. Occasionally, they may have a few white employees in the top jobs. The assigning of Negro employees to such occupational units without a meaningful opportunity to transfer out without the loss of benefits is discrimination. This conclusion flows without regard to the functional relation of the particular department. Hiring practices which segregate on racial grounds, coupled with restrictions on transfer opportunities, effectively confine the Negro employees in the departments into which they were hired, thus perpetuating the discriminatory job assignment which was originally given them.

The proof process in this type of case is similar to that in the line of progression situation, and involves identification of the segregated nature of the unit and evaluation of restrictions on meaningful transfer opportunities. If all employees can move whenever there is a vacancy to any job in the plant, then the departmental lines lose their significance as barriers to promotion. However, in most cases the facts will show that the Negro employee, to transfer from one department or line, must suffer three losses: (1) a reduction in pay, (2) loss of accumulated seniority in the Negro department, and (3) he will become the junior man in the white department. Experience confirms that Negro employees will not give up their job security and economic position to take a lower-paying and less-secure job because it was a white job once. Nor should they be required to do so. An employer who has been discriminating may not require the victims of discrimination to pay for the privilege of exercising their rights to be free of discrimination by taking a cut in pay or job security. The opportunity for a lower-paying, less-secure job is not the kind of equal employment opportunity which the statute was designed to provide.

5. Plant seniority. The plant is generally the widest seniority unit available in a given location. Its use in the typical Southern context will rarely constitute a violation of the statute. However, there may be a violation where the parties have historically treated contiguous operations as separate. For example, in one case in Alabama, the company and the union had, for historic reasons not related to discrimination, treated two contiguous operations as two separate plants. This meant that there were no transfer opportunities between plants, and new employees could be hired in one plant in preference to transfers of old employees from the other plant. One plant engaged in heavy-metal processing, the other in more sophisticated operations. The Negro em-

ployees were concentrated in heavy operations. There were separate collective bargaining agreements covering the two plants. This is an illustration of a state of facts in which plant seniority would work to the disadvantage of Negro employees in much the same way that the smaller classification could operate, and would be susceptible to the same analysis.

However, in the usual case, the Negro in the South will be benefited by a larger seniority unit because he has worked in the establishments in Negro jobs for years. The broader the seniority unit, the more opportunity he will have.

In one case in which Negroes had been confined to the sanitation department and could not transfer or be promoted to other departments without loss of seniority, company and union renegotiated the seniority provisions and established a system of plantwide seniority. The Commission held that, because of the new agreement, there was no cause to believe that discrimination existed.

6. General method of proof in seniority unit cases. From the foregoing, there emerges a pattern of analysis which is appropriate to all seniority discrimination cases. This analysis requires: (1) the identification of various seniority units, (2) the identification of those in which whites were hired and those in which Negro employees were hired, and (3) the description of barriers to promotion and transfer from the Negro to the white jobs and units and the operational consequences of those barriers in terms of the confinement of Negroes to Negro jobs.

The importance of this last element cannot be overstated. One basic purpose of seniority is to provide job security. Promotion and transfer opportunities without this element are not meaningful. In assessing the opportunity for transfer between seniority units, there are at least two ways in which the union and the company may attempt to preserve the job security of the Negro employee. One is by allowing him to carry his Negro-unit time into the white unit. The other is by allowing him to bump back into the Negro unit and reassert his claims there if he should be laid off from the white unit into which he transferred. But if the Negro employee is simply treated as a new employee when he enters the white line, subject to the risks of layoff, this is not a satisfactory elimination of discrimination. The Negro will reject the spurious opportunity thus presented, and with good reason.

7. Destruction of Negro seniority rights. There have been several

cases in which employers and unions have destroyed Negro seniority rights at the time that promotional opportunities were opened to them. This incongruous situation has arisen where the collective bargaining agreement appeared to confer broad seniority rights on Negroes but where these rights were not actually recognized. Once the color bar was dropped, the Negroes could exercise these broader rights at the expense of white employees, unless these rights were diluted. For example, seniority rights may have been recognized on a departmental basis but Negroes were confined to the lowest jobs in the department. When the color bar was dropped, if nothing else was done, Negroes could use their full departmental seniority to take and hold jobs ahead of whites who had lesser department seniority. To avoid this, the company and the union altered the system of seniority to assure that white employees maintained a preference on previously white jobs, ahead of the newly liberated Negroes.

In this situation, the proof of discrimination is simplified because of the additional element of destruction of pre-existing Negro seniority rights. The obviously wrongful quality of this action needs no explication. This was the situation in *Steele v. Louisville & N. Ry.* In shaping the remedy, however, one must be careful *not* to seek simply the restoration of the status quo ante, but to assure the full range of appropriate opportunities.

V. Remedies

The question of the extent of transfer, promotion, and other rights which must be granted the Negro as relief from previously segregated lines in order to satisfy Title VII is the key issue in this field, and is the point of sharpest conflict between labor and civil rights interests.

The power of the courts to order a meaningful, effective, and complete remedy is fully spelled out in the statute. Once discrimination is found, the federal district court "may enjoin the respondent from engaging in such unlawful employment practice and order such affirmative action as may be appropriate, which may include reinstatement or hiring of employees, with or without back pay. . . ." [59] There are two antecedents to the phrase "affirmative action." One is the provi-

---

[59] See §706(g).

sion of section 10(c) of the National Labor Relations Act, which has been given a broad interpretation by the Supreme Court.[60] The other is a somewhat more specialized meaning in the field of employment discrimination. In this field, the term embraces a wide range of activities of employers, unions, and others, aimed at increasing the rate and level of participation by minorities in the labor force.[61] This meaning should be read into the phrase "affirmative action" as it appears in Title VII. Congress rather clearly intended that the court require meaningful remedies to correct the social problem to which the statute is addressed, and not to remedy the wrong only to particular plaintiffs. This interpretation is supported by recent procedural decisions which broadly define the class action under Title VII and the issues to which a Title VII proceeding may be addressed.[62]

A. *The Process of Decision*

In the process of shaping a remedy, the interests of *all* parties must be consulted. The government and the civil rights groups should not execute an agreement with the employer which the employer then imposes on the union without prior consultation. By the same token, the union, the employer, and the government should not execute an agreement without full consultation with representatives of the Negro employees, which frequently will be the NAACP or the Legal Defense Fund. If the suit is under section 706, identification of the representatives will be no problem; but if the suit is by the Attorney General under section 707, he may have to work to identify those with whom to consult. The national labor and race relations policy requires full consultation with all parties prior to the institution of any change. This consultation should take place at the informal level, but if the matter

---

[60] Phelps Dodge Corp. v. NLRB, 313 U.S. 177 (1941), Virginia Electric & Power Co. v. NLRB, 319 U.S. 533, Fibreboard Paper Products Corp. v. NLRB, 379 U.S. 203 (1964); *but see* Local 60, Carpenters v. NLRB, 365 U.S. 651 (1961).

[61] See, *e.g.*, Plans for Progress Statements of Bethlehem Steel, Olin Mathieson Chemical Co., and the Great Atlantic & Pacific Tea Co., BNA Lab. Rel. Rep. LRX 2592 (a–g) (1965); Price, *The Affirmative Action Concept of Equal Employment Opportunity*, 16 Lab. L.J. 603 (1965).

[62] Jenkins v. United Gas Corp., 58 Lab. Cas. ¶9154 (5th Cir. 1968); Oatis v. Crown Zellerbach Corp., 58 Lab. Cas. ¶9140 (5th Cir. 1968), Miller v. International Paper Co. 59 L.C. ¶9211 (5th Cir. 1969).

reaches litigation, then the court should insist on full consultation regardless of whether the union or civil rights group has been made a party to the litigation. The court should insist that the union be made a party to the litigation so that its interests can be consulted and it will be bound by the order.

The Commission's practices of full consultation in conciliation plus the availability of the class action in court should assure that the three interests in any discriminatory seniority system in fact do negotiate together concerning the remedy for discrimination. Trilateral negotiation is a key element of Title VII. The legal rules concerning rights and remedies furnish the framework for such negotiations. The negotiations can take place either in an EEOC conciliation conference or in the process of preparing a proposed order for the court once discrimination is found. In these negotiations the parties can take account of any facts and circumstances peculiar to their situation.

The discussion which follows suggests patterns of relief which the courts may order and the parties then utilize as a framework for settlement.

B. *Promotion from Within*

Rejecting the principle of the *Whitfield* case does not answer vexing questions of remedies, but it clears the underbrush and suggests a direction. I think it clear, once we have freed ourselves of *Whitfield* thinking, that any remedy must be based on the principle of promotion from within. This principle will require the employer, to the maximum extent possible, to promote his incumbent Negro employees before he hires from the outside. This principle is consistent with general principles of labor relations which favor incumbents over strangers to the employment relation.[63] This principle will cut off the employer from his former access to the white labor market for white jobs until he has promoted his Negro employees into those jobs. For this principle to operate, the remedy must (1) allow Negroes to compete presently with whites for jobs at any point in the previously white unit where their seniority and ability, with training, can carry them, and (2) allow Negroes to carry

---

[63] See NLRB v. Babcock & Wilcox Co., 351 U.S. 105 (1956) and text, *supra*, at note 52.

with them their Negro-unit seniority when they enter the white line. Thus, in the event of layoff, they will be the first out only if their Negro-unit seniority plus their white-unit seniority is less than the white-unit seniority of the whites. Otherwise, they will not be the first out. These points are necessary if the Negro employee is to have a meaningful opportunity to advance, as distinct from a purely formal opportunity.

C. Rightful Place

A perceptive note in the *Harvard Law Review* in 1967 [64] discussed three possible alternative remedies: (1) "freedom now," (2) "rightful place," and (3) "follow the white man." After rejecting the "freedom now" solution in which Negroes would bump white employees to assume their proper position in seniority lines, and the "follow the white man" theory, which would "grandfather in" all whites ahead of all Negroes, the Harvard note comes down for "rightful place" arrived at as rapidly as future vacancies permit. This view has the benefit of sloughing off apparent extreme positions and sitting comfortably in the middle.

The three views of the Harvard note are inadequate today. In the early years of the administration of Title VII, these three views, expressed less elegantly than in the Harvard note, were often expounded by various interests. But these views were expounded against a background of pre-July 2, 1965, facts. It might have been appropriate to say that a Negro employee could not displace a white employee who assumed his position prior to the effective date of Title VII and that the Negro should, as rapidly as possible after July 2, 1965, assume his rightful place. But what of discriminatory promotion actions which took place *after* the effective date of Title VII? As to those actions, taken in the last three years, there must be added a fourth dimension—that of *present illegality*. It seems to me that, subject to the limitations periods in Title VII, no promotion action taken after July 2, 1965, in furtherance of a discriminatory promotion system, can be allowed to stand without remedy.[65] The precise remedy, injunction, damages, or other

---

[64] 80 HARV. L. REV. 1260 (1967).

[65] This limitation period requires that a charge be filed within ninety days after an act of discrimination. However, it is now clear that a charge by an individual

relief, will be discussed later. The point here is that as to post-July 2, 1965, promotion actions which discriminated against Negro employees, there is present illegality which requires a present remedy. This feature of the operation of the seniority system was not the subject of the Harvard note, nor has it yet been noted in race discrimination decisions. It has, however, been noted in a sex-seniority case, *Bowe v. Colgate-Palmolive Co.*,[66] in which the district court awarded money damages for illegal operation of the seniority system between the limitations period specified in the Act and the date at which the court concluded that the discrimination had ended.

Rightful place remedies which include remedies for the effects of post-July 2, 1965, discrimination seem appropriate standards under Title VII.

The remedy on the promotion side is that framed by Judge Butzner in the *Philip Morris* case;[67] it is substantially the remedy recommended by the Commission in numerous cases, and occasionally adopted; it is analogous to a remedy adopted by the court in the *Crown Zellerbach* case.[68] It has taken nearly three years of negotiating to arrive at this remedy; but I find it difficult to conceive of any lesser remedy meeting the standards of present effective relief. I think that this may entail a rather extensive reworking of many seniority systems to shake out the discrimination which has been built in over the years. The remedy does not involve bumping of whites by Negroes in the first instance, but it does require the insertion of senior Negroes in previously white lines ahead of the junior whites who were there first. This may lead to a

---

may be the foundation for a class action on behalf of all similarly situated employees, and that this will include all Negro employees adversely affected by a seniority system. Oatis v. Crown Zellerbach Corp., 58 Lab. Cas. ¶9140 (5th Cir. 1968); Jenkins v. United Gas Corp., 58 Lab. Cas. ¶9154 (5th Cir. 1968). Thus it would appear that, at the least, Negro employees would be entitled to relief reaching back ninety days prior to the filing of a charge with EEOC concerning the operation of their seniority system. These limitations do not apply to the Attorney General, who may sue under §707 of the act. Thus relief in a 707 suit may relate back to July 2, 1965, the effective date of the act. For some purposes relating to relief, however, the courts may wish to utilize the time limit in §706, with respect to §707 proceedings. Since many §707 proceedings are initiated after the EEOC process has been unsuccessfully invoked by private parties, the date of filing with EEOC may be considered relevant by the court in determining the scope of the remedy under a §707 suit.

[66] 416 F.2d 711 (7th Cir. 1969).
[67] Quarles v. Philip Morris, 279 F. Supp. 505 (E.D. Va. 1968).
[68] Local 189, Paper Makers v. United States, 416 F.2d 980. (5th Cir. 1969).

second-generation bumping of junior whites in the event of subsequent layoffs. (I will deal with that question separately.)

The adoption of the principle of promotion from within impliedly rejects the concept of freedom now, of initial displacement or bumping of the white employees by more senior Negroes. This "no bumping" rule can be justified with respect to promotion actions in favor of white employees taken before July 2, 1965, on the grounds that, despite the illegality of the seniority system under *Steele*, it can be said that no one anticipated that the jobs of these whites would be jeopardized, and that the price of labor support for the passage of the statute was at least this no bumping rule.

D. *Damages for Post-July 2, 1965, Delay in Promotion*

But the same considerations do not hold with respect to discrimination occurring after the effective date of Title VII. In those cases, the illegality of the system having been established, the possible remedies include (1) immediate access of Negroes to jobs from which they were denied access *after July 2, 1965*, by the operation of a discriminatory seniority system, (2) back pay consisting of the difference between actual earnings and what they would have earned if they had had the jobs, or (3) a lump-sum award plus a continuing payment reflecting past and current losses until vacancies develop.

In short, once post-July 2, 1965, discrimination is established, the plaintiff and members of his class are entitled to an immediate remedy. This remedy may or may not be that of specific performance of the statutory obligation. It would be consistent with the no bumping philosophy of Title VII to provide for money damages in lieu of immediate promotions, which would continue to accrue until the promotional opportunities became available. I believe this distinction between pre- and post-July 2, 1965, discrimination is crucial. If the rights of miniorities after July 2, 1965, are formally recognized, then there will be a major incentive for both labor and management to promptly resolve these seniority issues. If the rights under Title VII are not treated as present, there will be less pressure for resolution and the realistic possibility of a long-drawn-out period before enforcement of the statutory obligations. The kind of disaster which resulted from the adoption of the "all deliberate speed" formula in the field of school desegregation[69] should not be repeated. While in the field of constitutional law there may have been some justification for such doctrine, there is none in the field of enforcement of statutory obligations such as those imposed under Title VII. It is true that both legislative and administrative moratoriums have been utilized from time to time to provide for adjustment by the regulated parties to their new legal obligations. But we have been through the moratorium period. The Truman Committee of 1947 recommended that labor and management be given a year's grace to adjust to the new statutory obligations not to discriminate, which the committee recommended at that time.[70] This moratorium suggestion was in fact adopted by Congress in 1964, delaying the effective date of the law to 1965.[71] It is too late now for the cry of "I didn't know it was illegal" to carry weight in the law.

The "no bumping" rule can be applied in this situation by providing for money damages as part of a remedy which includes a revision of seniority rights and provides for promotion of Negroes as vacancies develop in previously white jobs.

The allocation of the costs of this remedy would rest in the discretion of the court. In the absence of other specific considerations, it would seem equitable for the employer to bear the costs of this remedy, keeping in mind that the white employees are giving up some promotional rights.[72] The injection of the damage issue into the seniority

---

[69] Green v. County School Board, 391 U.S. 430 (1968); Raney v. Board of Education, 391 U.S. 443 (1968); Monroe v. Board of Commissioners, 391 U.S. 450 (1968).

[70] PRESIDENT'S COMMITTEE ON CIVIL RIGHTS, TO SECURE THESE RIGHTS, 167 (1947).

[71] See §716(a).

[72] On the problem of allocation of financial responsibility, see Vaca v. Sipes, 386 U.S. 171 (1967); Local 60, Carpenters v. NLRB, 365 U.S. 651 (1961). This is not a problem to be resolved by some mechanical process of characterizing both unions and employers as "wrongdoers" and then splitting the financial responsibility equally between them for want of a more exact method of measurement. To do this would be to overpenalize the union. For the monetary remedy would be but part of a systematic revision of seniority which would require white employees, normally the majority in the union, to give up certain expectations under the seniority system. If, in addition to this, they must pay for the financial obligation of the union in the damage remedy, they are being subjected to a very heavy burden. It would seem, in the absence of special considerations, appropriate to impose most or all of the financial responsibility on the employer, since the white employees will bear the costs of lost opportunities. For an analogous differential remedy in a different historical context, see 4, HOLDSWORTH, HISTORY OF ENGLISH

situation provides that measure of flexibility which, I believe, makes these difficult problems solvable. The damage remedy allows the white employee to retain his preferred position, but to pay the Negro for his losses while he waits for a vacancy. It thus reduces the friction between white and black employee, and between civil rights and labor movement interests. It introduces the element of practical responsibility of the employer for the discrimination in employment practices, which has heretofore been lacking.[73] The issues are thus focused differently, and the conflict is no longer solely between whites and blacks. Requiring the employer to share the costs of the remedy for discrimination makes it possible to both give present protection to the victim of discrimination and to honor the initial "no bumping" principle.

Once this is realized, then a financial solution may also be useful in dealing with second-generation bumping. Under our proposed remedy, once a Negro employee has acquired a position in the white line, he may use his combined seniority for the purpose of further promotion and protection against layoffs. This means, in the event of subsequent layoffs, that junior whites will be displaced. May they assert priority over Negroes in the Negro line? In short, may they bump down?

I think it clear that they are not entitled to displace Negroes senior to them in terms of plant seniority. This would simply be shifting the cost of ending discrimination from one group of Negroes to another, and giving the whites superseniority in Negro jobs. Then may the whites displace in Negro jobs Negroes who are junior to them in terms of plant seniority? I think here the answer is less clear, but it is probably no, because this would have the effect of making the junior Negroes pay for creating equality of opportunity for senior Negroes. Therefore the white employees displaced in second-generation bumps may fall behind the incumbent Negro employees. However this problem is resolved, either the junior Negro or junior white employees will lose their position. Either way, this loss falls where it does because of the effort to remedy discrimination. It is appropriate to devise some way to make the employer share in this burden, for example by maintaining the income of employees by these bumps, using the same red circle system in

---

LAW, ch. 2, explaining and justifying differential treatment of breaches of employment contracts by employers and workers.

[73] The employer's legal responsibility was spelled out in Steele v. Louisville & N. Ry., 323 U.S. 192 at 203–04 (1944). See Blumrosen, *supra*, note 49 at 1469–70.

which Negro incomes should be maintained on opening transfer rights into white lines. Placing the entire burden on the white employee seems no more equitable than placing it on the junior Negro.

Does the introducion of the damage remedy, the conventional "legal remedy," require a jury trial and thereby defeat the entire process? In sensitive areas of social legislation, one juror out of sympathy with the program can render it ineffective in the particular case. If the jury trial right is extended to Title VII matters because complete relief, including damages, is to be afforded, then Congress must create an administrative hearing mechanism when it wishes to implement the legislation without jury trial.

It would be unfortunate for the nation if the Supreme Court deprived Congress of the opportunity to use the judicial process to enforce social legislation. The administrative process, as we have learned over the last generation, is not necessarily the savior of mankind.[74] Congress *should* be able to value the strengths of the judicial process more highly than its weaknesses and to utilize the courts rather than create another bureaucracy. Yet the effect of a requirement of jury trial in a Title VII matter would be to foreclose this option. While the question is not free from doubt from the perspective of the precedents, I submit that there is no jury trial right under Title VII, even if the relief sought includes monetary compensation. The matter of compensation is simply part of a larger remedial program to eliminate systematic discrimination within the traditional broad framework of equitable discretion.[75]

---

[74] See Jaffe, *James Landis and the Administrative Process*, 78 HARV. L. REV. 319–28 (1964).

[75] See Johnson v. Georgia Highway Express, Inc. 417 F.2d 1122 (5th Cir. 1969). No congressional intention to permit jury trial under Title VII can be discerned in the legislative history. In moving toward the present structure of Title VII, Congress discarded the administrative agency approach in favor of judicial proceedings, but not with respect to the jury issue. A provision for the appointment of masters was initially inserted. Representatives Poff and Cramer, for the minority, spoke clearly to this issue in their objection. The employer, they said, would have to prove his innocence and, "in the process of attempting to do so, he will enjoy no right of trial by jury." (LEGISLATIVE HISTORY 2110). The provision for a special master was later eliminated. The history clearly reflects an emphasis on specific relief through the injunctive power, but does not support the concept of jury trial. The short statute of limitations means that the damage remedy could not be a major aspect of court relief. The express provision for jury trial with respect to contempt proceedings, set forth in Title XI, stands as evidence that no intent exists to recognize jury trial under Title VII.

The expansion of the jury-trial right and the consequent contraction of the doctrine that equity may award damages incident to the granting of injunctive

E. *Training Programs—The Ability Factor*

We have thus far discussed the "length of service" component of seniority systems. But few seniority systems overtly operate on the basis of length of service alone. There is usually a component of skill or ability or some other term which relates to the capability of the individual to learn or perform the job to which his length of service would presumptively entitle him. The exact relationship between length of service and ability is dependent on the collective bargaining agreement in particular cases. Whatever that relationship is, many minority employees will be at a disadvantage compared to white employees in the measurement of ability because of patterns of discrimination either in employment or in education. If experience is used as a component for measuring skill or ability, then blacks will lose out to whites because only whites could have gained such experience in the time of overt discrimination, in which blacks were excluded from white jobs. If educational requirements for the job exceed the requirements under which blacks were hired, to impose these requirements at the time when discrimination is abolished perpetuates the restriction of minorities to lower jobs. These are but two illustrations of the difficulties which are encountered in administering the ability factor of seniority. I think the remedies here are threefold: (1) In comparing the ability factor, between whites and blacks, it is discriminatory to "count" experience gained when only whites could gain it. (2) Where at all possible, in remedying discrimination in seniority, carefully supervised probationary training periods

---

relief without jury trial (disparagingly called the "clean up" doctrine) are expounded in Beacon Theatres, Inc. v. Westover, 359 U.S. 500 (1959) and Dairy Queen, Inc. v. Wood, 369 U.S. 469 (1962), *discussed in* 2(B) BARRON & HOLTZOFF, FEDERAL PRACTICE AND PROCEDURE §871 (Wright, ed.). This doctrine of jury-trial right has not been extended to the administration of such social legislation as is now presently administered by the federal courts. The courts have rejected the jury-trial right argument under the Landrum-Griffin Act, McCraw v. United Ass'n of Journeymen, 341 F.2d 705 (6th Cir. 1965), *but see* Simmons v. Avisco Local 713, 350 F.2d 1012 (4th Cir. 1965); and, more importantly in point, under the Fair Labor Standards Act, Wirtz v. Jones, 340 U.S. 901 (5th Cir. 1965); Sullivan v. Wirtz, 359 F.2d 426 (5th Cir. 1966) *cert. den.* on this issue, 385 U.S. 852. The FLSA cases are closely in point because the statute has been interpreted to make possible both prospective relief by way of injunction and retroactive compensation. See note, 37 U. OF CHI. L. REV. 167 (1969).

should be provided for minorities who are entitled to upgrading by length of service. (3) The employer should be required to make upgrading training generally available to minority group employees so that when the time comes for them to exercise their newly acquired rights to promotion, they will be equipped to do so.

The employer should bear the cost of training Negroes to the point where they have the requisite ability to exercise their Title VII seniority, although governmental cost-sharing programs may be availabile to him. In many cases, Negro employees have had neither on-the-job training nor formal educational experiences to equip them to handle the jobs which their Title VII seniority would otherwise entitle them. The entire processes of Title VII can become a mockery if the employer is simply allowed to certify that all or most of his Negro employees do not have the requisite ability without giving them opportunities to develop that ability which are the practical equivalent of the training and familiarizing opportunities which were in fact given to the white employees.

The requirement for provision of training opportunities provides a point of parallelism between the antidiscrimination policy and the national manpower policy, which tries, through a variety of programs, to upgrade the national manpower skills.[76] The integration of a remedy for discrimination with various manpower training programs is a major objective of the EEOC. It was only occasionally achieved. There are two anecdotes, pointing in opposite directions. In one success story, a basic metals fabrication plant in Birmingham with plantwide seniority adopted a MDTA (Manpower Development and Training Act) training program to equip Negroes for formerly all-white jobs. Within a year, significant transfers to these jobs had been accomplished.

In the other direction, a chemical processing firm tried, with the assistance of the EEOC, for one full year, to secure government funding of a basic education program to assist workers in learning reading and writing skills. The efforts floundered in the morass of the various bureaucracies involved. I told the story in detail to a high administration official whose agency was involved. He sounded as if he had heard it many times before as he said, "Oh, tell the company they should pay for it themselves, they will never get through the bureaucratic maze."

---

[76] See Blumrosen, ch. 9 *infra.*

Chrysler Corporation has recently taken the view that they will do just that.[77]

In any event, in the formulation of a remedy for discriminatory seniority lines, the existence of these manpower programs means that the court may give the respondent employer his choice of developing his own program, or, failing that, may order the employer to enter into a MDTA-type program with the appropriate unit of the federal government, which will assure that the Negro employees have the practical equivalent of training and experience provided the white employees. The cost may be borne either by the employer or by both the employer and the government. If these programs did not exist, the task of designing and supervising them would tax the time and ingenuity of the most able federal judge. But with their existence, he can simply order the employer to participate, and rely on the bureaucracy to labor through the details.

F. *The Equal Opportunity Fund*

Many of these proposals will entail significant costs. If Negro employees can bump whites at any point, then the whites will take a cut in pay. If Negro employees cannot bump whites, then the Negro employees will be paid less than they are entitled to. If, in a layoff situation, white employees cannot bump down into previously Negro jobs, they will lose employment status. If, on the other hand, they can, the junior Negro employees will pay for the promotional opportunities of senior Negroes by being laid off. Thus far, this has been the nature of most discussions of the seniority problem. It has been assumed that Negro and white employees were pitted against each other for a few jobs, and that the loser in the struggle would have to bear the costs of his loss. The employer has been viewed as a sort of innocent bystander. This analysis is incorrect. No discrimination seniority system could operate

---

[77] The Washington Post, Sunday, Dec. 24, 1967, at A3:

Detroit, Dec. 23—Chrysler Corp. doesn't want any more federal money to train automobile mechanics as part of the war on poverty.

Company officials, who said they were unhappy with government red tape, are ending their joint program with the Labor Department. They said the apprenticeship program has been a success despite federal regulations but are convinced they can do the job better alone.

without employer instigation, or active approval. There is no reason to allow the employer to avoid facing his share of the responsibility for the correction of a discriminatory system which he helped to engender.[78] Thus the availability of money damages to assist that person, either Negro or white, who has suffered as a result of the adjustment of the seniority system to meet the new demands of the present era, is rooted in the shared responsibility of the employer for the initial discrimination. However, there will be difficulties in computing exact sums which might be due to a given employee under a corrected system. This involves extensive guesswork and virtually requires a computer simulation of what "might have been" to determine who is entitled to what position. To ease this difficult mechanical burden, I suggest that the three parties—labor, management, the civil rights interest representative—plus the government, develop a special fund to deal with problems of displacement of workers and loss of earnings arising out of the need to meet the current demands of social justice. This fund, properly payable by the employer as its share of the costs of readjustment, would be comparable to the automation funds developed to defray a wide variety of costs to workers arising from the introduction of automated equipment.[79] The technological changes of automation generated this idea of a fund to defray the human costs of technological change. The impact of a change in legal and social thinking about discrimination is as significant as the impact of technological change. Devices which have proved their worth in one context of change may be appropriate in others. The challenge of developing such a fund may well demonstrate whether collective bargaining has retained sufficient creativity to cope in a meaningful way with contemporary problems.[80]

---

[78] See Doerringer, *Promotion Systems and Equal Employment Opportunity,* in Industrial Relations Research Ass'n, PROC. OF THE 19TH ANN. WINTER MEETING 278 (1966). The damage remedy under the *Steele* doctrine of fair representation is discussed in Central of Georgia Ry. v. Jones, 229 F.2d 648 (5th Cir. 1956) *cert. denied,* 352 U.S. 848 (1956); Richardson v. Texas & N.O. R.R., 242 F.2d 230 (5th Cir. 1957).

[79] See KENNEDY, AUTOMATION FUNDS AND DISPLACED WORKERS (1962); Weber, "Collective Bargaining and the Challenge of Technological Change," in INDUSTRIAL RELATIONS, CHALLENGES AND RESPONSES (Crispo ed., 1966); Kossoris, *1966 West Coast Longshore Negotiations,* 89 MO. LAB. REV. 1067 (1966); see Volkswagenwerk v. Federal Maritime Commision, 390 U.S. 261 (1968) for a sidelight on the West Coast longshore agreement.

[80] See HENDERSON, HINTZ, JARRETT, MARBUT & WHITE, CREATIVE COLLECTIVE BARGAINING, ch. 2, 3, 6 (Healy ed. 1965); WIRTZ, LABOR AND THE PUBLIC INTEREST 37–57 (1964).

The equal opportunity fund could bear the costs of equalizing wages where that was required, of maintaining wages in the event of layoffs, and of other costs associated with the operation of a nondiscriminatory system. It could also bear the back-pay liability of the employer. Such funds could come into being through conciliation or, I suspect more likely, through a court ordering the defendant to either establish such a fund or suffer the calculation of individual claims of all of his minority employees from the date of post-July 2, 1965, discrimination until they obtained their rightful place in the seniority system.[81]

It is true that the automation funds were developed to provide a sharing of income which resulted from automation. Labor and management anticipated a cost saving from which such funds could be created. In the seniority discrimination case, this factor is absent. However, the risk, or the actuality, of a significant damage award may provide a substitute incentive for the possibility of gain through automation which

---

[81] Justice Brennan, in dealing with a comparable problem of complexity in determining the appropriate reduction in union dues for member who objects to political expenditures, said, in Brotherhood of Ry. & S.S. Clerks v. Allen, 373 U.S. 113, (1963):

While adhering to the principles governing remedy which we announced in Street, see 367 U.S., at 771–775, we think it appropriate to suggest, in addition, a practical decree to which each respondent proving his right to relief would be entitled. Such a decree would order (1) the refund to him of a portion of the exacted funds in the same proportion that union political expenditures bear to total union expenditures, and (2) a reduction of future such exactions from him by the same proportion. We recognize that practical difficulties may attend a decree reducing an employee's obligations under the union-shop agreement by a fixed proportion, since the proportion of the union budget devoted to political activities may not be constant. The difficulties in judicially administered relief, although not insurmountable (a decree once entered would of course be modifiable upon a showing of changed circumstances), should, we think, encourage petitioner unions to consider the adoption by their membership of some voluntary plan by which dissenters would be afforded an internal union remedy. There is precedent for such a plan. If a union agreed upon a formula for ascertaining the proportion of political expenditures in its budget, and made available a simple procedure for allowing dissenters to be excused from having to pay this proportion of moneys due from them under the union-shop agreement, prolonged and expensive litigation might well be averted. The instant action, for example, has been before the courts for ten years and has not yet run its course. It is a lesson of our national history of industrial relations that resort to litigation to settle the rights of labor organizations and employees very often proves unsatisfactory. The courts will not shrink from affording what remedies they may, with due regard for the legitimate interests of all parties; but it is appropriate to remind the parties of the availability of more practical alternatives to litigation for the vindication of the rights and accommodation of interests here involved.

would motivate the parties to establish such a fund. While this would, of course, increase labor costs, two points should be made: First, discrimination in seniority systems is so widespread that I doubt that any employer would gain a competitive advantage with respect to these costs. Second, the employer would consider the costs of the equal opportunity fund as a part of his overall labor costs. In the subsequent collective bargaining on general economic issues, he will consider that he has already allocated the amount of the equal opportunity fund to his labor costs and will, to that extent, resist general wage demands. The effect of this resistance then may be to pass some part of the cost of the fund back to all of the employees in the form of lower wage increases or other benefits. But this consequence, to the extent that it takes place, is appropriate. For the union representing the employees has had a duty through the years to bargain away the features of illegal discrimination, even at a cost to the other employees.[82]

VI. A Summary of Remedies

The conclusions reached in the preceding discussion can now be summarized.

Remedies for discrimination in seniority systems should include at least four common elements:

1. In the South, or wherever there are substantial numbers of nonwhites in lower-rated jobs, the adoption of the principle of promotion from within.

2. No reduction in pay for the Negro worker transferring into a previously white line even if the starting rates in that line are lower than the rate the Negro had in his line. This principle, is commonly known in industrial relations as "red circling" of rates of transferred employees. It has been adopted in several conciliation agreements, notably the Newport News Agreement.[83] It assumes that the top rate in the white line is higher than the Negroes prior earnings and the Negro line.

3. Training programs which are the functional equivalent of the

---

[82] Central of Georgia Ry. v. Jones, 229 F.2d 648 (5th Cir. 1956), *cert. denied*, 352 U.S. 848 (1956).

[83] See ch. 9 *infra*.

experience which the white employees have had, in order to equip the Negro employees for the likely vacancies in the previously white line. The details of the training programs may be worked out with MDTA officials.

4. There shall be no increase in qualification required for the Negro employees over those required for whites. All qualifications must meet nondiscriminatory standards.

In addition, the following remedies seem appropriate to the problems presented by the various types of seniority:

1. Dead-End Jobs—These jobs must be associated with promotional opportunities which are the functional equivalent of those available to white employees of similar pay and qualifications. This will mean allowing holders of these jobs to bid into certain other seniority units, such as departments and lines of progression, which will have to be identified on a case-by-case basis. The employee should carry with him his accumulated seniority for purposes of both further promotion in the line and for purposes of layoff.

2. Job or Occupational Seniority—This system is at war with Title VII. The total unit seniority of Negro employees should entitle them to promote to any vacancy anywhere on the line of jobs, regardless of whether they were the most senior man on the next lower job, and to carry their Negro seniority with them into the job. I think this will mean the abandonment of the pure principle of job or occupational seniority for the time being in those establishments with a historic pattern of discrimination.

3. Line of Progression Seniority—The remedy here is twofold:

   a) Previously segregated lines must be merged on the principle that the Negro employees should have the equivalent promotional opportunities available to white employees hired during the period of discrimination. This is where the concept of functional relationship may be relevant. Merging can be a difficult problem, requiring perhaps the assistance of a conciliator to suggest particular arrangements and full consultation with all parties.

   b) In the merged line, the Negro employee takes with him his Negro-line seniority plus any acquired in the white line for purposes of further promotion or protection against layoffs. The question of whether he reserves bump-back rights to his Negro job or the question of whether the displaced white employee can bump a Negro employee from a Negro job remains unclear. My inclination is in the direction of not allowing the displacement of the junior Negro employees, but rather allowing the whites to come in at the bottom of the Negro line, with some compensation paid them for the loss of income as a result of the change in situation. Alternatively, the parties may wish to provide income protection for Negroes who are displaced by whites who are, in turn, displaced by Negroes. There is no magic in either of these solutions. The employer contribution in the form of maintenance of income payments means that he must share the cost of a remedy along with the white employees.

4. Departmental or Other General Unit Seniority—Here the same principles apply; the units to which the Negro unit is to be associated, or to which Negro employees may transfer, must be identified, and the principles of rights on transfer are the same as those stated with respect to Line of Progression seniority.

5. The Equal Opportunity Fund—As a part of the "affirmative action" required under Title VII, there should be established an equal opportunity fund to deal with the various costs associated with the elimination of discrimination in seniority, and to avoid much litigation over the details of the damage remedy which might otherwise ensue. Details should be worked out through multi-interest bargaining between labor, management, and civil rights groups with the assistance of administrative agencies.

VII. Conclusion

It is a tragic irony that the success of the labor-liberal-civil rights coalition in passing the Civil Rights Act of 1964 laid a foundation for its own destruction. But there is no doubt that the problems emerging under the statute, including the seniority problem, have contributed importantly to the breakdown of this coalition, which has achieved no significant legislation since the 1964 Civil Rights Act. Yet the liberal-labor coalition has been an important instrument in the adoption of most of the program of modern social legislation under which we live.[84]

The foregoing survey suggests that the relations between labor and the civil rights movement on the question of seniority will be difficult over the next few years, but that the problem is solvable. The key ingredient which makes a solution possible is the financial responsibility of the employer. With this additional element in mind, the parties, with the aid of the government, can proceed to promptly eliminate the vestiges of discrimination in seniority units as they affect incumbent employees.

The broader implications of the foregoing discussion are optimistic. Once some fundamental rules are laid down, the parties can play their accustomed role in collective bargaining. In that role, the union will support the claims of Negro employees and the gap between labor and civil rights interests can be closed.

I have seen this happen both under conscious leadership of a labor-lawyer statesman and under the instinctive reaction of a tough union representative who was by no means a labor liberal. In the first case, under the aggressive leadership of labor-lawyer, (now) professor of law David Feller, the International Chemical Workers (ICW) brought a Title VII suit to obtain major wage increases for employees of the Planters Manufacturing Company. In the process the union first overcame the initial resistance of EEOC to treating the union as an aggrieved party and later persuaded the federal district court of its view.[85] Postsuit use of the EEOC conciliation service produced a very significant wage increase for Negro employees as the price of settlement.

The other case involved one of my few experiences in conciliation of arranging a confrontation between charging parties and corporate officials. The union representative was present, but in the background.

After a few minutes, the management official became aggressive in his questioning of the complainants. I was about to interrupt him when the union representative came to life. His sense of duty or fitness over-

---

[84] See BAILEY, CONGRESS MAKES A LAW (1950).

[85] See International Chem. Workers v. Planters Mfg. Co., 54 Lab. Cas. ¶9025 (N.D. Miss. 1966) denying motion to dismiss for want of standing by plaintiff union, 55 Lab. Cas. ¶9046 (N.D. Miss. 1967), *dismissed by consent* after execution of conciliation agreement which increased rates of pay of Negro employees by changing job classifications.

came his dislike of the complainants, who had also filed charges against his union. His interruption provided them with experienced protection against the abrasive attitude of the managers.

I have often pondered on this experience and wondered how to galvanize this aspect of the labor movement in the seniority area. It seems that here are the roots of an accommodation which will rebuild the liberal-labor-civil rights coalition.

The tangible achievement of such accommodations is a difficult and time-consuming process. In the summer of 1968, I served as a special attorney for the Civil Rights Division of its Department of Justice, advising on employment discrimination. In the process, I went to Birmingham in connection with the trial of *United States v. H. K. Porter & United Steel Workers*, which involved seniority. I found myself on an elevator with an important person in the steel workers. He told me the government should accept an unacceptable settlement offer. I responded by avoiding the question.

"Look," I said, "suppose you lose the case. Won't you turn to management to make them share the cost of the remedy? Management has let labor and civil rights people fight each other. I think that is the wrong position for you to be in."

I had repeated this theme over the last three years, to this same man, and to others. This time I thought his silence was more thoughtful. It made timely this formal presentation of this concept.

The introduction of employer financial responsibility into the picture of remedies for discriminatory seniority systems provides that measure of flexibility which will enable solutions with reduction of tensions between white and black, and between labor and the civil rights movement. Movement in this direction will also spur the prompt adjustment of these seniority disputes to minimize the costs of adjustments.

And thus I remain optimistic that we can reach an adequate solution to the seniority dilemma. To achieve this, however, we need the clear articulation of the law on the seniority issues. Once we have this articulation, the parties in industrial relations can sit down and arrive at practical steps to implement them.

An episode in the paper industry makes this point clearly. The paper industry seniority system has been the target of the federal government antidiscrimination program at least since 1963. Then the

PCEEO tried its hand at ending discrimination through its administration of the government contracts obligation. Some token mergers of seniority lines were achieved. When Title VII was passed, EEOC Chairman Roosevelt tried personal intervention in the dispute involving Crown Zellerbach in Bogalusa, and achieved some change in the position of Negro employees.[86] A group of Title VII proceedings were instituted, both by individuals and by the government. Then the OFCC threatened to and, for a time, did suspend contracting by the government with Crown. Crown secured an injunction against this kind of activity,[87] but then agreed to make the changes OFCC sought. The union threatened to strike, and the government secured an injunction against the strike.[88] Finally, the Title VII cases were heard and decided in a broad-based decision which invalidated job seniority and required a transfer to a system of mill (plant) seniority.[89]

During all this time, International Paper had been another target, though a less active one, of governmental action. After watching the above-described events, and after several EEOC and OFCC efforts, International Paper and the unions negotiated changes in the seniority system at all their southern facilities to conform to the requirements of the *Crown* decision.[90] This action achieved, with little government effort, a result which otherwise might have taken years. This demonstrates the radiating effect of broadly and soundly written judicial decisions, which can provide a basis for achieving practical results without protracted proceedings. Labor relations personnel are sharply attuned to developments in the legal system, and are quick to react to these developments. There are effective communications media in the field which rapidly transmit information to cadres of personnel officers, union officials, labor relations advisors, and attorneys. This law transmission system can speed the process of ending discrimination if the decisions are written in a comprehensive manner.[91]

---

[86] See EEOC News Release, in CCH EMPL. PRACTICES, ¶8032 (Dec. 30, 1965).

[87] Crown Zellerbach Corp. v. Wirtz, 281 F. Supp. 337 (D.D.C. 1968).

[88] Local 189, United Paper Makers v. United States, 416 F.2d 980 (5th Cir. 1969).

[89] *Id.*, Hicks v. Crown Zellerbach Corp., 58 Lab. Cas. ¶9145 (E.D. La. 1968).

[90] Dep't of Labor, News Release, Aug. 5, 1968, CCH EMPL. PRACTICES, §8004 (1968).

[91] This radiating effect is already noticeable under the Civil Rights Act of 1964. In Newman v. Piggie Park Enterprises, Inc., 390 U.S. 400, 402, the Supreme Court

If this is done, the frictions between labor, management, and civil rights interests may be displaced, or at least lessened, by the emphasis on the search for practical solutions in particular cases.

---

held that a prevailing plaintiff in a case involving discrimination in public accommodations under Title II of the act would normally be entitled to attorney fees. In its short decision, the Court stated:

> If he [plaintiff] obtains an injunction, he does so not for himself alone but also as a "private attorney general" vindicating a policy that Congress considered of the highest priority. . . . Congress therefore enacted the provision for counsel fees. . . . to encourage individuals injured by racial discrimination to seek judicial relief under Title II.

The breadth of this conception, that the public interest is involved in and to be vindicated in private proceedings under the Civil Rights Act of 1964, has already spilled over into Title VII cases, particularly with respect to procedural matters. See the broad opinion in Jenkins v. United Gas Co., 400 F.2d 28 (5th Cir. 1968).

For a fuller description of the "law transmission system" which notes the "private attorney general" conception in the labor field, see ch. 1 *infra*. On the general problems of communication and implementation of legal norms, see Laswell, *Toward Continuing Appraisal of the Impact of Law on Society*, HABER AND COHEN, ed's, THE LAW SCHOOL OF TOMORROW (1968).

6   The Duty of Fair Recruitment Under
the Civil Rights Act of 1964

Discrimination in recruitment and hiring is the chief measurable evil against which the modern law of employment discrimination is directed. The crucial social fact giving rise to this legislation is that Negro unemployment rates have been at least double those of whites in nearly every significant category for most of the last quarter century. The Truman Committee on Civil Rights cited this multiple unemployment rate as a basic reason for a federal program to end job discrimination in 1947. Since then, every study, every legislative proposal has underscored the higher unemployment rates for minorities. This pattern remains.[1] Unless it is broken, all other efforts at regulation of discrimination and at manpower planning are bound to fail. The sense of relative deprivation and injustice will persist, and the dimensions of the social problem which confronts us will continue to expand.

The administrative process has failed in this field because it has been unable to make a significant change in the relative unemployment rate. This conclusion applies to federal programs such as the contracts compliance program dealing with government contractors, the Equal Employment Opportunity Commission, and various manpower planning programs. It applies as well to state and local fair employment practice commissions. The law will be deemed successful only when the unemployment rate for minorities comes more into line with the unemployment rates of the rest of the community. The elimination of minority differential in unemployment rates will be a true signal that equal employment opportunity does in fact exist. Moreover, a host of other

---

[1] For a selection of these reports and studies over the last twenty years, see app. I this chapter.

social and cultural changes will result if true equality of opportunity comes into being.

This test of success is also accepted by those who have a sociological rather than a legal perspective on the problem. The now famous *Moynihan Report* and the *President's Riot Commission Report* can both be read in support of this conclusion.[2]

I. The Question of Priorities—Program Planning

In light of these facts and of the implications of the problem, the assault on the outrageously high unemployment rate of minorities should take first priority over administrative efforts to remedy discrimination in other fields. The enforcement energies of public agencies such as the Attorney General, the Office of Federal Contract Compliance, and the Equal Employment Opportunity Commission, as well as state agencies, should focus on recruitment and hiring practices, to the extent that their resources are not committed to the processing of individual complaints.

The plight of the underemployed minority person, while tragic, may be less demanding of the limited resources of government than the plight of those totally without work. A man with a job has a toehold and can begin to fight his way up. He can file complaints with government if he faces discrimination. In some considerable numbers he has done so in recent years. A man unemployed for any significant length of time begins to become an economic outlaw, unwanted by the economic system. He finally reaches the point where he rejects the values of the economic, social, and political system because it has rejected him. Thereafter he will not seek help from the established system of laws. Therefore, self-initiated governmental activity is necessary to provide opportunities for him.

My earlier conclusion was that the complaint process is generally ineffective because of the reluctance of minorities to seek the assistance of government—a reluctance rooted deep in the culture.[3] This con-

---

[2] See RAINWATER & YANCY, THE MOYNIHAN REPORT AND THE POLITICS OF CONTROVERSY (1967); REPORT OF THE NATIONAL ADVISORY COMMISSION ON CIVIL DISORDERS (1968), reprinted in part, app. I(E) this chapter.

[3] Blumrosen, *Antidiscrimination Laws in Action in New Jersey: A Law-Sociology Study*, 19 RUTGERS L. REV. 189 (1965); see Zeitz, *Survey of Negro Attitudes To-*

clusion is now subject to a limitation. Minorities, like the rest of us, are more likely to fight to preserve tangible benefits than for intangible opportunities. They are more likely to use the complaint process to protect against loss of visible job opportunities than to gain new ones. Employed persons are more likely to use the complaint process to protest unfair treatment on the job than to protest refusals to hire in the first instance. The difficulty of proof in discriminatory recruitment cases buttresses this tendency. Those who do not trust the legal system to redress the wrongs of discrimination will, of course, not file complaints because they believe the act to be futile. But those who would rely on the legal system tend to accept burdens they believe it imposes. Thus they will not complain because they have no "evidence" of discrimination, only a suspicion, when they are turned away from a job. More basic is the fact that they cannot complain if they are unaware of the opportunity in the first instance. Thus the Negro who wishes to operate within the system lacks evidence of discrimination; the Negro who does not believe in the system will not seek its help. Where the discrimination takes the form of concealing notice of job opportunities from the minority community, there is no one who can complain, because no

---

ward Law, 19 RUTGERS L. REV. 288 (1965). This reluctance was vividly demonstrated by an exchange at the EEOC New York hearings:

> COMMISSIONER XIMENES. Mr. Rodriguez, after having been interviewed by these 30 or 40 large corporations, and after having come to the conclusion that there was something wrong even though you weren't told by the company employment manager or personnel officer that he was not hiring you because you were Puerto Rican or your surname was Rodriguez, did you do anything to try to get back at the company? Did you complain to someone? Did you write out a complaint of discrimination? Would you be able to do that sort of thing at some point?
> MR. RODRIGUEZ. No sir. I have never done it.
> COMMISSIONER XIMENES. Do you think it would be a wise idea?
> MR. RODRIGUEZ. No sir.
> COMMISSIONER XIMENES. You don't think it would be wise to complain did you say, sir?
> MR. RODRIGUEZ. That is correct, sir.
> COMMISSIONER XIMENES. Why would you say that?
> MR. RODRIGUEZ. For the simple reason that you do not know, as I stated before, why the company did not hire you, so you cannot write back to them and say, "You did not hire me because I am a Puerto Rican, because I am a Negro."

EQUAL EMPLOYMENT OPPORTUNITY COMMISSION, DISCRIMINATION IN WHITE COLLAR EMPLOYMENT 198 (1968).

Negro knows of the opportunities which are passed around within the white community.

The result is the same in all three instances. The complaint is not filed, and discriminatory hiring and recruitment systems remain unchallenged unless the government initiates the proceedings itself. Until recently, there was no effective mechanism by which this could be done, because the government simply could not identify the sources of discrimination in recruitment and hiring. The requirement that the employers subject to Title VII of the Civil Rights Act of 1964 report the racial and ethic composition of their work force has provided information to the government on the basis of which it can seek out discrimination.[4] This information, developed and organized by the Equal Employment Opportunity Commission, provides, not only insights into the problem of discrimination, but also a source of subjects for further investigation into possibly discriminatory patterns of recruitment and hiring.[5]

There are practical advantages to government-initiated proceedings with respect to recruitment and hiring systems. The problems of investigation, decisionmaking, and the development of remedies are easier to solve in recruitment and hiring cases than they are in cases of promotion and layoff. The latter involve complex individual decisions in cases which often involve a collectively bargained seniority system and always involve the subjective judgment of a supervisor. Investigation, proof, and remedial problems arise because of the unique features of each case. Recruitment and hiring practices, on the other hand, are more likely to fall into patterns which can be more readily identified, evaluated, and remedied. Thus again, given the limited resources available, the payoff appears to me to be greater in terms of man hours invested into this area.[6]

---

[4] 78 Stat. 253, 42 U.S.C. §2000(e) (1964). Hereinafter, references will be given to the section number in the official version of the statute only. The reporting requirements and their limitations are found in §709(c)-(d).

[5] Commission regulations relating to reporting requirements are found in 29 C.F.R. §§1602.7-14 (1968).

[6] Thus I believe my conclusion is compatible with the "Planning-Programming-Budgeting" approach, which attempts to rationalize government program decisionmaking. For a review of this program, see ASSOCIATION OF AMERICAN LAW SCHOOLS, REPORT OF THE COMMITTEE ON RESEARCH 65 (1967). See also Held, *PPBS Comes to Washington*, 4 PUB. INTEREST 102 (1966). Many of the concepts discussed in this chapter have been incorporated into the EEOC state-grant program under the direction of Peter Robertson.

For the above reasons, I opt for emphasis on recruitment and hiring rather than promotion and transfer. The counterargument has some attractive features. First, the injustice of a discriminatory promotion system is clear and lasts into the indefinite future, thus circumscribing opportunities for a man's entire working life. Second, the employed persons who are restricted in their promotional opportunities have demonstrated their attachment to the work ethic. There is no question of their desire to work. No charge of malingering can be brought against the incredibly patient, long-suffering, and hardworking Negro steel workers in Birmingham whose lives have been confined by the network of hiring practices and seniority rules. Third, at least some of these men will assert their interests through the filing of complaints, thus making a claim on governmental resources toward the solution of their problem. Fourth (and this argument appealed to the Riot Commission), if the underutilization of minorities were abolished, the increase in minority group income would be very substantial. Fifth, the problems of seniority and promotion have a professional appeal to lawyers that the correction of a system of recruitment and hiring cannot have. Our professional temptation will be to think and act in terms of individual cases, rather than system reform. These cases are more easily identified in the area of seniority and promotion because of the presence of individual complainants. In comparison, a recruitment system seems a nebulous quantity to bring before the bar of a federal district court.

Taking account of all these factors, I conclude that the emphasis of uncommitted government resources should be placed on recruitment and hiring. Complaints should be given priority under the federal statute, but not to the exclusion of governmental initiation of proceedings in this area. My judgment in the end is influenced by the principle of maximizing individual freedom, particularly for youth. We all walk in paths delineated by decisions made early in life, some of which relate to employment. If maximum freedom for the individual is not present when these decisions are made, some avenues of growth and choice are forever foreclosed.

This discussion is a bitter critique of the appropriation policies of federal and state legislatures. They have starved agencies which deal with employment discrimination. This has contributed to the failure of the agencies to develop programs and has stunted the growth of professionalism in this complex and difficult field. The obvious and important answer is to develop enough money and manpower to do the job. But, on the evidence of history, this answer is unlikely to be forthcoming.

II. The Procedural Context

The procedural context in which discriminatory recruitment and hiring issues are raised will include the individual action by a person refused a job. But the context may be much broader. The law may be developed in part under an orderly government-inspired program. This program will include computer analysis of employer reporting forms to identify employers whose hiring practices should be investigated. The substantive law here may emerge through several avenues:

1. Suit by an individual denied employment or access to employment, after processing his case through the EEOC;[7]
2. Suits based on EEOC commissioner charges alleging discriminatory recruitment or hiring practices;[8]
3. Class actions on behalf of minorities denied access to employment opportunities;[9]
4. Suits by the Attorney General under section 707 of the Civil Rights Act alleging that recruitment and hiring practices constitute an unlawful pattern or practice of resistance to the enjoyment of employment opportunity;[10]

---

[7] Section 706(e) provides that an aggrieved party who has pursued the EEOC processes without securing redress has thirty days from receipt from the Commission of a notice of right to sue in which to institute suit in Federal District Court. Section 706(g) authorizes the court to grant relief to the complainant and to "order such affirmative action as may be appropriate."

[8] Section 706(a) provides that a member of the EEOC may file a charge and thus initiate an investigation if he has reasonable cause to believe the statute has been violated. Section 706(e) provides that, in such a case, suit may be brought "by any person whom [sic] the charge alleges was aggrieved by the alleged unlawful employment practice." It is unclear whether the word "person" includes organizations, although both the literal wording §701(a), and a case on a related point, International Chem. Workers Union v. Planters Mfg. Co., 259 F. Supp. 365 (N.D. Miss. 1965) (standing of union to be aggrieved person), suggest that this is the proper construction.

[9] Such class actions could arise either from an individual complaint (see Hall v. Werthan Bag Corp., 251 F. Supp. 184 [M.D. Tenn. 1966]) or from a commissioner's charge, note 8 supra.

[10] Section 707(a) provides that the Attorney General may sue in federal court for appropriate relief, including an injunction, when he has reasonable cause to

5. Enforcement activity by the Office of Federal Contract Compliance implementing the antidiscrimination clause in government contracts;[11] and

6. Administrative proceedings at the state and local agency level.[12]

Thus the issues of discriminatory recruitment and hiring may be raised by individual, group, or governmentally instituted proceedings. The nature of the procedure should not influence the development and application of substantive law in this crucial field. As the Supreme Court has recognized in a cognate area, private litigation is intended to vindicate the public interest under the Civil Rights Act fully as much as the initiation of proceedings by government.[13] The variety of proce-

---

believe persons are engaged in a "pattern or practice of resistance to the full enjoyment of any of the rights secured by this title . . . [which is] of such a nature and is intended to deny the full exercise of the rights herein described. . . ." Obviously, a discriminatory recruitment and hiring pattern of the type discussed in the text would fit within the language of the statute. The text discussions of intent would also apply to §707.

[11] The Office of Federal Contract Compliance in the Department of Labor exercises the powers conferred in Executive Order No. 11246 and some other orders, through working with the individual departments and agencies who engage in government contracting. Each employer who holds a government contract is assigned, for compliance purposes, to one such agency, which is known as the "predominant interest agency" for that employer. The Department of Defense is the largest single predominant interest agency. See generally 113 Cong. Rec. 1536–40 (daily ed., Feb. 29, 1968), remarks of Representative Ryan.

[12] For a full discussion of the sweep of federal and state law as of 1965, see Sovern, Legal Restraints on Racial Discrimination in Employment (1966). I disagree with some of his conclusions; Blumrosen, Book Review, 14 U.C.L.A.L. Rev. 721 (1967). Professor Bonefield has engaged in the most intensive and detailed study of state legislation and administrative procedures. His works are well worth reading. Bonefield, *The Substance of American Fair Employment Practices Legislation I: Employers,* 61 NW. U.L. Rev. 907 (1967); *The Substance of American Fair Employment Practices Legislation II—Employment Agencies, Labor Organizations, and Others,* 62 NW. U.L. Rev. 19 (1967); *An Institutional Analysis of the Agencies Administering Fair Employment Practices Laws,* 42 N.Y.U.L. Rev. 823, 1035 (1967).

[13] In Newman v. Piggie Park Enterprises, 390 U.S. 400 (1968), the Court stated:

> . . . If he [plaintiff] obtains an injunction [under Title II of the Civil Rights Act of 1964], he does so not for himself alone but also as a "private attorney general," vindicating a policy that Congress considered of the highest priority. If successful plaintiffs were routinely forced to bear their own attorneys' fees, few aggrieved parties would be in a position to advance the public interest by invoking the injunctive powers of the federal courts. Congress therefore enacted the provision for counsel fees—not simply to penalize litigants who deliberately advance arguments they know to be untenable but, more broadly, to encourage individuals injured by racial discrimination to seek judicial relief under Title II.

dures emphasize the different interests involved in this field. There is the individual interest in employment opportunity, the group interest in employment opportunity, the group interest in freedom from class discrimination, and the social or public interest in the expansion of freedom of opportunity.[14] Each has its procedural avenue of expression in this field.

III. Identification of Discriminatory Recruitment and Hiring Practices

The Southern pattern of discrimination involves restricting Negroes and other minorities to certain menial or low-paying jobs and reserving the better jobs for whites. The basic discriminatory pattern outside the South has consisted of not recruiting or hiring Negroes at all. The resulting segregation has been nearly absolute with many employers. This segregation is the main focus of this study. The "100 companies" statistics of the EEOC are illuminating. EEOC studied the white-collar employment practices of employers based in New York City. The study demonstrates the exclusionary activities of major corporations. Of special significance is the record of those among the 100 companies who are members of Plans for Progress, a highly publicized organization of blue-chip corporations dedicated to improving minority employment opportunities. Their record was the worst of the group studied, which in turn was worse than that of all New York City employers.[15]

Many companies who have engaged in the Northern practice of exclusion of minorities have also added the Southern twist by hiring some minorities but confining them to minor jobs. This pattern of nonrecruitment of minorities is one basic element responsible for the multiple minority unemployment rate. Once the pattern is broken, the employer

---

It follows that one who succeeds in obtaining an injunction under that Title should ordinarily recover an attorney's fee unless special circumstances would render such an award unjust. . . .
Id. at 402 (footnotes omitted). These principles appear operative under Title VII as well.

[14] The group interest concept is especially useful in analyzing problems in this area. See Cowan, *Group Interests*, 44 VA. L. REV. 331 (1958); *A Symposium on Group Interests and the Law*, 13 RUTGERS L. REV. 429–602 (1959); Blumrosen, *Group Interests in Labor Law*, *id.* at 432.

[15] For the EEOC summary of its analysis of white collar employment in New York City, see app. II this chapter.

may take a real interest in improving schools and other institutions supplying the labor market. If the employer may take the labor force as he finds it, he will skim the cream and treat the question of improvement of such institutions as a matter of civic virtue. If, however, he must recruit and hire from all sectors of the labor market, he has a practical interest in improving the quality of these institutions. Self-interest occupies a higher priority in business planning than does a demonstration of civic virtue. The failure of Plans for Progress to produce expanded minority employment in the New York white-collar job market demonstrates that the approach through civil virtue can become a shield for inaction.

The law of discrimination in recruitment and hiring thus stands at the intersection of the educational system and the labor market. It may make a crucial contribution to the reduction of the unemployment differential between Negroes and whites and at the same time set in motion forces which will contribute to the practical improvement of our school systems. A few judicial decisions in this area can have a radiating effect on our society which is difficult to measure. This is one of the most profound tributes to the legal system imaginable. It imposes an extraordinary obligation on the judicial and administrative system to understand, appraise, and respond to the problem.

IV. The Language of Title VII

Sections 703(a)(1) and (2) bear on discriminatory recruitment and hiring practices. They establish that it is unlawful for an employer to "fail or refuse to hire," to "otherwise discriminate" against an individual, and to "limit, segregate or classify" employees so as to "deprive or tend to deprive" individuals of employment opportunities or otherwise "adversely affect" their status as employees because of race, color, religion, sex, or national origin.[16]

---

16 Section 703(a) states:

It shall be an unlawful employment practice for an employer—
1) to fail or refuse to hire or to discharge any individual, or otherwise to discriminate against any individual with respect to his compensation, terms, conditions, or privileges of employment, because of such individual's race, color, religion, sex or national origin; or
2) to limit, segregate, or classify his employees in any way which would deprive

Most of the state antidiscrimination laws simply use the term "refuse" to hire. Title VII uses "fail or refuse." Why the two words? Does "fail" simply cover the case of an employer who does not respond to an application by a minority group member ("Don't call us, we'll call you.")? Or does it suggest an additional dimension of statutory obligation; a dimension which encompasses a duty to reach out and provide employment opportunities? "Fail" could connote the use of restrictive recruitment systems which do not give the minority community notice and opportunity to apply for jobs, and "refuse" could connote the rejection of an applicant on grounds of his minority status. The legislative history is helpful.

While there were many debates on a variety of the issues involved in Title VII as it passed through the legislative process, and while the procedures for enforcement of the antidiscrimination obligation were changed through political bargaining and compromise, the substantive language of the bill as reported out by the Committee on Labor and Public Welfare remained virtually unchanged. The "fail or refuse" language appeared in that, as in earlier drafts.[17]

The Committee stated that its bill operated on four "basic principles" which dealt with coverage, definition of equal employment opportunity, enforcement procedures, and initiatory power of the government. Only the enforcement procedures aspect of the bill was seriously changed in the legislative process. The coverage and substantive provisions remained unchanged. Thus the Committee statement of principle is entitled to considerable weight. The Committee stated: "The bill defines equal employment opportunity in broad terms to include a wide range of incidents and facilities, and encompasses all aspects of discrimination in employment because of race, color, religion, or national origin." [18]

The distributive reading of "fail or refuse," while not conclusive, better serves the legislative intent which can be gleaned from the pre-

---

or tend to deprive any individual of employment opportunities or otherwise adversely affect his status as an employee, because of such individual's race, color, religion, sex, or national origin.

[17] S. Rep. No. 867, 88th Cong., 2d Sess. (1964). See the comparative analysis of Senate and House bills prepared under the supervision of Representative McCulloch, 110 Cong. Rec. 15453–58 (daily ed., July 6, 1964), in Bureau of National Affairs, The Civil Rights Acts of 1964, at 305 (1964).

[18] S. Rep. No. 867, 88th Cong., 2d Sess. 10 (1964).

enactment history of the statute. High minority unemployment rates were a primary reason for passage of Title VII. Both House and Senate committee reports cited the unemployment statistics and indicated that these were the fundamental grounds for the adoption of Title VII.[19] This is cogent evidence of congressional intent that the evil to be addressed starts with discriminatory recruitment.[20]

The words "fail or refuse" must be read in conjunction with the "otherwise discriminate" language in section 703(a)(1), and perhaps more importantly, they must be related to the provisions of section 703(a)(2), which make it unlawful for an employer to "limit, segregate, or classify" in such a way as to "deprive or tend to deprive" individuals of employment opportunities or otherwise "adversely affect" their status as employees because of race, color, religion, sex, or national origin.

Where an employer perpetuates a substantially all-white labor force by the use of a variety of recruitment and hiring practices, this may constitute "segregation" under section 703(a)(2) and also his "failure" to provide opportunities for hiring under section 703(a)(1). The relationship between the two provisions is as follow: If an employer has an all-white labor force to begin with, he may perpetuate that segregated force by using recruitment methods which fail to notify the minority community of job vacancies in a meaningful way and to give them a realistic opportunity to apply for employment. This is the "failure" envisioned under 703(a)(1). The result of this system of recruitment is that his labor force remains all white. This constitutes segregation of his employees. This segregation in turn has an adverse effect on employment opportunities of minorities under 703(a)(2) because they are cut off from the expanded employment and promotional opportunities as-

---

19 See app. I, B, this chapter.

20 For literalists, the definition of "fail" may be interesting. WEBSTER'S THIRD INTERNATIONAL DICTIONARY 814–15 (1968) defines it as to "miss performing [an] expected or hoped-for service" or "to leave some possible or expected action unperformed or some condition unachieved." The courts have so construed the term. United States v. Heikkinen, 240 F.2d 94 (7th Cir. 1957) involved the crime of violating a deportation order. The indictment charged the defendant with "willful failure" to depart from the country. The court said that the word "failure" connoted "an omission to perform a duty or appointed function" (*id.* at 100) and imposed an affirmative duty to act on those subject to the law. See also state statutory interpretation cases, *e.g.*, State v. Gasque, 241 S.C. 316, 321, 128 S.E.2d 154, 156 (1962) ("fail" in tax statute means "an omission or the nonperformance of something due or required to be done."); State *ex rel.* Brown v. Butler, 81 Minn. 103, 106, 83 N.W. 483, 484 (1900) ("failure" in publication of notice statute referred to the "nonperformance of a duty").

sociated with employment. As long as the employer maintains a segregrated labor force, the network of informal communication about job vacancies and other opportunities is denied to the minority groups. They themselves do not hear of or cannot tell their friends of jobs which become available; they are unable to recommend them for employment or help them over the difficulties of a new and strange situation. They are excluded from the picture altogether. This is the "adverse effect" to which the statute speaks. The results "deprive" or at least "tend to deprive" minorities of employment opportunities.

Where an employer has a segregated labor force and uses recruitment methods which perpetuate it, it is fair to assume that he is aware of the consequences of his recruitment system. All employers required to file reports with the Equal Employment Opportunity Commission *must* be aware of the consequences of their recruitment system because they are required to state these consequences in statistical terms. The EEO-1 form requires the employer to state the number of racial and ethnic minority employees and the number of each sex in each of the standard job classifications as of a certain date. The employer who fills out such a form cannot then claim lack of knowledge of the consequences of his recruitment system. In fact, employers do not claim to be insensitive to the problems of minority hiring. Most say they are aware of the problem and are taking steps which, from their point of view, are reasonable to meet it.

The conscious maintenance of the segregated labor force discriminates against minorities as a class by denying them notice and opportunity to apply for employment. The awareness of the consequences of the recruitment system establishes the intent necessary for judicial proceedings under Title VII. No subjective prejudice or negative feeling toward minorities is required under the statute. Few employers purposefully seek or desire to discriminate against minorities. Moreover, such a purpose or desire is not an element of a Title VII proceeding. Title VII is not a criminal statute requiring *mens rea*. It is regulatory social legislation designed to change conduct and eradicate discriminatory practices. Its operation does not turn on the subjective feelings of employers, unions, and other respondents. This has been clearly established under the National Labor Relations Act by the Supreme Court.[21]

---

[21] Under §8(a)(3) of the National Labor Relations Act, many cases have arisen

The point has been raised and resolved under Title II of the Civil Rights Act as follows: "The Civil Rights Act is not concerned with the subjective racial prejudices of the people affected. Instead it is directed toward discrimination against certain classes of persons when those classes are determined on the basis of race, color, religion, or national origin." [22]

V. The Duty of Fair Recruitment

Where an employer is aware that his past hiring practices, combined with his present recruitment practice, have produced and maintained a segregated labor force, he is in violation of sections 703 (a) (1) and (2) of Title VII, unless he can justify his conduct. Title VII prohibits him from closing his eyes to the consequences of his recruitment practices and from perpetuating segregation by denying minorities a meaningful opportunity to secure employment with him.

Title VII thus proscribes recruitment practices which deny minorities the notice of and opportunity to secure employment with employers who have a substantially segregated labor force. It may be useful to

---

concerning the interpretation to be given the term "intention to discriminate." In a series of cases, the Supreme Court has held that the intention under that regulatory social legislation is satisfied if the consequences were foreseeable. See NLRB v. Fleetwood Trailer Co., 389 U.S. 375 (1967); NLRB v. Great Dane Trailers, Inc., 388 U.S. 26, 33 (1967) ("'unavoidable consequences which the employer not only foresaw but which he must have intended . . . bears its own indicia of intent'"); NLRB v. Erie Resistor Corp., 373 U.S. 221 (1963); Radio Officers Union v. NLRB, 347 U.S. 17 (1954). See also Prosser, Torts §8 (3d ed. 1964); Restatement of Torts §13, comment d at 29 (1934); Restatement (second) of Torts §8(A), comments a, b at 15 (1965).

An effort was made by Senator McClellan to add the word "solely" in front of each phrase of §703 so that it would be necessary to prove that discrimination had occurred "solely" because of race, etc. Had this amendment been adopted it might have affected the intent requirement under the statute by requiring "specific intent" to discriminate on racial grounds. It was defeated. 110 Cong. Rec. 13837–38 (1964). The same proposal had been defeated earlier in the House of Representatives. Id. at 2728.

The intent required under §706(g) can be established by inference from facts. See 110 Cong. Rec. 14270 (1964) (remarks of Senator Humphrey). Senator Humphrey explained that the intent requirement in §706 "does not involve any substantive change in the title. The express requirement of intent is designed to make it wholly clear that inadvertent or accidental discrimination will not violate the title. . . ." 110 Cong. Rec. 12723–24 (1964).

[22] United States v. Gulf-State Theaters, Inc., 256 F. Supp. 549, 552 (N.D. Miss. 1966).

crystalize this reasoning by stating that Title VII imposes on employers who have a substantially segregated labor force the duty of fair recruitment.

It would be unfortunate if this shorthand expression were to become involved in those interminable arguments about misfeasance versus nonfeasance. The arguments could be made that Title VII imposes no affirmative duties, but merely assures that what an employer chooses to do, he must do in a nondiscriminatory manner. The futility of this line of argumentation should be clear to any first-year torts student.[23] The short answer is that the distinction is without substance. In fact, employers do have recruiting systems; they notify, advertise, post notices, interview applicants, and hire people. All of these things constitute activity. They are measurable and controllable. Where these activities perpetuate segregation, they are unlawful under Title VII. The duty of fair recruitment is simply a way of expressing the legal conclusion that a recruitment system utilized *in action* by the employer is unlawful if its consequence is the denial of employment opportunity to minorities and the segregation of the labor force.

The duty of fair recruitment as thus defined is composed of three elements: (1) the requirement that an employer who has a substantially segregated labor force recruit in a manner affording realistic notice of job vacancies and opportunity to apply for them to the minority community; (2) the requirement that the qualifications for hiring used by the employer do not exclude minorities unfairly and without justification; and (3) the requirement of fair and prompt processing of minority applicants. A carefully worked out system of recruitment along with a realistic set of qualifications can be skewed if it is not administered sensitively and fairly.

VI. Discriminatory Recruitment Systems

A. *"Whites Only" Recruiting through Obvious Devices*

An employer who advertises that he will hire "whites only" obviously violates the law; similarly an employer who says: "I will recruit

---

[23] The difficulties inherent in the misfeasance-nonfeasance distinction can usually be solved by manipulating the manner of stating the situation. See PROSSER, TORTS §54 (3d ed. 1964).

only from a school which has white students," violates the law. An employer who employs only through an agency which he knows will send him whites only violates the law. An employer who limits the residential area of his employees so that only whites may be employed violates the law. In all of these cases, the employer has set up the conditions for his recruitment in such a way to exclude the possibility that he will consider employment of minority persons.

The same principle applies to the use of any pool of prospective employees as the source for recruiting which to the knowledge of the employer contains no or very few minorities. Putting aside problems of recruitment through certain unions, particularly in the construction trades, the principle is simple and relatively easy to apply. The restriction of the pool of possible applicants to exclude minorities is itself discriminatory.

B. *Word-of-Mouth Referrals*

What of the most common recruiting system of them all, which is no formal system at all? Word-of-mouth recruiting, whereby one employee tells a friend about the job and, when he applies, vouches for him to the boss, is probably the most common recruitment device in the nation.[24] The discriminatory, or rather, exclusionary, operation of this system is easy to visualize. A machine shop has a total of 250 white employees. The average annual turnover rate of the establishment is approximately 10 percent, or say 25 employees. The bulk of the remaining employees are relatively satisfied with their jobs and are willing to say so to their friends in the trade or their neighbors. If a vacancy develops, the employees become aware of the opening through highly informal information systems. Each of them becomes a potential recruiter in his own circle of friends and acquaintances. Since, in most places, these circles of friendship and residence are segregated by race, the employees will refer whites because they know them or know of them. But it is unlikely that the employees will know a Negro lathe operator whose former boss just went into bankruptcy, or the Negro

---

[24] WAYNE STATE UNIVERSITY, INSTITUTE OF LABOR AND INDUSTRIES RELATIONS, PATTERNS OF DISCRIMINATION IN EMPLOYMENT 223 (1966) suggests that personal referrals were the primary source of recruitment used to fill 40% of blue-collar, 32% of white-collar, and 14% of managerial positions.

truck driver who has just been discharged from military service, or the Puerto Rican youngster working at the corner gas station who has mechanical ability. Hence, these people are simply not included in the pool of possible applicants. The segregated social and residential patterns in the nation make it unlikely that minorities will be included in the "web of information" which flows around opportunities in the white society.

Thus the employer who starts off with a substantially all-white labor force and relies on the system of employee referral will end up with a segregated labor force, all with little or no effort on his part. In addition, this system will generate applicants whom existing employees are willing to recommend. The employees thus not only recruit, but screen as well before they will go out on a limb to the extent of recommending men for employment. For they know that the recommendation means that their judgments are involved in the initial success of the applicants. A more efficient and less expensive and cumbersome system would be hard to devise. Some employers promote the process through a system of bonuses.

As long as the work force is largely or exclusively white, the system discriminates because of patterns of residential and social segregation. But the word-of-mouth system can also perform the function of integrating the work force, once a sufficient number of minority employees begin to refer their friends and acquaintances along with the whites. Once this happens, the system will then tend to be self-operating in the maintenance of an integrated labor force. I believe this is an important part of the success stories of companies who have integrated their work force. These companies have reached the takeoff point where their recruitment systems, including word-of-mouth referrals, tend to perpetuate integration rather than segregation.

But, while the basic work force is all white, the system is discriminatory. An employer who uses it is "failing to hire" from the available labor market because he is restricting his recruitment efforts to the white labor market. The foreseeable, and hence intended, consequence of his action is the restriction of his labor force to whites only.

This analysis makes clear that the scope of the "duty of fair recruitment" is commensurate with the problems of recruitment faced by an employer. The use of news media which is used by the majority, but not the minority; the use of radio or television time on stations other than those which cater to minorities; the selection of schools, employment agencies, or other sources which are relevant to the majority only —all come under the ban of the duty of fair recruitment if they are used in a way which in fact favors the majority part of the labor market at the expense of the minority.

C. Walk-In Applications

Ranking with word-of-mouth referrals as the primary sources of hire in blue-collar and white-collar jobs are walk-in applications.[25] The applicant may have read the newspaper, or be going past the establishment, or on the basis of its general reputation, decided to seek employment. The use of walk-in applications is, for the employer, a painless, expenseless method of obtaining employees. If his reputation is sufficiently good, or if the labor market is tight enough, he will have a steady flow sufficient for his needs. If an employer has an all-white labor force, and this steady flow is substantially all white, has he violated Title VII by relying on this system of recruitment?

The principles described earlier are applicable here. The employer is using a system which he knows will perpetuate the segregated character of his labor force. The precise mechanism by which the all-white character of the labor force is perpetuated through walk-in applications may vary. For example, the reputation of the employer as one who does not hire minorities may be known in the minority community. Under these circumstance, most minority group persons will not seek employment with the employer at all, because they do not wish to have a confrontation with one whom they believe to be a bigot. On the other hand, the employer may not be known in the minority community at all. That community, not having any experience with him, may be unaware of his existence, his location, his functions, or the type of jobs or qualifications for these jobs. In still other situations, where the employer uses want ads, the evidence suggests that whites rely on want ads as a method of job search substantially more than do Negroes.

Thus the mechanisms by which the flow of job applicants is all

---

[25] *Id.* See In the matter of Allen-Bradley Corp., *recommended decision,* OFCC Docket No. 101–68, Dec. 17, 1968, CCH EMPLOYMENT PRACTICES, NEW DEVELOPMENTS (1968–69) ¶8065, *aff'd* by Secretary of Labor, Jan. 16, 1969, *id.* at ¶807.

white may vary, but the result of these mechanisms is the same. The all-white character of the labor force is perpetuated to the knowledge of the employer. The system violates Title VII.

VII. Remedies for Improper Recruiting

A. *Recruiting*

It has been commonplace in the field to propose to a respondent who underutilizes minorities that he make his willingness to hire minorities known to sources from which they might come. Letter or personal contacts with the Urban League, for example, have become common. The corporate EEO officials (a new breed of corporate men designed for this problem) have tended to take a minority group representative out to lunch, explain entry-level requirements, and make it publicly clear that their posture is equal opportunity. They also say, on the side, "If you have any qualified ones, we will hire them." At the same time it is made clear that the employer will not appreciate applicants who are "unqualified." These contacts of the employer with minority referral sources are duly memorialized by letter and memorandum. At the next governmental review of the EEO posture, they are brought out and read verbatim and *ad nauseum* to the reviewing official. Very frequently these contacts are unproductive. Minority applicants and employees do not appear. After being exposed to this corporate treatment a number of times, I developed a standardized response, which was to suggest to the corporate officials that their program was inefficient and that they were not getting their money's worth out of the "knock on all doors" policy in that it did not produce minority employees, but only a record of trying.[26]

Part of the reason for corporate failure involves the failure to use all possible sources of minority group employment. But part of the reason lies in the feeble nature of the relationship established between the employer and the civil rights organization. It is appropriate to insist that a "continuous relationship" be established between the relevant

---

[26] Compare the basic thrust of United States v. County Bd. of Educ., 372 F.2d 836 (5th Cir. 1966). *"The only school desegregation plan that meets constitutional standards is one that works." Id.* at 847.

sources of minority group recruitment and the employer involved, a relationship which transcends the annual or semiannual letter to the Urban League along with the occasional lunch.

The elements of this regularized relationship should include (a) the standing job order, (b) notification of specific vacancies, and (c) estimates of future vacancies in the months ahead so that the minority organization can plan for them or for their likelihood. Reporting the results of the recruiting process is essential in assuring that the remedy is effective.

This relationship must have a formal information flow for review purposes. The applicants sent must carry cards, which are returned to the sending agency. A form of this system is currently in use by the employment services. The expansion of advertising of vacancies to include minority media is also commonplace.

Finally, cessation of certain exclusive dealings, and possibly any dealings, with tainted sources of recruitment should be required. The employment agency which refers only whites should not be a recruitment source for an employer who has breached his duty of fair recruitment.[27]

B. *Strengthening the State Employment Services*

Outside the South, where the employment services tend to participate in discriminatory recruitment patterns, the employment service is the poor man's employment agency, and particularly the Negroes' employment agency. A study of the unemployed in Newark recently revealed that 26 percent of whites but 56 percent of Negroes used the service. The extremes were even sharper with respect to males in the labor market, for 25 percent of whites and nearly 61 percent of Negroes used the service.[28]

Thus a requirement outside the South that all employers utilize the

---

[27] An outline of a conciliation agreement covering these and other matters appears after a critical comment by Senator Fannin in his dissent from a report of the Senate Committee recommending amendments to Title VII. S. REP. No. 1111, 90th Cong., 2d Sess. 23, 28 (1968), in app. III this chapter. I was involved in the preparation of the material which Senator Fannin placed in the report.

[28] CHERNICK, INDIK & STERNLIEB, NEWARK, NEW JERSEY, POPULATION AND LABOR FORCE, SPRING, 1967, at 15 (1967).

employment service with respect to all jobs will benefit Negro jobseekers to a proportionally greater extent than white, and should be imposed. The importance of referrals through civil rights sources should not be denied, but neither should the findings of a Wayne State survey of employment practices in eight states. This study, commissioned while I was Chief of Liaison with State Agencies for EEOC, revealed that public employment agencies were used as referral sources by 44 percent of employers with respect to blue-collar and 35 percent with respect to white-collar jobs. Civil rights organizations were used for 4.3 percent of employers with respect to white-collar and 3.6 percent of employers with respect to blue-collar jobs.[29] This, coupled with the Wayne State finding that the most common form of affirmative action was for an employer to consult with civil rights organizations, makes it clear that much effort in this field has been fruitless. The public employment service is frequently used by both employers and minorities. It is the only existing formal channel where this is the case. As such it must be strengthened.

There are many problems accompanied with such strengthening. In the South, there is evidence that the employment agencies participate in the Southern pattern of discrimination in their referral activities. Outside the South, there is evidence that such agencies participate in the Northern style of discrimination, which is based on residential segregation. Employment agency offices are regionalized, and job opportunities arising in each region are offered first to applicants in that region. This means that vacancies in a plant which is located in a lily-white suburban area will first be offered to the unemployed of the area, thus perpetuating the segregated character of the work force and restricting minority opportunities.

Progress has recently been made toward identifying problems within the public employment service structure and in making the agency capable of assisting employers who seek to increase their utilization of minorities. The Secretary of Labor has ordered the employment service to code the race of the applicant for employment, so that records can be maintained and action taken with respect to the problems discussed here. This forward step means that employment service practices can be reviewed and that employer requests for assistance in providing equal opportunity can be honored.

---

[29] See note 24 *supra.*

VIII. Discriminatory Hiring Processes

Once the available pool of manpower has been freed of its bias against minorities, attention can be turned to the impact of Title VII on the employer's hiring practices.

The hiring process may be understood in a sequence of steps leading to employment. We are now dealing with the handling of a "warm body" produced through a nondiscriminatory recruitment system. Obviously all varieties of administration of hiring procedures which discriminate are condemned by the statute, from the refusal to allow a minority group person to apply to the rejection of a fully completed application on discriminatory grounds. Disparate treatment in the administrations of hiring practices carries its own indicia of discrimination and is condemned. Rarely is one turned away because of his race; more frequently he is simply turned away and a white hired. Proof that this happened to a qualified minority applicant in the context of a substantially all-white labor force would suffice for a finding of discrimination.

The hiring process includes the stages of application, review of application, qualification, and hiring. Discrimination can take place at any of these stages.

A. *Applications*

Must an employer take applications at all? The easy case is one in which he takes applications from whites, not from minorities. This is classic and obvious discrimination. It is, however, uncommon. The more difficult case is one in which he does not take applications at all, but operates under a "hire only when there are vacancies" policy which is equally applicable to all. Can this "equal treatment" policy constitute discrimination? Since we define discrimination as an "adverse effect" on employment opportunities related to race, and so forth, we can answer this question only by examining the operational consequences of the policy. For example, if we find that the employer has an all-white labor force and fills vacancies through word-of-mouth referrals by existing employees who simply do not refer Negroes, we have identified a discriminatory hiring system. As part of this system, the "hire only when vacancies exist" policy may mean that the word-of-mouth referral system works quickly when vacancies develop. If so, it contributes to the maintenance of a segregated labor force and is discriminatory. Under these circumstances, the employer's refusal to take the application of a minority group member is discriminatory regardless of whether he would have taken the application of a white. The "no application" policy is discriminatory because it is part of a system of exclusion of minorities. Thus the duty of fair recruitment is breached if the employer rejects the opportunity presented by the minority applicant. The duty of fair recruitment requires that an employer with a substantially segregated labor force accept applications from minority group members.

B. *Fair Processing of Applications*

If an employer does accept applications, then he must receive and process them fairly. To turn away a minority applicant on false grounds, such as the absence of vacancies, or to falsely deny that there is a waiting list, is obviously discriminatory. The administration of most hiring procedures will appear fair on the surface. The crucial issues involve identification of circumstances under which such programs perpetuate forbidden discrimination through their operation. Any system is capable of distortion, and it would deny the ingenuity of man to attempt to catalogue the ways in which a system could be maladministered.[30] In exploring the administration of recruitment and hiring systems, comparisons of treatment of majority and minority applications are in order. Cultural biases may have crept into the process so that minority applications are not reviewed by as generous standards as white applications. The employer may have indulged in some presumptions of

---

[30] Thus the necessity for administrative flexibility. As the New York Court of Appeals noted 14 years ago in Holland v. Edwards, 307 N.Y. 38, 119 N.E.2d 581 (1954):

> One intent on violating the Law Against Discrimination cannot be expected to declare or announce his purpose. Far more likely is it that he will pursue his discriminatory practices in ways that are devious, by methods subtle and elusive —for we deal with an area in which "subtleties of conduct * * * play no small part." . . . All of which amply justifies the legislature's grant of broad power to the commission to appraise, correlate and evaluate the facts uncovered.

Id. at 45, 119 N.E.2d at 584.

competence with respect to the majority group applicants which he withheld from minorities. In addition, account should be taken of the effect of personnel procedures on minority applicants. A personnel officer hiring young men for heavy summer work may call all of them, Negro and white, "boy." To the white youth, this is meaningless; to the Negro, it may seem a badge of servitude.

C. *Order of Processing Applications*

If an employer who has excluded minorities through discriminatory practices maintains a waiting list, may he process applicants in the order in which they apply? This depends on whether to do so will perpetuate discrimination. To place Negroes at the end of an all-white waiting list with a firm of virtually all-white employees obviously perpetuates the segregation of the labor force which has been produced by discrimination in recruiting and hiring. It would amount to providing a "grandfather clause" type of protection for the white applicants who had gotten onto the list and would bar consideration of minority applicants until the white applicants had all been hired.

IX. Remedies fo Discriminatory Hiring Procedures

Remedies for discriminatory hiring procedures may be appropriate in at least two situations: (1) where the employer has engaged in discriminatory *recruitment* rather than discriminatory hiring practices, but remedial action in connection with hiring is necessary to dissipate the effects of the discriminatory recruitment system and (2) where discriminatory hiring procedures have been established. In constructing remedies for discriminatory practices, it is frequently necessary to go beyond mere nullification of the particular unlawful practice which has been identified. Nullification sometimes leaves the situation with all the active consequences of discrimination still in operation. These consequences must be modified by remedial devices tailored to that end.[31]

---

[31] Compare the concept of freezing voting requirements in order to assure that federally protected voting rights are recognized in a meaningful way. Thus the power of a state to prescribe new voting requirements is foreclosed until the inequities of past discrimination are eliminated. See South Carolina v. Katzenbach,

Thus a discriminatory recruitment system which failed to provide notice and opportunity to apply for minorities would not be adequately modified unless the hiring procedures which followed the application and the qualification standards which were applied during the hiring process were also reviewed and revised where necessary to eliminate the possibility that the discrimination in recruitment would simply be replaced by discrimination further down the line. The failure to anticipate this possibility was responsible, I believe for the government giving tacit approval to the practice in the early 1960's in the South, where employers lifted formal racial barriers to certain jobs but instituted testing practices for admission to those jobs which had the effect of perpetuating the exclusion of Negroes.[32] To avoid this type of response, where the discrimination suppressed at one point reappears again under a different label, careful analysis and comprehensive remedies are the order of the day.

---

383 U.S. 301, 334–35 (1966); United States v. Duke, 332 F.2d 759, 768–69 (5th Cir. 1964).

[32] See decision of EEOC on discriminatory testing procedures, Dec. 2, 1966, in CCH EMPLOYMENT PRACTICE GUIDE ¶17,304.53, at 7413–27:

On August 24, 1966, the Commission adopted *Guidelines on Employment Testing Procedures* [¶16,904]. In light of the *Guidelines,* the Commission concludes that reasonable cause exists to believe that Respondent's testing procedures are in violation of Title VII of the Act.

The following facts are undisputed. Respondent employs approximately 2,465 persons in its Paper Mill and Converter Plants. . . . While Negroes constitute approximately 40% of [the local] population, they constitute 6% of Respondent's work force. Commencing in 1958 Respondent has administered various tests to applicants for employment. From the beginning of 1957 through April 1964 Respondent hired 386 whites and 12 Negroes; of the Converter plant employees hired since then, between April 1964 and November 1965, 75 are white and 4 are Negro.

. . . In 1964 Respondent commenced administering tests to employees desiring to move from dead end jobs to line of progression jobs or from one line of progression to another. Employees who were in line of progression jobs were not required to take the tests to keep their jobs or to be promoted within lines of progression. Since 1964, 94 white employees and 17 Negro employees have taken the transfer tests. Of these, 58 white (58%) and one Negro (6%) passed. The one Negro who passed was outbid for the job he was seeking by a higher seniority white.

Employment Practices

It is significant that until 1963, shortly before the transfer tests were instituted, Respondent maintained segregated jobs and lines of progression, so that Negroes were categorically excluded on the basis of their race from the more skilled and better paying jobs which were reserved for "whites only." While the bars are no longer expressly in terms of race, it is plain that Respondent's testing procedures have had the effect of continuing the restriction on the entrance of Negro employees into "white" line of progression jobs.

Our discussion of remedies assumes that the recruitment system has been opened up in order to assure that an employer with a substantially segregated labor force now receives a significant group of applicants from the minority community. If he has vacancies, the question of qualification standards is intertwined in the question of how he will process his applicants, and therefore this matter will be deferred to our discussion of qualification standards. Let us deal first with the process of handling applicants where there are no vacancies at the time of the minority group application.

A. *The Duty To Maintain a Waiting List*

Many employers do not maintain waiting lists of applicants. Instead, when vacancies occur employers hire from those applicants who present themselves. Obviously the maintenance of a waiting list for whites, but not for Negroes, is discriminatory. But what of the employer with a substantially all-white labor force who has in fact applied his "no waiting list" policy to both Negroes and whites? May he simply advise the minority applicant that there are no vacancies and send him away? If so, then the laborious process of generating minority applications will have proved futile, the statutory purpose will have been frustrated, and the multiple minority employment rate will not be affected. To avoid this result, we must conclude that the employer with a substantially segregated labor force may not reject minority applicants because he lacks a vacancy. He may not apply his "no waiting list" policy where this would perpetuate the segregated character of his labor force. He must maintain a register of minority employees to consider for hiring vacancies which arise in the future.[33]

---

[33] In an interpretive memorandum of Title VII submitted by Senator Case and Senator Clark, it was stated:

Title VII would have no effect on established seniority rights. Its effect is prospective and not retrospective. Thus, for example, if a business has been discriminating in the past and as a result has an all-white working force . . . the employers obligation would be simply to fill future vacancies on a non-discrimination basis. He would not be obliged—or indeed, permitted—to fire whites in order to hire Negroes, or to prefer Negroes for future vacancies, or, once Negroes are hired, to give them special seniority rights at the expense of the white workers hired earlier. (However, where waiting lists for employment or training are, prior to the effective date of the title, maintained on a discriminatory basis,

B. *A Minority Group Waiting List?*

What is the breadth of this requirement? May an employer keep a waiting list of minority applicants and continue to apply his "no waiting list" policy to whites? Support for this view can be developed. The requirement that an employer take applications is a remedial device to correct hiring practices which discriminated against minorities. It is not imposed because it is someone's idea of sound personnel practices in the abstract. Therefore, it should be confined to the narrowest scope necessary to achieve the objective of ending discrimination. This is achieved if the employer is simply required to take minority applications. It is not necessary to the achievement of the statutory purpose that he also accept majority group applications where there are no vacancies. It is true that this would create a double standard of application practices, but this is simply a necessary consequence of the adoption of a narrowly drawn remedy to correct the system which discriminated against minorities.

Furthermore, the "no waiting list" policy has generated a sufficient flow of white applicants in the past to permit the employer to operate under it. Presumably this flow would continue. Thus the employer would have two sources of applicants when a vacancy arose: the Negroes on the waiting list and the Negro and white applicants who showed up at the time of the vacancy. Since these white applicants are the only ones who had expectations of employment under the employer's old policy, they suffer no deprivation if the employer considers them in competition with the Negroes who have applied at any time. They are obviously not entitled to be considered separately or apart from the Negro applicants. This was the past practice, but it was this practice which was the heart of the illegal system.

These arguments have more appeal than I supposed when I set out to articulate them. Even so, I believe they will prevail only if the employer agrees with them, or if a less severe order proves ineffective.

---

the use of such lists after the title takes effect may be held an unlawful subterfuge to accomplish discrimination.)
BUREAU OF NATIONAL AFFAIRS, THE CIVIL RIGHTS ACT OF 1964, at 329 (1964). This discussion, however, has no relevance to remedies for systems which discriminated after the effective date of Title VII.

Thus a negotiated settlement by which the employer agrees to place minority applicants on a waiting list and hire from a combination of that list and the applicants who come forth at the time of the vacancy will be lawful as a remedy under the statute.

However, the employer may resist this remedy on the grounds that, if his "no waiting list" policy was part of his illegal system, he should be able to abandon it altogether and accept applications from all persons. He will argue that if he is forced to maintain a "double standard" he will be "forced" to hire Negroes except where, by a quirk of fate, whites apply at the time of a vacancy. This, he will claim, constitutes "discrimination in reverse" against the white applicants who were not at fault in the situation. The argument, of course, contains major elements of exaggeration. White applicants have shown up in sufficient numbers in the past to fill the employer's needs. They can be expected to continue to come forth. Furthermore, the employer can, by informal means, make sure that desired applicants are in fact notified of vacancies so that they are on tap when the vacancies occur. Thus the argument that a dual system would force minority hiring almost exclusively does not, on its face, seem likely to be borne out. Finally, the employer might argue that the hostility engendered by this particular form of remedy, both among applicants and among his own personnel staff, would be considerable and that this form of remedy is not necessary to correct the discrimination. These arguments have, in combination, considerable merit.

There is no doubt that an employer who has illegally discriminated in recruitment and hiring can be required to increase his hiring of minorities under the concept of "affirmative action" under Title VII. However, the adoption of two different formal procedures with respect to receipt of application which bars *any* consideration of whites who apply in advance of vacancies is probably unacceptable. It bears too heavily the stamp of segregationist thinking and does not appear necessary under present conditions to achieve significant increases in minority employment. The employer guilty of discrimination in recruitment and hiring who wishes to abandon his "no waiting list" policy altogether should be permitted to do so, provided that his new system (1) contains safeguards against continued discrimination under any other guise and (2) provides procedures to eliminate the present segregation which has resulted from discriminatory recruitment and hiring.

C. *Alternate Hiring*

Short of the dual system for receipt of applications, there are many intermediate points on a spectrum of remedies for discriminatory recruitment and hiring practices. For example, the employer might be required to hire Negro and white applicants alternately from his integrated waiting list until the effects of discrimination have been dissipated. This remedy is analogous to that ordered by the Federal District Court in *United States v. Local 53, Asbestos Workers*.[34] There the court found that the union had discriminatorily excluded Negroes from both membership and job referrals. As a part of the remedy, the court ordered alternate Negro and white referrals as long as Negoes were available. Assuming qualifications, this appears to be a practical and workable approach to the problem.

D. *The Takeoff Point Analysis*

One difficulty which this and other remedies engender is the problem of defining the circumstances under which the remedial system may be discontinued. No technical or mathematical answer to this question can be provided. There is a concept, however, which should enable us to handle this problem wherever it arises; that is the concept of the "takeoff point."

In dealing with the developing countries, the United States has functioned for some time under a concept of a takeoff point: a level of economic activity which is sufficiently self-generating so that massive aid might be reduced or withdrawn. A similar analysis is available in the field of employment discrimination. When there are sufficient minority employees to assure that the informal channels of recruitment and hiring are in fact open to the minority community so that they do have reasonable and realistic opportunities for employment in an environment which is not hostile, the effects of a discriminatory recruitment and hiring system are dissipated, and the remedies may be modified and ultimately removed. Major employers who have in fact

---

[34] Local 53, Asbestos Workers v. Vogler, 407 F.2d 1047 (5th Cir. 1969); order issued, 62 Lab. Cas. ¶9411 (D.C. La. 1970).

achieved substantial minority employment have reached this point. At this juncture, Negro employees begin to refer other Negroes, and the informal job search now includes the employer. This is the point at which governmental pressures should be relaxed and ultimately withdrawn. The question of when a given employment situation has reached this takeoff point is a matter for judgment in individual cases. There is not a sufficient body of experience to provide us with guidelines for an answer. The ratio of Negroes to whites in the population has no necessary relation to the question of takeoff point. Possibly the court faced with the need to make such a judgment will wish to gradually withdraw from the situation by reducing or modifying the remedies imposed, but retaining jurisdiction until it is assured that the takeoff point has in fact been reached and that minority recruitment is proceeding through the processes which assure that the discriminatory exclusion of Negroes will not be reestablished.

E. *The Affirmative Action File*

A milder measure to remedy discriminatory recruitment and hiring practices is the use of the "affirmative action file." This contemplates a recruitment procedure whereby the employer seeks applications from minorities, reviews them, and places the presumptively qualified minority group applications in a separate file. He reviews this file first when vacancies arise and will hire from it unless he has compelling reasons not to. These compelling reasons might include the opportunity to hire a hot-shot white employee who is clearly superior in his potential contributions to the employer. This remedial device has been negotiated by the EEOC.[35]

The affirmative action file works as follows: All minority applicants are asked to fill out an application form, regardless of whether there is a vacancy. This form is then reviewed by the employer, who makes a tentative judgment regarding the qualifications of the applicant. If he is qualified, the application form is placed in the affirmative action file. As vacancies develop, this file is consulted, and persons are hired from it unless there is some overriding reason to bypass the file. Reports on the

---

[35] See app. III this chapter.

operation of the file are kept so that top management and the government can be aware of its operations. This is a practical device which enables the employer to hire qualified minority applicants, yet leaves flexibility in the event the company has an opportunity to hire someone whom they cannot afford to pass up. The successful operation of the file requires a good faith effort by management. Given this, the use of the file will increase minority employment without seriously disrupting management functions. The affirmative action file represents a practical minimum order that might be entered in a fair recruitment case. Regular reports on the operation of the recruitment and hiring system, including the affirmative action file, will indicate to the court and agency whether it is being used in good faith and whether it is achieving the desired results. If it is not, the residual powers of equity are available to shape a remedy which might be more effective.

In administering the affirmative action file, the court might call upon the EEOC to receive and evaluate the reports of the employer on the operation of the recruitment and hiring system, and advise it on matters concerning the systems which come before it.

This remedial device poses certain philosophical and practical problems. These problems are common to every remedial device which seeks to actually change the pattern of treatment of minorities.

F. Discrimination in Reverse

The individualistic ideology on which the philosophy of Title VII does depend states that "merit" and not an irrelevant characteristic such as race should govern the allocation of employment opportunities. Employers are supposed to seek out the best-qualified person from the manpower available to fill the vacancy. The affirmative action file appears to alter that policy by providing that an employer who has discriminated will normally hire his qualified persons from the file, rather than from elsewhere. This may mean that equally or more-qualified white persons will not be employed while minority group persons secure scarce-work opportunities. This poses the classic issue of "discrimination in reverse." The issue is, of course, a red herring designed to distract attention from the fact that the employer involved has been discriminating and that this discrimination has denied to the minority employment opportunities over substantial periods of time, which in many cases have gone to members of the white community only. The discrimination in reverse argument, in effect, reflects a desire to maintain the privileged sanctuary for white employees which the employer had established by his past discriminatory practices.

Since the employer has been adjudicated to have engaged in illegal discriminatory hiring and recruiting practices which have perpetuated a segregated work force and discriminated against minorities, the remedy should require him to provide opportunities to those in the class against which he has discriminated. He cannot provide opportunities for those persons who, over the years, were denied notice and opportunity to obtain employment, because they cannot be identified. Therefore, the remedy must benefit other members of the class. This is the only way in which the discrimination against the class which has produced the multiple minority unemployment rate can be remedied.

The concept of group interest is useful in understanding this aspect of the remedy.[36] Antidiscrimination laws are intended to protect minority groups as a class and individuals who are members of the class. Discrimination in recruitment and hiring denies the group and its members the opportunities to participate fully in the economic life of the nation. This denial has consequences which range far beyond the impact on the individual. They permeate the entire social and economic fabric of the minority community. Remedies, to be meaningful, must provide the opportunities to both the group and the individual. Obviously, the group is an abstract concept. Only by helping individuals can the group be assisted. Thus the individual protected by antidiscrimination legislation is important, both for himself and as a vehicle for the protection of the group interest. Where an individual has been denied a specific employment opportunity because of his minority status, the relation of the remedy to the group is clear. But where there is no individual complaint, and only the group interest requires vindication, the remedy should be no less broad. Those who argue that the white applicant who is not hired because of the affirmative action file was not responsible for the prior discrimination and hence should not suffer now miss this point. Whites as a group are not entitled to continued

---

[36] See note 14 *supra*.

preference in employment with an employer who has engaged in discriminatory recruitment and hiring practices. Thus the future opportunities of these white persons may be restricted while the effects of discrimination are remedied.

The Supreme Court has dealt with the problem of remedies running to classes of employees in connection with violations of the National Labor Relations Act. These court decisions are relevant here for two reasons. First, the remedial language of the National Labor Relations Act was the apparent antecedent of Title VII.[37] The phrase "affirmative action" in Title VII appears in the earlier act. Second, under the NLRA, the court deals with a group interest of employees, the interest in organizing for purposes of collective bargaining. Under Title VII, we have the same statutory language and a different group interest, that of freedom from restriction of opportunities.

Some of the decisions of the court under the NLRA have turned on the question of whether there was "discrimination" as that term is used under that statute. Where discrimination has been found, the court has allowed broad remedies if it was satisfied that they were related to the wrong done to the class. Thus where a union was unlawfully foisted upon employees, the court upheld a broad dues-reimbursement order,[38] but where there was no showing that employees as a class had been harmed by unlawful employer support to a union, the court refused to permit such a remedy.[39] In the duty of fair recruitment cases, there is no

---

[37] See Phelps Dodge Corp. v. NLRB, 313 U.S. 177 (1941). The National Labor Relations Act §10(c), 29 U.S.C. §160(c) (1964) states:

The testimony taken by such member, agent or agency or the Board shall be reduced to writing and filed with the Board. Thereafter, in its discretion, the Board upon notice may take further testimony or hear argument. If upon the preponderance of the testimony taken the Board shall be of the opinion that any person named in the complaint has engaged in or is engaging in any such unfair labor practice, then the Board shall state its findings of fact and shall issue and cause to be served on such person an order requiring such person to cease and desist from such unfair labor practice, and to take such affirmative action, including reinstatement of employees with or without back pay, as will effectuate the policies of this Act. . . . Such order may further require such person to make reports from time to time showing the extent to which it has complied with the order. If upon the preponderance of the testimony taken the Board shall not be of the opinion that the person named in the complaint has engaged in or is engaging in any such unfair labor practice, then the Board shall state the findings of fact and shall issue an order dismissing the said complaint. . . .

[38] Virginia Elec. & Power Co. v. NLRB, 319 U.S. 533 (1943).

[39] Local 60, Carpenters v. NLRB, 365 U.S. 651 (1961).

difficulty in demonstrating how the minority group as a class has been harmed; hence there will be no difficulty in supporting a remedy which relates to the class.

The employer has only a limited number of opportunities to allocate. If he now "begins to treat everyone equally," he will fail to provide any remedy for the group against which he has discriminated. The group interest which the statute was intended to protect will not be vindicated. The only way in which the class or group interest secured by the statute can be protected is by providing opportunities to members of the group. Since these opportunities would have been available all along had there not been discrimination, the requirement that they now be made available in a meaningful way is reasonably related to the purpose of the statute.

Thus viewed, the affirmative action file fits within the framework of the statute. Whites who are delayed or denied employment because of the operation of the file are in no position to complain. Their status is analogous to an applicant denied employment because an employer has an affirmative duty to rehire strikers at the end of a strike. The applicants for new employment may have had no responsibility at all for the strike or its causes. Nevertheless, they are denied opportunities for employment by operation of the rights of reinstatement of strikers, rights which, if not voluntarily recognized by the employer, will be protected by the Board and the courts in order to vindicate the public policy of protecting the right to organize and bargain collectively.[40] So here remedial devices designed to vindicate the public policy against discrimination are valid, although they may result in the delay or denial of employment opportunities to white applicants.

At another level, the concept of "hire the most qualified" must be carefully understood. It was never to be taken literally. At the maximum, the concept referred to the best man an employer could get considering the state of the labor market, the information available concerning jobs and employees, and the price he was willing to pay. Where an employer practices racially exclusionary recruitment, he has failed to consider an entire segment of the labor market. No employer, least of all one guilty of discrimination, can claim to "hire the most qualified."

And finally, the identification of the "best qualified" is a difficult and

---

[40] See, e.g., NLRB v. Fleetwood Trailer Co., 389 U.S. 375 (1967) (citations listed).

subjective matter. "Qualification" is not the talisman that some would make it. The concept is a shield for managerial discretion and a challenge to entrenched privilege based on birth or status. It creates flexibility for decisionmaking, but cannot, itself, resolve difficult cases.

Thus the discrimination in reverse argument, stripped of its emotional content, appears as an argument to preserve an illicit privilege, to prevent the operation of meaningful remedies to correct discrimination in recruitment and hiring. It should be rejected. In statutory guise, it arises in connection with the so-called no-quota provision of Title VII.

G. *The "No Quota" Provision*

Section 703(j) prohibits the imposition of a numerical quota for employment based on the proportion of minorities in the population or in a given labor market.[41] But no authority to impose such quotas is given under the statute. Remedial authority is limited to cases where discrimination has been found. There is no general remedial authority to remedy imbalances in minority employment in the abstract. Thus the proviso is addressed, not to a real possibility, but to a mythical one —the fear that the government would overreach. The provision is intended to prevent the substitution of arithmetic for evidence of discrimination. The section has no literal application to a remedial device which imposes a quota in order to remedy discrimination, rather than because of population statistics. However, the no-quota provision does relate to the question of remedies under Title VII in at least one respect. It reflects a congressional disinclination to solve difficult problems of adjusting industrial relations systems to eliminate discrimina-

---

[41] Section 703(j) states:

Nothing contained in this title shall be interpreted to require any employer, employment agency, labor organization, or joint labor-management committee subject to this title to grant preferential treatment to any individual or to any group because of the race, color, religion, sex, or national origin of such individual or group on account of an imbalance which may exist with respect to the total number or percentage of persons of any race, color, religion, sex, or national origin employed by any employer, referred or classified for employment by any employment agency or labor organization, admitted to membership or classified by any labor organizations, or admitted to, or employed in, any apprenticeship or other training program, in comparison with the total number or percentage of persons of such race, color, religion, sex, or national origin in any community, State, section, or other area, or in the available work force in any community, State, section, or other area.

tion by simple mathematical formulas. It suggests that Congress wished individually tailored remedies rather than uniform rigid solutions. This suggestion is honored by both the affirmative action file and the alternate referral system, and by other remedial devices based on judgment rather than mathematics.

This construction of the no-quota provision provides a clear coordination with the remedial section of the statute. Section 706(g) provides that the courts are not only to afford specific remedies for the benefits of plaintiffs but may direct the defendant to take, in addition, "such affirmative action as may be appropriate." [42]

The phrase "affirmative action" has two relevant antecedents in this field. First, it is the phraseology of the National Labor Relations Act. This language has received a generous interpretation by the Supreme Court of the United States in a series of cases beginning with *Phelps Dodge*.[43] The footnote references make it clear that the court considers this language an appropriate vehicle for remedial orders tailored to meet social needs, confined by concepts of "appropriateness" and bounded by the forbidden hinterland of "punitive" remedies.[44]

Second, the phrase has evolved a specific meaning in the field of employment discrimination. This is the form of the requirement imposed on government contractors under executive orders and the form of statements of good intentions made by members of Plans for Progress that they will "do more" than avoid discrimination and will "reach out" into the minority community to improve employment opportunities.[45] This gloss should be read into the phrase "affirmative action" as it appears in Title VII. Congress should be assumed to have intended that the courts and the Commission would require meaning-

---

[42] Contractors Ass'n of Eastern Pennsylvania v. Shultz, 62 Lab. Cas. ¶9421 (E.D. Pa. 1970).

[43] Phelps Dodge Corp. v. NLRB, 313 U.S. 177 (1941).

[44] See generally Note, *The Need for Creative Orders Under Section 10(c) of the National Labor Relations Act*, 112 U. Pa. L. Rev. 69 (1963); cases cited notes 38, 39 *supra*. The reestablishment of contracted out operations and the offer of employment at other establishments to employees discharged through plant closure have been ordered under this section. NLRB v. Darlington Mfg. Co., 380 U.S. 263 (1965); Fibreboard Paper Prods. Corp. v. NLRB, 379 U.S. 203 (1964).

[45] For some examples of a statement of good intentions, see BNA, Lab. Rel. Rep. LRX 2592a–(g) (1965) (Bethlehem Steel Co., Olin-Mathieson Chem. Corp., The Great Atlantic & Pacific Tea Co.); N.Y. Times, Jan 22, 1968, at 23, col. 1 (N.J. Bell Telephone Co.).

ful remedies—in addition to those for plaintiffs—which would reach and remedy the social problem to which the statute is addressed.

Viewed in this light, the affirmative action provision is related to the no-quota provision as follows. Neither the courts nor the Commission can insist on mathematical nicety of employment by an employer who has discriminated. The devices to remedy discrimination remain within the discretion of the courts and agencies, so long as they are sensitively administered and tailored to meet the real problems of the minority labor force and the employer.

X. Reporting as a Tool for Enforcement

The affirmative action file solves practical problems of personnel officers by requiring reporting on the disposition of applicants, who must be identified by race and national origin. The reports include information of vacancies which arise, whether the file was used, list of persons and their qualifications included in and excluded from the file, and other such information. A number of employers have indicated their interest in using such a file because it gets around an old rule which prevented them from keeping records regarding the race of job applicants. Without this information, they could not effectively control lower management in the recruiting and hiring area.

Not so long ago it was bad form to note race on applications. The theory was that minority group members would stand a better chance of employment if their status was unknown to the reviewers of the application. The theory ran afoul of reality at several points. Obviously a personal interview made hash of it. Similarly, the ability to identify many minority group members by distinctive names, by address, or by school attended made it relatively easy for reviewers of paper to exercise such subjective judgments as they wished.

This paper color blindness accomplished virtually nothing except to make information gathering more difficult. The pendulum has now swung, and the maintenance of racial data is now appropriate and in some instances required. The reasoning is simple. If it is national policy to increase minority employment, all concerned must know how that policy is being effectuated. The only way this can be fully achieved is by racial identification. Hence, racial identification for the purpose of increasing minority employment is no violation of the law. At this writing, a racial and ethnic census must be taken annually of employees. Still, the applicant's race remains, if not taboo, at least not encouraged or required on his application form. Yet it seems obvious that an employer who has a segregated work force and is seeking to comply with congressional policy will need to know who his minority applicants are in order to hire them; and the government will want to know their identity in order to protect them from discrimination. The collection and recording of such data concerning applicants is, at this juncture, desirable as an adjunct to the elimination of segregated employment patterns and should be permitted (or required) of employers with this problem.

Whether the remedial device be the affirmative action file, alternate referral, or some other mechanism, its operation should be accompanied by detailed reports by employers. Only in this way will it be possible for the court or agency to know whether the system is operating in the manner anticipated at the time it was instituted. Employers traditionally complain of the burden of paper work which such reports entail. This argument is specious when made by large employers, which have a personnel office and computerized employment records. Such employers are already equipped to develop records and produce the needed information, provided they know in advance what is required. Data collection is now standard for large corporations. The "burden of paperwork" argument is one of the most overworked in this field. It masks a desire to keep the details of the recruitment and hiring practices from governmental scrutiny. Yet clearly, where the employer has operated a discriminatory recruitment and hiring system, disclosure of how his revised system operates is an essential part of any remedy which purports to be meaningful and to respond to the problem of the unemployment rates of minorities. This information flow is especially important in connection with the operation of a revised system where, with the best of intentions, the designer of the system is uncertain whether it will work as he intends. Furthermore, employers normally require detailed information of the type involved in reviewing the operation of a recruitment system for cost control purposes. A vivid example of this is the detailed statistics kept by General Electric Company on their "voluntary" program to train and employ the hard-core unemployed.[46] This kind of information, necessary for informed business judgment, is also necessary for informed administrative and regulative judgment. An example of a type of reporting requirement which will illuminate the operation of a recruiting and hiring system appears as an appendix to Senator Fannin's dissent from the report of the Senate Labor Committee proposing amendments to the Civil Rights Act of 1964 (reproduced in appendix III, this chapter).

XI. Fair Qualification Standards

There are three basic issues with respect to the question of qualifications raised in connection with an employer who has discriminatorily excluded minorities: (1) Does the standard in operation exclude a higher proportion of minority group members than majority group members? (2) If so, is this exclusion justified by business necessity to have a man capable of certain tasks? (3) Is the employer entitled to require this capability in his applicants without providing training programs to develop the necessary capability? These three issues are intertwined in most cases. They demonstrate clearly the relationship between the law against discrimination and other aspects of our national manpower policies.

A. *Education and Experience*

In every age group, the proportion of Negroes with a given level of educational attainment is uniformly lower than that of whites.[47] The unemployment rates for Negroes are at least double that of whites in virtually every age grouping.[48] Thus if the employer establishes educational and prior-experience standards as conditions for employment, he will necessarily exclude from consideration proportionately more Negroes than whites.

---

[46] James, *Learning To Work: GE Finds the Unskilled Pose Problems at Start, But It Sights Progress,* Wall Street Journal, May 21, 1968, at 1, col. 1.

[47] See app. IV this chapter, which includes information prepared by the United States Dept. of Labor comparing Negro and white educational levels and attainments.

[48] See app. I this chapter.

This means that the efforts to improve recruitment and hiring procedures described earlier will have but limited effect on the minority employment rate. The use of such educational and experience standards has an adverse effect on minority employment and perpetuates segregation where the employer begins with a substantially all-white labor force. We may take note of these social facts concerning minority educational and employment rates without awaiting proof in individual cases.

Under the circumstances described here, with employer awareness of the exclusionary consequences of the use of educational and experience requirements, the elements of a prima facie case of discrimination arise and shift the burden of explanation to the employer. His claim must be that his standards are so appropriately related to his employment activity that they are necessary for successful operation of his business; in short, the claims that the adverse effect on minorities is justified by business necessity.[49] The employer whose use of such criteria has produced or contributed to a segregated labor force may be unable to demonstrate a rational relationship between the standard and the work to be done. In that case, his action constitutes discrimination, and his standards must be suspended.

Those employers who have been most successful in integrating work forces have disregarded formal requisites in favor of a more functional analysis of the capabilities of applicants associated with careful training and indoctrination programs. Indeed, the piece of paper issued on completion of high school may not be valid evidence of a given level of competence in a particular skill.

Obviously, there is something counterproductive here. A better-educated labor force is desirable because a better-educated citizenry is desirable. In addition, higher educational levels are necessary to operate our sophisticated economic system. National manpower policy should encourage higher educational aspirations at all levels. We should not design a national manpower program which will encourage the dropout with the promise of employment, particularly where the

---

49 This is the analysis which operates under the National Labor Relations Act in comparable situations. See NLRB v. Fleetwood Trailer Co., 389 U.S. 375 (1967); NLRB v. Great Dane Trailers, Inc., 388 U.S. 26 (1967); NLRB v. Erie Resistor Corp., 373 U.S. 221 (1963); Local 357, Teamsters v. NLRB, 365 U.S. 667 (1961); Radio Officers Union v. NLRB, 347 U.S. 17 (1954); NLRB v. Macaky Radio & Telegraph Co., 304 U.S. 333 (1938).

future opportunities for the dropout are limited. The depression of entry-level standards for minority group employees, which reduces the significance of educational attainment is contrary to longrun interests of the nation and to the not-so-longrun interests of youth—minority group youth in particular.

However, a generation of experience has demonstrated that, as long as the business and industrial community can, they will adapt to the quality of educational product emerging from the status quo. They will skim the cream, usually white, and leave the rest as society's problem, not theirs. They may hire overqualified people who may be promotable. Thus they avoid facing the consequences of our inadequate educational system. They insulate themselves from these consequences with entry standards designed, not necessarily with efficient business practices in mind, but rather in order to avoid facing the problems arising from the failures of the educational system and the general culture. These standards reject persons for reasons related to the general cultural, educational, and experience levels of the minority community rather than the requirements for the job. Thereby the minority unemployed pattern is perpetuated.

In one sense "business convenience" *is* served by a screening system whereby the employer disregards the cultural context in which he operates. He may have fewer "business problems" in production if he can restrict his labor force to the better-equipped whites.[50] But does the "business necessity" justification encompass practices which will perpetuate the evils which the statute was intended to remedy? This justification should be limited to the functional abilities necessary for production. It should not allow the employer to remain aloof from the social problems of our time even if he encounters difficulties and costs along the way.

Congress has determined that employers must share the responsibilities for correction of the social evils arising from discrimination as they effect employment. This may entail costs and the facing of real problems. It certainly requires that the "business necessity" justification be narrowly construed to cover only the essentials of the production process, not the costs associated with accepting and integrating into employment those excluded by discriminatory process. In fact, it could be argued that the concept of business justification has no place under

---

[50] See the problems described in James, *supra* note 46.

Title VII in any guise. The elements of business justification in areas of
sex, national origin, and religion are recognized in the statute under the
concept of a "bona fide occupational qualification reasonably necessary
to the normal operation of that particular business or enterprise." [51] No
such privilege is recognized with respect to race or color. Thus it could
be argued that business convenience is simply not applicable to discrimination cases under Title VII involving race or color. However, I
think this argument goes beyond the concept of bona fide occupational
qualification intended in the statute. This provision was intended to
eliminate questions of customer preference, employee preference, and
the like as grounds for discrimination. I think it sufficient to allow the
concept of justification as an element within the concept of discrimination, but to hold it to narrow limits relating to the processes of production and excluding the general considerations arising from cultural disadvantage.

Thus prior-experience requirements must be demonstrated to be
relevant to the job, and not a substitute for training programs which the
employer should provide. Educational standards must be demonstrated
to be germane to the work at hand. Frequently, unrealistic formal educational requirements conceal a functional requirement. For example,
an employer may require high school graduation, but need a fifth-
grade reading level. This can be judged without the high school degree
requirement. The remedies here should be intimately related to the requirements of the employer's operation.

B. *Testing Practices*

Employers utilize preemployment testing to improve the quality of
their employees and to minimize subjectivity in the selection process.
These efforts are not necessarily motivated by discriminatory purpose;
however, when tests are introduced at the time formal barriers based
on race are removed, the purpose becomes suspect.[52] Both skill and ability testing may have discriminatory implications.

---

[51] Section 703(e)(1).
[52] See note 32 *supra*.

1. TESTING OF EXISTING SKILLS

A man seeking a job as an experienced welder may be required to prove that he knows how to weld. A sales clerk may be required to prove that he can add and subtract; a clerk typist must be able to type at a certain rate, and engage in filing and other clerical tests. If Negroes have never been allowed to become welders, if typing is taught for the first time in the twelfth grade of the Negro school while in the white schools it begins in the tenth grade, and if the attainment levels in the Negro schools are lower than those in the white schools, all of these standards will exclude proportionally more Negroes than whites.

Nevertheless, business necessity may provide a justification. The question of whether there is justification depends on (a) the nature of the operation and (b) the resources of the defendant. An employer whose practices have produced a segregated labor force may find its entry level requirements under review and may thus be put to the issue of justification. If the government uses 40 words per minute as standard entry typing level, how can a higher level be justified by big industry? If a large firm does not have multiple levels of welders so that it can hire less-experienced men and upgrade them, how valid is the justification that it must employ only experienced men who know how to weld? Contrast the small retail store whose capability does not include multiple levels of store clerks and training programs. The giant corporation should not be allowed to use the small businessman as a stalking horse to avoid its responsibility to provide upgrading training.

Once it has been determined that the skills tested for are reasonably related to the job for which the applicant has applied and that the employer is not required to provide training, the matter is at an end, even if the effect is exclusion of a disproportionate number of minority group members. The issue in skills testing is the relationship between the skill tested for and the job applied for, in light of national policies intended to increase minority group labor force participation and to increase the manpower training activity of large industry. The rule which emerges is that skill testing which has a disproportionate impact on minorities may be justified if it (1) tests a skill necessary for the job and (2) is a skill which the employer is entitled to seek in the labor market without providing training.

The obligation to provide training for skills is a complex one. First, it depends on the resources of the employer. Most employers of significant size today have training programs for some purposes. The failure to establish such programs for entry level jobs may be discrimination where the skills in question are not adequately developed in both majority and minority groups. But a small employer who does no training should not be saddled with such an obligation unless cost-absorbing programs are available. Second, the requirement depends on the availability of training programs to provide the skill. Today there are government and privately sponsored programs to provide upgrading training in virtually every field, with the government being willing under the Manpower Development and Training Act to absorb at least the training costs.[53] These programs should be considered part of the same basic natural manpower policies which give rise to the antidiscrimination laws and should be considered a part of the range of remedies available to the court or agencies administering the antidiscrimination law. The workability of such programs under governmental auspices vastly expands the range of judicial or administrative relief because there exists the administrative capability to design and supervise them—a capability which neither the court nor the antidiscrimination agencies alone possesses.

2. Ability testing

If skill is not required, the ability to absorb training may be, as well as the ability to do the job. The identification of ability by testing involves us in matters which must be considered from several perspectives. Management frequently as resorted to the use of ability tests to avoid the subjectivity which otherwise characterizes the hiring process. These tests are scored on some simple mathematical scale. Hiring policies have turned on the score received, either in terms of "we hire the highest" or "you must make a minimum score" to be further considered, or the score becomes one factor taken into consideration. Sometimes, the tests are introduced with as much scientific validity as the psychological testing profession can muster. The tests are calculated to measure characteristics which have been determined after careful study to be requi-

---

[53] See U.S. Dep't of Labor, Manpower Report of the President 47–70 (1967).

site for the jobs for which the applicants are tested. Such tests are deemed to be job related; they have been shown to have a high degree of reliability, as measured by, not only the success of those who pass the tests, but also by the failures of those who do not. The tests not only screen-in successes; they screen-out failures. Both functions have been demonstrated.

Much of industrial testing, however, was not instituted on such a rational basis. Personnel officers are faced with the necessity of staffing an operation. They purchase a predeveloped and fully printed test in sufficient multiple copies to use for some time. The test comes with instructions which can be understood by the average competent secretary who becomes the test administrator. The relationship between the abilities measured by the test and the abilities required for the job for which the test is used is speculative at the beginning and remains speculative thereafter. Those who pass the test may do well on the job. This is taken as proof of the validity of the test, without reference to the real possibility that some who failed the test might have done fully as well.

Where this system bears proportionally heavier on minorities, it is called into question under Title VII. Thus far, most of the cases before the Commission involving testing have concerned the situation in which the employer has administered tests to both Negroes and whites, with Negroes failing the tests in a much higher percentage of the cases than whites. Thus the potential of the test to exclude a higher proportion of Negroes than whites has been proved. Where the administration of a test is a part of a pattern of recruitment and hiring which has historically excluded Negroes from the recruitment phase of the hiring process, there may be no such experience because few Negroes have even reached the stage of taking the tests. Under these circumstances, there are two choices: (1) try to correct other phases of discriminatory recruitment and hiring and await the application of the test before challenging its use, or (2) rely on the accumulated experience of the EEOC to establish the likelihood that a given test in a given job situation will tend to screen out a higher percentage of minorities. The Commission is in a good position to make such judgments after reviewing the testing matters which have come before them. In this way, the experience of the Commission will enable the telescoping of the problems of testing and the other phases of recruitment and hiring so they can all be disposed of in a single proceeding. I believe it is reasonable at this point in history for the Commission to make these judgments and for the courts to accord significant weight to them.[54]

C. *The EEOC Guidelines*

The EEOC guidelines are designed to point out the pitfalls in ability testing. The guidelines begin as follows:

> Title VII of the Civil Rights Act of 1964 provides that an employer may give an act upon the results of "any professionally developed ability test provided that such test . . . is not designed, intended or used to discriminate because of race . . ." (Sec. 703(h)). The language of the statute and its legislative history make it clear that tests may not be used as a device to exclude prospective employees on the basis of race. The Commission accordingly interprets "professionally developed ability test" to mean a test which fairly measures the knowledge of skills required by the particular job or class of jobs which the applicant seeks, or which fairly affords the employer a chance to measure the applicant's ability to perform a particular job or class of jobs. The fact that a test was prepared by an individual or organization claiming expertise in test preparation does not, without more, justify its use within the meaning of Title VII.[55]

The Commission's view is that where such testing discriminates against a class of minorities, it is invalid unless the business using it can demonstrate its validity.[56] Frequently such demonstration is unavailable. Thus

---

[54] Compare the Health, Education, and Welfare guidelines, which require school boards to affirmatively abolish the existing effects of de jure segregation in public schools. 45 C.F.R. §§80.1–.13 (1967). This issuance of these guidelines has been declared to be within the congressional mandate of Title IV of the Civil Rights Act of 1964. They are to be accorded "great weight" in future adjudications in the area of school desegregation. United States v. County Bd. of Educ., 372 F.2d 836, 847 (5th Cir. 1966), aff'd en banc, 380 F.2d 385 (5th Cir.), cert. denied, 389 U.S. 840 (1967); Comment, 21 RUTGERS L. REV. 753 (1967). For an exhaustive treatment of the many aspects of employment testing, see Note, *Legal Implications of the Use of Standardized Ability Tests in Employment and Education,* 68 COLUM. L. REV. 691 (1968), Cooper & Sobel, *Seniority and Testing under Fair Employment Laws,* 82 HARV. L. REV. 1598 (1969).

[55] EEOC, *Guidelines on Employment Testing Procedures,* BNA, LAB. REL. REP. LRX 2051 (August 24, 1966).

[56] The decision, quoted in part in note 32 *supra,* goes on as follows:

> We stated in our *Guidelines:* "If the facts indicate that an employer has discriminated in the past on the basis of race . . . the use of tests in such circum-

Title VII becomes a vehicle for civilizing the use of ability tests which have often been introduced throughout industry, not because of their validity, but because they provided a mathematical way to avoid making difficult human judgments.

The so-called objective criterion of a successful passage of a test replaced the subjective judgment of management and the possible bi-

---

stances will be scrutinized carefully by the Commission." Accordingly, where, as here, the employer has a history of excluding Negroes from employment and from the better jobs because of their race, and where, as here, the employer now utilizes employment tests which function to exclude Negroes from employment opportunities, it is incumbent upon the employer to show affirmatively that the tests themselves and the method of their application are non-discriminatory within the meaning of Title VII.

Title VII permits employers to use ability tests which are "professionally developed" and which are not "designed, intended or used" to discriminate. As we have stated in our *Guidelines*, to be considered as "professionally developed," not only must the tests in question be devised by a person or firm in the business or profession of developing employment tests, but in addition, the tests must be developed and applied in accordance with the accepted standards of the testing professions. Relevant here are the requirements that the tests used be structured in terms of the skills required on the specific jobs in question and that the tests be validated for those specific jobs. In other words, before basing personnel actions on test results, it must have been determined that those who pass the tests have a greater chance for success on the particular jobs in question than those who fail. Moreover, where the work force, or potential work force, is multiracial, the tests should be validated accordingly.

In the instant case, all prospective Converter Plant employees are required to pass the Otis Employment Test 1A or 1B. Applicants for jobs "requiring mechanical ability" are also required to pass the Bennett Test of Mechanical Comprehension Form AA and PTI Numerical Test A or B. For transfer, employees are required to pass or have passed one or more of the above tests plus the Wonderlic Personnel Tests Form A. The Otis and Wonderlic tests measure "general intelligence," with particular loading on verbal facility; the PTI test measures skill in arithmetic; the Bennet test measures knowledge of physical principles. There is nothing in the voluminous materials submitted by Respondent to indicate that the traits measured by these tests are traits which are necessary for the successful performance of the specific jobs available at Respondent's plant. Nor does it appear that any of the tests have been validated properly in terms of the specific jobs available at Respondent's plant, or in terms of the racial composition of Respondent's work force. In the absence of evidence that the tests are properly related to the jobs and have been properly validated, Respondent has no rational basis for believing that employees and applicants who pass the test will make more successful employees than those who fail; conversely, Respondent has no rational basis for believing that employees and applicants who fail the tests would not make successful employees. Respondent's testing procedures, therefore, are not "professionally developed." Accordingly, since Respondent's testing procedures serve to perpetuate the same pattern of racial discrimination which Respondent maintained overtly for many years before it began testing, we conclude that there is reasonable cause to believe that Respondent, thereby, has violated and continues to violate Title VII of the Civil Rights Act of 1964.

ases and favoritism which such subjective judgments make possible. Objective criteria enable higher management to review the decisions below. This review is more difficult if the managerial judgment is based on subjective factors which are largely unreviewable.

The problem, in the context of the civil rights controversy, is that these particular objective tests are carriers, which translate discrimination in education into discrimination in employment. The use of tests constitutes an effort of the employer to insulate himself from the effects of discrimination in other areas of life. This is the fundamental reason why the civil rights interests challenge testing practices.

The challenge creates an interesting dilemma for the civil rights interest. "Objective" criteria are rejected in favor of a "total personnel assessment" of the "whole man" in order to avoid the adverse effect on minorities of testing practices. But obviously the concept of a total personnel assessment provides a fertile field for the free play of subjective factors of discrimination. For years, civil rights interests opposed use of subjective judgment in employment cases because they enabled and sometimes concealed discrimination. Thus civil rights supporters favored objective criteria because such criteria reduced the chance of subjective discrimination and made it possible to discern differential treatment. Now the shoe begins to pinch the other foot as the objective criteria are shown to have discriminatory consequences.

Thus, the civil rights interests are poised on the horns of a dilemma —existing objective criteria discriminate, but a shift to subjective judgment of management creates a fertile field for more discrimination. At this point, the civil rights interests must seek some other objective criteria to avoid giving a new license for discrimination.

I suggest that the objective criterion to which the civil rights interest is moving is the number of minorities employed in various job classifications. This corresponds to my suggested standard for measurement of effectiveness of the antidiscrimination laws. The reduction of differential in unemployment rates between the minority and majority requires that employees hire greater proportions of minorities. This becomes the objective criterion by which to measure overall performance by the employer in hiring and promoting minorities.

This stardard, rather than the development of a "culture free" or "culture fair" testing system, is likely to be the way out of the dilemma posed by the fact that objective tests discriminate and subjective judgments may discriminate too. If, whatever his standards, the employer's performance is measured by the extent to which he has acquired substantial numbers of minority employees, the civil rights interest is satisfied and the "affimative duty" is met. This conclusion has the further advantage of reducing the degree of detailed scrutiny over the employer's personnel practices. This does not imply anything as mechanical as a quota of minorities in employment. We can leave it to management to determine a way out of the dilemma posed by the need to increase minority employment on the one hand and to avoid a quota system on the other. I suspect the basic way out is to obtain a sufficient number and proportion of minority employees so that the recruiting system is self-operating because of the word-of-mouth referral mechanism. At this point, the basic background facts will be less favorable to a finding of discrimination, and the government may leave the employer alone.

If this is the conclusion which management reaches, then the net work of rules discussed here concerning recruiting and hiring will have been appropriate to the task of the Commission and the courts. The efficacy of each such rule then should be measured by its potential for inducing the employer to increase minority employment. Whether he has contributed to the solution to the social problem will be measured by his performance as charted in annual reports to the EEOC.

D. *The Protective Amendment*

When dealing with testing, however, the matter cannot rest on the issue of discrimination and justification. Here, we face the first of the Dirksen amendments to Title VII, designed to assure that consequences deemed obnoxious to the opponents of the bill would not result from its passage. There are several of these provisions, mostly concentrated in sections 703(e)-(j).

One section relates to testing, and was generated by the *Myart v. Motorola, Inc.*[57] decision. There are numerous problems created by the

---

[57] No. 63C—127 (Ill. F.E.P.C. 1964), in 110 Cong. Rec. 5662 (1964), *modified sub nom.* Motorola, Inc. v. FEPC, 58 L.R.R.M. 2573 (Ill. Cir. Ct. 1965), *rev'd,* 34 Ill. 2d 266, 215 N.E.2d 286 (1966). Section 703(h) states: "[N]or shall it be an unlawful employment practice for an employer to give and to act upon the results of any professionally developed ability test provided that such test, its administration or action upon the results is not designed, intended or used to discriminate be-

proviso. Does the proviso apply to "nonprofessionally developed" tests? Does it apply to tests which measure or purport to measure something other than ability? Is a professionally developed test one which was written by one who holds himself out as a test writer or one which has been measured and tailored by the standards of psychological testers to the needs of a particular job? And, finally, is the "intended, designed, or used to discriminate" clause simply another way of stating the existence of a violation of the statute? In short, is the whole proviso meaningless once discrimination is found?

I think this is nearly the answer. The other questions can be easily disposed of if this provision is viewed as laying a ghost which never walked. Unless the test "discriminates" as we have used the word, its use does not violate the proviso. If it does discriminate, by the terms of the proviso, its use is not protected. The proviso must be meaningless unless it uses the term "discrimination" in a sense different from sections 703(a)-(d). The real issue here is what constitutes discrimination. On this question the proviso is silent. It does not give a privilege to perpetuate discrimination through the use of a test. Thus, a nonprofessionally developed test, such as an arithmetic test, would be measured by the same standards as the Wonderlic test to determine if discrimination exists. A test measuring general intelligence rather than ability would be measured in the same way as an ability test. The term "professionally developed" must refer to the test as applied, since the user of the test and not its writer is subject to the jurisdiction of the Commission and the courts.

The testing proviso and the provision dealing with quota and seniority arrangements are both designed to make clear congressional fears of governmental excess in the enforcement of this legislation. In light of the failure to enforce the law in the field, fears of administrative zeal may have been groundless. Administrative incompetence may exist where zeal is lacking. The difficulty is that the provisos fail to protect anyone against administrative incompetence, and since they do not pro-

---

cause of race, color, religion, sex, or national origin." For the history of this section, see Berg, *Equal Employment Opportunity Under the Civil Rights Act of 1964*, 31 BROOKLYN L. REV. 62, 74 (1964). For an EEOC criticism of pre-employment testing devices, see Address by EEOC Chairman Shulman, Greater Philadelphia Chamber of Commerce Seminar, June 8, 1967, in BUREAU OF NATIONAL AFFAIRS, LABOR RELATIONS YEARBOOK—1967, at 438–43 (1968).

tect conduct made unlawful by the statute, they do not really temper administrative zeal.

Perhaps Congress, in adopting the protective provisions, was saying as best it could that mechanical quota arrangements are undesirable; seniority systems are important, and testing is an important element in a personnel system. Where these arrangements have a discriminatory effect, they must be dealt with by the Commission and the courts. No privilege to discriminate is given the tester or the user of an illegal seniority system. Yet, in light of the provisos, the Commission and the courts ought to think out and to carefully document their actions in these areas. Congress spotlighted the sensitivity of these institutions. The burden on those who would question them is therefore heavier.

The elements of the serious consideration with respect to testing, however, are often easily satisfied because of the slipshod fashion in which many of these tests have been introduced and applied in industry. In many situations the tests were instituted without any serious advance planning or validation and were applied purely as a screen-out device, which has no relation to the job for which they are given. One simply does not need the skills measured by the Wonderlic test to catch bags coming off a paper machine in Louisiana or to change tires on trailer trucks in a terminal in New Jersey. When this is pointed out, business frequently resorts to the presidential syndrome, stating that the tests are really to determine the extent of upward mobility of workers to rise through the ranks from janitor to president. There are four difficulties with this explanation.

First, often these tests are given for jobs which have no significant promotion opportunities attached. Promotion will be determined by factors other than the holding of the job. Thus, the logic of the defense is lopped off at its base. Even under a standard seniority system, promotion invokes a judgment as to ability based on past performance as one factor along with length of service.

Second, the tests may be no more related to the jobs which are up the line of promotion than the entry-level job for which it is applied.

Third, it is generally agreed that tests are substitutes for evaluation based on experience. They may be necessary with new hirees, because there is no experience. But, with a man on the job, the judgmental process which determines whether he will be promoted involves primarily the reasoned assessment of his superiors on the job, not the abstract analysis provided by test results.

Fourth, since promotions come some time after initial hiring and since experience may improve ability to perform on higher jobs, the employer builds in unfairness when he uses an entry-level test aimed at determining ability to do higher jobs. He denies the applicant the opportunity to improve by working at the entry job. If it is true that Negroes and other minorities are not as test-wise as white youths, this unfairness is particularly likely to perpetuate their restrictions to lower-range jobs, because it does not allow them to demonstrate their improvement based on enhanced skills developed through working. In short, this argument assumes that the applicant should be prepared (from the perspective of testing) for promotion *before* he begins to work at all. This cuts off from possibility of employment those who might prepare themselves for promotion by developing skills while at work. And thus is a man's future gauged, not by his abilities or capabilities, but by some abstract system designed for the convenience of administrators and the simplification of the processes of internal corporate review and control.

I do not believe that our society can afford this kind of rigidity for long; certainly it has no place in labor relations. In the most sensitive area of race relations and labor policy, where the future of the nation as well as the future of individuals is concerned, the argument has been given short shrift by the Commission and should be similarly treated by the courts.

E. *Remedies for Unfair Qualification Standards*

The most obvious remedy is to drop the offending entrance requirement, substitute nothing for it, and hire the minorities who come through the standard screening without it. One difficulty may be that a qualification standard is necessary, although not the one used by the employer. The employer should be permitted to show, in an attempt to avoid a remedy which abolishes his standard, that some other standard is necessary. The burden of proof here would be on the employer, and the duty would be to validate the proposed standard with present employees, in accordance with some rational standards. For example, the employer may have imposed a high-school graduation requirement for work which required reading at the third-grade comprehension level. He should be able to establish some kind of a check on reading ability, even after abandoning the discriminatory high school requirement.

The second level requirement relates to the institution of training programs for those who need training for upgrading as a result of change in the admission standards. If government or other subsidy is available, the training should be provided on the job. This means the employer may be required to hire the qualifiable, if training programs are available which are likely to make applicants eligible for the work. This, in turn, requires close relations between the courts, the agencies, and the elements in the Department of Labor and Health, Education and Welfare, and the Office of Economic Opportunity which deal with these matters. These are questions of administrative practices which can be worked out.

Here, at the conclusion of our exploration of the duty of fair recruitment, is the nexus between Title VII and the national manpower policies which are being painfully and slowly forged out of our national need and national tragedy. To carry out the mandate of Title VII, the courts should feel free to require the manpower programs to come to their assistance and to require the Secretary of Labor to make his personnel available to design the kind of training program which the employer is to be required to undertake as a part of the remedy for breach of the duty of fair recruitment.

XII. Conclusion

Is the law relevant to the demands for social change manifest in our time? Given the creativity, inventiveness, and practical sense which the law can muster on occasion, it can, I believe, make a meaningful contribution to the resolution of the dilemmas of our time. I fear that, without this contribution, we may be immobilized and unable to resolve our problems. The clash of interests is enormous; the technical problems rise to the highest levels of intensity. Principled and enforceable legal solutions to these problems are, in my view, essential. The creative lawyers and judges from Coke through Mansfield, Marshall, Shaw, Holmes, and Warren all saw this great need in their own times. The problems of employment discrimination require all of the wisdom, technical skill, and practical sense that the law can bring to bear. The recruitment and hiring problem, if solved through the imposition of the duty of fair recruitment, will alter, for the better, the dimensions of the total problem before us.

Appendix I: Selected Reports on Minority Unemployment, 1947–68

A. The report of PRESIDENT TRUMAN'S COMMITTEE ON CIVIL RIGHTS, TO SECURE THESE RIGHTS, was published in 1947. The Rights to Equality of Opportunity was discussed beginning at 53. Here is the substance of the discussion of the problem:

4. The Right to Equality of Opportunity

THE RIGHT TO EMPLOYMENT

A man's right to an equal chance to utilize fully his skills and knowledge is essential. The meaning of a job goes far beyond the paycheck. Good workers have a pride in the organization for which they work and feel satisfaction in the jobs they are doing. A witness before a congressional committee has recently said:

Discrimination in employment damages lives, both the bodies and the minds, of those discriminated against and those who discriminate. It blights and perverts that healthy ambition to improve one's standard of living which we like to say is peculiarly American. It generates insecurity, fear, resentment, division and tension in our society.

In private business, in government, and in labor unions, the war years saw a marked advance both in hiring policies and in the removal of on-the-job discriminatory practices. Several factors contributed to this progress. The short labor market, the sense of unity among the people, and the leadership provided by the government all helped bring about a lessening of unfair employment practices. Yet we did not eliminate discrimination in employment. The Final Report of the federal Fair Employment Practice Committee, established in 1941 by President Roosevelt to eliminate discrimination in both government and private employment related to the war effort, makes this clear.

. . . .

Discriminatory hiring practices.—Discrimination is most acutely felt by minority group members in their inability to get a job suited to their qualifications. Exclusions of Negroes, Jews, or Mexicans in the process of hiring is effected in various ways—by newspaper advertisements requesting only whites or gentiles to apply, by registration or application blanks on which a space is reserved for "race" or "religion," by discriminatory job orders placed with employment agencies, or by the arbitrary policy of a company official in charge of hiring.

. . . .

Discrimination in hiring has forced many minority workers into low-paying and often menial jobs such as common laborer and domestic servant. This has done much to bring about the situation reported by the Bureau of the Census in 1940—

Striking differences between the occupations of whites and Negroes were shown in 1940 census statistics. Farmers, farm laborers and other laborers constituted 62.2 percent of all employed Negro men and only 28.5 percent of all employed white men. Only about 5 percent of all employed Negro men, compared with approximately 30 percent of employed white men, were engaged in professional, semiprofessional, proprietary, managerial, and clerical or sales occupations. Skilled craftsmen represented 15.6 percent of employed white men and only 4.4 percent of employed Negro men. More than half of the Negro craftsmen were mechanics, carpenters, painters, plasterers and cement finishers and masons.

On-the-job discrimination.—If he can get himself hired, the minority worker often finds that he is being paid less than other workers. This wage discrimination is sharply evident in studies made of individual cities and is especially exaggerated in the South. A survey, conducted by the Research and Information Department of the American Federation of Labor shows that the average weekly income of white veterans ranges from 30 to 78 percent above the average income of Negro veterans in 26 communities, 25 of them in the South. In Houston, for example, 36,000 white veterans had a weekly income of $49 and 4,000 Negro veterans had average incomes of $30—a difference of 63 percent. These differences are not caused solely by the relegation of the Negroes to lower types of work, but reflect wage discriminations between whites and Negroes for the same type of work. The Final Report of the FEPC states that the hourly wage rates for Negro common laborers averaged 47.4 cents in July, 1942, as compared with 65.3 cents for white laborers. [See chart No. 1 *infra*.]

B.   H. Rep. No. 914, pt. 2, 88th Cong., 1st Sess. (1963) contained the views of supporters of the House version of the bill, which eventually became the Civil Rights Act of 1964. That report contained the following analysis at 26-27:

Testimony supporting the fact of discrimination in employment is overwhelming. The following table contained in the Manpower Report of the President, 1963, prepared by the Department of Labor, presents the dramatic contrast: [See chart No. 2 *infra*.]

In 1962, nonwhites made up 11 percent of the civilian labor force, but 22 percent of the unemployed. Approximately 900,000 nonwhites were without jobs during the year—thereby constituting an unemployment rate of 11 percent. This was more than twice the rate of white unemployed workers. The breakdown among age, sex, and occupational categories is even more striking as the above table reveals. Moreover, among Negroes who are employed, their jobs are largely concentrated

[Chart No. 1] Unemployment Hits Minority Groups Hardest
(percent of total white or non-white* labor force unemployed)

Prewar Spring, 1940	White	Nonwhite
Baltimore, Md.	9%	17%
Charleston, S.C.	10%	16%
Chicago, Ill.	13%	35%
Louisville, Ky.	12%	22%
Mobile, Ala.	12%	19%
Newark, N.J.	18%	35%
New York	18%	27%
Philadelphia, Pa.	17%	35%
Pittsburgh, Pa.	20%	41%
St. Louis, Mo.	13%	30%
Postwar Fall, 1946		
Baltimore, Md.	4%	12%
Charleston, S.C.	8%	17%
Chicago, Ill.	3%	8%
Louisville, Ky.	3%	7%
Mobile, Ala.	6%	13%
Newark, N.J.	7%	12%
New York	6%	10%
Philadelphia, Pa.	6%	12%
Pittsburgh, Pa.	6%	13%
St. Louis, Mo.	4%	14%

* Nonwhites consists of Negroes, Indians, Chinese, Japanese, and other nonwhite races.

SOURCE: United States Bureau of the Census (Reports on the Labor Force, 1946).

[Chart No. 2]   Table 1.—*Unemployment Rates by Color, Age, Sex, and by Selected Major Occupational Group, 1962*

Characteristics, Age and Sex	White	Nonwhite
Total	4.9	11.0
Male	4.6	11.0
14 to 19 years	12.3	20.7
20 to 24 years	8.0	14.6
25 years and over	3.6	9.4
Female	5.5	11.1
14 to 19 years	11.5	28.2
20 to 24 years	7.7	18.2
25 years and over	4.3	4.8
Selected major occupational group:		
Clerical workers	3.8	7.1
Craftsmen and foremen	4.8	9.7
Operatives	6.9	12.0
Nonfarm laborers	11.0	15.8
Private household workers	3.1	7.1
Service workers, except private household	5.3	10.8

among the semiskilled and unskilled occupations. This has the effect of severely retarding the economic standards of the Negro population. Likewise, concentration at the lower levels of employment heightens the chances of early and long duration layoffs. This is particularly evident today with the rapid upgrading of job skills which is closely associated with automation. The table which follows, included in the manpower report, clearly reflects this unbalanced occupational distribution: [See chart No. 3 *infra.*]

C. S. Rep. No. 867, 88th Cong., 2d Sess. 6-8. (1964) concerning the Equal Employment Opportunity Act, S. 1937, which ultimately became Title VII of the Civil Rights Act of 1964, included the following explanation:

The precarious position of the Negro American in today's labor market is dramatized further by the nonwhite unemployment rates. The startling fact is that one out of every five of the unemployed and one out of every four of the long-term, hard-core unemployed is nonwhite. Stated somewhat differently, approximately 900,000 of the 7 million nonwhites in the labor force are unemployed, a figure which represents more than 22 percent of the total unemployment figure. Thus although Negro and other nonwhite Americans constitute only 10 percent of the labor force, they make up more than twice that figure in the ranks of the unemployed. The unemployment rate of the nonwhite, particularly the Negro, is cur-

[Chart No. 3]   Table 2.—*Employed Persons by Occupational Group and Color,*
1948 and 1962

Major Occupational Group	White		Nonwhite	
	1948	1962	1948	1962
Total	100.0	100.0	100.0	100.0
White-collar workers	39.1	47.3	9.0	16.7
Professional and technical	7.2	12.6	2.4	5.3
Managers, officials, and proprietors	11.6	11.9	2.3	2.6
Clerical workers	13.6	15.8	3.3	7.2
Sales workers	6.7	7.0	1.1	1.6
Blue-collar workers	40.5	35.4	39.7	39.5
Craftsmen and foremen	14.6	13.6	5.3	6.0
Operatives	21.0	17.5	20.1	19.9
Nonfarm laborers	4.9	4.3	14.3	13.6
Service workers	7.9	10.6	30.3	32.8
Private household	1.5	2.1	15.6	14.7
All other	6.4	8.5	14.7	18.1
Farmworkers	12.4	6.8	21.0	11.0
Farmers	7.8	4.0	8.5	2.7
Laborers	4.6	2.8	12.5	8.3

rently running at almost 2½ times the unemployment rate of the white worker. In heavily industrialized areas, such as Chicago and Detroit, the differential is even more striking. Furthermore, the duration of unemployment is generally longer for the Negro than for the white, and if the nonwhite ultimately manage to find work, it is generally in the unstable unskilled, and semiskilled occupational sector most vulnerable to repeated layoffs. Three out of 10 of the nonwhite unemployed who worked during 1962 experienced 3 or more periods of unemployment during the 1962 year. This is 66 percent higher than the white rate.

The situation of the Negro youth is even more pessimistic in its outlook. Approximately 250,000, or 1 out of 5 of the youths between the ages of 16 and 21, out of school and out of work, are nonwhite. The rates of unemployment for nonwhite teenagers have risen steadily throughout the decade and are currently running as high as 25 percent for boys and 33 percent for girls. Their employment opportunities, like those of their fathers, are severely restricted to the dead-end, lowskill and unskilled jobs, and as a consequence, they remain unemployed for substantial periods of time because of their youth and inexperience.

Discrimination in employment thus begins at the top of the economic system and filters down through the lower levels despite educational

[Chart No. 4] Estimated Lifetime Earnings for Males in the Experienced Civilian Labor Force, by Years of School Completed, Color, and Major Occupation Group, for the North and West

[Earnings from age 18 to 64 years. Thousands of dollars. These data are from Herman P. Miller, Trends in Income Distribution in the United States; 1960 census monograph being prepared under the joint sponsorship of the Bureau of the Census and the Social Science Research Council]

Occupation and years of School Completed	North				West			
	Total	White	Non-white	Ratio of Nonwhite to White	Total	White	Non-white	Ratio of Nonwhite to White
Total Experienced Civilian Labor Force								
Total	240	247	150	61	254	263	166	63
Elementary:								
Less than 8 years	171	177	136	77	164	171	131	77
8 years	192	195	142	73	206	211	150	71
High school:								
1 to 3 years	220	226	150	66	231	237	163	69
4 years	249	254	160	63	263	269	184	68
College:								
1 to 3 years	299	306	175	57	294	300	159	63
4 year or more	433	441	229	52	401	409	265	65
4 years	403	410	199	49	369	378	226	60
5 year or more	469	478	254	53	436	445	326	73

Unemployment as Percent of Civilian Labor Force, by Color, by States, 1960

	Total	White	Non-white		Total	White	Non-white
Alabama	5.7	4.7	8.4	Montana	6.8	6.4	24.8
Alaska	12.8	10.5	25.4	Nebraska	3.1	3.0	7.7
Arizona	5.3	4.7	13.2	Nevada	6.2	5.9	10.1
Arkansas	6.1	5.3	9.1	New Hampshire	4.3	4.2	10.2
California	6.1	5.8	10.0	New Jersey	4.6	4.1	9.5
Colorado	4.0	3.9	6.6	New Mexico	5.9	5.5	13.6
Connecticut	4.6	4.4	8.9	New York	5.2	4.9	7.4
Delaware	4.6	3.8	9.2	North Carolina	4.5	3.6	7.4
District of Columbia	4.1	2.5	5.7	North Dakota	5.6	5.4	25.2
Florida	5.0	4.6	6.7	Ohio	5.5	4.9	11.9
Georgia	4.5	3.8	6.3	Oklahoma	4.4	4.0	9.0
Hawaii	4.2	4.8	4.0	Oregon	6.0	5.9	9.5
Idaho	5.7	5.6	8.6	Pennsylvania	6.2	5.8	11.3
Illinois	4.5	3.8	11.5	Rhode Island	5.3	5.2	10.0
Indiana	4.2	4.0	8.5	South Carolina	4.1	3.4	5.7
Iowa	3.2	3.1	9.3	South Dakota	4.1	3.7	23.8
Kansas	3.7	3.4	8.5	Tennessee	5.2	5.0	6.5
Kentucky	6.0	5.9	8.1	Texas	4.5	4.1	7.1
Louisiana	6.1	4.7	9.5	Utah	4.1	4.1	5.7
Maine	6.5	6.4	17.8	Vermont	4.5	4.5	10.6
Maryland	4.8	3.8	9.5	Virginia	4.2	3.5	7.1
Massachusetts	4.2	4.1	7.8	Washington	6.6	6.4	13.4
Michigan	6.9	6.0	16.3	West Virginia	8.3	8.2	11.4
Minnesota	5.0	5.0	12.8	Wisconsin	3.9	3.7	11.4
Mississippi	5.4	4.5	7.1	Wyoming	5.1	5.0	10.1
Missouri	4.1	3.7	3.6				

attainment. The Negro youth, observing this, becomes demoralized and disinterested in educational achievement and drops out of school at alarming rates, ranging as high as 20 percent. He is caught in a vicious cycle in which, untrained, undereducated and undermotivated, he is rarely prepared for an employment opportunity should one arise.

. . . .

The State record indicates substantial achievement, but the vast amount of work yet to be done is apparent from the economic facts developed in the course of the hearings on the bill. Gross disparities in earnings and employment opportunities continue to prevail in States having fair employment practice legislation and statewide unemployment rates do not appear to differ substantially from those in States without such legislation. [See chart No. 4 *supra*.]

D. In October 1967, the United States, Department of Labor issued Bureau of Labor Statistics REPORT No. 332, SOCIAL AND ECONOMIC

[Chart No. 5]   Number of Employed and Unemployed Persons,* 1960-1967
(numbers in millions)

	Employed*		Unemployed*	
	Nonwhite	White	Nonwhite	White
1960	6.9	58.9	.8	3.1
1961	6.8	58.9	1.0	3.7
1962	7.0	59.7	.9	3.1
1963	7.1	60.6	.9	3.2
1964	7.4	61.9	.8	3.0
1965	7.6	63.4	.7	2.7
1966	7.9	65.0	.6	2.3
1967 †	8.0	66.1	.6	2.3
Change 1960–1967:†				
Number	+1.1	+7.2	− .2	− .8
Percent	+ 16	+ 12	− 25	− 26

* The information on unemployment is obtained from a monthly sample survey of households. All persons 16 years and over are classified as employed, unemployed, or not in the labor force for the calendar week containing the 12th of the month.

The unemployed are persons who did not work or have a job during the survey week, and who had looked for work within the past 4 weeks, and were currently available for work. Also included are those waiting to be called back to a job from which they had been laid off or waiting to report to a new job.

The sum of the employed and the unemployed constitutes the civilian labor force.

† Average of first 9 months, seasonally adjusted.

SOURCE: United States Department of Labor, Bureau of Labor Statistics.

CONDITIONS OF NEGROES IN THE UNITED STATES. The report on employment appears at 29–42 and includes the following:

Employment has increased almost steadily in the past 7 years and unemployment has declined for both nonwhite and white workers. The number of nonwhite employed rose 1.1 million in the 7-year period, a 16 percent increase. [See chart No. 5 *supra.*]

The nonwhite unemployment rate in 1966 and 1967 has been the lowest since the Korean War, but the ratio of nonwhite to white unemployment has remained roughly the same: 2 to 1. Since 1961, the most recent recession year, the nonwhite unemployment rate has dropped by more percentage points than the white. [See chart No. 6 *infra.*]

Married men—the largest component of both the nonwhite and white labor force—have the lowest unemployment rates. Unemployment rates for nonwhite married men have been declining more rapidly than those for white married men. However, the nonwhite rate is still twice the

[Chart No. 6]   Unemployment Rates,* 1949-1967

	Nonwhite	White	Ratio: Nonwhite to White
1949	8.9	5.6	1.6
1950	9.0	4.9	1.8
1951	5.3	3.1	1.7
1952	5.4	2.8	1.9
1953	4.5	2.7	1.7
1954	9.9	5.0	2.0
1955	8.7	3.9	2.2
1956	8.3	3.6	2.3
1957	7.9	3.8	2.1
1958	12.6	6.1	2.1
1959	10.7	4.8	2.2
1960	10.2	4.9	2.1
1961	12.4	6.0	2.1
1962	10.9	4.9	2.2
1963	10.8	5.0	2.2
1964	9.6	4.6	2.1
1965	8.1	4.1	2.0
1966	7.3	3.3	2.2
1967 (First 9 months seasonally adjusted)	7.3	3.4	2.1

* The unemployment rate is the percent unemployed in the civilian labor force.

SOURCE: United States Department of Labor, Bureau of Labor Statistics.

[Chart No. 7]   Unemployment Rates for Married Men, 1962-1967
(20 years old and over)

	Nonwhite	White
1962	7.9	3.1
1963	6.8	3.0
1964	5.3	2.5
1965	4.3	2.1
1966	3.6	1.7
1967 (First 9 months)*	3.4	1.6

* Average, not seasonally adjusted.
SOURCE: United States Department of Labor, Bureau of Labor Statistics.

white rate. Of every 100 nonwhite married men in the labor force, 96 have a job. [See chart No. 7 *supra*.]

Nonwhite teenagers have the highest unemployment rates in the labor force. The total unemployment rate among nonwhite teenagers was over 26 percent in 1967, more than double the white teenage rate. [See chart No. 8 *infra*.]

[Chart No. 8]   Unemployment by Sex and Age, 1967
(first 9 months)*

	Number Unemployed (thousands)		Unemployment Rate	
	Nonwhite	White	Nonwhite	White
Total	634	2,315	7.3	3.4
Adult men (20 years and over)	194	870	4.3	2.1
Adult women (20 years and over)	236	827	7.0	3.8
Teenagers†	204	618	26.5	10.6

* Average, seasonally adjusted.
† Teenagers include those 16–19 years old.
SOURCE: United States Department of Labor, Bureau of Labor Statistics.

An increasing proportion of unemployed nonwhite teenagers are enrolled in school and also looking for work—1 in 3 compared with 1 in 5 a few years ago. However, this is still less than among white teenagers. [See chart No. 9 *infra*.]

Most nonwhite tenagers are in school. Of those out of school, a fifth are unemployed, and a third are not at work or looking for work. The majority of these latter are keeping house. [See chart No. 10 *infra*.]

Nonwhite men are less likely to be in the labor force than white men, except for ages 18–24. Among women, participation in the labor force

[Chart No. 9]   Unemployed Teenagers* and Percent Still in School, 1963, 1966, and 1967

	Unemployment Rate		Unemployed Number (thousands)		Percent Still in School	
	Nonwhite	White	Nonwhite	White	Nonwhite	White
1963	30.2	15.5	175	708	22	34
1966	25.4	11.2	185	650	27	39
1967 (First 6 months)†	26.3	11.2	182	615	32	38

* Teenagers include those 16–19 years old. Full-time students are also counted as unemployed if they want a job and have been actively looking for work during the 4-week period prior to interview in the monthly survey of the labor force.
† Not seasonally adjusted.
SOURCE: United States Department of Labor, Bureau of Labor Statistics.

is much greater for nonwhites except for those under 20. [See chart No. 11 *infra.*]

The reasons men are not in the labor force are roughly the same for whites and nonwhites in most age groups. Young people are likely to be in school, and white youth especially so; most old people are retired. In the middle and older working years, a larger proportion of nonwhites than whites are not at jobs because they are disabled. [See Chart No. 12 *infra.*]

[Chart No. 10]   Work and School Status of Nonwhite Teenagers, 1967
(first 6 months)*

	Number (thousands)	Percent
Out of school	703	100
Unemployed	124	18
Employed	347	49
Not in the labor force	232	33
Keeping house	137	19
Unable to work	10	1
Other reasons†	86	12
In school	1,083	100
Unemployed	58	5
Employed	165	15
Not in the labor force	860	79

* Average, not seasonally adjusted.
† Includes many waiting to be called to military duty.
SOURCE: United States Department of Labor, Bureau of Labor Statistics.

[Chart No. 11]   Labor Force Participation Rates,* by Age and Sex, 1966

	Men		Women	
	Nonwhite	White	Nonwhite	White
Total, 16 years and over	79	81	49	39
16 and 17 years	41	47	24	32
18 and 19 years	67	65	44	53
20 to 24 years	90	84	55	51
25 to 34 years	96	98	55	38
35 to 44 years	94	98	61	45
45 to 54 years	91	96	61	51
55 to 64 years	81	85	49	41
65 years and over	26	27	13	9

* The "labor force" is composed of those at work or looking for work. A person "not in the labor force" is neither at work nor looking for work. Participation rates equal percent of population group in labor force.

SOURCE: United States Department of Labor, Bureau of Labor Statistics.

[Chart No. 12]   Men Not in the Labor Force, by Age, 1967
(average first 8 months)

	Total Not in Labor Force (thousands)	Reason Not in Labor Force (percent)			
		Total	Going to School	Unable to Work*	Other†
16 to 19 years:					
Nonwhite	407	100	79	1	20
White	2,349	100	80	1	19
20 to 24 years:					
Nonwhite	85	100	58	7	35
White	769	100	77	4	19
25 to 54 years:					
Nonwhite	200	100	9	40	52
White	878	100	14	37	49
55 to 64 years:					
Nonwhite	155	100	—	45	55
White	1,134	100	‡	31	69
65 years and over:					
Nonwhite	465	100	—	20	80
White	5,226	100	‡	10	90

* Includes only those who have serious, long-term physical or mental illness.

† Includes retired workers, those keeping house and a large number preparing to enter or reenter the labor force or awaiting military service.

‡ Less than 0.5 percent.

— = Represents zero.

SOURCE: United States Department of Labor, Bureau of Labor Statistics.

[Chart No. 13]   Average Unemployment and Long-Term Unemployment*
in the Labor Force, 1967
(first 9 months)†
(numbers in thousands)

	Total	White	Nonwhite	Percent Nonwhite
Total civilian labor force	77,095	68,482	8,613	11
All unemployed workers	3,015	2,370	646	21
Percent of labor force	3.9	3.5	7.5	(X)
Long-term unemployment*	461	353	108	23
Percent of labor force	0.6	0.5	1.3	(X)

* Unemployed for at least 3½ consecutive months, 15 weeks or more.
† Not seasonally adjusted.
X = Not applicable.
SOURCE: United States Department of Labor, Bureau of Labor Statistics.

Nonwhite workers are twice as likely as white workers to be unemployed and among the longterm unemployed. About one and one half percent of the total nonwhite labor force is among the longterm unemployed. [See chart No. 13 *supra.*]

The Census Bureau estimates that its Current Population Surveys miss about 13 percent of the nonwhite population of working age and 2 percent of the white (the "undercount"). The undercount is greatest among nonwhite men in prime working years. Assuming that unemployment rates for the undercounted are twice those for the counted, the adjusted total unemployment rate would change by less than half a percentage point. For any particular group, the greatest difference from the current unemployment rate would be 2.5 percentage points. The undercount also has the effect of reducing the nonwhite birth and death rates. [See chart No. 14 *infra.*]

The percent of nonwhite workers in the high-skill, high-status, and good-paying jobs, and jobs in manufacturing increased much more sharply than among white workers from 1960 to 1966. Nonwhite employment in most of the less desirable occupations tended to stabilize or decline. [See chart No. 15 *infra.*]

The upward movement of nonwhite workers since 1960 has resulted in a gain of over one million jobs in white-collar, skilled, and semiskilled occupations. [See chart No. 16 *infra.*]

Despite 6 years of occupational advances, over two-fifths of the nonwhite men and three-fifths of all nonwhite women workers in 1966 remained in service, laboring, or farm jobs—substantially more than twice the proportion among whites. [See chart No. 17 *infra.*]

The increased penetration (percent of total) of nonwhite workers has been notable since 1960 in professional and technical occupations, especially in teaching and health work. Nonwhites are also a larger percentage now of workers in construction crafts. Despite the progress nonwhites remain a far larger than average percent in the lower-paid, lesser-skilled jobs. [See chart No. 18 *infra*.]

[Chart No. 14]   **Estimated Effect of Survey Undercount**

	Reported	Adjusted†
Unemployment rates, 1967 (First 8 months):*		
All workers	3.8	4.0
All nonwhite workers	7.3	8.2
Nonwhite males:		
16 to 19 years	24.0	25.8
20 years and over	4.4	5.2
20 to 24 years*	7.7	10.0
Birth and death rates, 1965:		
Nonwhite birth rate	28.5	26.0
Nonwhite death rate	9.6	8.8

* Seasonally adjusted except for nonwhite males 20 to 24 years old.

† In making the adjustment, it was assumed that the unemployment rates for those not covered by the employment survey were twice those interviewed and the percentage not covered was 6 percent for all persons in the labor force, but as much as 30 percent for nonwhite males 20 to 24. These estimates of undercoverage were obtained by noting the difference between the initial, unadjusted survey estimates and independent estimates of the population adjusted for net census undercount. Inasmuch as nothing is known about the labor force characteristics of the population not interviewed, the assumption made about unemployment is arbitrary though thought to be a maximum. Unemployment rates may not be much if any higher for those not interviewed than for those interviewed, since persons missed include people who may be away at work when the interviewer calls and in occupations which the missed persons may not wish to discuss.

SOURCE: United States Department of Commerce, Bureau of the Census.

E.   The REPORT OF THE NATIONAL ADVISORY COMMISSION ON CIVIL DISORDERS (1968) devotes chapter 7 to employment problems. The following appears at 124–26:

UNEMPLOYMENT AND UNDEREMPLOYMENT
THE CRITICAL SIGNIFICANCE OF EMPLOYMENT

The capacity to obtain and hold a "good job" is the traditional test of participation in American society. Steady employment with adequate compensation provides both purchasing power and social status.

[Chart No. 15]   Employment by Occupation,* 1966, and Change, 1960-1966
(numbers in thousands)

| | Employed, 1966 | | Change, 1960–1966 | | | |
| | | | Number | | Percent | |
	Nonwhite	White	Nonwhite	White	Nonwhite	White
Total	7,968	66,097	+927	+6,457	+13	+11
Professional, technical,						
and managerial	758	15,968	+251	+1,893	+50	+13
Clerical	751	11,095	+244	+1,791	+48	+19
Sales	149	4,610	+ 36	+ 316	+32	+ 7
Craftsmen and foremen	602	8,996	+187	+ 825	+45	+10
Operatives	1,786	12,093	+371	+1,537	+26	+15
Service workers, except						
private household	1,558	5,881	+326	+ 991	+26	+20
Private household workers	941	1,308	− 66	+ 115	− 7	+10
Nonfarm laborers	934	2,756	− 38	+ 72	− 4	+ 3
Farmers and farm workers	488	3,389	−384	−1,144	−44	−25

* Data on occupation are annual averages.
SOURCE: United States Department of Labor, Bureau of Labor Statistics.

[Chart No. 16]   Employment by Broad Occupational Groups 1960 and 1966

| | White-Collar Workers Craftsmen, and Operatives | | All Other Workers | |
	Nonwhite	White	Nonwhite	White
Number (in millions):				
1960	3.0	46.4	4.1	13.3
1966	4.1	52.8	3.9	13.3
Change, 1960–1966:				
Number (in millions)	1.1	6.4	− .2	(Z)
Percent	37	14	− 4	*

* Less than 0.5 percent.
Z = Rounds to less than 50,000.
SOURCE: United States Department of Labor, Bureau of Labor Statistics.

It develops the capabilities, confidence, and self-esteem an individual needs to be a responsible citizen, and provides a basis for a stable family life. As Daniel P. Moynihan has written:

The principal measure of progress toward equality will be that of employment. It is the primary source of individual or group identity. In America what you do is what you are: to do nothing is to be nothing;

to do little is to be little. The equations are implacable and blunt, and ruthlessly public.

For the Negro American it is already, and will continue to be, the master problem. It is the measure of white bona fides. It is the measure of Negro competence, and also of the competence of American society. Most importantly, the linkage between problems of employment and the range of social pathology that afflicts the Negro community is unmistakable. Employment not only controls the present for the Negro American but, in a most profound way, is creating the future as well.

[Chart No. 17]   Employment by Occupation and Sex, 1966
(percent distribution)

	Nonwhite		White	
	Male	Female	Male	Female
Total employed (in thousands)	4,655	3,313	42,983	23,114
Percent	100	100	100	100
Professional, technical, and managerial	9	10	27	19
Clerical and sales	9	15	14	43
Craftsmen and foremen	12	°	20	°
Operatives	27	16	20	15
Service workers, except household	} 16	26	} 6	14
Private household workers		28		6
Nonfarm laborers	20	°	6	°
Farmers and farm workers	8	4	7	2
Other	(X)	2	(X)	2

° A few workers included in "Other."
X = Not applicable.
SOURCE: United States Department of Commerce, Bureau of the Census.

For residents of disadvantaged Negro neighborhoods, obtaining good jobs is vastly more difficult than for most workers in society. For decades, social, economic, and psychological disadvantages surrounding the urban Negro poor have impaired their work capacities and opportunities. The result is a cycle of failure—the employment disabilities of one generation breed those of the next.

NEGRO UNEMPLOYMENT

Unemployment rates among Negroes have declined from a post-Korean War high of 12.6 percent in 1958 to 8.2 percent in 1967. Among

[Chart No. 18]   Nonwhites as a Percent of All Workers in Selected Occupations,
1960 and 1966
(penetration of nonwhites into each occupational group)

	Percent Nonwhite 1960	Percent Nonwhite 1966
Total, employed	11	11
Professional and technical	4	6
Medical and other health	4	7
Teachers, except college	7	10
Managers, officials, and proprietors	2	3
Clerical	5	6
Sales	3	3
Craftsmen and foremen	5	6
Construction craftsmen	6	7
Machinists, jobsetters, and other metal craftsmen	4	6
Foremen	2	4
Operatives	12	13
Durable goods	10	11
Nondurable goods	9	12
Nonfarm laborers	27	25
Private household workers	46	42
Other service workers	20	21
Protective services	5	5
Waiters, cooks, and bartenders	15	16
Farmers and farm workers	16	13

SOURCE: United States Department of Labor, Bureau of Labor Statistics.

married Negro men, the unemployment rate for 1967 was down to 3.2 percent.[1]

Notwithstanding this decline, unemployment rates for Negroes are still double those for whites in every category, including married men, as they have been throughout the postwar period. Moreover, since 1954, even during the current unprecedented period of sustained economic growth, unemployment among Negroes has been continuously above the 6 percent "recession" level widely regarded as a sign of serious economic weakness when prevalent for the entire work force.

While the Negro unemployment rate remains high in relation to the white rate, the number of additional jobs needed to lower this to the level of white unemployment is surprisingly small. In 1967, approximately 3 million persons were unemployed during an average week, of whom about 638,000, or 21 percent, were nonwhites. When corrected

[1] Adjusted for Census Bureau undercounting.

for undercounting, total nonwhite unemployment was approximately 712,000 or 8 percent of the nonwhite labor force. To reduce the unemployment rate to 3.4 percent, the rate prevalent among whites, jobs must be found for 57.5 percent of these unemployed persons. This amounts to nearly 409,000 jobs, or about 27 percent of the net number of new jobs added to the economy in the year 1967 alone and only slightly more than one half of 1 percent of all jobs in the United States in 1967.

THE LOW-STATUS AND LOW-PAYING NATURE OF MANY NEGRO JOBS

Even more important perhaps than unemployment is the related problem of the undesirable nature of many jobs open to Negroes. Negro workers are concentrated in the lowest-skilled and lowest-paying occupations. These jobs often involve substandard wages, great instability and uncertainty of tenure, extremely low status in the eyes of both employer and employee, little or no chance for meaningful advancement, and unpleasant or exhausting duties. Negro men in particular are more than three times as likely as whites to be in unskilled or service jobs which pay far less than most: [See chart No. 19 *infra.*]

This concentration in the least desirable jobs can be viewed another way by calculating the changes which would occur if Negro men were

[Chart No. 19]

Type of Occupation	Percentage of Male Workers in each Type of Occupation, 1966		Median Earnings of all Male Civilians in Each Occupation, 1965
	White	Nonwhite	
Professional, technical and managerial	27	9	$7,603 [1]
Clerical and sales	14	9	5,532 [1]
Craftsmen and foremen	20	12	6,270
Operatives	20	27	5,046
Service workers	6	16	3,436
Nonfarm laborers	6	20	2,410
Farmers and farm workers	7	8	1,669 [1]

[1] Average of two categories from normal Census Bureau categories as combined in data presented in UNITED STATES BUREAU OF LABOR STATISTICS, DEP'T OF LABOR, BULL. No. 332, THE SOCIAL AND ECONOMIC CONDITIONS OF NEGROES IN THE UNITED STATES.

employed in various occupations in the same proportions as the male labor force as a whole (not solely the white labor force). [See chart No. 20 *infra*.]

Thus upgrading the employment of Negro men to make their occupational distribution identical with that of the labor force as a whole would have an immense impact upon the nature of their occupations. About 1.3 million nonwhite men—or 28 percent of those employed in

[Chart No. 20]

| Type of Occupation | Number of Male Nonwhite Wokers, 1966 | | | |
| | As Actually Distributed [1] | If Distributed the Same as all Male Workers | Difference | |
			Number	Percent
Professional, technical, and managerial	415,000	1,173,000	+758,000	+183
Clerical and sales	415,000	628,000	+213,000	+ 51
Craftsmen and foremen	553,000	894,000	+341,000	+ 62
Operatives	1,244,000	964,000	−280,000	− 23
Service workers	737,000	326,000	−411,000	− 56
Nonfarm laborers	922,000	340,000	−582,000	− 63
Farmers and farm workers	369,000	330,000	− 39,000	− 11

[1] Estimates based upon percentages set forth in UNITED STATES BUREAU OF LABOR STATISTICS, DEP'T OF LABOR, BULL. No. 332, at 41.

1966—would move up the employment ladder into one of the high-status and higher-paying categories. The effect of such a shift upon the incomes of Negro men would be very great. Using the 1966 job distribution, the shift indicated above would produce about $4.8 billion more earned income for nonwhite men alone if they received the 1965 median income in each occupation. This would be a rise of approximately 30 percent in the earnings actually received by all nonwhite men in 1965 (not counting any sources of income other than wages and salaries).

Of course, the kind of "instant upgrading" visualized in these calculations does not represent a practical alternative for national policy. The economy cannot drastically reduce the total number of low-status jobs it now contains, or shift large numbers of people upward in occupation in any short period. Therefore, major upgrading in the employment status of Negro men must come through a faster relative expansion of higher-level jobs than lower-level jobs (which has been occurring for several decades), an improvement in the skills of nonwhite workers so they can obtain a high proportion of those added better jobs, and a drastic reduction of discriminatory hiring and promotion practices in all enterprises, both private and public.

Nevertheless, this hypothetical example clearly shows that the concentration of male Negro employment at the lowest end of the occupational scale is greatly depressing the incomes of United States Negroes in general. In fact, this is the single most important source of poverty among Negroes. It is even more important than unemployment, as can be shown by a second hypothetical calculation. In 1966, there were about 724,000 unemployed nonwhites in the United States on the average, including adults and teenagers, and allowing for the Census Bureau undercount of Negroes. If every one of these persons had been employed and had received the median amount earned by nonwhite males in 1966 ($3,864), this would have added a total of $2.8 billion to nonwhite income as a whole. If only enough of these persons had been employed at that wage to reduce nonwhite unemployment from 7.3 percent to 3.3 percent—the rate among whites in 1966—then the income gain for nonwhites would have totaled about $1.5 billion. But if nonwhite unemployment remained at 7.3 percent, and nonwhite men were upgraded so that they had the same occupational distribution and incomes as all men in the labor force considered together, this would have produced about $4.8 billion in additional income, as noted above (using 1965 earnings for calculation). Thus the potential income gains from upgrading the male nonwhite labor force are much larger than those from reducing nonwhite unemployment.

This conclusion underlines the difficulty of improving the economic status of Negro men. It is far easier to create new jobs than either to create new jobs with relatively high status and earning power, or to upgrade existing employed or partly employed workers into such better quality employment. Yet only such upgrading will eliminate the fundamental basis of poverty and deprivation among Negro families.

Access to good-quality jobs clearly affects the willingness of Negro men actively to seek work. In riot cities surveyed by the Commission with the largest percentage of Negroes in skilled and semiskilled jobs, Negro men participated in the labor force to the same extent as, or greater than, white men. Conversely, where most Negro men were heavily concentrated in menial jobs, they participated less in the labor force than white men.

Even given similar employment, Negro workers with the same education as white workers are paid less. This disparity doubtless results to some extent from inferior training in segregated schools, and also from the fact that large numbers of Negroes are only now entering certain occupations for the first time. However, the differentials are so large and so universal at all educational levels that they clearly reflect the patterns of discrimination which characterize hiring and promotion practices in many segments of the economy. For example, in 1966, among persons who had completed high school, the median income of Negroes was only 73 percent that of whites. Even among persons with an eighth-grade education, Negro median income was only 80 percent of white median income.

At the same time, a higher proportion of Negro women than white women participates in the labor force at nearly all ages except 16 to 19. For instance, in 1966, 55 percent of nonwhite women from 25 to 34 years of age were employed, compared to only 38 percent of white women in the same age group. The fact that almost half of all adult Negro women work reflects the fact that so many Negro males have unsteady and low-paying jobs. Yet even though Negro women are often better able to find work than Negro men, the unemployment rate among adult nonwhite women (20 years old and over) in 1967 was 7.1 percent, compared to the 4.3 percent rate among adult nonwhite men.

Unemployment rates are, of course, much higher among teenagers, both Negro and white, than among adults; in fact about one-third of all unemployed Negroes in 1967 were between 16 and 19 years old. During the first 9 months of 1967, the unemployment rate among nonwhite teenagers was 26.5 percent; for whites, it was 10.6 percent. About 219,300 nonwhite teenagers were unemployed. About 58,300 were still in school but were actively looking for jobs.

F. The report of the Senate Committee considering amendments to Title VII, S. REP. No. 1111, 90th Cong., 2d. Sess. 3. (1968), made the same point as follows:

NEED FOR THE BILL

Four years ago, recognizing the prevalence of discriminatory employment practices in the United States and the need for federal legislation to deal with the problem of such discrimination, Congress adopted Title VII of the Civil Rights Act of 1964 (42 U.S.C. 2000e-2000c-15). The present bill consists of amendments to Title VII. Its primary effect is to grant to the Equal Employment Opportunity Commission authority to issue judicially enforceable cease and desist orders. Two basic factors explain the need for the bill.

First, despite progress which has occurred since the implementation of Title VII began, Negroes and other minority groups continue to be denied equal employment opportunity. In his testimony in May 1967 before the subcommittee considering proposed amendments to Title VII, Secretary of Labor W. Willard Wirtz stated the following:

Nonwhite workers comprise over 10 percent of the labor force, but about 22 percent of the unemployed, they are 25 percent of those jobless for 6 months or longer, and 18 percent of those working part time involuntary. In general, the rate of unemployment among nonwhite workers is twice or more the rate for white workers.

The March 1967 unemployment rate for men 20 years old or over was 2 percent for whites and 5 percent for nonwhites. Among teenagers (16 to 19 years) the unemployment rate is 23.6 percent for nonwhite youth compared to 9.1 for white youth.

For women, the story is the same—with both white and nonwhite unemployment levels standing higher than male rates.

Adult white women currently have a 3.6 unemployment rate; for nonwhite adult women the rate is at 7 percent. The rate is 10 percent for white teenage girls and 23.5 percent for nonwhite teenage girls.

Appendix II

EQUAL EMPLOYMENT OPPORTUNITY COMMISSION, DISCRIMINATION
IN WHITE COLLAR EMPLOYMENT 593 (1968):

This is to summarize conclusions and findings from the study of minority and female employment patterns in 100 major companies in New York City presented on January 16, 1968, at the Commission's N.Y.C. Hearings on Discrimination in White Collar Employment (full text attached).[1]

Each of the 100 companies employs at least 500 white collar employees—officials/managers, professional, technical, sales and office/clerical workers—in the City of New York. The group includes companies in a variety of manufacturing and service industries, but excludes "finance" and "communications" which are covered separately in other Commission reports presented at the N.Y.C. hearings. The 100 companies account for 15.8 percent of the Gross National Product and employ approximately 10 percent of the 26 million employees covered by the EEO-1 reporting system nationally. They account for about 163,000 white collar workers reported in N.Y.C. in 1966 under EEO-1, or about 25 percent of the city's white collar employment outside the retail and medical service industries.

Principal Conclusions and Findings

1. *The 100 major companies clearly fail to match their economic leadership role with leadership in equal employment opportunity. They lag significantly behind the N.Y.C. average in the employment of Negroes and Puerto Ricans in all levels of white collar jobs, and in utiliza-*

---

[1] Employment figures cited herein are based on Employer Reporting Forms (EEO-1) filed annually with the Commission by employers of 100 or more people (or 50 or more in companies with federal contracts or $50,000 or more).

tion of white collar jobs at the officials/managers, professional and tech-nician level. The city average for minority employment itself is far below the proportion of minorities in the population.

Negroes, representing approximately 18 percent of N.Y.C. population in 1966, fill 5.2 percent of white collar jobs[2] reported under 1966 EEO-1 in the city as a whole. They fill only 2.6 percent of such jobs in the 100 major companies.

Puerto Ricans, representing an estimated 10 percent of city popula-tion in 1966 filled 2.9 percent of white collar jobs city-wide in 1966, but only 2.0 percent in the 100 companies.

A comparison of 100 major corporations and all New York City em-ployers in utilization of Negroes, Puerto Ricans and women is shown below. [See chart No. 21 *infra.*]

2. *The 100 companies trail most major segments of New York City's large "financial" and "communications" industries in white collar utiliza-tion of Negroes and Puerto Ricans. They trail all with respect to women above clerical level.* [See chart Nos. 22, 23 *infra.*]

[Chart No. 21]

Occupational Category	Precent Negroes		Percent Puerto Ricans		Percent Women	
	City	"100"	City	"100"	City	"100"
All White Collar	5.2	2.6	2.9	2.0	42.5	30.9
Officials & Managers	1.3	0.7	1.0	0.7	11.9	3.8
Professionals	1.6	0.7	1.3	1.2	14.4	4.7
Technicians	5.1	2.4	3.2	1.7	14.1	8.3
Sales Workers	1.6	1.4	1.0	0.9	10.3	11.2
Office & Clerical	7.9	4.5	4.2	3.4	67.8	62.5

3. *The absence of leadership in equal employment opportunity by the 100 companies is further illustrated by comparison of N.Y.C. white collar employment in these companies vs. a comparable group of N.Y.C. nonprofit organizations (excluding hospitals) reporting employment to the Commission in 1966.* The 100 major companies employ about 163,000 white collar workers and the non-profit organizations about 28,000 or about one sixth as many white collars in total. Yet the nonprofits employ about *one half as many* Negro officials and managers, *four times as many* Negro professionals, and *one and a half times as many* Negro technicians.

4. *At higher levels of white collar employment, the majority of the top 100 companies appear to be implementing equal employment policies less effectively in their headquarters city of New York than in company installations elsewhere.* Among those 78 companies with large white

---

[2] Excluding retail trade and medical services.

[Chart No. 22]

	1966 Negro White Collar %		1966 Puerto Rican White Collar %
Banking	6.7	Banking	5.1
Insurance	5.9	Insurance	2.8
Radio-TV Broadcasting	3.9	Book Publishing	2.5
Book Publishing	3.7	Periodical Publishing	2.4
Brokerage	3.4	Brokerage	2.2
Newspaper Publishing	3.0		
Periodical Publishing	2.9	100 COMPANIES	2.0
100 COMPANIES	2.6	Advertising Agencies	1.8
		Newspaper Publishing	0.9
Advertising Agencies	2.5	Radio-TV Broadcasting	0.9

[Chart No. 23]

	1966 Female Officials & Managers %		1966 Female Professionals %
Periodical Publishing	24.6	Periodical Publishing	55.2
Book Publishing	18.2	Book Publishing	42.3
Insurance	14.3	Advertising Agencies	20.2
Advertising Agencies	11.5	Banking	15.0
Radio-TV Broadcasting	10.5	Insurance	11.1
Banking	8.8	Radio-TV Broadcasting	10.0
Brokerage	4.9	Newspaper Publishing	9.6
Newspaper Publishing	4.8	Brokerage	9.0
100 COMPANIES	3.8	100 COMPANIES	4.7

collar work forces throughout the country as well as in N.Y.C., only 19 have a better record in Negro employment as officials and managers in N.Y.C. vs. the balance of the country.

5. *While there were individual exceptions, those companies (46) within the 100 which are signatories of a "Plan for Progress"—a public posture of affirmative action in minority employment—utilized minorities in 1966 at a substantially lower rate as a group than the 54 companies not party to a comparable public pledge.* For example, while non-members had 1.2 percent Negroes in positions as officials and managers, Plans members had only 0.3 percent in these jobs.

6. *There are wide variations in minority employment among the individual companies comprising the group of 100. These variations indicate that some of the companies have successfully located and utilized minority workers in a manner (a) which belies an allegation that qualified and qualifiable minority workers are seldom available; and (b)*

which could be emulated by the majority of companies which have not.

In Negro clerical employment only 11 employers have a better record than the city as a whole at 7.9 percent. The bottom 12 have only 133 Negroes out of a total 8,366 clerical workers or 1.6 percent. Three other of the companies *each* have more Negro clerical workers than these 12 combined.

Unbelievably, 56 of the companies, with a total of 12,665 officials and managers in N.Y.C., had not in 1966 a single Negro in that category. The other 44 had 221 Negroes among a total 19,500 officials and managers, an average of five each. One of the 44 alone employed 27 Negro managers.

Forty-eight of the companies, with 8,857 officials and managers in N.Y.C. employed not a single Puerto Rican in this capacity. The other 52 reported 235 Puerto Rican managers out of 23,308 in total. One of these companies alone reported 59 Puerto Ricans among its officials and managers.

7. *Changes in minority employment in 1967 vs. 1966 showed a slight improvement among the 100 companies, but nowhere near that seen in the "financial" group analyzed separately.* For the 70 companies for which 1967 statistics could be matched against 1966, the figures were as follows, compared to the city's nine largest banks, 10 insurance companies and 15 brokerage firms (which collectively employ about the same total number of white collar workers as the 70 corporations—about 112,000): [See chart No. 24 *infra*.]

[Chart No. 24]

Negro % Total White Collar				Puerto Rican % Total White Collar			
	1966	1967	Increase		1966	1967	Increase
70 Corporations	2.5	3.2	+0.7	70 Corporations	1.9	2.2	+0.3
9 Banks	7.1	10.2	+3.1	9 Banks	5.2	5.4	+0.2
10 Insurance				10 Insurance			
Companies	6.7	8.3	+1.6	Companies	2.5	3.2	+0.7
15 Brokerage Firms	3.6	4.8	+1.2	15 Brokerage Firms	2.4	3.3	+0.9

Among the 70 corporations, the improvement in 1967 in overall white collar participation for Negroes was confined largely to the clerical category. For example, thirty-eight of the seventy corporations showed no change between 1966 and 1967 in Negro participation as officials and managers. Of these, thirty-five had *no* Negro officials or managers either year.

Appendix III

S. Rep. No. 1111, 90th Cong., 2d. Sess. 28 (1968) contains the following exhibit:

EXHIBIT A. EXCERPTS FROM TEXT OF TYPICAL
CONCILIATION AGREEMENT

EXPLANATION OF PROPOSED AGREEMENT

The attached proposed agreement is intended to assist employers in taking affirmative action to provide Equal Employment Opportunity under Title VII of the Civil Rights Act of 1964. The provisions deal with recruitment, hiring procedures, and qualifications for employment. Because of the detailed nature of the proposed agreement, it appeared useful to provide this general explanation.

I. General principles: In this section, the purposes of the agreement are made clear, along with the statement that the signing of the agreement does not constitute any admission by the employer of any violation of Title VII.

II. Recruitment practices: This section establishes a continuous relationship between the establishment and various sources from which minority group applicants for employment may come. These sources include the State employment service, and various private organizations which have as an object, the expansion of employment opportunities for minorities. In this relationship, the employer will notify the listed organizations in advance of expected vacancies, will also notify them of other vacancies as they develop. When the listed organization refers an applicant, records will be kept of the disposition of the application by both the employer and the sending agency.

III. Hiring practices: The employer agrees to the prompt and fair processing of applications of minority group members. Where no vacancy exists, but the applicant may be qualified, the employer will place the application in an affirmative action file, and when vacancies develop, will give every consideration to hiring applicants from this file, prior to seeking applicants from other sources.

IV. Review of qualifications: After a review of qualifications, certain requirements previously maintained by the employer may be changed. This section provides for the listing of such changes as are agreed to.

V. Reporting: This section deals with quarterly reports of compliance with the above provisions of the agreement. Reporting forms are included.

VI. Other provisions: This section deals with the effect of the agreement, provides for reexamination of the agreement, and for procedures for enforcement of the agreement.

Appendixes contain various forms relating to the carrying out of the agreement.

I. GENERAL PRINCIPLES

A. Whereas the above establishment is located in an area of substantial minority group population, but employs few minority group persons; and whereas the employer wishes to employ more minority groups persons than he has been employing under his existing recruitment and hiring practices* * * the employer hereby agrees with the Commission to establish a specific program of affirmative action set forth below* * * :

* * * * * * *

IV. QUALIFICATIONS FOR EMPLOYMENT

A. In recognition of the fact that requirements which appear to be fair on their face may:

1. Not be related to the job or jobs for which they are applied, and

2. May have the effect of denying access to employment oppor-

tunities to minority group members in greater proportion than the minority,

a careful review of the requirements for each job * * * has been undertaken. * * * On the basis of this review, it is agreed that certain entry level qualifications heretofore required by the employer shall be suspended and that no other requirements shall be imposed without prior consultation with and approval by the Commission.

        ❋   ❋   ❋   ❋   ❋   ❋   ❋

C. Guidelines: The employer agrees to comply in all respects with the Guidelines on Employment Testing Procedures issued by the Commission on August 24, 1966, which are incorporated herein and made a part hereof.

D. Additional training periods and programs: It is recognized that the revision of entry level requirements accomplished under paragraph A, above, may require the introduction or expansion of training programs by the employer. The Commission hereby undertakes to provide the employer with continuing technical assistance to facilitate the introduction and financing of such other programs as the employer may be willing to undertake to provide for upgrading training for his employee. In his quarterly reports, the employer will identify any new or proposed training programs.

V. REPORTING

Ninety days from the date of this agreement, and each 90 days thereafter for a total of 2 years, the employer shall send to the Commission a written report which shall include the following information:

A. Copies of all correspondence with the State employment service and the organizations listed in II (H), and of correspondence from such organizations to the employer.

B. A report on the operation of the recruitment and hiring program outlined in sections II and III of this agreement which shall be submitted on a form to be supplied by the Commission, listed here as appendix 8. The report shall contain the following information:

    1. Name, address, and phone number of all applicants for employment during the quarter, with all minority group applicants listed first.

    2. Race, color, and national origin of each said applicant.

    3. Date applied.

    4. Indication of source from which applicant was referred, or how he applied.

5. If hired, starting date, job, and starting rate.

6. If rejected, date.

7. If held for further action, noted.

8. If applicant was minority group member and was rejected, the reasons for rejection.

9. If applicant was minority group member and placed in affirmative action file, the date so placed.

10. If applicant hired from file, date hired.

11. If applicant was removed thereafter from affirmative action file for reasons other than hiring, state the reason.

12. If minority group employee separated within 90 days of employment, explanation of circumstances of separation.

C. A statistical summary containing:

1. The number of applicants in the file at the beginning of the period.

2. The number added during the period.

3. The number removed during the period.

4. The number hired during the period.

5. The total at the end of the period on the form provided as appendix 9.

D. Copies of all correspondence with minority group applicants required under section III of the agreement.

E. Copies of company statements circulated as in section I(C).

F. Copies of notices to employment services as required in section II(F).

G. Report on advertising practices as required in section II(G).

VI. OTHER PROVISIONS

A. The execution and implementation of this agreement shall have no effect upon the handling or disposition of individual complaints of employment discrimination.

News Release, EEOC, July 17, 1969:

"AFFIRMATIVE ACTION FILE" AGREEMENT TO INCREASE MINORITY HIRES

A major conciliation agreement increasing white collar job opportunities for minorities was announced today by William H. Brown III, Chairman of the U.S. Equal Employment Opportunity Commission and F. Raymond Peterson, Chairman of the Board of the First National Bank of Passaic County, New Jersey.

"This agreement pioneers a powerful technique for employers to increase minority employment systematically and efficiently," stated Brown.

Under the Agreement, the Bank will expand its minority recruiting efforts, and promptly process minority applicants. The heart of the procedure, however, is an "affirmative action file" to be maintained by the Bank. This file would comprise the names of qualified or qualifiable minority applicants for whom no jobs were available at the time of application. The Bank will consult the file and give consideration to persons in it, before looking elsewhere when a vacancy develops.

The Agreement also includes provisions whereby the Bank will require a high school diploma only for jobs which reasonably require it, and will request the American Bankers Association to validate a battery of tests which it uses.

The Agreement grew out of a Commission project involving the New Jersey Division on Civil Rights and the Rutgers Law School in developing procedures for employers having a low utilization of minorities. Rutgers Professor Alfred W. Blumrosen, former EEOC Chief of Conciliations, coordinated the project.

Appendix IV

UNITED STATES DEPARTMENT OF LABOR, SOCIAL AND ECONOMIC CONDITIONS OF NEGROES IN THE UNITED STATES 43–46 (1967):

The nonwhite dropout rate among 16 and 17 year olds has fallen sharply. The school enrollment gap has narrowed for these ages and for kindergarteners, but has widened for persons in the late teens and early twenties. [See chart No. 25 *infra.*]

[Chart No. 25]   Percent Enrolled in School, by Age, 1960 and 1966

	1960		1966	
	Nonwhite	White	Nonwhite	White
5 years	51	66	66	74
6 to 15 years	98	99	99	99
16 and 17 years	77	85	83	89
18 and 19 years	35	40	39	48
20 to 24 years	8	10	14	21

SOURCE: United States Department of Commerce, Bureau of the Census.

Six years ago the education gap between nonwhite and white young men was 2 years of school experience. Today the gap is one half year of school experience. A majority of nonwhite young men 25 to 29 years old now have a high school diploma, and, unlike 6 years ago, they tend to have more years of schooling than nonwhite young women. [See chart No. 26 *infra.*]

[Chart No. 26]   Educational Attainment of Persons 25 to 29 Years Old,
by Sex, 1960 and 1966

	Male		Female	
	Nonwhite	White	Nonwhite	White
Median years of school completed:				
1960	10.5	12.4	11.1	12.3
1966	12.1	12.6	11.9	12.5
Percent completing 4 years of high school or more:				
1960	36	63	41	65
1966	53	73	49	74

SOURCE: United States Department of Commerce, Bureau of the Census.

7   The Construction Industry Problem

Testimony of Alfred W. Blumrosen on June 25, 1969 Before the Massachusetts Advisory Committee to the United States Civil Rights Commission on Equal Employment Opportunity in the Construction Industry

My name is Alfred W. Blumrosen. I am a Professor of Law at Rutgers University, Newark, New Jersey. My field of specialization is labor law and race relations law. I am a labor arbitrator and have served several government agencies dealing with employment discrimination. In 1963–64 I was a consultant to the New Jersey Civil Rights Commission and conducted a critical study of the New Jersey Division on Civil Rights, the State antidiscrimination agency, which was published in *Rutgers Law Review*.[1] At the same time, I advised Rutgers University as it faced problems of discrimination in the construction of the University's new campus in Newark. From 1965 to 1967 I was on leave with the Equal Employment Opportunity Commission, which had just been established. I served as consultant, as first Chief of Liaison with Federal and State Agencies and, for most of the time, as first Chief of Conciliations. In that capacity, I was responsible for the development of remedies in cases where the EEOC found reasonable cause to believe discrimination existed under Title VII of the Civil Rights Act of 1964. The single major case which marked that period was the Newport News Shipbuilding Agreement under which some 3,000 Negro employees received promotions or wage increases and 100 were promoted or to be promoted to supervision. I remained a consultant to the EEOC after returning to Rutgers in 1967 and developed a program to deal with employers who had few minority employees in areas of high-minority population. In the summer of 1968, I served as Special Attorney in the Civil Rights Division of the Department of Justice, advising the De-

---

[1] Blumrosen, *Antidiscrimination Laws in Action in New Jersey: A Law-Sociology Study*, 19 RUTGERS L. REV. 187 (1965).

partment on its employment discrimination litigation, and assisting in the trial of *United States v. H. K. Porter Co.* in Birmingham. I am currently a Consultant to the Office of Equal Opportunity, Department of Housing and Urban Development.

I consider the problem of remedying discrimination in the construction industry to be one of the most difficult in the field of civil rights. Yet it is one of the most important because the construction process is a visible one; and has become symbolic in our time of the question of whether equality will prevail in employment and the more fundamental question of whether our laws against discrimination will be faithfully executed.

I believe the first step in any attempt to remedy patterns of discrimination in construction is to identify that discrimination. Once discrimination has been established, then a wide range of remedies is available. Until discrimination is established, it is difficult to discuss the extent of remedies which are appropriate. The concept of discrimination is substantially the same whether one discusses Executive Order No. 11246 or Title VII of the Civil Rights Act of 1964. Discrimination is to be broadly defined to achieve the aims of the Congress and the President, to eradicate racial bias from our employment system. Therefore, I will first discuss the concept of discrimination as it applies to the construction industry, and then turn to the question of remedies.

I. General Background

The patterns of exclusion of minorities in some of the construction trades will be detailed for you during the course of these hearings.[2] Similarly, the various relationships between the unions and the general contractors and subcontractors will be outlined to you, along with the various hiring hall arrangements which permeate the industry. An understanding of the hiring hall arrangements, the subcontracting system, and the concept of territorial and work jurisdiction of craft unions is essential to the identification of discriminatory patterns on the part of unions and employers.

A. *The hiring hall* is the key to union security and job opportunities

---

[2] See appendix I of this chapter for EEOC statistics on minority participation in the construction industry.

in the construction industry. For most employees in construction, there is no seniority with a single employer, such as is enjoyed in manufacturing industries. Men are hired by a contractor for one project, and discharged at the conclusion of their work. They then return to the hiring hall and wait for assignment, in some order of priority, to the next job. For this system to provide job security, the union must embrace as much of the construction work in the area as possible within its jurisdiction, and then assign men to these jobs in a manner which will assure job security for them, just as the seniority systems assures job security in manufacturing industries.

B. Each craft union has *exclusive territorial jurisdiction* and *exclusive work jurisdiction.* Controlling this jurisdiction and limiting the numbers of men in the trade who can perform work within gives the craft union its basic bargaining power with employers. If employers were free to hire from outside the union hall, they would not be under pressure to meet the wage demands of the craft unions in construction.

C. Construction contracts are usually let to one or more general contractors who then subcontract most of the work to specialty contractors. These contractors in turn hire labor from the hiring halls.

The local contractors and their counterpart unions arrange, in many cases, for apprenticeship programs, which are often administered on an area basis by a Joint Apprenticeship Committee (JAC).

All of these parties—union, contractors, and joint apprenticeship committees—are subject to Title VII of the Civil Rights Act of 1964, which prohibits unlawful employment practices which "adversely affect" employees or potential employees, in their employment opportunities, because of race, color, religion, sex, or national origin. Employers, including general and subcontractors in federally supported construction, are subject to Executive Order No. 11246, which imposes both a "nondiscrimination" and an "affirmative action" requirement. Indirectly, unions are affected by this executive order, but are not directly subject to it, since, in theory, it is part of the contracting process with the employers. Apprenticeship programs are subject to regulation of sorts by the Bureau of Apprenticeship and Training under regulations promulgated by that agency. And, within a state like Massachusetts, all parties are subject to state laws against discrimination in employment.

II. Establishing Discrimination

In most cities, many of the construction unions will be fairly integrated, and in some, often the trowel trades, minorities may predominate. But, in most areas, there are some locals which have either no minority members, or very few such members. Frequently this will include the more highly paid and sometimes the more sophisticated trades, such as electricians, sheet metal workers, and elevator constructors. Frequently the plumbers and iron workers will be found to have virtually all-white membership. Since the construction unions have been a fraternal, and often a family type, institution, the privileges of membership often include the privilege of bringing in new members, including family members. Thus the segregated construction local tends to restrict information concerning its activities to members and friends, to give breaks to members and friends of members in its admissions and other policies, and to perpetuate its segregated character.

Whether consciously or subconsciously, these various unions developed segregated characteristics, and retained them as the nation entered the era of equal employment opportunity. This era dawned in the mid-1940's, with the Supreme Court's decision on *Steele v. Louisville & N. Ry.*, 323 U.S. 192 (1944), and the passage of Fair Employment Practice laws in many states, as well as the first of the executive orders prohibiting discrimination by government contractors. These orders were progressively broadened until the Kennedy order, Executive Order No. 10925, and its successor, the Johnson order, Executive Order No. 11246, reached their present form in 1961 and 1965. The Civil Rights Act of 1964 added the congressional decision that employment discrimination was unlawful.[3] This law went into effect on July 2, 1965, and has now been in effect for four years, minus a week. The passage of all this time, and the present discriminatory practices of some construction unions, have eroded public confidence in the efficacy of law to solve or assist in solving racial discrimination problems, and have contributed to the civil unrest of our time.

One of the evidences of this tragedy is that we have few judicial decisions as to what constitutes discrimination by construction unions.

---

[3] See, in general, SOVERN, LEGAL RESTRAINTS ON RACIAL DISCRIMINATION IN EMPLOYMENT (1966).

The following analysis is based on my study of court decisions and of decisions of the EEOC finding reasonable cause to believe that discrimination exists which is illegal under Title VII.

Discrimination in those construction unions whose practices are of concern in a given community *consists largely of devices which are designed to or have the effect of maintaining the substantially segregated character of these unions. When dealing with a substantially segregated union, any device or procedure which has this effect is discriminatory, unless it can be justified.*

For example, when dealing with a substantially all-white local union,

1) a decision not to admit new members at all has the effect of perpetuating segregation;

2) a decision to admit new members (as apprentices or journeymen) without notifying the minority community, has such an effect, because only part of the white community will be aware of the opportunities;

3) a decision to commence an apprenticeship program without recruiting in the minority community has the effect of perpetuating discrimination;

4) a decision to enroll new members or open an apprenticeship class at a certain time, without notifying and recruiting in the minority community, perpetuates segregation;

5) decisions not to refer applicants of minority groups for work, has a similar effect;

6) the establishment of the barriers of delay, of subjectively evaluated tests, of unreasonable test standards not uniformly applied to whites, as a similar effect;

7) a decision to refer to work in order of seniority in the local, or in the trade in the area, may have this effect if there has been a pattern of exclusion of minorities in the trade;

8) any decision to "blanket in" a group of whites has a similar effect in that it delays the time minorities may be included.

This is a partial catalogue of tactics which have been used. All these tactics, when engaged in by locals with substantially all-white membership, have the effect of perpetuating segregation, and therefore violate the executive order, Title VII, and state laws against discrimination. For purpose of contract compliance, the presence of such tactics, and hence the determination of discrimination, can be made informally in the administrative process. Unions which wish it may be entitled to a more formal hearing under the executive order. Under Title VII, the employer is in violation, not because the union discriminated, but because he knows that if he uses the union as an exclusive or primary referral source, he will in fact secure only white or substantially all-white employees. Thus he is using a tainted source, and is therefore in violation of the law. For the purpose of Title VII, "reasonable cause" decisions on these lines are made administratively by the EEOC, and judicially by the courts.

III. Shaping Remedies for Discrimination

Effective remedies for discrimination should make complainants whole for losses resulting from discrimination, establish procedures for the future which will assure that minorities do in fact have employment opportunities and prevent the development of other modes of discrimination or delay.[4] These objectives are mandated by Title VII which, after a finding of discrimination, directs the federal courts to, "enjoin the respondent from engaging in . . . unlawful employment practice, and order such affirmative action as may be appropriate . . ."

The breadth of the remedial requirement imposed by substantially similar language in the New Jersey Law Against Discrimination has recently been explained by the New Jersey Supreme Court in a housing discrimination case, *Jackson v. Concord Co.* 54 N.J. 113 (1969), as follows:

> From all of this it is patently clear that the Legislature intended to create an effective enforcement agency in order to eradicate the cancer of discrimination. Even in the case of an individual complainant, it is plain that the public interest is also involved. Discrimination, by its very nature, is directed against an entire class in the particular circumstances and wrongful conduct against a complaining individual is indicative of such a state of mind in the wrongdoer against the class. Common knowledge and experience dictate the conclusion, for example, that an apartment owner found to have discriminated because of race in one instance may well have discriminated, and proposes to discriminate, against all others of the class seeking to rent his accommodations . . . So the law

---

[4] Dobbins v. Local 212, IBEW, 292 F. Supp. 413 (D.C. Ohio 1968).

seeks not only to give redress to the individual who complains, but moreover to eliminate and prevent all such future conduct on the part of the landlord by enjoining further discriminatory practices as to all persons, as well as to deter others similarly situated from engaging or continuing to engage in such courses of conduct.

A more specific discussion of remedies for discrimination must be based on an understanding of decisions in three cases: *Local 53, Asbestos Workers v. Vogler,* 407 F.2d 1047 (5th Cir. 1969); the Seattle Iron Workers case, *Lewis v. Local 86, Iron Workers* (1969 CCH EMPLOYMENT PRACTICES ¶8083); and a school teacher case, *United States v. County Board of Education* 395 U.S. 225, decided a week ago Monday by the United States Supreme Court.

In *Asbestos Workers* the federal district court was sustained by the court of appeals for the Fifth Circuit in an order which required that the union abandon its preference for family relations, its requirement of a recommendation by an existing member and its membership vote for admission, that it operate its hiring hall so as to refer one white and one minority person alternately for employment, and that it develop a plan to increase the size of membership.

In the Seattle *Iron Workers,* the union was ordered by the Washington State FEPC to cease discriminating and to pay for losses suffered by black applicants who had been delayed and rejected for membership to the extent of thousands of dollars.

In the *County Board of Education* case, the Supreme Court upheld a district court decision requiring specific ratios of black to white teachers in the Montgomery County school system as a remedy for past discrimination. Note that this use of targets, goals, or specific numbers of persons of various races is not the mechanical quota which is proscribed in employment cases by the so-called no-quota provision of section 703(j) of the Civil Rights Act of 1964.

This method of increasing minority employment is not prohibited, because the statute only prohibits mechanical requirement of proportion of minority employees based on population or labor force participation rates. It says nothing about the use of goals or standards as remedies for segregation and discriminatory exclusion. Where segregation and discrimination are found, the statute speaks only of the "affirmative action" required to correct it. Obviously, if the discrimination consists of excluding or substantially excluding minorities, the remedy, if it is to be meaningful, must be aimed at increasing the numbers of minorities involved. The only remaining question is whether the method used to increase minority participation rates is reasonably necessary to achieve the result, and is reasonably related to this purpose. In the Montgomery *County Board of Education* case, the Supreme Court recited five years of efforts by the District Court, short of the application of numerical standards, to accomplish this result, to no avail. Under those circumstances, said the court, the application of a numerical standard was sound, because it was necessary to remedy the past discrimination. The court assumed that the standards used in that case would be fairly and reasonably administered.

The history of some unions in the construction trades exactly parallels the history of the Montgomery *County Board of Education* case. Efforts going back to 1961 to persuade, cajole, and encourage these unions to abandon their segregation practices have failed. If a construction trades union today, in 1969, remains substantially segregated, it is not because there have been no efforts at persuasion. Against this background, stronger medicine is obviously called for, and numerical targets are appropriate because they are clear and definite, and give all parties guidance in what is likely to be required of them.

I can give personal testimony to the importance of numerical standards, in addition to the experiences of the National Alliance for Businessmen. Since 1960 my law school has been making efforts to increase minority participation in the school. We thought we were doing well, but between 1960 and 1967 we graduated twelve black students, while graduating eight hundred whites. This was obviously inadequate in the face of our modern needs. In 1968, we adopted numerical targets: twenty minority students in the fall of 1968, and forty in succeeding years. Our internal organization was revised to centralize control over this program in a committee of which I am chairman. We met our target last fall, and will meet it this fall. We will in this way substantially increase the participation of minority persons before the bar. The numerical targets cleared the air and permitted effective implementation of a policy which we had long stated, but had not implemented. The need for such targets will lessen as more minority group persons become aware of their opportunities before the bar. Incidentally, we increased the size of our classes so that no nonminority person who otherwise would have been admitted was excluded.

So I can testify to the administrative effectiveness of such targets or goals, where there has been a history of ineffective efforts, or no efforts, to eliminate segregation in an institution.

With this introduction, let us turn to the areas of remedies which are required here, of both unions and contractors, and their joint agents, the JAC's:

A. RECRUITMENT. It is generally believed in the minority community that construction unions discriminate. Therefore, the employers and their unions must make efforts to convince minority persons, both youths in school and men working in the trade, that they are welcome and are encouraged to participate, to join the union, and to secure employment. The unions and employers in the area may wish to organize and coordinate this program with local institutions such as vocational high schools, the Workers Defense League, the Urban League, or other. Failure to engage in these activities constitutes, in my view, the perpetuation of segregation. I have described this problem in more detail in chapter 6.

Recruitment in this area must include assistance in equipping young men with such qualifications as are reasonably necessary to enter the trade, by advising them of reasonable standards, and assisting them in meeting these standards.

B. PROCEDURES FOR ADMISSION AS APPRENTICE OR JOURNEYMAN. These procedures provide ample room for discrimination, as the *Asbestos Workers* and Seattle *Iron Workers* cases attest. They must be carefully evaluated so as to wring out the opportunities for discrimination. This can be done only by judging the procedures in terms of their results. The various admissions standards, from the necessity for filling out an application form, through the need for references, or other subjective evaluations based on interviewing and the like, all can be used to perpetuate discrimination. Where the subjective factors in admissions procedures operate in this manner, they must be overridden.

But admissions standards also involve, with respect to apprentices, written and manual tests. I have expressed my views on testing by employers in the same article already referred to. Unless the test is reasonably related to entry requirements, if it excludes minorities, it should be stricken or revised.

C. INCREASING THE SIZE OF THE LABOR FORCE. The result of increased minority recruitment, and eased admission standards, will be that more minority persons will seek admission as apprentices or journeymen. Unions normally seek to keep down the numbers of men in the trade, and often there is an apprentice-journeyman ratio, intended to prevent employers from overusing apprentices with their lower rates. The size of the union and this ratio may have to be altered to permit the entry of more minority persons. More nonminority persons as well may be admitted under the required relaxation of numerical limitations. I realize that this increase in numbers may weaken the bargaining position of the union, but these unions which have been perpetuating segregation cannot expect the minority community to subsidize their high-wage structure by remaining out of their part of the labor market.

D. ADMISSION OF EXPERIENCED WORKERS AS JOURNEYMEN. In some trades and areas, minority personnel have become experienced in the trade by working in the nonunion sector. These men should be entitled to full journeyman status and membership in the union upon establishing that they meet the standards of the least-qualified white journeyman, or the minimum standards necessary for performance in the trade.[5]

E. ALTERNATIVES TO APPRENTICESHIP. In the Boston area, a limited route to journeyman status, called trainee, has been instituted in a very limited way in the model cities program. I will not defend or criticize the particular arrangement, but will support the principle that it may now be appropriate to develop an alternative route to journeyman status aside from the ordinary apprenticeship system, and to insure that substantial numbers of minorities are included. In addition, to the extent that apprenticeship requirements are not reasonably related to the needs of the trade, these requirements themselves should be revised. The duration and conditions of some apprenticeship programs suggest that they are more important as a low-wage restriction on access device than as an educational institution.

All of the foregoing are intended as remedies to increase minority participation in the construction trades labor supply. If minority participation is assured, we turn to the problem of assuring that the minority labor supply is in fact put to work by referral to the various construction sites. This aspect of the remedial problem involves contractors and the operation of the hiring hall. We will assume that there exists a supply of the type of labor required for construction in question.

---

[5] *Dobbins, supra.*

F. Qualification of Contractors and Bidders on Government Contracts. If a contractor is aware that the source of his labor is such that he will operate with a substantially segregated labor force, and is prepared to continue to use that source, he intends to have a substantially segregated labor force. Such a contractor should not be permitted to bid on government contracts. Virtually all competing contractors in a given trade deal with the same union, and if that union has all-white membership and referrals and an exclusive hiring hall arrangement, none of the contractors who have such arrangement should be permitted to bid. I realize this is strong medicine, but I see no alternative but to insist that there can no longer be federal construction under such conditions. The unions and the employers, under such a rule, will have a mutual interest in increasing minority participation, because without that participation, there may be no federally supported construction in a given area. Unions and employers may respond to this rule by relaxing the exclusivity of the hiring hall, altering the referral processes from the hall, increasing minority participation in the union or by using other methods of avoiding the perpetuation of segregation. But the rule should be clear that a segregated union plus an exclusive hiring hall arrangement means that the contractor is not qualified to bid on government contracts.

G. Specification of Numbers or Ratio of Minority Participation in Trades Which Have Been Found to Discriminate in the Bidding Stage of Contracting. This is the theory of the "Philadelphia Plan." It requires that the government indicate minimum acceptable numbers of minority workers on projects in an area, *with respect to those trades and crafts where there is discrimination.* Only in this way can it be assured that the operation of the hiring hall will not be skewed to perpetuate discrimination. If the unions know that they must refer certain numbers of minorities, they will undertake to do so. If they are left to their own devices, the hiring hall arrangements are apt to work in a discriminatory manner. *I repeat that this remedy is appropriate after an administrative finding of discrimination or segregation.*[6]

H. Direct Control of Operation of Hiring Hall. Another ap-

---

[6] This view was sustained in Contractors Ass'n of Eastern Pennsylvania v. Shultz, 62 Lab. Cas. ¶9421 (E.D. Pa. 1970) which upheld the Philadelphia Plan.

proach is to directly regulate the operation of the hiring hall. For example, in the *Asbestos Workers* case, the court ordered alternate referrals, one black and one white. In *Iron Workers,* the union was enjoined from refusing to refer Negroes based on length of service in the trade because this had an exclusionary effect. Another example has just come to my attention. This is a consent order in the case of *United States v. Local 520, Operating Engineers,* in East St. Louis, Illinois. This decree seems to require the establishment, on an interim basis, of a minority group referral list, with priority given to referrals from that list in a certain defined geographic area.

I. USE OF AFFIRMATIVE ACTION FILE. A more modest device than the ones mentioned above is the affirmative action file utilized in some cases by the EEOC with employers. In this system, qualified or qualifiable minority group applicants are placed in a separate file which is consulted when vacancies develop. This could be used as a basis for direct employer hirings, for employer referrals to the union, or for union referrals to employers.[7]

J. TO USE OR BYPASS THE HIRING HALL. Ane additional question is of basic importance. In remedying the segregation, should public policy urge employers to use the union hiring hall provided it is reformed, or to bypass it and hire directly? Hiring halls can be used by employers who have engaged in recruiting through an understanding between the union and the employer that, if the employer refers a minority applicant who has sought work at the work place, the union will refer the applicant back to the employer. In this way the union retains some influence in the employment system.

Hiring halls are an integral part of the collective bargaining process in construction, and they serve valid purposes for both labor and management. If they can be reformed, I would prefer to see them operate in a fair way. Therefore, I would not propose *at this time* the bypassing or abolition of hiring halls. I remain hopeful that the trade union movement, for all of its failure in this area, can reform; and I am not optimistic about the alternatives of greater government involvement in the labor market institutions, or the ability of employers to operate fairly without the pressures of unionism. It would be tragic, indeed, if the trade union movement were to flounder to the point of self-destruction

---

[7] See Ch. 6 *supra.*

over this issue of racial equality. But the issue is present and must be resolved now. I believe that public policy should support instant reforms of hiring hall arrangements, but should tolerate no longer the delays we have seen over the years.

I realize that reforms may be difficult. The electricians, for example, refer from the hiring hall in the order of priority dictated by whether a man is in one of four classes. Class I members have worked in the trade under the same contract for a long time. They are referred first. Where membership in such a local was limited to white employees, this referral procedure excludes minorities from any but the leavings. Such a procedure applied against minority employees perpetuates the past discrimination and cannot be allowed to continue. This at least is my view, shared by the Seattle Iron Workers decision.

K. REPORTING. (1) In general: In order to determine whether the law is being complied with, reporting of several types is essential. For government contract projects, the general reporting responsibility should rest on the general contractor. At present, contractors must report the number and racial composition of their employees; and unions and joint apprenticeship committees must report on Forms EEO-2 and 3 the numbers and racial composition of members and apprentices. No contractor should be eligible to bid on any government contract if his offer does not include a copy of the latest EEO-1 form he has filed and copies of the EEO-2 and EEO-3 forms filed by unions and joint apprenticeship committees with whom he will deal in the course of building the project on which he is bidding.

2) By Project. In addition to the above reporting requirements, there should be periodic and frequent reports on the racial composition of the construction crew as it erects the project, to determine if manning tables are being complied with or if there is a form of discrimination and exclusion not previously noted. I would recommend monthly reports indicating the number of journeymen in each craft on the job by race, the number of apprentices by race, and the amount earned by race during the month (to avoid tokenism for reporting purposes). There exist various monthly reporting forms which can be used for this purpose. Before a bidder qualifies on a subsequent project, his record of performance on the most recent completed project should be examined and compared with that of other bidders, to determine if he is "responsible."

The above program is only an outline of possibilities.[8] Man can turn his creative imagination to the ending of discrimination, as well as to its perpetuation. When he does so, he may produce many new ideas and ways of solving the social problem before us which we have not even thought of. It is the function of law at this time to create conditions under which men will solve this problem. If the law fails in this—and thus far it has not succeeded—then indeed, the very fabric of American traditions, institutions, dreams, and ideals has rotted apart. I cannot accept this conclusion and have therefore devoted the last six years of my life in the law to the quest for equality in employment. During this period, we have learned how to solve the problems of discrimination, and we must now immediately put our experience to work to break the back of the patterns of discrimination in the land. I fear very much the polarization of American society which I see on every hand. Employment opportunity is the crucial key to a revived, dynamic, and idealistic America, and it must be brought to reality by law forthwith. Our laws have been on the books and ineffective for twenty-five years. That is long enough. We must now make real, in the fabric of life, what has been long stated as our policies. That is, I hope and must believe that there is still time to do this, if we act at once. For this reason, I appreciate the opportunity of testifying before your committee.

Thank you.

---

[8] See appendix II to this chapter for an application of these and other concepts to the construction industry problem in Chicago by HUD Assistant Secretary Samuel Simmons.

Appendix I: Equal Employment Opportunity Commission Report, September 28, 1969

Minority Group Membership in Referral Local Unions, as Reported in 1967

International Union Trade	Membership in Referral Units				
	Total	Negro	% Negro	SSA*	% SSA
ALL UNIONS	2028052	198358	9.7	127797	6.3
ALL BUILDING TRADES UNIONS	1257929	106263	8.4	56062	4.5
Asbestos Workers	6104	61	0.9	75	1.2
Boilermakers	23946	934	3.9	917	3.8
Bricklayers	34069	3300	9.6	733	2.1
Carpenters	315538	5284	1.6	8692	2.7
Electrical Workers	133904	915	0.6	2490	1.8
Elevator Constructors	6728	33	0.4	89	1.3
Operating Engineers	103677	4200	4.0	1456	1.4
Iron Workers	70273	1197	1.7	2406	3.4
Laborers	266243	81457	30.5	26350	9.8
Lathers	4660	177	3.7	147	3.1
Marble, Slate & Stone Polishers	4355	387	8.8	699	16.0
Painters	66714	2498	3.7	4502	6.7
Plasters	28182	3947	14.0	3568	12.6
Plumbers	147862	320	0.2	2038	1.4
Roofers	10807	1461	13.5	357	3.3
Sheet Metal Workers	34867	92	0.2	1543	4.4

* Spanish-surnamed American

SOURCE: Equal Employment Opportunity Commission, Local Union Report EEO–3.

Appendix II: Statement of Assistant Secretary Simmons before Department of Labor Hearing on Discrimination in the Construction Industry in Chicago, Sept. 25, 1969, Arthur A. Fletcher, Assistant Secretary of Labor, Presiding

My name is Samuel Simmons. I am Assistant Secretary for Equal Opportunity, Department of Housing and Urban Development. I have been assigned by Housing and Urban Development secretary George Romney the responsibility for administering the antidiscrimination clause included in the Department's federal and federally assisted construction contracts pursuant to Executive Order 11246.

At the request of some concerned citizens in Chicago, I came to this city on September 5 in an attempt to help bring the building industry, both union and employers, and the United Coalition for Community Action to the negotiating table to work out a solution to the serious problem of providing meaningful minority employment opportunities in the construction industry in this city.

While we succeeded in bringing the parties to the table, they were not able to agree on a program for Chicago. Under those circumstances, it became clear to me that it would be necessary to further carry out my obligation to see that Executive Order 11246 was enforced in the construction industry. To achieve that end, on September 9 I directed that an investigation be conducted concerning compliance with the Executive Order. It has involved examining the relationship between some 20 HUD assisted construction contractors and six of the craft unions in this city who have very few minority group members. These six unions are Iron Workers Local 1, Sheet Metal Local 73, Operating Engineers Union 150, Plumbers Local 130, Pipefitters Local 597 and the Electrical Workers Union 134. In the course of this investigation, we learned much, Mr. Secretary, about the relationship between the building contractors and the labor unions which goes far to explain why so few minority group persons are employed in the construction industry.

As a result of these investigations, I recommend to you that enforcement action to impose economic sanctions, in the form of prohibition of future contracts and cancellation of existing contracts, be taken pursuant to the Executive Order upon 17 of the contractors whom we investigated and upon other contractors who may after investigation be found to have engaged in similar practices.

Our findings here in Chicago also lead me to the following general conclusions:

1. The Federal Government's present program to insure equal opportunity for individuals regardless of factors of race, color, religion, national origin and sex is inadequate. It does not adequately or effectively succeed in correcting the effects of the historical patterns of racial exclusion or other practices which have the same effect, nor does it achieve success in establishing a system insuring equal and just participation by minority groups in the future.

2. The present manpower utilization system prevailing in the construction industry makes it next to impossible for even the most creative and just employer to consistently provide equal employment opportunity. There has to be major institutional reform of the system. New methods of recruitment, training, and referral have to be developed and implemented.

My recommendations to correct these problems are as follows:

1. The Offices of Federal Contract Compliance should require each Federal agency with compliance responsibilities under construction contracts in the Chicago area to immediately undertake compliance reviews of each contractor, to insist upon immediate compliance with the Executive Order.

2. The Federal Government should establish specific goals and performance standards for compliance in all metropolitan areas. Standards should be set for each craft and compliance with these standards should be a precondition for the award of new contracts. In setting the standards consideration should be given to the projected number of job slots needed in the future as well as present opportunities. In those situations where it is obvious that

there are few or no available minority group journeymen or persons who can qualify as journeymen, employers should be permitted to be in compliance through the utilization of individuals in legitimate training programs.

3. The obligation to provide equal opportunity must be effectively administered with respect to all work of any contractor who has a Government contract and not be limited to federally financed and assisted projects.

4. The Federal Government should cease to be a passive participant in terms of training or certification of persons in the construction industry. On all direct and federally assisted construction the Government must require an alternative to the present union controlled apprenticeship training system and set goals for the number of persons to be trained. In view of the requirements of many Federal programs to provide economic opportunities for low income residents of the area and the needs of the industry for greater numbers of trained workers, the government cannot continue to sit idly by and see persons over 27 who are the victims of inferior education be denied an opportunity to become a skilled worker in the construction industry. Whatever alternative system is developed must contain the following three elements:

a) Control of the training system cannot be abdicated to the union, or to unions and management. The Government must be an active partner. The training program must also provide for the adequate involvement of majority and minority group general and subcontractors, unions, and minority group communities.

b) The Federal Government must make a commitment to share the cost of this expanded training. It cannot expect the employers or the sponsors of the construction project to assume this economic burden. Present Labor Department manpower programs must be restructured to provide funds for recruiting trainees, providing counselling and related classroom instructions and costs of on-the-job training for the period it takes to develop a journeyman or an individual who can at least perform most of the functions of a journeyman.

c) The Federal Government must develop procedures to insure

that once a person is recruited as a trainee systematic training opportunities will be available on every federally supported construction project. After the successful completion of a certain number of hours of on-the-job training the trainee would be successively advanced on the pay scale until such time as he receives 100% of journeyman pay. The Federal Government must certify to the competence of an individual completing the training program and require that he be given an opportunity on all construction undertaken by a Federal contractor. These standards should apply regardless of whether or not the individual is a member of a union.

It is only when all of the factors I have outlined are put into effect that minority group individuals can expect to realize equal opportunity in the construction industry.

Those, in summary, are my conclusions and recommendations, Mr. Secretary.

Now, with your permission, I should like to explain the background of the problems in the community, the nature and extent of our investigation and the reasoning by which we arrived at the conclusions which I have just stated. I will take as my starting point the year 1962 when GSA contracted for the construction of the U.S. Court House building in Chicago. The construction contracts specifically included by reference the terms of Executive Order 10925, the immediate predecessor of the Order presently administered by the Labor Department. The whole shoddy story of discrimination by Iron Workers Local 1 was revealed in a law suit which was filed as a result of the alleged discrimination in the building of that Court House. Judge Campbell, after reviewing the evidence, concluded as follows:

. . . Based upon rational and reasonable inferences I find that either negroes were refused application blanks by the Joint Committee, or if permitted to file such applications they were never acted upon. I find that the negro community as such knew of this policy of the Joint Committee and the Union and that because of the inherent and patent futility of such action sent few applicants in recent years to the Joint Committee or the Union.
To make my position clear, I should observe that the mere absence of members of the negro race on the roles of this specific Union or on the

roles of that Union's apprenticeship list would not in and of itself be proof of discriminatory membership policies.

However, the evidence before me, including but not limited to the history and general policies of the Union and the Joint Committee, manifest a definite policy and history of discrimination against those of the negro race. These facts present a clear picture not of racial segregation but of racial exclusion. The above-cited facts and figures evidence a systematic policy on the part of Union and Joint Committee to exclude negroes solely on the basis of their race.

The Judge also found that the Joint Apprenticeship Committee and the union discriminated against Negroes who sought admittance to the union and further found that the facilities and equipment of the Chicago Board of Education (The Washburne Trade School) were utilized to educate classes of all-white apprentices.

And, beyond that, the Judge found that both the General Services Administration and the Bureau of Apprenticeship and Training of the Department of Labor "directly and significantly made possible and aided in the perpetuation of the Joint Committee and Union's discriminatory policies. The GSA by making it possible for the Union and Joint Committee to function on the Government Building project, the violent alternative of course, unfortunately would be to stop construction; and the Bureau by extending direct aid and assistance and recognition and in effect giving its blessing to the practices of the Joint Committee."

This clear condemnation of the union and the Joint Apprenticeship Committee, and the inadequate response of those Federal agencies charged with the duties of enforcing the Executive Order should have produced a prompt and widespread response in the construction industry. It should also have produced a vigorous and effective program of governmental supervision and enforcement of the Executive Order.

Unfortunately, it produced neither. We investigated three contractors during the week of September 10 of this year who had relations with this same union, Iron Workers Local #1. That investigation disclosed that the first black employee was taken into the union in 1966—three years after the Chicago Court House decision. These contractors today do not expect to secure meaningful numbers of minority employees from this union. This state of affairs exists despite the fact that in 1965 the Department of labor undertook to establish an Apprenticeship Recruitment Program for the building trades in connection with the Washburne Trade School.

Information available to the Department makes it clear that Local #1 remains substantially all-white. The compliance review makes it clear the contractors generally obtain their employees through the union and that the union refers union members before it refers nonmembers. Under these circumstances, the situation with respect to minority employment in the Iron Workers trade is little changed since 1963.

I mention the Iron Workers Apprenticeship Program because that program has been the subject of searching judicial scrutiny and because the apprentice system has been viewed as the method by which young men could become journeymen craftsmen. The evidence with respect to the Iron Workers established that the apprentice route to journeyman which was officially closed in 1963 and was opened a trifle in 1966, is still not genuinely available to minority youth. Six years of effort since the Chicago Court House case have brought us only to the point where, of the 222 structural Iron Workers apprentices, 20 are Negro, two American Indian and 11 of Spanish descent as of June 30 of this year. These figures graphically demonstrate why it is necessary to develop an alternate route by which interested young men can become journeymen. The apprenticeship program is simply inadequate to provide meaningful equal opportunity under the Executive Order taking into consideration the fact that there are only 12 minority journeymen out of a total of 2,300 current members of Local #1. Furthermore, the apprenticeship training program is associated with the Washburne Trade School which has a discriminatory past, and the School's admission standards depend upon the judgment of those who until recent years overtly excluded minorities from the trade.

Let me turn now to a general summary of the findings of our investigation into the six trades and the contractors who dealt with the six unions involved.

First, we found that the unions involved had relatively few minority group members. In no case did any union have more than 4.6% minority group members. If the operating engineers are excluded, the proportion of minority group members in the remaining five trades is 1.5%. Secondly, we found that the unions invariably referred members for work before they did refer a nonmember. This was stated to us again and again by contractors dealing with each of the trades. It follows from these two factors that to the extent the contractor relies upon the union as a referral device, he will inevitably secure a white labor force.

When we examined the extent to which the contractors use the union as a referral device, we found a variety of answers. One union, Operating Engineers Local #150 has an exclusive hiring hall arrangement written into the collective bargaining agreement.

The Electrical Workers also have an exclusive referral system which they describe as a "seniority system," which requires referral by certain categories of employees which are established in relation to their length of service in the trade.

The other unions did not function in the same manner. These unions, the Sheet Metal Local 73, the Iron Workers, Local 1, the Plumbers, Local 130 and the Pipefitters Local 597 tended to permit employers to seek employees where they wished, so long as the employers secured the permission of the union before a nonunion man was put to work.

From these facts it can be concluded that all of these unions maintain control over the labor supply through the following techniques: 1) direct union referral, and 2) union approval of individuals recruited by the employer. The existence of this system made it difficult for employers to secure minority employees because it required them to not only make special recruiting efforts to obtain minority employees, but then to send those employees or their names through for approval by the union. In other words, the employers would simply not place men on the job who had not been approved by the union.

As a result of the system which I have described, very few employers whom we investigated had made any real or substantial effort to obtain minority employees. They knew that they could not get such employees through the union and few of them actively sought minority employees by recruiting or by upgrading their own labor. In our investigations we did encounter three cases where it appeared that employers had, in fact, exercised options to recruit and upgrade minority employees.

As to the other employers, their reliance, whether required or not, on the union referral system has guaranteed that they would secure a substantially all-white labor force. This, in fact, has happened and Government contracts are being executed today in Chicago with a substantially all-white labor force in some crafts, which is exclusionary, segregationist, and discriminatory against minority employee persons. Many of the employers whom we investigated had, as required, submitted affirmative action statements to HUD as a part of an effort to secure compliance with Executive Order 11246. Their performance was in the main in sharp contrast to their affirmative action statements. With respect to the 17 contractors against whom we are recommending sanctions, the figures show that these contractors have 1,445 journeymen employees of whom 101 are minority group individuals.

These facts are well known in the trade and are known to the contractors. In effect, they enter upon the performance of federally financed contracts vowing nondiscrimination and affirmative action but knowing that their collective bargaining relations and their other recruitment practices will produce a substantially segregated labor force.

Employers in the construction industry are not immune from the obligations of the Executive Order. Even if these obligations cannot be fulfilled within the framework of the collective bargaining system operated in the construction industry, the Executive Order must be obeyed. It is clear that except for three of the employers investigated, these obligations are *not* being fulfilled. This is true whether the employer utilizes the union as a referral source, or functions on his own as a recruiter within the framework of a system which requires the approval of the union before a man can be put to work.

In light of all of this background and other material which I am submitting to you, it is clear to me that the time has come for the Government itself to take the kind of affirmative action which it has long stated is required of contractors. Court suits, training programs financed by the Department of Labor, informal efforts at mediations urged on by and supported by Government officials at the highest level have all been tried. All have failed to produce meaningful adjustment to the situation.

The contractors and unions must understand and believe that the Federal Government now means to implement the powers which Judge Campbell pointed out some six years ago were available to it to assure equality of opportunity. At this late date the credibility of the Federal effort can be established only by the application of sanctions. Those sanctions, once applied, should facilitate effective and meaningful action to provide for a rapid increase in minority employment opportunities in the construction trades.

It is no light matter to make proposals for action which may result in some disruption of the Federal construction program. But, I cannot perform my responsibilities under the Executive Order without noting that repeated efforts to solve this problem the softer way have failed.

Mr. Secretary, on behalf of Secretary Romney and myself, I wish to thank you for the opportunity to present to you the results of the investigation conducted by my staff, and the opportunity to present our recommendations. Thank you.

8 The Newport News Agreement

One Brief Shining Moment in the Enforcement of Equal Employment Opportunity

I. Introduction

In March of 1966 the United States Government conducted negotiations with the Newport News Shipbuilding and Dry Dock Company to remedy the pattern of racial discrimination against the Negro workers at the shipyard. During these negotiations the government utilized its total power, including the Equal Employment Opportunity Commission, the Departments of Justice, Labor, Defense, and Navy, to combat employment discrimination. The result was a detailed written agreement providing for substantive revisions in the industrial relations structure at the shipyard and establishing procedures for its administration.[1] The initial administration of the Agreement took approximately one year. During that year, more than 3,000 of the 5,000 Negro employees at the yard were promoted, and 100 became or were designated to become supervisors.[2] The EEOC staff estimate was that the agreement added approximately one million dollars a year in income to the Negro community in the Newport News area.[3] Later, this agreement came under sharp criticism from Senator Fannin of Arizona and *Barron's* business magazine.[4]

---

[1] The full text of the agreement appears as app. 1 to this chapter.

[2] The figures are conservative. In my analysis for the EEOC entitled "The Impact and Significance of the Newport News Shipbuilding Agreement," I reported that the shipyard has confirmed that 3,890 promotion actions had taken place with respect to the Negro employees at the shipyard. Some of these involved multiple promotions for the same individual. See app. III this chapter.

[3] Precise figures showing the increase in wages to Negro employees are not available at this time.

[4] *Barron's* initial criticism (see app. II this chapter) was later inserted in the

As this article is written in the fall of 1968, the Newport News agreement stands alone. The various government agencies have not combined their resources to repeat the type of performance demonstrated there. For those involved in the struggle to end employment discrimination through law, this fact represents the greatest frustration. The government has the power, and it has the machinery and the experience, to end discrimination in major concerns across the country without relying on the long-drawn-out administrative and judicial process. Newport News points the way to an efficient, thorough, and fair method of eliminating discrimination in industrial relations systems. But is has not been duplicated or seized upon as an example. Rather, we seem bent either on judicializing these problems through formal judicial and administrative hearings or on holding high-level general conferences.[5]

One of the reasons for writing this chapter is to prevent the lesson of Newport News from being lost in the rapid personnel changes among those who administer equal employment opportunity laws. Already many of the people involved in the original agreement have left the government, either voluntarily or otherwise.[6] Once the agreement came

---

Congressional Record by Senator Fannin. On Aug. 22, 1967, Senator Javits published in the Congressional Record a reply to the charges of *Barron's* magazine which called the criticisms of the EEOC "unjustified." This reply (see app. III) included my analysis of "The Impact and Significance of the Newport News Agreement." On Sept. 18, 1967, Senator Fannin responded with further criticism (see app. IV) and continued his attack on the EEOC in "*Does Washington Force Racial Bias?*", NATION'S BUSINESS, Mar. 1968, p. 77, and in his minority report to S. 1111, 90th Cong., 2d Sess., 1968, opposing a bill to give the Commission cease and desist powers. App. V contains my detailed response to these attacks.

[5] The Office of Federal Contract Compliance in the Dep't of Labor, which administers the antidiscrimination clause in government contracts, made an effort at a systemwide settlement in connection with the Crown Zellerbach Corporation. See the aftermath in Crown Zellerbach Corp. v. Wirtz, 281 F. Supp. 337 (D.D.C. 1968) and in United States v. Local 189, United Paper Makers and Paper Workers, 282 F. Supp. 39 (E.D. La. 1968). Since then, it has moved in the direction of formality by calling hearings with respect to the issue of compliance with the executive order involving five companies. At present writing, September 1968, two of the hearings are underway.

The Civil Rights Division of the Dep't of Justice, acting under §707 of the Civil Rights Act of 1964, has instituted more than thirty suits and is concentrating on this activity. The EEOC has held a public hearing on the Textile Industry in the Carolinas and on White Collar Discrimination in New York (see EEOC, HEARINGS ON DISCRIMINATION IN WHITE COLLAR EMPLOYMENT (1968), and has conducted interagency confrontations with employers in cooperation with such other federal agencies as the Food and Drug Administration.

[6] The following is a partial list of the positions whose occupants have been re-

under senatorial attack, most administrators hesitated to duplicate the performance lest senatorial ire be directed at them. The effect of Senator Fannin's attack has been to force administrators to balance gains and losses carefully before undertaking another such effort. In this administrative calculus, the path of least resistance is to lose sight of the gains made at Newport News and to reach the conclusion that the agreement was, not a model, but an aberration which brought down senatorial wrath without compensating advantages. It is even simpler to "forgot" this approach altogether and never face the question of whether the gains are worth the risks. To stem a tide which I sense is beginning to run in this direction, this chapter is devoted to a study of the Newport News agreement, and the context in which it was reached and administered. It is important to the enforcement of antidiscrimination laws to retain the concept of a massive change directed toward ending discrimination and reached through careful negotiation in a context in which the government exercises all of its existing powers.

While the judicial process is essential to develop the law, and to protect those individual rights which the government is unable or un-

---

placed since the negotiation of the Newport News agreement in March 1966 in the department of government concerned with it.

A. *Justice Department:* Assistant Attorney General for Civil Rights; First Assistant A.G., several trial attorneys.

B. *Equal Employment Opportunity Commission:* Only one of the five commissioners in office at the time of the agreement remains as of this writing. Dr. Luther Holcomb. Commissioners Graham's and Jackson's terms were not renewed, and Chairman Roosevelt and Commissioner Hernandez resigned before their terms expired. The Executive Director of the Commission, Mr. Herman Edelsberg, was succeeded by Staff Director Gordon Chase. Deputy Executive Director Walter Davis resigned; Special Assistant to the Executive Director Winn Newman resigned. The Director of Compliance, George Holland, resigned; General Counsel and Deputy Counsel resigned; Directors of Congressional Liaison and Public Affairs resigned. I was succeeded as Chief of Conciliations by Kenneth Holbert, who assisted in the negotiation and administration of the agreement as my deputy.

C. *Department of Defense:* Contract compliance programs have been completely reorganized, and personnel have been scattered. Mr. Girard Clark, Dep't of the Navy, who was instrumental in laying the groundwork for the agreement, was "reorganized out of existence" and has left the government. An account of the episode involving Mr. Clark's departure was inserted in the Congressional Record by Congressman Ryan (see app. VI this chapter).

D. *Department of Labor:* Edward Sylvester, Director of the Office of Federal Contract Compliance, resigned to become Assistant Secretary of HEW. Several attorneys in the Solicitor of Labor's office, including Jack Caro and Henry Rose, who were active in connection with the agreement, have either left or have assignments outside the civil rights field.

willing to assert, it does not follow that, where the government is willing to act, it must do so only after a judicial-type procedure. Those who
contract with the government must abide by the equal opportunity requirements of the laws and regulations. The procedures to assure that
there is compliance should be as swift as is consistent with fairness,
because delay works to perpetuate discrimination. While fairness
would require a trial-type hearing before cancelation of existing contracts, it would not require a full hearing prior to a temporary suspension of the privilege to undertake future contracts. The temporary suspension of the privilege of undertaking future government contracts
while questions of racial discrimination are resolved may be analogous
to a temporary restraining order or preliminary injunction, which can
be issued without a full hearing. This was the procedure used in the
Newport News case. If carefully administered, it is both efficient and
fair, and does not penalize the victims of discrimination by the delay
inherent in the adjudicatory process.

The elimination of employment discrimination is one of the most
important tasks of this decade. Newport News demonstrated that it can
be done quickly, fairly, and efficiently through tough-minded negotiation and sensitive administration. If we use this as a model for changing
industrial relations systems, we can move quickly throughout the land
to end employment discrimination. If we judicialize the entire process,
and thus assure the business and labor community that we will do nothing until the courts have acted on a case-by-case basis, we are perpetuating the problem of discrimination and the tensions and difficulties
which it generates. Yet this seems to be the course we are taking. Both
the Labor and Justice Departments are moving toward more formal
hearing activity and away from any concept of massive-negotiated system change. I consider this a fundamental error of government strategy
in dealing with employment discrimination.

II. Background

Newport News, Virginia, sits across Hampton Roads from Norfolk.
Downtown Newport News is shabby and unimpressive. It is crowded
in on the west by the shipyard, which seems to run for miles along the

main highway into town. The yard, reputedly the largest in the free world, produces major naval vessels, such as the carriers *Enterprise* and *Kennedy*, and an important part of the nuclear submarine fleet. It also produces heavy equipment for industry. It employs 22,000 workers, including some 5,000 Negroes. It is the largest single employer in Virginia.

The Newport News Shipbuilding and Dry Dock Company had not been the typical Southern employer. Its employment practices differed in three important respects from, for example, those of the steel industry around Birmingham, Alabama. First, the company had not followed the traditional Southern pattern of confining its Negro employees to lower-paying, lower-skilled jobs. In 1965 there were at least 400 Negro employees who were in the top group of job classifications called mechanic. This meant that there was a reservoir of trained skilled manpower from which supervisory employees could be identified. In most Southern plants three years ago it would have been impossible to find a substantial number of Negroes who had been promoted to first class mechanic status.

The second major difference between Newport News and the typical Southern plant was the lack of any seniority system for promotions and only a minumum system of seniority in operation for purposes of layoff. The broad range of company discretion with respect to promotions in this situation made it possible to reach solutions at the yard without facing difficult questions of seniority rights as between incumbent Negro and white employees. These questions have prevented settlement of racial discrimination cases in many plants throughout the South. The workers at the shipyard were represented by the Peninsular Shipbuilders Association, an independent union. The collective bargaining agreement in effect at the yard in 1966 was brief. To one familiar with industrial relations practices in the manufacturing industry, the brief coverage of issues in the contract suggested a broad range of managerial discretion.

Third, the company was at least 75 percent dependent on government contracts and therefore had to be especially sensitive to its relations with the government.

I know little of the efforts of the government to deal with problems of discrimination at the shipyard before 1965. As a major government contractor, the shipyard had been subject to executive orders prohibiting discrimination in employment since those orders were first promulgated.[7] There was no significant effort at enforcement of these orders until the adoption of the so-called Kennedy order, Executive Order No. 10925, in 1961. This order created the President's Committee on Equal Employment Opportunity (PCEEO), which was supposed to secure compliance with both the "no discrimination" and the "affirmative action" provisions of the order by supervising the work of the specific contracting agencies. The theory of the order was that the primary responsibility for assuring compliance rested with that agency which was the dominant contractor with the particular company. That agency was called the Predominant Interest Agency (PIA) for that employer. Each government contractor was thus assigned to one of the agencies for compliance purposes. Each agency was supposed to establish its own office of contract compliance, and to supervise the actions of the employers under its jurisdictions by answering complaints and by conducting periodic compliance reviews. In addition, each agency was to report its findings and recommendations to the PCEEO for approval and for review. This awkward system was devised because Congress refused to establish and fund a single agency for this purpose. The above system functioned within the appropriations to each of the specific agencies. The PCEEO itself functioned within the administrative framework of the Department of Labor. The system as described remains largely intact, although the PCEEO has been abolished and replaced by the Office of Federal Contract Compliance in the Labor Department.

The Navy Department was the PIA for the shipyard. It engaged in little activity until 1965. Rumor had it that discriminatory practices at the government-owned and -operated shipyard in Norfolk were so bad that it would have been embarrassing for the Navy to have pressed Newport News before cleaning its own house. At any rate, the new era dawned in 1965, when two events of significance took place.

First, Title VII of the Civil Rights Act of 1964 became effective on July 2, 1965.[8] This gave individuals and groups aggrieved by discrimination a new forum, the Equal Employment Opportunity Commission. The EEOC was to investigate, decide whether reasonable cause existed

---

[7] See M. SOVERN, LEGAL RESTRAINTS ON RACIAL DISCRIMINATION IN EMPLOYMENT, ch. 5 (1966), for a description of the operation of the executive orders dealing with discrimination by government contractors.

[8] Pub. L. No. 88–352, §716(a), 78 Stat. 253, 42 U.S.C. §2000(e) (1964). Hereinafter, sections of Title VII will be cited by official section number only.

to believe that the title had been violated, and then make an informal effort to settle the matter through conciliation. If this failed, the aggrieved party could litigate the question of discrimination in the federal district court.[9] In addition, the Attorney General could institute suits, either on his own motion or on referral from the EEOC, if he had reason to believe there existed a pattern or practice of resistance to the full enjoyment of Title VII rights.[10]

The NAACP and the Legal Defense Fund both organized group efforts to make use of the provisions of Title VII. In Newport News the local NAACP chapter was headed by the Reverend J. C. Fauntleroy, who was a minister and also an employee of the shipyard. Shortly after Title VII went into effect, the Reverend Fauntleroy and some forty other Negro employees filed charges of discrimination under Title VII.

The second relevant event of 1965 at the yard was the launching of the *George Washington Carver,* a large nuclear submarine. The yard decided to make an important public affair of the launching of a vessel named after a distinguished Negro. All high federal officials concerned with equal employment opportunity were invited, including Secretary of Labor Wirtz and the five newly appointed members of the Equal Employment Opportunity Commission.[11] Rumors of discontent among the Negroes at the shipyard seeped back to the office of the Secretary of Defense so the Equal Employment Opportunity Office of the Navy was directed to make a quick check at the yard, primarily to assure that there would be no embarrassment to cabinet-level personnel from any manifestations of Negro discontent. The Navy office, under the direction of Girard Clark, conducted a compliance review and found the yard to be in noncompliance with the executive order. However, the review also established that it would be "safe" for government personnel to participate in the launching ceremonies. These ceremonies went off without a hitch.

As a result of the activities of the summer, therefore, two government agencies, EEOC and the Navy Department, were for the first time actively concerned with the problems of discrimination at the shipyard.

---

9 See §706.

10 See §707.

11 The Commission originally consisted of Chairman Franklin D. Roosevelt, Jr., Vice-Chairman Holcomb, Commissioners Hernandez, Jackson, and Graham.

After 1965, the decisionmaking functions tended to change hands. First, they were delegated to the staff in Washington, and then, gradually, to the field offices. Thus, as I write today, the draft decisions are no longer prepared in the commissioners' offices but are a staff function in Washington. I predict it will not be long before decisions are drafted in the field offices. Individual commissioners no longer sign the Commission decisions; rather the secretary to the Commission does so. But the essential high-level consideration of the question of "reasonable cause" expressed in the written decisions does remain the hallmark of the Commission.

The use of written decisions on the reasonable cause issue has the twin effect of forcing development of rules of law concerning discrimination and of laying the foundation for meaningful conciliation efforts. As the first Chief of Conciliations for the Commission, I was adamant in insisting that we should never undertake conciliation without a written decision on reasonable cause, because without that we had no basis on which to insist on relief or on changes in industrial relations system. The history of soft settlements in the field, plus my own study of the failures of the New Jersey antidiscrimination agency, had convinced me that only with the foundation of a written, official Commission decision could meaningful settlement agreements be achieved.[12] Without this foundation, employers would deny discrimination and then agree to a nuisance settlement to get rid of the conciliator. The conciliator and the complainants would be hard put to resist this technique. With the written decision the concilator could assume the existence of discrimination and move on to discuss settlement. Furthermore, the decision became a basis for our insistence that the rights involved were individual rights and for refusing to accept any settlement which was not signed by the charging party. The written decision became part of a process by which the Commission administratively determined that it would honor the concept of individual rights and would not follow the path of predecessor agencies of informally settling claims of discrimination regardless of the wishes of the victim of discrimination. We rejected the paternalistic theory of administrative action in favor of a theory which tried to rein-

---

12 See M. SOVERN, *supra* note 7, ch. 3; Blumrosen, *Antidiscrimination Laws in Action in New Jersey: A Law-Sociology Study,* 19 RUTGERS L. REV. 189 (1965); Hill, *Twenty Years of State Fair Employment Practice Commissions: A Critical Analysis with Recommendations,* 14 BUFFALO L. REV. 22 (1964).

force the individual right to be free of discrimination—a right which had, we thought, been written into Title VII.[13]

The written Commission decision in the *Newport News* case was developed within the framework I have just described. The Commission found reasonable cause to believe that:

1. Wages of Negro employees doing the same work as white employees were lower than white employees;
2. Negro employees were promoted at a slower rate than white employees;
3. Negro employees were not promoted to supervisory status under the same circumstances as white employees;
4. Negro employees were restricted in their access to the apprenticeship program, and
5. Locker and shower facilities were segregated.[14]

Once this decision had been rendered, it was sent to my office. At that time I had only two persons to assist me: Kenneth Holbert, who had come from a Dallas law practice with a Negro firm to the Labor Department in 1961 and who transferred to the Commission in September of 1965; and Herbert Belkin, who had been one of my students at Rutgers and who came to Washington after graduating in 1965. To cope with the mass of cases for conciliation, we drafted persons from other parts of the Commission. The *Newport News* file was given to Delano Lewis, a young Negro attorney with little prior experience. He and I discussed the remedies he was to seek, and he went to Newport News.

His visit was treated lightly. The company representative, an elderly vice-president in charge of labor relations, denied the discrimination, and the union also declined to conciliate. After several trips, Lewis gave up.

I reviewed the file, recommended that it be referred to the Attorney General for possible suit under section 707 of the act, dispatched "notice letters" to the complainants indicating that the conciliation efforts had failed and that they had thirty days in which to file suit under Title

---

[13] The compliance process of the EEOC is more fully explored in ch. 2, pt. V, *supra*.

[14] See app. III this chapter.

VII, and sent the file to the office of the General Counsel. That was November 1965. I heard no more of the case until the following March.

III. The Foundation for Negotiation

In the interim the processes of government ground on. The Department of Defense continued the investigation which had begun before the launching of the *Carver* and reached the conclusion that action should be taken. The PCEEO was abolished and its functions transferred to a new institution, the Office of Federal Contract Compliance (OFCC). Its new energetic director, Edward Sylvester, Jr., sitting on top of substantially the same staff and organization as the PECCO, was prepared to exercise the contract suspension power which had been rarely used in the past.

At the same time, the EEOC file on *Newport News* was referred by the Commission to the Department of Justice. Attorneys from the Civil Rights Division went to Newport News and conducted extensive interviews. By March 1966 the Department was prepared to institute litigation against the shipyard. In the meantime the Negro employees who had complained to the EEOC filed suit on behalf of themselves and similarly situated employees in the federal district court. Their local attorney was affiliated with the Legal Defense and Education Fund of the NAACP.

Through unofficial channels, the company learned of the impending suit by the Justice Department and attempted to head it off. Mr. Holden, who had met Commissioner Hernandez at the launching of the *Carver,* came to her office. She indicated to him that she was aware that the shipyard was in difficulty and referred him to me.

Our posture was that, as far as we were concerned, conciliation had failed but we would always be glad to discuss the problems of discrimination with him if that was appropriate. He indicated he wanted to negotiate a solution. I called Herman Edelsberg, then Executive Director of the Commission, and learned that the Department of Justice was within days of filing suit. I so advised Mr. Holden, and told him that we would be prepared to work with him to reach an agreement if it was appropriate, but that we could do nothing at that time.

The activities of the company precipitated an interdepartmental meeting in the office of John Doar, then Assistant Attorney General for Civil Rights. Present were representatives from the OFCC (including Ed Sylvester), the Department of Defense (Mr. Jack Moskowitz), the Navy Department (Mr. Girard Clark), and the EEOC (Mr. Herman Edelsberg, Mr. Richard Berg, and myself). In all there were about twenty people sitting in a simicircle around Mr. Doar's desk. For an hour we discussed the pros and cons of whether to file suit and then negotiate, or whether to accept the current offer of the company to negotiate first. EEOC's view was that Justice should file suit and that we would negotiate afterward. Our theory was that when a company turned down the Commission's offer to concilate, they should not be given another opportunity before the Justice Department filed suit. To give this opportunity would weaken the incentive to negotiate with the EEOC.

After an hour, Doar announced his decision. He would not file suit, but would allow opportunity for negotiation. During these discussions, Sylvester pressed the Department of Defense (DOD) officials for a memorandum which would enable the Department of Labor to suspend further contracting with the shipyard, and DOD and Navy officials agreed to supply a memorandum of noncompliance with the executive order dealing with government contractors. When Doar announced his decision, Herman Edelsberg stood up and said, "Very well, EEOC will conduct the negotiations." This was agreed to by everyone in the room, and we promised to be in touch with the various agencies as we moved toward the negotiations.

Edelsberg had grabbed the ball, figuratively speaking, from the other agencies, and thereby stamped the entire effort as an EEOC venture. It became my responsibility to develop proposals to remedy discrimination at the shipyard, and to shepherd these proposals through the bureaucratic maze of the Commission and of three other government agencies before we could begin to negotiate.

This responsibility was significant. Unlike the manner in which a collective bargaining agreement details the operation of a plant, there was here no satisfactory history for the preparation of binding agreements which detailed the responsibility of employers to make massive changes in industrial relations systems to eliminate discrimination. Most employer statements made at the request of the government up to that time had consisted of generalities concerning equal opportunity.[15]

I sat down with Delano Lewis and prepared a first draft of a proposal based on our analysis of the file and his discussions with the charging parties. We sent it to the General Counsel's office, where additions were made. We were then ready for a meeting with Executive Director Edelsberg and his staff and others in the Commission concerning the proposals. One of our proposals had been to establish a preferential promotion list for Negro employees who were the victims of discrimination. We heard that this was to be opposed by some on the Executive Director's staff on the theory that the agreement should provide for equal treatment in the future without remedying the past discrimination. On this key issue Ken Holbert suggested that we needed allies so our final preparation for the meeting consisted of outlining to Commissioner Hernandez our proposals and the difficulties we expected to face. She agreed with our approach and indicated that, if we had trouble with the staff in the office of the Executive Director, we could come back to her and she would, if necessary, take the matter up at a formal meeting of the fall Commission.

To the uninitiated, our action seemed a breach of the bureaucratic tradition. We had deviated from channels by going around the Executive Director to one of the commissioners. At that time in the history of the Commission, there was a serious dispute as to the role of the commissioners vis-à-vis the Chairman concerning who "ran the Commission" and as to the relation between the commissioners and the staff. The Chairman and the Executive Director felt that they ran the staff and that the commissioners should be advisors to the Chairman, while the commissioners thought that they were entitled to participate in important day-to-day decisions. The resulting confusion allowed staff people to seek the most favorable forum for various positions they wanted to take; this was our reason for going to Commissioner Hernandez. Such a maneuver would be unlikely today. The commissioners are now much further removed from the day-to-day operation of the Commission, which is largely centralized under the Staff Director, who reports to the Chairman. The flexible days of the first year of the Commission are no more.

---

[15] Blumrosen, *supra* note 12. For a follow-up study, see Frakt, *Administrative Enforcement of Equal Opportunity Legislation in New Jersey*, 21 RUTGERS L. REV. 422 (1967).

At any rate, armed with the support of Commissioner Hernandez, Holbert and I went to the staff meeting and won our point concerning the scope of the remedy sufficiently so that we did not feel it necessary to seek the Commissioner's assistance in the formulation of the proposals. The proposals were broad and included remedies for past discrimination as well as system changes for the future. They dealt extensively with all of the problems of the shipyard which we had identified and ran some twenty pages double-spaced. Over the weekend we had them duplicated and called an interagency meeting for early the following week. Meanwhile, we advised the shipyard that our negotiating sessions would take place in Washington rather than in Newport News because of the numbers of government personnel who would be involved.

On the Sunday before the negotiations several of us flew to Newport News to meet with the leaders of the charging parties to make sure that our proposals for solution to the problems of discrimination made sense to them. Discussion of proposals with charging parties prior to submission to respondents was and is part of the Commission's procedure. This assures that the interests of complainants will not be ignored and makes it more likely that an agreement based on such proposals will later be acceptable to the charging parties.

We met the charging parties in the office of their attorney, Phillip Walker. They ran the gamut from the Reverend Fauntleroy, a veteran of civil rights efforts, and Thomas Mann, the first Negro graduate of the apprenticeship school of the yard, who had not been promoted as had his white colleagues, to Arthur Ford and James Lassiter, long-time employees at the yard who had seen their white contemporaries promoted past them. We discussed the tentative proposals and returned to Washington that night.

Early the following week, we held an interagency meeting and distributed our proposals. Present were representatives from Labor, Defense, Justice, OFCC, and Navy. We discussed the proposals for nearly two hours, and secured informal acquiescence in them from the other agencies involved. For the first and the only time thus far in the history of federal efforts to end employment discrimination, we had a firm position from which to negotiate, agreed to by *all* of the government agencies involved and the aggrieved parties. The concept of a single government position in the field of employment discrimination usually is a myth. There is not one government; there are several agencies, each with its institutional viewpoint and each reflecting the viewpoints of dominant personnel. It is a most difficult feat to secure a "government position" in this field. But this one time it was obtained.

IV. The Negotiations

The negotiations began on a Wednesday. Mr. Edelsberg opened them with a short statement and then turned the session over to me. Sitting next to me was Ken Holbert, my Deputy. Around the end of the table was Girard Clark, the aggressive Navy Contracts Compliance Chief. To my left was a representative of the Justice Department, sometimes Stephen Pollock, then First Assistant and later Assistant Attorney General for Civil Rights, or Gerald Choppin, Executive Assistant to the Assistant Attorney General for Civil Rights. The entire federal governmental structure dealing with employment discrimination was thus represented at the government end of the bargaining table. At the other end were the president of the company, Mr. Holden, the company's counsel, Mr. Pat Gibson, and various company officials.

I made a short opening statement indicating that our proposals had been carefully worked out and were seriously presented, but that we were prepared to discuss the details of each of them in terms of their practicality in light of the conditions at the shipyard. We distributed copies of the proposals and then recessed to allow the company time to consider them.

At this point, the statute draws a curtain over our initial proposals and the discussions which followed.[16] Nothing "said or done during and as a part of" conciliation efforts may be made public without the written consent of the parties. My files reflect four separate and distinct drafts of the conciliation proposals which emerged during our discussions which took more than a week. The point I wish to make is that in fact these were serious negotiations, and there were many changes made in the initial government proposals before the agreement was finalized. The government, despite its array of "power," did not purport to have a monopoly on wisdom or on the most practical method of effectuating equal opportunity at the shipyard. No "take it or leave it"

---

[16] See §706a. See also §III(6) of the agreement, app. I this chapter.

attitude was expressed by the government during the negotiations. Someday it may be practical to compare the initial government proposal with the agreement as signed to make clear that negotiations did take account of issues raised by the shipyard. It was this factor which contributed, I believe, to the decision by the company to implement the agreement in good faith.

On the day after the negotiations opened, the Secretary of Labor issued his order suspending further contracting by any government agency with the Newport News Shipyard. The suspension order interrupted contracting for several naval vessels, of which the Navy Department was aware, as well as a Maritime Commission contract, of which the Labor and Defense Department officials were unaware. At the last minute there was hesitancy in the government channels as to whether to suspend contracting—after all, the officials of the yard had come up to negotiate and were thus demonstrating "good faith." My opinion was sought on this question, and I was strongly of the view that the contracting should be suspended. I was doing the negotiating, and I was fully aware that all that had happened up to this point was that the company had received our proposals. Their past performance and the manner in which they had brushed off prior proposals did not suggest to me that there was any great willingness to take all steps necessary to end the discriminatory system at the shipyard. I wanted to negotiate from strength, and the strongest position was one in which the shipyard was under great pressure to settle. Thus the suspension was, in my view, crucial to the outcome of the negotiations. Without the suspension I do not believe we would have achieved the full-scale solution to the system of discrimination at the shipyard. With the suspension we were able to negotiate from strength. This view prevailed, and the suspension order was issued.

There is another feature of our system which made these negotiations genuine even though the contracts were suspended. The company had the option at all times to seek judicial intervention against the disruption of contracting. They thus had a choice even though the contracts were suspended. This presence of judicial control is a healthy limitation on any risks of administrative excess.[17]

One must always be careful not to confuse bargaining power with wisdom. The fact is that there was considerable give and take on var-

---

[17] See Crown Zellerbach Corp. v. Wirtz, 281 F. Supp. 337 (D.D.C. 1968).

ious issues after the order had been issued. The negotiations took at least a week, the discussions were serious, and extensive changes were made in the government proposal. Finally, agreement was reached. This agreement was reviewed by the Navy, Defense, and Labor Departments and was considered a comprehensive plan justifying the lifting of the contracting bar. Justice decided, on the strength of the agreement, not to institute suit. The agreement led to the settlement of the private litigation. In short, the agreement was approved by the various government agencies as well as by the company and the charging parties and the Legal Defense Fund, the civil rights organization backing the litigation. Since the Reverend Fauntleroy was the NAACP official in Newport News, it is fair to say that the agreement received the endorsement of the concerned civil rights community. Finally, the agreement was approved by the Commission and made public.

V. Correcting an Error of Omission

In all of this flurry of activity which took place within a two-week period, the Peninsular Shipbuilders Associations (PSA) was not consulted by the government. We had been rebuffed once by the PSA, and we were inclined to accept the view that the proposed changes could be made within the framework of the existing labor agreement as a matter of management's discretion. This was a feasible position in light of the facts that the collective bargaining agreement left so many matters to the discretion of management, and that it contained no provision dealing with seniority for promotions and only limited protection for long-service men in cases of layoff. In retrospect, it is clear that we erred in not consulting with the PSA prior to the signing of the agreement with the company.[18]

We paid an appropriate penalty for this omission. The AFL-CIO became worried that we might not consult its affiliates before signing with companies in cases where there were substantial issues at stake, and we revised our conciliation procedure to make sure this would not happen again. The PSA officials were insulted and upset, and threatened to take the company to the NLRB for making unilateral changes in working conditions without negotiating. I marked on my private cal-

---

[18] See NLRB v. Katz, 369 U.S. 736, 82 S. Ct. 1107 (1962).

endar the point in time six months from the signing of the agreement as the period within which the PSA could file with the NLRB and thus cast a cloud over all of our work.[19] We then began a protracted course of negotiations with the PSA itself. Ultimately these negotiations paid off. PSA and the company signed a supplemental agreement shortly before the six-month period expired. In it the PSA recognized the conciliation agreement. PSA then began to process grievances under the agreement. This not only constituted a waiver of any objections to procedure the PSA might have had, but also brought the union in as an agency to enforce the agreement, an agency closer at hand than the EEOC offices in Washington.

What prompted the union to give up a claim which might have shattered the agreement and left the whole concept of a major negotiated system change in jeopardy? I believe it was the self-interest of the union and of the employees in the yard, for the agreement gave to all of the employees in the yard, not just the Negro employees, two important benefits which they had never had before. First was the posting of notices of vacancies so that men could seek to improve their own position in the yard. This posting of vacancies increased intraplant mobility for all of the employees, white and black. Second, the agreement provided that vacancies were to be filled on the basis of length of service where "skill, ability, and efficiency are fairly equal." [20] This provision benefited all except those who preferred the principle of supervisory favoritism as a basis for promotions.

And so this one fumble in the processing of the Newport News agreement was recovered. Strangely, in a subsequent proceeding the Labor Department did not involve the Paper Makers Union in negotiations to change the seniority system at Crown Zellerbach and was, on that account as well as others, enjoined from suspending government contracts with Crown.[21] The lessons from that experience were two: first, be sure to involve the union even where the agreement seems to fall within the ambit of management prerogatives; and second, many mistakes by government can be corrected by patient and careful action.

---

[19] The National Labor Relations Act requires that a charge be filed within six months of the unfair labor practice. See §10(b) of the National Labor Relations Act as amended, 61 Stat. 136, 29 U.S.C. 141 (1964).

[20] See §II(3)(a) of the agreement, app. I this chapter.

[21] Crown Zellerbach Corp. v. Wirtz, 281 F. Supp. 337 (D.D.C. 1968).

VI. The Administration of the Agreement

The signing of the agreement was hailed by EEOC Chairman Roosevelt as a milestone and as a model for others. But the signing was only the beginning of a year of administration which taxed the feeble resources of the EEOC to the limit. In discussing the administration of the agreement, it is necessary to sketch the procedural posture of the agreement, and the strengths and weaknesses of the administering agencies.

The agreement provided that its general administration would be in the hands of the EEOC. This meant, for practical purposes, that it was administered through the office of conciliations. However, the agreement provided that the provisions relating to promotions of Negroes to supervisors (called quartermen) would be handled by the Department of Defense. Futher, it provided that a number of crucial questions relating to promotion of Negroes in nonsupervisory positions would be determined by an expert, to be retained at company expense, who would be acceptable to the Commission. Thus the administration of the agreement involved a substantial number of parties: the charging parties and the NAACP, the union, the company, the expert, the Defense Department, and the Commission. To manage all of these relationships, my office had expanded somewhat. Jules Gordon and Andrew Muse, both attorneys, joined the office during the administration of the agreement and participated in it. Holbert and Belkin also spent time at Newport News. Newport News administration thus consumed an important part of the time of the entire office of conciliation during the 1966–67 year. Toward the end of the period, when the Defense Department dropped out of the picture, I worked nearly full time with five DOD staff persons to conclude the administration of the agreement. To say that we were spread thin in the administration of the agreement is to put it mildly. But government usually functions this way. Much government service involves routine and dull activity requiring no great talent or energy. This is suddenly displaced by extraordinary demands requiring all concerned to function far above their expected capacity.

In addition to having to cope with all of the groups involved, our office was faced with a shifting superstructure above us. Chairman Roosevelt resigned shortly after the agreement was negotiated to run, unsuccessfully, for governor of New York. Vice-Chairman Holcomb took over for several months, to be replaced by Steven Shulman. Shulman's administration replaced Mr. Edelsberg as Executive Director with Mr. Chase. The Director of Compliance at the beginning of the agreement, Mr. Holland, left the Commission and was succeeded by my deputy, Ken Holbert, in an acting capacity.

I emphasize all these difficulties to attempt to place the administrative process in its human context. Government is not an impersonal mindless bureaucracy, at least at the level in which I encountered it. On the contrary, it is an intensely personal process. This of course reinforces the necessity for fully documented written agreements. Only in this way is there some likelihood that matters will be carried forward in some relation to the original intention of the negotiating parties. This applies to the government side as well as to the position of the charging parties and respondents.

VII. The Results Summarized

Shortly after I returned to Rutgers Law School in the summer of 1967, I was asked to prepare a discussion of the impact of the Newport News agreement for EEOC staff members. This analysis was later placed in the Congressional Record by Senator Javits, and it is reproduced at the end of this chapter as appendix III. I insert a part of that document here to give substance to what has gone before and to the remainder of this account. One of the great difficulties in evaluation of governmental action is that frequently there is no followup or feedback, and thus it is impossible to determine the effectiveness at any level of a given program. To deal with this problem of evaluation of the Newport News agreement, I prepared a three-column chart which was included in the Congressional Record[22] under the following introduction:

> There follows a table indicating the nature of the problem of discrimination at the shipyard, the solution reached in the conciliation agreement and the results of the application of the act.

---

[22] See app. III this chapter.

PROBLEM	SOLUTION	RESULTS
1. Negro employees were underpaid for doing the same work as white employees and were promoted at a slower rate than white employees.	Retention of an expert, (Case & Co.) approved by the Commission to prepare job descriptions to determine the rate and conditions for promotions of white employees, and to determine which Negro employees were underpaid and had been promoted at a slower rate than white employees.	Case & Company conducted an intensive study of each of the more than 30 departments at the shipyard. It then issued a report on each department to the company and commission indicating which Negro employees should have been promoted and the positions they would have reached if their rate of progress had equaled that of the white employees. The company promoted these employees or placed them on a list for future promotion. While promoting these employees, the company continued its normal promotional practice with respect to white employees. Actually, nearly half of the Negro employees whom Case & Company found entitled to promotion had already been advanced by the Company before the study was completed. This indicated the company's cooperative attitude. This provision of the agreement accounts for the nearly 3,900 promotion actions on behalf of Negro employees during the year after the agreement was executed.
2. Negro employees restricted to certain departments, not permitted to transfer to higher paying jobs in previously white departments.	Company to post notices of job vacancies so that employees can bid for them and allow Negro employees to transfer to previously all-white departments.	Company posted vacancies for the first time in its history and employees, both white and Negro, began to take advantage of the transfer provisions.

PROBLEM	SOLUTION	RESULTS
3. Negro employees alleged they were passed over for promotion.	Establishment of proposal that promotions are henceforth to be given by seniority and ability.	Application of this proposal on behalf of both Negro and white employees.
4. Negro employees were restricted in promotion to supervisor. At the time of the agreement, only 32 of the nearly 2,000 officers and managers were Negro although 25% of the labor force was Negro.	DOD and company developed a profile of the qualifications of the last 100 white employees promoted to supervisors. Selected Negro employees to be measured against this profile and those who matched or exceeded it, to be promoted prior to promotion of others. Company could request exceptions in special circumstances. Disputes between company and DOD to be submitted to Case & Co.	This provision requires substantial interpretation in light of problems which arose after the agreement was executed. Rather than the last 100 white employees, it was agreed to use the last 5 whites promoted in each department as the basis for the profile because of variation in standards. EEOC assumed responsibility for administration. Company promoted more than 20 Negroes to supervision during the administration of the agreement, and at the end of the period agreed to promotions of an additional 75 Negroes who had been certified by their own supervisors as qualified to become supervisors. Exceptions were granted in two instances by the Commission, one of which involved a white employee who was the lead foreman handling scaffolding on the carrier *Kennedy*, and the other man with special technical skills. The extensive promotions to supervisors were possible because the company had, over the years, permitted some Negro employees to advance to mechanical status

PROBLEM	SOLUTION	RESULTS
		and thus had a reservoir of high skilled men who were available for promotion. All promotions were worked out by agreement between the Commission and the company and it was not necessary to submit any disputes to Case & Company.
5. Restriction of Negro applicants to apprentice schools, segregation of apprentice school staff and selection of committee. Only 6 of the 500 students were Negro. The apprentice school is a 4-year advanced technical school.	Negotiation of staff and committee, recruitment efforts among Negro schools, elimination of restrictions on married students, those with prior college education, and raise maximum entry age to 25 years, with notification to present Negro employees who might qualify under these standards, of their new opportunities.	Nearly 50 Negros admitted to the school during the first year after the agreement; prompt integration of staff and selection committee; identification of employees who might qualify, and as part of the closing administrative phase of the agreement, notification to them by the Commission of their opportunities under the agreement. The company engaged in recruiting contacts with the various NAACP branches in the labor market area.
6. Segregated locker, shower, and toilet facilities.	Reconstruction of toilet facilities in accordance with a diagram attached to the agreement to eliminate their segregated character. Reassignment of locker and shower facilities on an alphabetical basis.	This was accomplished by company action within 30 days of the signing of the agreement. No serious difficulties were reported.
7. The specific complaints of the 4 individual charging parties regarding re-	Agreement to promote 3 of the 4 individuals to supervisor and to promote	This provision was implemented the week after the signing of the agreement.

PROBLEM	SOLUTION	RESULTS
striction on their promotional opportunities because of race.	the 4 to a higher paying job class.	The private law suit was dismissed with payment of cost and attorney fees by the company.
8. Resolution of the other 37 complaints which involved rate of pay and promotional opportunities problems.	Agreement on an expedited procedure to resolve these problems.	Charges were satisfactorily adjusted within 3 months of the agreement.

VIII. The Company Takes the Initiative

Some phases of the administration of the agreement were over quickly. The company desegregated the toilet facilities and reassigned locker space in accordance with the agreement. There was some grumbling from the union, but this was promptly done. The policy statement of the president was distributed in pay checks; group meetings were held to explain the agreement to all employees; bulletin boards for posting job vacancy notices were erected and put into operation.

In the most meaningful sense of the word—that is, in their actions— the company demonstrated "good faith" in the initial administration of the agreement. Those things which they could do at once they did. They established procedures to anticipate the formal enforcement of the agreement and executed them. Where there were serious difficulties, they did not hesitate to say so and to negotiate firmly with us to the end that their own interest in flexibility was maintained as much as possible, while complying with the agreement.

In anticipation of the enforcement of the specific provisions of the agreement, the company made a major undertaking of its own. First, it promoted a great many Negroes. I believe the figure was between 1,200 and 1,500. Second, it scoured the yard for Negroes who were already mechanics to determine how many it could promote to supervisory status. It then promoted some 20 Negroes to supervisory positions without awaiting the enforcement of the agreement. This reflected both good faith and good sense on the part of the company. By acting in anticipation of the administration of the agreement, the company was able to exercise more of its discretion in selection of personnel, and thus retain the sense of control over the operation of the yard, and at the same time demonstrate to the government that it was carrying out the spirit of the agreement. Later, however, others used the fact that the company had gone ahead as minimizing the role of the government with respect to all of these promotions.[23] It is clear, however, that but for the major gov-

---

[23] Thus *Barron's* magazine suggestion that only a few Negroes were promoted under the agreement is explainable only if all the other promotion actions of the company are treated as unrelated to governmental action.

ernmental effort which culminated in the agreement, this mass of promotions of black employees would not have taken place.

A. *Promotions to Nonsupervisory Positions—Enter the Experts*

The Commission had found cause to believe that Negroes were promoted at a slower rate than were whites. This finding was not based on
an examination of the rate of promotion of all blacks in the yard compared to whites. Rather it was based on a number of specific situations.
In order to determine which Negroes had in fact been promoted at a
slower rate than whites, the conciliation agreement provided for the
selection of an expert, who could either be an individual, a management consultant firm, or an operations research institution. The expert
was to be knowledgeable in race relations and acceptable to the Commission. The expert was given various roles under the agreement and
was central to its successful administration.[24] Thus the identification of
the expert became a matter of great concern to both the company and
the government. During the negotiations we did not agree either on a
mutually acceptable expert or to agree on a formula for selection of
such an expert. Thus it was left that both the company and the government could nominate experts, the company could select, and the Commission could veto. If the process did not produce an expert within
forty-five days, the parties would reconvene for the limited purpose of
solving the problem.

The government nominated a group of individuals, and the company, after reviewing proposals from several management consultant
firms, nominated Case and Company. One senior official of Case had
been president of the Urban League of New Jersey some years previously. Case retained a Negro adviser to assist it in carrying out the
assignment. With these considerations Case and Company was deemed
acceptable. Again, this demonstrates the advantage which the company
gained by taking the initiative in the selection of the expert. If it had
engaged in foot dragging, the entire arrangement could have come un-
stuck and they might have been saddled with an outsider not of their
choosing. As it was, Case and Company has performed generally useful

---

24 See §§II(i)(4), III(5)(c) of the agreement, app. I this chapter, for provisions relating to the expert.

work for the shipyard. Case assigned Mr. Robert Montgomery with a staff to undertake the preparation of job descriptions and the analysis of the rate of promotion of Negro and white employees, and to carry out the other tasks under the agreement. The company provided working space near its records and cooperation through its knowledgeable personnel.

The task of preparing the various analyses took nearly a year. One phase of the task was the receipt of complaints from Negro employees of slow promotion or underpayment compared to whites. The analysis of the rate of promotion of Negro versus white employees had the effect of resolving most of the questions of depressed rates of pay. This was because of the wage structure at the shipyard. Employees were divided into four major job groupings, called classifications. These were in descending order: mechanic, handyman, helper, and laborer. Within each of these groups were three levels, first, second, and third class, each carrying a corresponding rate of pay. Thus there were in effect twelve rates, and a promotion ladder up these rates from laborer to first class mechanic. The company had retained considerable flexibility with respect to assignments to specific tasks so that it was possible that a first class mechanic and a third class helper could be working together on the same job. If the third class helper was a Negro whose rate of promotion up the ladder had been discriminatorily retarded, as compared to the white mechanic, a correction of his rate of pay would automatically correct the "inequity" of Negroes doing the same work as whites but at lower rates. None of us had realized this fact until the concluding phase of the administration of the agreement. This made it considerably easier to conclude the administration than it would otherwise have been.

The task of Case and Company was of considerable magnitude. There were basically two problems arising from the agreement, and they gave both the government and the company substantial difficulty. The theory of section II (4) of the agreement was that the expert would develop a profile of the "rate and conditions" of promotion of white employees in selected departments in cooperation with the Defense Department. The history of progression and promotion of Negro employees would then be compared with this profile; if the Negro had not been promoted in accordance with the rate and conditions for promotion of whites, he would forthwith be placed in the first grade in his present job classification (*e.g.*, if he was a third class handyman, he would be made first class) and would be put on a preferential promotion list to move into the higher classification if that was indicated by the expert.

The agreement provided a mechanism by which the company could demonstrate that the employee had not been promoted "for reasons of physical handicap, improper attendance, or other conduct on the premises." The company had the burden of proof on this issue. Then the agreement provided that "considerations of skill and ability are not germane to this section." [25] The theory of this section was that the expert would adduce a standardized rate of promotion of whites, based largely on length of service, and that this movement up the wage ladder should be considered as automatic within each group of jobs. In the administration of this provision it was argued that since the profile of the white employees included "rate and conditions" for promotion, some questions of skill and ability were properly included in the calculation as to whether employees were promotable. We finally decided not to resolve this question of interpretation. The considerations leading to this conclusion were as follows: first, we found variations in the criteria used for promotions in the various departments in the yard; and second, the argument on the language was not wholly without merit, although the specific language of Section 4(f) would seem to be more persuasive than the generality of the term "rate and conditions." At any rate, for the purposes of administration, we did not press the issue. The effect of this was that some Negro employees were not promoted. But the number rejected on grounds of lack of ability was, I believe, far smaller than would have been the case if the "skill and ability" language had not been included in the agreement.

I think this was sound administration. It would have been awkward to litigate this question. Our posture would have smacked too much of the views attributed to EEO programs by their opponents—of attempting to secure promotion of incompetents. Our argument, that the rate of promotion was really an automatic wage increase and that we were simply correcting past inequities, might well be lost in the resulting furor. At any rate, we made the judgment to back away from literal application of the clause during the administration of the agreement, leaving the issue to be raised, perhaps, another day.

---

[25] See §II(4)(f) of the agreement, app. I this chapter.

The other issue with respect to the administration of the agreement dealt with the measurement of rate of promotion. The argument was as follows. If, for example, the sample disclosed that the average time in grade of white employees before promotion from third to second class handyman in a given department was eleven months, I took the view that all Negroes who had been in the third class more than eleven months were entitled to promotion insofar as the time element was concerned. This was a literal reading of the agreement.[26] The contrary view was that the number of Negroes considered for promotion should be such that the overall average time in grade for both Negro and whites equaled eleven months.

These two competing interpretations of section 4(f) were discussed. Finally, I asked Case and Company to identify the individuals whose promotions were at stake depending on which view prevailed. Once this was done, we found we were talking about relatively few employees. As a part of the wrap-up of the administration of the agreement, the company acquiesced in my view on this issue, and the promotions were made.

I hope these two illustrations suggest the degree of informality and practicality involved in the administration of the agreement and dispel the concept that it was administered on a wooden "take it or leave it" basis. I do not suggest that we were soft or easy in our approach, but we did take realistic account of genuine issues and considerations. At the same time, since we were dealing with group claims, we always ran the risk of doing less than full justice to the individual claims involved. I will discuss this aspect of administration later.[27]

The result of the course of action described above was a total of 3,980 promotion actions for Negro employees during the first year of the agreement.

B. *Promotions to Supervisor*

The problem with respect to promotions to "quarterman"—the term for foreman in the yard—was that there were 25 percent Negro employees but only 1½ percent of the persons listed as officers and man-

---

26 *Id.*
27 See §IX of this chapter.

agers were Negro. The Commission had found that Negroes were not promoted to supervisor under the same circumstances as whites. This finding was based on a few cases, not on an exhaustive investigation of all situations. Three of the four principal charging parties, Fauntleroy, Mann, and Lassiter, were promoted to quartermen as part of the settlement agreement.[28] But more importantly, procedures were established under sections II (2) (a)-(e) of the agreement to review all of the skilled Negro employees in the yard and provide for their promotion to quartermen if they met the criteria applied to the promotion of the last one hundred whites who had been made quartermen. The implementation of this agreement was to be done by the Department of Defense and the company jointly.[29]

Promptly after the agreement was signed, the company examined its roster of Negro employees for those who had supervisory capability, and proceeded to promote some twenty of them to quartermen, in addition to the three appointments of the charging parties. The Department of Defense was slow in implementing this phase of the agreement, and shortly the company found itself in need of additional quartermen.

The company believed it had promoted all the qualified Negroes to quartermen, and therefore the provision of Section II (2) (d) for the appointment of Negroes to vacancies as quartermen was no longer applicable.[30] Faced with the need to make additional quartermen, the company took two important steps. First, it pressed persistently in Washington, both with DOD and with the EEOC, for the government to come and administer this phase of the agreement, and second, it began to promote whites to temporary quartermen positions.

During late 1966, DOD made a beginning at solving the quarterman problem by sending some men to the shipyard, but it soon developed that the provisions of the agreement were simply unworkable. Since criteria for promotion to quarterman varied from department to department, the use of the last one hundred whites promoted as the basis for establishing criteria did not work. Thus DOD and the com-

---

[28] See §II(7)(c) of the agreement, app. I this chapter.

[29] §II(2)(b) of the agreement, app. I this chapter.

[30] In the agreement there is a provision under which the company would promote qualified Negroes in the interim period. We had not provided for the contingency of slow government action and an arguable case that there were no more qualified Negroes available.

pany agreed, with EEOC approval, to substitute a profile based on the last five appointments in each department prior to July 2, 1965, as the basis for determining qualifications. Having gotten this far, DOD then bogged down.

As 1967 began, the company pressure mounted to finish this aspect of the agreement. Many employees had been temporary quartermen for months, and they were restive in their position. I believed the company was rapidly moving into a position where, with justice, they could say that the government had defaulted on its obligations to administer the agreement; that they had promoted all the qualified Negroes they could find, and that they would consider this phase of the agreement at an end. They then might have made their temporary promotions permanent. This would have created additional problems and would have publicly discredited the agreement and the efforts of the government. We began to pressure the DOD to complete the inventory. Suddenly we found that an internal struggle over the EEO program in the Department of Defense had crippled DOD's ability to administer the agreement. As a part of this struggle (which resulted ultimately in the elimination of Girard Clark, the aggressive Navy EEO Chief who had pressed so insistently for the action against the shipyard[31]) we were notified that DOD personnel would not go back into the yard. This caused a major crisis in the office of conciliation. The entire concept of a systemwide change through a master agreement was again jeopardized. The government effort would be discredited if we could not deliver on our promises made in the agreement. Chairman Shulman agreed with our estimate of the seriousness of the situation, and contacted high officials in the office of the Secretary of Defense. The upshot of his conversations was a typical bureaucratic solution. DOD would not go back to the yard, but it would detail five men to work for EEOC for one month to conclude the administration of the agreement.

Thus it was that in March 1967 I began shuttling between Newport News and Washington to complete the administrative phase of the Agreement. The problem which had stalled the DOD personnel was this: once it had been agreed to utilize the last five whites promoted prior to July 2, 1965, as the basis for the development of a profile of those made supervisors in each department, it was necessary to determine the elements of that profile, and then to apply it to each of the

[31] See note 6(C), *supra.*

Negro mechanics in the department. The enormity of this task virtually stopped the DOD personnel cold. They spent weeks in a single department interviewing employees and supervisors, but did not simplify the mass of data so that they could apply specific criteria to the Negro mechanics. When I arrived and met the DOD men, most of whom had been in the yard before, I concluded that their prior work had not required sharp decisions; it merely urged better corporate action in general terms.

I organized a procedure to resolve the supervisor question. First, we took the formal criteria of performance ratings of the whites who had been promoted to supervisor and applied these criteria to the Negro mechanics. I resolved doubtful questions in favor of including Negro employees in the list of those eligible for promotion. When this was done, we reduced the group of Negro mechanics for consideration to somewhere between two and three hundred. I then instructed the DOD men to ask supervisors of these men whether, in their opinion, these Negro employees had the qualities to become quartermen. The decision to proceed this way was a calculated risk on my part. It was realistic because, when whites were promoted to quartermen, it was on recommendation of their supervisors in addition to certain formal standards of performance, but there was the danger that racism would infect the judgments of the supervisors. In effect, I was allowing a decision which should have been made by government to be heavily influenced by the supervisors. In lieu of any other practical approach, I was prepared to gamble on the integrity of the foremen, and their making an honest appraisal of the Negro employees. At least, I thought, we should try this approach. I left Newport News for Washington one day, leaving the five DOD personnel, who were highly skeptical of this procedure, under the immediate supervision of one of my staff, Jules Gordon. (This phase of the administration of the agreement tied up both Gordon and myself during the entire month of March, and thus immobilized one third of the conciliation staff of the EEOC from other activity.)

I returned two days later, and was met at the airport by a group of the DOD personnel who had a surprising story to tell me. They had expected the supervisors to report that none of the Negroes were qualified to be supervisors. This was not an unrealistic expectation for the reasons mentioned above and also because the company had asked the supervisors about promoting Negroes to quartermen when they made their first round of promotions. The report, however, contradicted the expectations. The supervisors were reporting that between 30 and 50 percent of the Negroes who met the formal criteria were qualified to be quartermen. The DOD personnel were stunned by the response. I was greatly heartened. The gamble had paid off. We carefully documented these answers, and I directed that we carry out this procedure in all thirty-one departments in the yard. When we were done, we had a list of around one hundred Negroes who met the formal requirements and had been "certified" by their supervisors as capable to be quartermen. As the information came in, I began feeding it to the company on forms which we had prepared for the occasion. The company cooperated fully in making personnel available for interviews, in making records available, and in providing secretarial and duplicating services. When the information was all in, the company indicated its willingness to promote some seventy of those whose names we had submitted but not the entire list. The time had come to decide whether to settle.

But there was one preliminary hurdle. The company was unwilling to demote white employees who had been promoted to temporary quartermen and who had been serving in that capacity for some time, due to the slowness of the government in resolving this issue. We were then faced with a serious problem of potential conflict between those Negroes who qualified by our standards and those whites who had been serving as quartermen. Once again, it appeared that the entire agreement was in jeopardy, and that, rather than assisting in solving the problems of discrimination, we were about to generate a new problem of great difficulty. We turned to the facts and were again happily surprised. In only three or four instances were there conflicts of the type we had anticipated. Otherwise, the Negroes whom we wished to see promoted were not in conflict with whites. The reason then became apparent—the bulk of the Negroes who were qualified for quartermen were in primarily Negro departments. The company had not placed white temporary quartermen in those departments, hence there was little conflict between white and Negro for quarterman positions.

What conflict there was could be resolved as a part of the wrap-up of the agreement. We gave two exemptions to the company for whites with specialized skills (one of whom was in charge of the scaffolding on the carrier *Kennedy*) allowing them to remain as quartermen ahead of

Negroes who were qualified. In another conflict situation the company agreed to promote the Negroes in such a way that it would not be necessary to demote the whites.

We were then down to the final issue: would we settle for the seventy additional Negro quartermen which the company was prepared to make or at least to place on a preferential promotion list, or would we insist on all of the one hundred or so names that we had submitted.[32] In submitting these names, and in the development of these lists, I had instructed the DOD personnel when in doubt to make decisions, as to whether the Negro employees met the criteria and in interpreting the comments of the foremen as to their qualifications, in favor of the Negro employees. I was thus satisfied that we had rejected few qualified applicants through the administrative process, and that we were probably pressing for promotion of a few men whose credentials were marginal.

As we pressed toward a narrowing of the list of promotable Negroes, I began to sense unrest among the DOD personnel. It was an integrated team, two Negroes, three whites, and they were becoming increasingly unhappy with me as we narrowed the list. My diagnosis of their unhappiness was as follows: they had not been in a decisional situation before. They had not had to make judgments securing promotions for some and not for others. Their prior activities had not produced these kinds of results, and they were not accustomed to the hard role of decisionmaking. Thus they resented the decisions which would strike men from the preferential promotion list, even though those decisions were necessary if others were to get on such a list.

The morning of decision I got up early and went for a walk in the late March sunshine. I had a sense that this was the day in which we would conclude the agreement's administration except for certain problems. I hoped that the conclusion would be one which could be viewed as a success by the government, the civil rights interests, and the shipyard. Yet I needed to be sure that my own desire to make the agreement work was not overcoming my judgment. I went back to the motel and sat down at a large table, waiting for the others to come down for

---

[32] In theory we could have submitted disputes to Case & Co. under §11(2)(e) of the agreement and then reviewed their decision under §III(5)(c), but I had no reason to expect that Case would have overruled the Newport News Shipbuilding & Dry Dock Co. on this issue.

breakfast. I posed two questions, individually, to the DOD personnel: (1) If we refused to settle, and the company then declined to promote the men we wanted promoted, did they think that DOD would cut off contracts with the company? The answer was uniformly no. (2) If we refused to settle, and those men who were not promoted sued, could they win a case of discrimination or of violation of the conciliation agreement? Again the answer was uniformly no.

I was convinced. They individually had given the same answer to each question. When they were all assembled, I interpreted their conclusions as dictating that we settle the promotion issue on the most favorable terms we could get, and explained to them that their answers to my questions meant that we had no more bargaining leverage on these issues. Somewhat unhappy at being made parties to the decision to settle, they reluctantly agreed that settlement was necessary.

Jules Gordon and I then went to the personnel office and sat down with William Myers, the Director of Industrial Relations, to work out the details of the settlement. Some seventy-five of the men on our list were placed on preferential promotion lists to become quartermen. The basic phase of the administration of the Newport News agreement was finished. The following week I resigned as Chief of Conciliations and began the process of withdrawal from the activities of the Commission which brought me back to teaching law at Rutgers in September 1967.

IX. Epilogue

In the months following our leaving Newport News, a strike occurred for the first time in the history of the yard. In an article which was, I thought, unfair to the Commission, *Barron's*, a conservative weekly, attributed this to the involvement of the EEOC. The article found its way into the Congressional Record, and Senator Javits, in rebuttal, inserted other material in the Record, making it clear that the strike was not over racial questions and including an analysis of the Agreement which I had prepared for the EEOC.[33] While the strike was not directly related to Commission activities at the shipyard, it is clear that our proceedings did cause a review and reconsideration of many aspects of labor relations at the yard which had been accepted in the

---

[33] *Supra* note 4.

period before the Agreement. In this sense, once the agreement had been executed and administered, industrial relations at the yard were on a new footing and new tensions could be expected to develop.

Senator Fannin and *Barron's* magazine have waged a sporadic attack on the operation of the EEOC in connection with the Newport News agreement since that time. These attacks have not been without effect. I think they have been one factor which has discouraged the government from operating since that time as it did in Newport News. There has been no such concerted effort with any company since the agreement was negotiated. Thus that week in March 1966 stands as the "one brief shining moment" when the government did marshal its resources and produce significant results with a major firm in ending a pattern of discrimination.

There are other reasons why this pattern of joint action (called "ganging up" by its detractors, as if employers had a vested interest in having the government act in an *uncoordinated* manner) has not been repeated. One reason has been bureaucratic jealousy; EEOC did get most of the public credit for the agreement. I think this was probably deserved, but surely there was enough to go around for Justice, DOD, Navy, and Labor. Also, general bureaucratic caution set in. Officials, particularly in DOD, pulled back from the concept of massive system changes to eliminate discrimination. They decentralized the contract compliance function and, within a year, eliminated Mr. Clark from any role in the program.[34] There were those in government who simply did not grasp the concept that discrimination could be sharply reduced through a comprehensive agreement such as that adopted at Newport News. Some staff people were deeply committed to a principle of gradualism. Finally, the administration did not give its endorsement to the concept of the Newport News agreement at the highest levels. This failure of a "signal" of intensive administrative support for and interest in the concept, meant that the administrative energy and courage necessary to its implementation could not be mustered. In short, the collective will of the government agencies which had joined for that brief moment could not be crystalized again during the time that I remained in government after the agreement. I have kept up my connections with the federal programs since leaving the EEOC staff and am in a position

---

[34] See app. VI this chapter.

to say that the joint effort mounted at Newport News has not been repeated as of September 1969.

Instead, each agency is going its own way, and the effect of the disjointed action of the federal government is to judicialize the administration of the antidiscrimination law and make it unlikely that many companies will be faced with the major system changes which confronted Newport News. The OFCC is now holding several hearings to decide whether to suspend contracting. The Department of Justice has filed a number of law suits under Title VII. Meanwhile, the contractors who are sued keep their contracts, and the contractors subject to hearings, deny discrimination and will have a trial and appeal on particular issues. Enormous amounts of government manpower go into each of these proceedings, leaving little government energy for other activities. The net effect of these proceedings will, of course, be healthy. There will be definitions of discriminatory conduct, and outlining of required remedies. Both of these are badly needed in the field.[35] And yet, this course of events means that very few companies will be subjected to systematic review and revision of their industrial relations systems such as was accomplished at Newport News with minimal investment of manpower, compared to that of the filing, preparation, and trial of a proceeding before OFCC or the federal court. And the range of solutions achieved in negotiation, as demonstrated at Newport News, is likely to be far broader than that which will issue from a judicial or administrative proceeding. Thus I think there remains today an important place in any sound program of administration of antidiscrimination laws for the Newport News type of joint governmental action, and I think it part of our national tragedy that the government has not followed the pattern established in that case.

The Newport News approach, however, did have its limitations. The administrative process settles large issues, and, of necessity, must sometimes ignore individuals. Perhaps some of those Negroes who were not placed on the list for promotion to quartermen are entitled to sue under the agreement as third-party beneficiaries. It is one of the consequences

---

[35] The first formal decision of the Secretary of Labor interpreting the requirements of the executive order was rendered on January 16, 1969, in Matter of Allen-Bradley Co. See CCH EMPLOYMENT PRACTICES GUIDE, NEW DEVELOPMENTS, ¶8070, 8065 (1969). A rather general settlement was tentatively approved by the new Secretary of Labor on Aug. 8, 1969. See CCH, NEW DEVELOPMENTS ¶8072.

of a negotiated solution that some possible beneficiaries will not receive the assistance that individualized attention to their situation would dictate. For this reason I am sharply in favor of the retention of the individual right to sue against employment discrimination, regardless of whether administrative agencies are given more power in the area, and I oppose amendments to Title VII which would restrict the individual right to sue.[36] The individual right is important for two reasons; first, it will "prop up" the administrator so that he is more likely to assist the individual than settle to get rid of his case, and second, it enables the individual who believes himself injured by a settlement agreement to secure de novo a judicial review of his rights. If administration has done a good job, the judicial review will uphold the settlement; if the administration has not done a good job, then the settlement should not be upheld. I do not fear that the individual right to sue will interrupt the settlement process; it will only deter the entering of meaningless settlements which should be discouraged anyway. If the settlement is a decent one, then it will be so recognized by all concerned parties. But my own experience as an administrator, disposing of bulk claims over a conference table as in the Newport News situation, has confirmed my belief in the importance of the individual right to sue with respect to these matters.

Finally, I would not leave the impression that the administration of the agreement brought repose to the shipyard. Problems of discrimination persist. Certain issues were never resolved. Promotion of some and the opening of opportunities have generated new ambitions and aspirations on the part of those who may not have had them before. The internal problems of the union have become complicated.

But repose is not an object of modern industrial relations. These relations are recognized by all as dynamic, as involving constant readjustments of positions and situations in light of the myriad of changes in circumstances which bear on any given system. The development of new methods of shipbuilding and the take-over of the shipyard by one of the conglomerates simply illustrate new factors which continually change and challenge the industrial relations situation at the shipyard. This is typical of modern industry. Men knowledgeable in industrial relations know this and are not ashamed of a temporary solution or of an adjustment for a limited period of time. A willingness to

---

[36] See chs. 1, 2 *supra.*

live with change is an essential ingredient in our ability to participate in the affairs of our time. What the Newport News agreement did, as it was administered, was to shatter the old system, shake up the patterns of wage rates, and provide a new basis, not tainted with discrimination, on which the business of the shipyard could be conducted. The affairs at the shipyard are not tranquil, but they are operating on a more civilized basis. Most major systematic discriminations built into the industrial relations systems over time have been shaken out by the Agreement and its administration. Future problems will look more and more like individual grievances under a collective bargaining agreement which can be resolved within the industrial relations framework, or as "ordinary" matters before the EEOC.

X. The Negotiated Settlement

This article has been concerned with the nexus between law and life in the new industrial state—with the points of contact between law, the administrative processes of government, and the intricate pluralism of union, management, civil rights groups, and individuals involved in any serious effort to untangle the web of racial discrimination and set employment matters off on a new nondiscriminatory footing. Coping with the myriad of personalities and interests, conceiving and developing substantive solutions which work, and seeing these solutions through the negotiation and administration of the Newport News agreement has provided a perspective on the negotiated settlement in the field of employment discrimination. I believe the objective of all such processes should be to force all parties to reach an agreement which will root out discrimination and its consequences. Whether this is done through administrative sanctions, such as the threat of suit or the suspension of government contracting as was the case in Newport News, or through a judicial decision that the law has been violated and that the parties should submit a proposed order, is a matter of highly important detail.

In the last analysis, system changes such as those achieved in Newport News are intricate and complex; they require careful negotiation to be workable. I believe that government should adopt a full enforcement approach in the field of employment discrimination by utilizing all of its power. Once this power has been applied, in most cases sensible negotiations will work an end to discrimination. But an enforcement policy without the negotiated solution as its objective may prove to be as sterile as the "soft" policies which government has historically followed in this field. A litigation program alone will not achieve the end of employment discrimination.

Except for the suggestion in *Crown Zellerbach Corp. v. Wirtz*[37] there is no right to a government contract; and it does not necessarily follow that a government contractor is entitled to a trial-type hearing on the question of whether he has discriminated before he loses the opportunity for future contracts. There are occasions on which the government can act without a trial-type hearing. I submit that in the field of employment discrimination a trial-type hearing *prior* to suspension of the opportunity to bid on government contracts is inappropriate. Suspension of contracting, on a temporary basis after informal administrative investigations which includes a full opportunity for respondent to present evidence and argument, can set the stage for major system changes such as those achieved at Newport News. After entering into a negotiated agreement for the kind of changes which the discrimination requires, the employer may comply with the agreement or seek judicial relief from its consequences. In the vast bulk of cases, the agreements reached will be honored, and discriminatory practice set aright. Where this is not a practical course, it is better to let the large institutions, the companies and the unions, seek judicial relief against overreaching by government rather than to leave the victims of discrimination with their burden pending judicial decisions. This structuring of the situation will facilitate negotiated solutions which can bring an end to employment discrimination. A trial-type hearing is not necessarily the most sensitive process for achieving the elimination of employment discrimination. I hope that the conference table will once again be utilized for that purpose by a government utilizing all of its powers to assure that the resulting bargain does in fact carry out the national purpose of establishing equal employment opportunity.

---

[37] 281 F. Supp. 337 (D.D.C. 1968) §208(b) of Executive Order No. 11246 requires a "hearing" prior to the issuance of a notice under §209(a)(6) prohibiting further contracting unless and until the Secretary of Labor is satisfied that the contractor will carry out the policies of the order. However, as §208(a) makes clear, the "hearing" contemplated under the order need not be a trial-type adversary proceeding. The order may mean no more than a requirement that contractors be afforded a full opportunity to present evidence and argument.

Appendix I: Conciliation Agreement Between Equal Employment Opportunity Commission et al. and Newport News Shipbuilding & Dry Dock Company, March 30, 1966

Equal Employment Opportunity Commission, Washington, D.C.: Case No. 5–7–235, 5–7–237, 5–7–520 and 5–7–521, in the Matter of the Conciliation Between Equal Employment Opportunity Commission; Thomas Mann; James Lassiter; Arthur Ford; Reverend J. C. Fauntleroy, et al.; Complainants and Newport News Shipbuilding & Dry Dock Company, Respondent

Charges having been filed under Title VII of the Civil Rights Act of 1964 by the Charging Parties, the Commission having found reasonable cause to believe the charges to be true and the matter having been conciliated, the parties hereby agree to and do settle the above matter in the following extent and manner:

I. STATEMENT OF PRINCIPLES

1. All hiring, promotion practices, and other terms and conditions of employment shall be maintained and conducted in a manner which does not discriminate on the basis of race, color, religion, or national origin in violation of Title VII of the Civil Rights Act of 1964. All present and future employees will be classified and assigned without discrimination on the basis of race, color, religion, or national origin. All job classifications shall be open to all employees without discrimination as to race, color, religion, or national origin.

2. The Company agrees that all facilities owned, operated, or managed by or on behalf of the Company shall be available for the use of any employee without regard to race, color, religion, or national origin; that there shall be no discrimination against any employee on said grounds with respect to the use of said facilities, and that the notice required to be posted by Title VII of the Civil Rights Act of 1964 will be posted.

3. The Company agrees that there shall be no discrimination or retaliation of any kind against any person because of opposition to any practice declared unlawful under Title VII of the Civil Rights Act of 1964; or because

of the filing of a charge; giving of testimony or assistance; or participation in any manner in any investigation, proceeding or hearing under or with respect to matters covered by Title VII of the Civil Rights Act of 1964, Executive Orders 10925 or 11246, and Regulations issued thereunder, or this Agreement.

II. GENERAL REMEDIAL ACTION

1. Evaluation of Jobs

a. The Company and the Commission shall forthwith undertake a general review to determine if Negro employees are improperly classified with respect to the job they are performing and the rates they are paid relative to white employees doing the same or substantially equivalent work. With respect to several job categories in which, predominantly, Negroes are employed and there is no direct basis for comparison with rates of pay of white employees, a review will be made of such categories to determine whether the rate of pay is discriminatorily depressed on the basis of race.

b. To conduct this review, the Company shall as soon as possible but not later than 45 days from the date of this Agreement, retain at its expense an expert in job evaluation and statements of work content, knowledgeable in race relations, who is acceptable to the Commission, to make this determination. In the event an expert acceptable to the Commission is not designated within 45 days, the parties shall forthwith reconvene for the sole purpose of designating the expert. The expert shall report his findings to the Company and the Commission. The company shall implement the decision of the expert by re-classifying such employees and/or adjusting the rate of pay accordingly within a period of 30 days from the date of determination. The Company shall supply said expert with adequate staff and facilities and shall make available all records and other information necessary to perform this function. Such review shall be concluded within 120 days of the appointment of the expert, unless the expert requests and the Commission agrees to a reasonable extension of time for this purpose.

c. The scope of the review is to be general, and shall not be limited by or to the complaint of individual employees. However, this review will encompass the rate and classification of any Negro employee who requests such a review. If, as a result of this review, the Commission believes that an employee's job is improperly classified relative to jobs held by white employees or that a rate is lower than that paid white employees performing the same or substantially equivalent work, the Commission shall so notify the Company which will take appropriate action to correct the situation. As a part of this review procedure, there shall be developed written statements of the work content for all jobs involved, which reflect the work actually performed.

d. The expert described above may be an individual, management consultant or operations research organization. Both the Commission and the

Company may nominate persons or organizations to be retained as the expert. It shall be the expert's responsibility to conduct the review set forth in the first paragraph of this section.

2. Promotion to Supervisor and Other Positions, Upgrading, and Vacancies

a. As the Company's last report to the Government showed that only 32 of 1,997 persons employed by the Company as "Officials and Managers" were Negroes, the Company agrees that, to comply affirmatively with Title VII of the Civil Rights Act of 1964, the Executive Order of the President and the Regulations of Departments and Agencies of the Federal Government, it will afford affirmative opportunities for promotion to and within supervisory levels, including staff supervisors, junior and senior quartermen, foremen and assistant foremen, assistant superintendent and superintendent, to qualified Negroes employed by the Company. Accordingly, the Company agrees to revise its promotion policies and practices with a view to improving opportunities for qualified Negro personnel for promotion to and within supervisory levels, as follows:

b. An inventory of the skilled Negro employees, indicating their seniority (defined as continuous service with the shipyard) and qualifications, and an inventory of the seniority and qualifications of the last 100 persons promoted to quarterman positions to July 2, 1965, will be conducted jointly by the Company and by Industrial Employment Policy Specialists of the Department of Defense as an interested party, and in the interests of contract compliance, commencing within 30 days of the date of this Agreement. Within 60 days of the conclusion of the inventory, a list of those Negro employees whose seniority and qualifications exceed those of white employees among the 100 persons described above will be developed jointly by the Company and by the Industrial Employment Policy Specialist and will constitute the order of placement, as supervisory positions open, for which the employee's qualifications are relevant, until the list is exhausted. Refusals of Negro employees to accept offers of promotions to supervision must be documented in each case.

c. Provided however that where the Company desires to fill a vacancy with an employee with greater seniority of qualifications than Negro employees on the list, the company may present has [*sic*] qualifications in writing to the Commission, along with a demonstration of special circumstances and unusual need for which it wishes to promote said employee. If the Commission is satisfied that the request is free of discrimination on the basis of race, color, religion, or national origin, it shall grant the request. All appointments to supervisory posts shall be made without regard to the race of the employees who will be subject to such supervision.

d. Prior to the completion of the list described above and its use as a basis for selection of supervisors, supervisory vacancies may develop. Said vacancies will be filled by qualified Negro employees. Where the Company has special reasons for desiring to fill any such vacancy with a white employee, it shall first notify the Commission in writing, stating its reasons. If the Commission is satisfied that the request is free of discrimination, it shall grant the request.

e. Any disagreement between the Company and the Industrial Employment Policy Specialists, with respect to matters described in the first paragraph of this section, shall be resolved by the expert mentioned above, if appointed and available, and otherwise by the Commission.

3. Promotion and Transfer to Nonsupervisory Positions

a. The Company agrees to post at the Employment Office, Yard Personnel Office, and at all normal access gates into the yard, notices of the existence of all job vacancies. Applications to fill such vacancies will be considered and qualified applicants for such jobs shall be selected on the basis of their length of service where their skill, ability, and efficiency are fairly equal.

b. The Company shall permit employees from predominately Negro job classifications to transfer to vacancies in other departments for which they are qualified. If, within two weeks, the employee is unable to perform in the new job, he may return to his old job. If the vacancy to which he transfers is a lower rate step in his classification, he will be transferred at his rate before the transfer.

c. Employees in predominantly Negro departments shall be given the first opportunity for training in programs in which they are qualified to enter.

d. The Company will apply a liberal policy in the application of this section to advance the basic purpose of this Agreement.

e. To comply affirmatively with Title VII and Executive Orders in the matter of promotion and training, the Company agrees to undertake an intensive re-evaluation of the skills of its Negro employees, to institute training programs to develop and improve the skill levels of such employees, and to promote and adjust compensation on the basis of such re-evaluation and/or training. Opportunities to acquire skills necessary for upgrading shall be afforded Negro employees on a non-discriminatory basis so that they acquire a rounded work experience.

f. The qualifications of all Negro applicants for employment will be reviewed and measured against minimum qualifications for all job classifications. Such applicants will be given full consideration for filling vacancies in all such job classifications for which they may qualify. Review of applicant qualifications shall be concluded within 60 days after the date of this Agreement.

4. Adjustment of Rate: Promotional Opportunities

In order to adjust the pay rate and classification of Negro employees who may have been discriminatorily denied or delayed in their advancement through the wage and job structure of the Company, the following is agreed to:

a. To determine Company practices with respect to the rate and conditions of promotions of white employees both within steps of job classifications and from one job classification to another, control groups will be picked by a random sample method from the Fitters Department (X–11), the Painters Department (X–33), and Storekeepers (O–53).

b. The sample selected from each department shall be sufficient to trace the pattern of employment history of white employees in the department from the time of their original hiring.

c. From this sample there will be derived a profile of the rate and conditions for promotion of white employees.

d. This profile shall be developed jointly by the expert described in section 1 and the Industrial Employment Policy Specialists, Department of Defense.

e. Thereafter, the expert would compare the history of progression and promotion of individual Negro employees in said departments with the profile.

f. Upon establishment that a Negro employee has not moved up through the grades within the classification in which he is presently employed as rapidly as the norm or standard derived from the sample for white employees, he shall forthwith be assigned the first grade in his job classification, or such other grade as he would have achieved had his history followed the normal progression indicated in the study unless the Company demonstrates from such records as it keeps which are themselves not the product or result of discrimination, that the employee was not promoted for reason of physical handicap, improper attendance, or other conduct on the premises. Considerations of the employee's skill and ability are not germane to this section. The burden of demonstrating that from Company records that the employee should not be upgraded is on the Company.

g. Where the expert finds that the Negro employee would have been promoted beyond his classification had the white rate of progress been followed, the Company may assert that the employee is not and cannot become qualified for promotion to the higher classification, using the same standard for promotion between classes heretofore used for white employees as derived from the sample.

h. If the evaluator finds that the Negro employee has such qualifications for promotion, or can achieve them through reasonable training, he shall be placed on a preferential promotion list and given at an appropriate time such training as may be reasonably necessary to equip him for promotion. Such promotion shall be given when need arises for additional members of the next higher class.

i. The sample and its results will apply to other departments to which reasonably applicable. Thereupon the expert shall apply the same standards of comparison of Negro employment records against the promotion and upgrading profile of white employees and the same actions will be taken as a result of that comparison as described in paragraph 6 and 7.

j. If a further sample is needed, the department or departments from which it is to be drawn shall be discussed with the Commission. The expert will apply the results of any such further sample alone or in conjunction with the previous sample in such departments as are agreed upon in the manner described in paragraph 6 and 7.

k. The entire Negro labor force will be reviewed in the manner set out above.

l. The Company may as a part of this process, and in its discretion, seek to determine if white employees have been unfairly treated in respect to in-grade progressions or promotions, and to attempt, in the event such unfairness is found, to correct it.

5. *Apprenticeship Programs*

As the Company's last report to the Government (Form 40) showed that only 6 of the 506 apprentices enrolled in the apprenticeship program were Negroes, the Company agrees that, to provide affirmatively for equal employment opportunity, apprenticeship classes shall henceforth be filled as follows:

a. The Company shall, within 30 days of this Agreement, estimate the number of vacancies in the program for the coming year. Similar estimates shall be made each succeeding 12 months.

b. The Company agrees that qualified employees now on the payroll shall have first opportunity to fill apprenticeship classes during the next two years. For these employees, the Company agrees to accept a high school diploma or academic equivalent for admission, to accept employees up to the age of 25 years as entering apprentices, to accept married students as apprentices, to keep such as apprentices should they marry during the course of apprenticeship, and not to debar any employee from the apprenticeship program because of previous attendance at college or other institution of higher education.

c. A list of Negro employees eligible for the apprenticeship program under these provisions shall be compiled and shall be available to the Commission. Rejections of this opportunity by employees on the list shall be obtained in writing, with a copy to the Commission.

d. In filling vacancies in the apprenticeship classes, the Company agrees to exercise its utmost efforts to see that substantial numbers of Negroes are included in such classes. To this end the Company agrees, (1) to include in its recruitment efforts the predominantly Negro schools in the labor market areas; and (2) to notify civil rights organizations in said area of this Agreement and to solicit such organizations to send qualified applicants for such programs. The Commission shall, upon request, supply a list of such organizations. Copies of such notices and solicitations shall be furnished by the Company to the Commission. The parties to this Agreement recognize as a natural result of this recruitment effort that the ratio of Negro to white apprentices in any given year should approach the ratio of Negro to white employees and the ratio of Negro to whites in the labor market area but this provision shall not be construed to require or permit the rejection of any qualified applicant on the basis of his race or color.

e. When the Company has filled one-third of the estimated vacancies in any apprenticeship class for each year through the foregoing procedures, it shall notify the Commission of the proportion of Negro employees enrolled in the class, and the Company shall not fill more than half the remaining vacancies until the Commission has responded. The commission's response can be expected within two weeks. If it appears to the Commission that adequate numbers of Negro employees will not be enrolled in the class, the Commission may propose additional reasonable recruiting steps which the Company shall undertake to assure the fulfillment of its obligations under this section.

f. The Company shall integrate the apprenticeship faculty by October 1, 1966, and the apprenticeship Selection Committee forthwith.

g. Apprenticeship requirements shall be reviewed by the Company and the Commission within the next 60 days to determine whether increased numbers of Negroes can be appointed consistent with the maintenance of the requirements for qualified apprentices. After this review, the Commission may propose other reasonable steps to increase the number of Negro apprentices, and the Company shall take such steps.

h. All other training programs, formal and informal, including crash training, patternmaking, and tack welding programs, shall be open to employees without regard to race or color.

The Company shall post in conspicuous places and otherwise publicize information to all its employees concerning the availability of these programs, and shall actively encourage Negro participation in these programs.

6. Facilities

In view of the desire of the Company to afford equal employment opportunity and to comply fully with the letter and spirit of the aforesaid Civil Rights Act of 1964 and the various Executive Orders and Regulations applicable to its activities, the Company agrees to take the following steps:

a. In addition to the elimination of a segregated facility in the Foundry, the Company agrees to alter the portable toilet facilities in the drawings attached hereto as Appendix II, and made a part hereof, in the manner indicated in such drawings. Such alterations shall be commenced within 30 days from the date of this settlement Agreement, and shall be completed not later than 75 days after work on such alterations has concerned.

b. Also, the Company agrees that all locker room facilities on the premises shall be available for the use of employees in that department without regard to race, color, religion, or national origin and there shall be no discrimination against any employee on such grounds with respect to the use of said facilities. All locker room space shall be reassigned in each department not later than the time specified in paragraph 1, on the following basis:

(1) Lockers in buildings devoted to locker rooms shall be reassigned to all employees on the basis of alphabetical order for all employees assigned to such buildings. Assignment to buildings shall be without regard to race.

(2) Locker rooms in other buildings shall be assigned alphabetically to employees using such facilities, in such manner as to eliminate segregated use of locker rooms and related facilities.

(3) Henceforth:

(a) Lockers are to be assigned on the basis of needs in the order of their vacancy regardless of race.

(b) An up-to-date record will be kept of lockers in all locker rooms with particular attention given to the following:

(i) Number and location of vacant lockers

(ii) Date of vacancy

(iii) Date of assignment

(iv) To whom assigned.

c. During such alterations and locker reassignments specified in paragraphs 1 and 2 and for a reasonable time thereafter, the Company will post on all Newport News Shipbuilding departmental bulletin boards a notice which, in substance, states that all employees have equal rights to use all such facilities. Any employee who interferes with or intimidates employees in the exercise of their rights hereunder and/or takes any other action which is intended to maintain segregated facilities shall result in disciplinary action including, where appropriate, discharge.

7. Other affirmative actions

Take the following affirmative action to effectuate the policies of Title VII of the Civil Rights Act of 1964:

a. Upgrade and advance qualified Negro employees to positions as first-class mechanics.

b. Full-time operators of cranes in the Foundry of 20 tons or above shall be paid first-class mechanics' rates, when they are qualified to operate such cranes in a proficient and safe manner.

c. The Company agrees to promote Thomas C. Mann, Reverend J. C. Fauntleroy and James E. Lassiter to the position of quarterman in their respective departments, effective the first Monday after the signing of this Agreement. The Company further agrees to promote Arthur Ford to the position of materialman, and advance him to mechanic, third class, effective the first Monday after the signing of this Agreement. The Company will review with Mr. Ford his experience and understanding of its operations to determine the most effective use which can be made of his capabilities.

d. Cooperate with the Equal Employment Opportunity Commission with regard to the investigation, conciliation, and processing of the charges of 38 other charging parties without regard to the time limitations of Section 706 of Title VII.

e. With regard to certain charging parties, waive the statutory period within which the charging parties may institute a civil action in the event conciliation is not achieved.

f. In addition, to cooperate with the Commission with regard to the investigation and conciliation of any charges which may hereinafter be filed.

g. Persons aggrieved, whose cases are subject to the job evaluation review under section 1 hereof, but who are not among those listed above, shall not be entitled to retroactive back pay in the event the expert determines that they have been improperly classified or paid.

h. Any person against whom a new act of discrimination is committed after the date of this Agreement shall be entitled to his full remedy under Title VII of the Civil Rights Act of 1964.

III. GENERAL PROVISIONS

1. Policy Statement

The Company agrees that its policy statement in support of the principle of equal employment opportunity, which was worked out with the Commission, and is attached to this Conciliation Agreement and marked Appendix III, is incorporated by reference herein as though fully set out. This statement emphasizes the Company's pledge of nondiscrimination with respect to recruitment, hiring, wages, hours, promotions, training, apprenticeships and all others terms and conditions of employment. This policy statement shall be published in full by the company within 30 days of the date of this Agreement by attaching said statement, signed by the President of the Company, to the pay check of each full-time employee of the Company. Copies thereof shall be displayed prominently on bulletin boards available to all employees.

2. Supervisory Employees

The Company shall within 30 days assemble all supervisory employees. It shall read the policy statement set forth herein, advise the supervisors of the contents of this Agreement, including the Company's policy of encouraging equal employment opportunities and a fully integrated work force. In addition, supervisors shall be instructed that they shall encourage the use of facilities on an integrated basis, and that terms of address used in the plant shall be the same for whites and Negroes. Further, supervisors shall be instructed that a violation of the policy set forth in this Agreement shall result in disciplinary action including, where appropriate, discharge.

The Company shall also call departmental or other group meetings for all employees for the same purpose. Meetings of supervisors and all employees shall be completed within 30 days from the date of this Agreement. The Commission shall be advised 5 days in advance of the date of meetings to be held in three representative departments. A representative of the Commission may attend any or all meetings held for this purpose.

3. *Implementing Procedures*

The Company shall establish implementing procedures which will include the assignment of responsibility within the Company for implementation of each and every provision of this Agreement, and a formalized feedback system to keep management apprised of the progress of the program by channeling to top management the substance of all decisions taken hereunder by officers, agents and employees of the company.

4. *Reports*

a. The Company shall prepare and furnish to the Commission not later than 90 days from the date of this Agreement a detailed report of the actions to comply with this Agreement. For 2 years thereafter the Company shall report at quarterly intervals its progress in complying with this Agreement. The initial and subsequent reports shall include the following statistical data broken down into the categories white and Negro:

(1) Applications for employment, by name, job applied for.

(2) New hires, by job title, department, name of employee, and date of employment.

(3) Changes in rate or job classification, by name of employee, date, and department.

(4) Promotions to nonsupervisory positions within each department and to supervisor by name of employee.

(5) Entrants into apprenticeship and formalized training and educational programs, by program, by name of employee.

b. The reports required by this paragraph are in addition to other reports required by this Agreement. All reports required to be furnished to the Commission under this Agreement should be addressed to the Chief of Conciliation, Equal Employment Opportunity Commission, Washington, D.C. 20506.

c. After the first 90 days the Commission shall consider simplifying these requirements by accepting in summary form the information contained therein.

5. *Review of Compliance*

a. The Company agrees that the Commission, on the request of any charging party named herein or in its own motion, may review compliance with this Agreement.

b. As a part of such review, the Commission may require written reports in addition to those otherwise provided for which are reasonably necessary to the audit of this Agreement, may inspect the premises, examine witnesses, and examine and copy records and documents.

c. The Commission shall determine whether the Company has complied with this Agreement, may review any finding or decision of the expert referred to in this Agreement, and may revise same where the Commission finds the revision necessary to prevent discrimination.

6. Publication of Agreement

The Company agrees that the terms of this Agreement and the proceedings before the Commission, but not including the content of conciliation discussions between the Commission and the Company, shall be made public by the Commission.

7. Federal District Court Proceeding

The signing of this Agreement shall not prejudice the right of the plaintiffs in the Federal District Court action embracing the same subject matter from seeking an award of costs, expenses and reasonable attorney fees in said action.

> NEWPORT NEWS SHIPBUILDING AND DRY DOCK COMPANY
> THOMAS C. MANN
> REV. J. C. FAUNTLEROY
> ARTHUR FORD
> JAMES LASSITER

I recommended approval of this Agreement; Alfred W. Blumrosen, Chief, Conciliations.

EQUAL OPPORTUNITY POLICY

I wish to emphasize the Company's fundamental policy of providing equal opportunity in all areas of employment practice, and in assuring that there shall be no discrimination against any person on the grounds of race, color, religion, or national origin.

This policy extends to hiring, working conditions, employee treatment, training programs, promotions, use of company facilities, and all other terms and conditions of employment. The Company encourages all employees to exercise their rights under this policy.

The importance of fulfilling this policy cannot be overemphasized. Any violation of the letter or spirit of this policy by any employee of this Company shall result in disciplinary action including, where appropriate, discharge. Specific instructions for affirmative action to implement this policy will be issued.

> D. A. HOLDEN,
> *President, Newport News Shipbuilding and Dry Dock Co.*

Appendix II: Barron's National Business and Financial Weekly

July 17, 1967 at 1, Official Bias: A Note on the Equal Employment Opportunity Commission. (Reprinted by courtesy of Barron's.)

As bureaucrats go these days, the Equal Employment Opportunity Commission has not gone very far. Created in mid-1965 to weed out discrimination
in employment based on either race or sex, the agency boasts a budget of
only $5.2 million and a staff of 314, smaller respectively than those of the
Office of Coal Research and the Federal Crop Insurance Program. Personnel-
wise, EEOC has been something of a revolving door: its first chairman,
Franklin D. Roosevelt, Jr., quickly resigned to run for Governor; his successor, Stephen N. Shulman, quit after nine months to go into private practice. While the Commission reportedly has received over 15,000 complaints,
it has cleared up only a few hundred. "We're out to kill an elephant," Mr.
Shulman recently was quoted as saying, "with a fly gun."

        ❃   ❃   ❃

In the wrong hands, however, even fly guns can be dangerous. Last
Monday Newport News Shipbuilding & Dry Dock Co., the nation's leading
builder of naval vessels, suffered the first strike in 81 years of doing business.
On the following midnight, a riot, which injured over a score of people and
was termed by local police the "worst disorder" in the placid history of
Newport News, Va., broke out at the company's main gate. Newspaper accounts of the affair, which interrupted the construction of the world's largest
aircraft carrier and led to the personal intervention of the Governor, were
scanty at best. The walkout apparently began in protest over relatively minor
grievances. However, union officials hinted that "other problems" lurk in the
background. A Washington paper reported cryptically that "the issues go
deeper."

Somehow nobody has chosen to identify the principal villain of the piece,
which is none other than the fly gun-totin' Equal Employment Opportunity
Commission. Backed by the firepower of the U.S. Department of Labor,
which threatened the shipyard's government contracts, the Commission 18
months ago moved in on management. In particular, the agency coerced
Newport News Ship into signing a so-called Conciliation Agreement, which,
by pointedly favoring Negroes for future apprentice training and on-the-job

promotion, made a new kind of discrimination official policy. "Shipyard in South Induced to Make Up for Past Bias," read the headline. Since then, in the words of an old hand at the yard, EEOC has done its worst to "set black against white, labor against management and disconcert everybody." In the alien world of bureaucracy, size is no measure of virulence.

Labor-management relations at Newport News Ship began to suffer in mid-1965, shortly after the Equal Employment Opportunity Commission set up shop. The company, which does roughly half a billion dollars worth of work per year, largely for the Navy or the subsidized merchant marine, was a logical target. It's also located in the South. The Commission swiftly set about building a case. According to our man in Washington (actually a charming lady named Shirley Scheibla, who was born and raised in Newport News), EEOC that summer began knocking on doors in Negro neighborhoods soliciting complaints of job discrimination. It managed to get 41, which, for one reason or another, ultimately narrowed down to four. Thus armed, EEOC began to negotiate with the company. After months of fruitless discussion, Washington got tough. Pleading a "pattern of discrimination," EEOC took the dispute to the Justice Department. At the same time, Labor Secretary W. Willard Wirtz ordered the newly organized Office of Federal Contract Compliance to crack down on the yard. A week later the company caved in and signed the notorious Conciliation Agreement, which some have called a "landmark in fair employment practices."

That's one way to describe a document which, in barring discrimination, moved to substitute favoritism. Thus, Newport News Shipbuilding agreed to hire an outside "expert in job evaluation . . . who is acceptable to the Commission" to determine whether Negro employes are improperly classified or working at rates set arbitrarily low. To arrive at his findings, the "expert" took a "random sample" of white employment histories, and, if a Negro worker's status lagged behind the resulting profile, he was deemed a victim of discrimination. Presumably to compensate for past sins, the company had to draw up a preferred promotion list consisting solely of Negroes (exceptions had to be cleared with the Commission). As to apprentice training, a company-run school, once the community's pride, was compelled to drastically change its admission practices. Though the number of applicants traditionally has far outstripped the available openings, Newport News Ship undertook to seek recruits in Negro schools and through civil rights groups. It also accepted a quota system under which "the ratio of Negro to white apprentices in any given year should approach the ratio of . . . Negro to white in the labor area."

The first outraged reaction came from the unaffiliated Peninsula Shipbuilders Association, which, though the recognized bargaining agent for most of the 22,000-man work force, was not consulted. Though subsequently made a party to the pact, the union has never overcome its resentment. Two months ago P.S.A., denouncing a Labor Department release on the company's promotion practices as self-serving and false, threatened legal action to set the record straight. The white community—Newport News Ship is far and away the leading local industry—has been equally aggrieved. One graduate of the Apprentice School wrote the local newspaper to protest against the lowering of admission standards to which, he argued, a quota system inevitably would lead. Another reader, the Rev. Richard B. Sisson of Hampton Roads, put the issue squarely in the moral realm. "I am for equal opportunity for all citizens in school, jobs, housing and all other matters. That is why I find the terms dictated by the government to the shipyard odious. The quota system is just as iniquitous as the exclusion of Negroes some have charged the Yard with practicing previously . . . It will result in very definite de facto discrimination against whites, Indians, Asiatics, and all other non-Negroes. Two wrongs do not make a right."

Even the Negroes, in whose behalf the whole exercise presumably was launched, have wound up frustrated and angry. Like all demagogues, the Equal Employment Opportunity Commission promised far more than it has been able to deliver. "You need a militancy in this community," Samuel C. Jackson, former NAACP bigwig and current EEOC Commissioner, told an audience in Hampton Roads. Thanks to official action, he added, 5,000 of the company's 5,800 Negro workers would get "substantial raises." Instead, according to the union, such rewards have gone to precisely 155. While trying to mind somebody else's business, moreover, the Commission has failed to attend to its own; some 78 cases of alleged discrimination brought by the union have dragged on far beyond the statutory 60 days. Linwood Harris, Negro co-manager of the Peninsula Shipbuilders Association, represents the voice of the people: "The good the EEOC has done," he told Barron's prior to the strike, "is minute and not worth it because of the bad they've done."

✻   ✻   ✻

Newport News is a relatively small place (though the company happens to be the sole remaining builder of U.S. capital ships). Yet what has happened there is a matter of national concern. Emboldened by its "success," EEOC is moving aggressively against other leading corporations. President Johnson has asked Congress to grant the agency power to issue cease-and-desist orders. Instead, to judge by the dismal record, we urge the lawmakers to hand down a stop order of their own.

Appendix III: Congressional Record

(daily edition) Aug. 22, 1967, S12001
Unjustified Criticism of the Role of the EEOC in the Recent
Newport News Shipbuilding & Dry Dock Co. Labor Dispute

MR. JAVITS. Mr. President, last week an article which appeared on the first page of Barron's, of July 17, 1967, was inserted into the RECORD. The article was very critical of the EEOC, and directly implied that the Commission's action in persuading the Newport News Shipbuilding & Dry Dock Co. to enter into a conciliation agreement which rectified longstanding racial discrimination against Negroes employed by the company was responsible for a recent labor dispute involving some violent episodes. The article suggested that the ostensible reason for the strike—the company's overtime policy— was not the real issue and that the strike was really attributable to resentment among white employees over the treatment of Negro employees pursuant to the conciliation agreement.

Mr. President, the article reading it carefully, does not actually state, in so many words, that the labor dispute involved the conciliation agreement, but it implies that this was the case.

Mr. President, the function of the EEOC is so critical to our overall fight against racial discrimination that I think the record should be set straight. The fact it seems to me demonstrates that racial discrimination and conciliation agreement negotiated by the EEOC really had nothing to do with the recent dispute. I call the Senate's attention to a letter dated August 11, 1967, from Mr. Willoughby Abner, Special Assistant to the Director of the Federal Mediation and Conciliation Service, to Mr. Chris Roggerson, a conciliator of the EEOC regarding the dispute. Federal mediators were involved in the negotiations which led to the settlement of the dispute. Hence, they are in the best possible position to know what were the actual issues. The letter specifically states that at no time during either the joint negotiating sessions of the parties at which Federal mediators were present, or at separate sessions between the mediators with the union and the company was racial discrimination or racial unrest even referred to. The letter also states that:

At no time during the course of the mediation of this dispute did the Federal mediators involved sense or detect racial unrest or racial discrimination as a factor in the dispute.

Finally, the letter states that the only reason it could even be written, in view of the confidentiality of the mediation process, is that the subject of racial discrimination "simply was not dealt with at the bargaining table or in separate meetings conducted by Federal mediators."

Mr. President, attached to the letter is a copy of a settlement agreement executed by the parties which seems to me to confirm the statements in the letter. The agreement covers the concerted refusal to work overtime, disciplinary action against employees who participated in the strike, a study of the "incentive problem" and a study of "rate ceilings." None of these matters has any real connection with racial discrimination.

Mr. President, I ask unanimous consent that the letter from Mr. Abner, the settlement agreement attached to the letter as well as a letter from Commissioner Holcomb to the editor of Barron's concerning the article be printed in the RECORD. I also ask unanimous consent that the original conciliation agreement, and an analysis of it by Prof. Alfred Blumrosen be printed in the RECORD.

Mr. President, it has been suggested, on the basis of the Barron's article, that the powers of the EEOC should be curbed rather than expanded. As the cosponsor of S. 1308 and S. 1667, the two bills now being considered by the Committee on Labor and Public Welfare which would give the EEOC cease and desist order power, I am particularly concerned to set the record straight on this article. It would indeed be a travesty of justice if this story had any real influence on the important legislation regarding the EEOC.

There being no objection, the material was ordered to be printed in the RECORD, as follows:

❊   ❊   ❊

THE IMPACT AND SIGNIFICANCE OF THE NEWPORT NEWS SHIPBUILDING AGREEMENT

(By Alfred W. Blumrosen, professor of law, Rutgers Law School, Newark, N.J., former Chief of Conciliations, EEOC.)

A major reason for the passage by the Congress of Title VII of the Civil Rights Act of 1964, and the establishment of the Equal Employment Opportunity Commission was that previous governmental activities had not provided full and adequate remedies for employment discrimination. The Conciliation Agreement signed March 30, 1966, by the Newport News Shipbuilding Company provided concrete and practical remedies tailored to meet the specific conditions and problems of racial discrimination in the shipyard. Under the agreement, more than 3,000 promotions of different kinds were received by the 5,000 Negro employees and 100 more are now supervisors or are in line to become supervisors. These figures are from Company records. In addition, the apprentice school has accepted nearly 50 Negro applicants, and the faculty of the school has been integrated. Lockers, shower rooms, and toilet facilities have been desegregated. A seniority system providing for future promotions on the basis of length of service and activity has been instituted.

No previous effort by the government approached this result. In achieving this result, the interest and concern of all parties—the company, union, civil rights organizations, employees, and the government—were fully taken into account. The cooperation of all these interests, while carrying out the mandate of Title VII, was the greatest achievement at Newport News.

I. BACKGROUND

The Newport News Shipyard is the largest privately owned shipyard in the free world. It employs 22,000 men, including some 5,000 Negro employees. It builds military ships, including nuclear aircraft carriers and submarines; repairs military and commercial ships and manufactures heavy machinery.

Charges of discrimination at the shipyard were filed in the late summer of 1965 with the Commission by 41 Negro complainants who work with the local chapter of the NAACP. The investigation of these complaints took place in the fall of 1965. On the basis of the investigation, the Commission found reasonable cause to believe that discrimination existed at the shipyard in the following respect:

(1) Wages of Negro employees doing the same work as white employees were lower than white employees;

(2) Negro employees were promoted at a slower rate than white employees;

(3) Negro employees were not allowed to become supervisors under like circumstances as white employees;

(4) Negro employees were restricted in their access in the company's apprentice program; and

(5) Locker rooms, shower rooms, and toilet facilities were segregated.

In November 1965, a conciliation effort was made by the Commission. It was rejected by the company and union. The Commission referred the case to the Attorney General with a recommendation that a "pattern or practice" suit be instituted under section 707 of the Act, and notified the charging parties of their rights to sue. They instituted a section 706 suit in the federal district court in Norfolk, Virginia, with the involvement of the Legal Defense Fund, Inc.

In March 1966, the Company learned that the Attorney General planned to institute suit and that the Department of Labor was considering suspending future government contracts. The company then sought to negotiate with the government. Assistant Attorney General John Doar decided to allow the opportunity for negotiation before filing suit. It was decided that EEOC would lead the negotiation with the participation of Justice, the Department of Defense, and the Department of Labor.

Initial conciliation proposals were developed by Alfred Blumrosen and Kenneth Holbert and refined by the EEOC staff. These proposals were then submitted to the other government agencies and accepted without substantial changes. The Department of Labor issued a letter suspending further government contracts as the negotiations began. The negotiations themselves consumed most of the last part of March. They were headed by Alfred Blumrosen, who was then Chief of Conciliation. They concluded on March 30 with the signing of the agreement. The Labor and Defense Departments accepted the agreement as a comprehensive plan to eliminate discrimination which justified the withdrawal of the suspension from government contracts. On the basis of the agreement, the Justice Department concluded that it would not institute suit. The agreement paved the way for the dismissal of the civil suit brought by the charging parties.

The signing of the agreement paved the way for its administration. First steps were quickly taken. Facilities were integrated and the parties moved toward the selection of the expert who had been assigned several tasks under the agreement. Case and Company, a management-consultant firm recommended by the shipyard, was selected and began to work. During the summer and fall of 1966, many problems arose which were hammered out in negotiation sessions between the Commission and the company. These sessions took place frequently.

The Peninsula Shipbuilding Association (PSA) which represented the employees, attacked the agreement at first. After several conferences with the Commission and the company, PSA, in late summer, signed an agreement with the company which recognized the conciliation agreement. Since then, the union has processed more than one hundred grievances relating to the conciliation agreement. By signing the agreement, the union relinquished whatever legal objections it might have asserted in connection with the conciliation.

In the winter of 1966, the administration of the agreement lagged with respect to the identification of Negro employees who were to become supervisors. This project was the responsibility of the Department of Defense under the agreement. Due to the pending reorganization, DOD could not devote adequate manpower to this project. EEOC Chairman Shulman and Mr. Moskowitz of DOD agreed that five DOD personnel would be detailed to the Commission for one month to conduct the administration of this phase of the agreement. Mr. Blumrosen assumed personal direction of this effort and, at the end of March 1967, secured agreement of the company to promote seventy-five Negro employees to supervisors, in addition to the twenty-five already promoted. The Commission then indicated that, except for certain problems, the administrative phase of the agreement was concluded.

The administration of the agreement was hampered by lack of adequate manpower. But all parties were understanding of the limitations of the Commission. The Negro employees and the NAACP understood that the Commission could devote but limited personnel to the administration of the agreement, and were patient with the Commission. The union came to understand that the Commission did not wish to supplant it as the representative of the employees, but rather was interested in seeing PSA act effectively on behalf of all employees. The company became aware that the Commission was sensitive to its basic needs and was prepared, in the administration of the agreement, to make adjustments to meet those needs as long as the basic thrust of the agreement was not blunted.

II. PROBLEMS, SOLUTION, RESULTS

There follows a table indicating the nature of the problems of discrimination at the shipyard, the solution reached in the conciliation agreement, and the results of the application of the act:
[The table is reproduced in the text, *supra* at pp. 347–50. The article concludes:]

III. SIGNIFICANCE OF THE AGREEMENT

The working out of the agreement has significance in several respects. First, it suggests that problems of employment discrimination can be solved through coordinated governmental activities, given the firm and courageous administration of Title VII. Secondly, it suggests that this can be done without serious harm to the interest of employers. Third, it suggests that in such actions, white employees may benefit as well as Negro employees. The addition of a system of seniority promotion and the posting of job vacancies is inured to the benefit of both Negro and white employees at the shipyard. Fourth, the agreement demonstrates that it is possible to design and execute practical remedies to eliminate the present effects of discrimination. Fifth, it suggests that employers need not await Commission action before adopting a management program to improve their employment practices.

Many employers have been greatly impressed by the detailed and technical approach in the conciliation agreement. This has facilitated acceleration of their own programs to eliminate discrimination, and in this sense is now a model for elimination of discrimination in employment. Other government agencies, Justice and OFCC, are using the agreement as a model as is the Commission. The agreement will continue to have these far-reaching implications in eliminating employment discrimination for years to come.

The agreement represented true government action. It was the only time during my stay in government when Justice, DOD, OFCC, and EEOC worked together with such harmony and unity. The result of this cooperation was truly striking. The moral is clear. The interlocking and mutually reenforcing joint action of these agencies can produce, under present laws, clear, complete, and meaningful remedies which will eliminate employment discrimination.

Appendix IV: Congressional Record

(daily edition) Sept. 18, 1967, S13106

OFFICIAL BIAS

MR. FANNIN. Mr. President, on August 8, 1967, I placed in the RECORD an article entitled "Official Bias," published in *Barron's National Business and Financial Weekly*. The article reported that the Equal Employment Opportunity Commission had coerced the Newport News Shipbuilding & Dry Dock Co., into signing an agreement which called for favoring Negroes in its hiring policies and with respect to its apprenticeship school—thus instituting a policy of discrimination in reverse. According to the report, this so-called agreement, in large measure, precipitated the first work stoppage in the company's 81 years of existence.

Subsequently on August 22, a statement by way of reply to this article was placed in the RECORD. Among material inserted to attempt to buttress this reply were the text of the conciliation agreement and an analysis of the background of the signing of the agreement written by professor Alfred Blumrosen, apparently the chief architect of the terms.

I had not seen either of these two documents before, and I am glad that they have been printed. They are shocking. To me the situation is worse than I originally thought. In fact it seems to me that the article in Barron's, told only about half the story for a careful reading of this material, leads inevitably to certain conclusions, which I ask unanimous consent to have printed in the RECORD.

There being no objection, the items were ordered to be printed in the RECORD, as follows:

(1) That the Equal Employment Opportunity Commission in negotiating this so-called "agreement" has in many respects completely exceeded any authority granted it under Title VII of the Civil Rights Act of 1964.

(2) That this so-called "agreement" was brought about by the most flagrant governmental coercion that has ever come to my attention. Had it been brought into being through the actions of any one other than a govern-

ment agency, it could have been characterized as "blackmail" and probably subject to nullification by court action.

(3) That this "agreement" implemented in accordance with its terms would result in what might be termed "reverse discrimination" to the disadvantage of all personnel except nonwhites singled out for preferential treatment.

(4) That since it is proposed that this so-called agreement be utilized as a model for elimination of discrimination in employment by not only the Commission but other government agencies such as the Department of Justice and the Office of Contract Compliance, a full and complete examination of the administration of Title VII of the Civil Rights Act of 1964 is in order to determine whether or not the administration of this Title by the EEOC is consistent with the authority granted it by the Congress and with the principles of fair play and due process of law.

MR. FANNIN. Mr. President, a brief reference to the contents of the aforementioned documents will demonstrate the validity of the conclusions I have outlined above.

It seems clear from Professor Blumrosen's analysis that the complaints in this case were in some measure simulated since he notes that "charges of discrimination at the shipyard were filed in the late summer of 1965 with the Commission by 41 Negro complainants who work with the local chapter of the NAACP." There followed an investigation by the Commission and in November 1965 a conciliation effort was made by the Commission which was rejected by the company and the union. Professor Blumrosen further states that in March 1966 the company learned that the Attorney General planned to institute suit "and that the Department of Labor was considering suspending future government contracts." The company then sought to negotiate with the government and Assistant Attorney General John Doar "decided to allow the opportunity for negotiation before filing suit," and it was then decided that the EEOC would lead the negotiation "with the participation of Justice, Department of Defense, and the Department of Labor."

Subsequently, the Department of Labor did, in fact, issue a letter suspending further Government contracts with this company as the negotiations began.

Given this kind of governmental pressure on a company almost totally involved in Government contract work, it is not surprising that an agreement was reached. Following the conclusion of the agreement, the Department of Labor came to the conclusion that this would justify the withdrawal of the suspension from Government contracts and, further, on the basis of the agreement the Justice Department concluded that it would not institute suit. In addition, it is stated by Professor Blumrosen that "by signing the agreement, the union relinquished whatever legal objections it might have asserted in connection with the conciliation."

Without question, this is governmental coercion of the highest order and

I am completely at a loss to find anywhere in Title VII of the Civil Rights Act of 1964 any such coercive authority granted to the EEOC.

Of equal importance, however, are some of the terms and conditions which apparently were insisted upon by the EEOC for inclusion in the so-called conciliation agreement.

For example, the company is required within 45 days of the date of the agreement to "retain at its expense an expert in job evaluation and statements of work content, knowledgeable in race relations who is acceptable to the Commission" to make a review of the company's personnel practices to determine whether non-whites are in any fashion being discriminated against. I am not aware of any statutory language in Title VIII which would authorize the Commission to require employment of an outside "expert" to examine a company's practices.

The company would then be required to implement the decision of the expert "by reclassifying such employees and/or adjusting the rate of pay accordingly within a period of 30 days from the date of determination." The company is further required to supply this said expert with adequate staff and facilities and to make available all records and other information necessary to the performance of this function.

This "expert," incidentally, must be acceptable to the Commission, and the profile of employment practices is to be developed jointly by this expert and the Industrial Employment Policy Specialists, Department of Defense, presumably without regard to company participation. In other words, the company would in effect be required to turn over to one outside expert and a group of individuals from the Defense Department the authority to analyze and change in any way they saw fit the personnel and employment practices of a company which has functioned for over 80 years without ever having had a strike.

Again, I am unable to find any such statutory authority in Title VII of the Civil Rights Act.

It should be noted that approval by the Commission is required at almost every step in this agreement which means, of course, a veto power over any actions which may be taken by the company. Continuing surveillance and participation by the Commission in company personnel actions is clearly provided for during the life of this agreement.

It is impossible to read this "agreement" without coming to the conclusion that it amounts to what might be called discrimination in reverse. Without question, this agreement makes other than nonwhite employees of this company the more or less "forgotten" man insofar as any protection he may seek pursuant to this agreement.

Notwithstanding statutory provisions designed to prevent the granting of "preferential treatment" to any individual or to any group because of his race, color, religion, sex, or national origin, this very preferential treatment is provided for in many sections of the agreement. As just one instance, in section 3(c) it is provided that "employees in predominantly Negro departments shall be given the first opportunity for training in programs in which they are qualified to enter." If I understand this correctly, this means that other than nonwhites need not apply, which to me is discrimination in reverse.

One of the most flagrant examples of abuse of authority by the Agency is found in section 4 of the Conciliation Agreement dealing with Adjustment of Rates and Promotional Opportunities.

Under this section, the so-called expert and the "Industrial Employment Policy Specialist" establish a profile of the rate and conditions for promotions for white employees, a so-called norm. Thereafter, a Negro employee who has not moved up through the grades as rapidly as the "norm" for white employees would be assigned "the first grade in the job classification or such other grade as he would have achieved had his history followed" the norm. Section 4(f) states "conditions of the employee's skill and ability are not germane to this section. The burden of demonstrating that from company records that the employee should not be upgraded is on the company."

As a further example, in section 4(h):

If the evaluator finds that the Negro employee has such qualifications for promotion or can achieve them through reasonable training, he shall be placed on a preferential promotion list and given at an appropriate time such training as may be reasonably necessary to equip him for promotion. Such promotion shall be given when need arises for additional members of the next higher class.

As is well known, the Congress in Title VII specifically provided that comparisons with, or quotas related to, the percentages of various races in the available work force in any community, State, section, or other area could not be required. Notwithstanding this, the Commission in section 5(d) of this "agreement" included a section which in practical operation would have no other effect. The section is as follows:

The parties to this agreement recognize as a natural result of this recruitment effort that the ratio of Negro to white apprentices in any given year should approach the ratio of Negro to white employees and the ratio of Negro to whites in the labor market area but this provision should not be construed to require or permit the rejection of any qualified applicant on the basis of his race or color.

Obviously, the disclaimer in the last few lines is designed to try and bring this provision within the language of the statute. I submit, however, that this comes in the "fine print" category and would be of questionable effect in forestalling the basic purpose outlined in the earlier part of this provision.

The company is further required to waive some of its statutory rights provided in Title VII as set forth in Section 7 (d) and (e) of the agreement which states as follows:

d. Cooperate with the Equal Employment Opportunity Commission with regard to the investigation, conciliation, and processing of the charges of 38 other charging parties without regard to the time limitations of Section 706 of Title VII.

e. With regard to certain charging parties, waive the statutory period within which the charging parties may institute a civil action in the event conciliation is not achieved.

This statutory period was inserted by the Congress with a definite design and purpose to eliminate stale claims and, in effect, fix a statute of limitations within which complaints must be filed. Notwithstanding, the Commission arrogates onto itself by the device of this so-called agreement to nullify the statutory protection provided by the Congress.

The foregoing is only a brief and quite incomplete indication of the lengths to which the EEOC has gone in bringing about this coercive agreement without statutory authority and in many cases in complete disregard of the language the Congress enacted. To me, the conclusion is inescapable that before the authority of this Commission is in anywise broadened a close examination of this Commission's activities is required in order to determine whether and to what extent the Commission is circumventing and ignoring the intent of Congress when it enacted Title VII of the Civil Rights Act of 1964.

Mr. President, finally I ask unanimous consent that there be printed in the RECORD *Barron's* reply to the charge that the EEOC was unjustifiably criticized. This is an excellent reply and points up a frightening situation:

BARRON'S REPLY TO THE CHARGE OF UNJUSTIFIED CRITICISM OF THE ROLE OF THE EQUAL EMPLOYMENT OPPORTUNITY COMMISSION AT THE NEWPORT NEWS SHIPBUILDING & DRY DOCK CO.

Barron's remains convinced that the Equal Employment Opportunity Commission (EEOC) was the principal villain in the first strike in the 81-year history of the Newport News Shipbuilding & Dry Dock Co. The record proves beyond doubt that the EEOC seriously damaged labor-management relations which heretofore had been noted as a model of harmony. It also created racial unrest and caused employee morale to sink so low that it resulted in a substantial drop in productivity. Under such conditions, it is not surprising that grievance procedures, which always had worked in the past, were inadequate to avert a strike.

Significantly, the dispute which led to the walk-out began in the company's transportation department, which has a work force comprised 80% of Negroes. In addition, the union meeting which passed the strike vote was attended 85% by Negroes, and we have pictures to prove it.

Under the threat of withholding federal contracts, which make up most of the business of Newport News Ship, EEOC ordered it unilaterally to take certain so-called antidiscriminatory actions. The Commission moved without even consulting the Peninsula Shipbuilders' Association (PSA), the independent union which represents most of the 22,000 workers at the yard.

This was in violation of the National Labor Relations Act, which says a company must not change working conditions or pay without bargaining with the certified representative of the workers. Too, the Commission violated an order of the National Labor Relations Board certifying the PSA as the sole collective bargaining agent of the employees of Newport News Ship.

Thus the company had conflicting orders from two federal agencies, with one saying the firm should change working conditions only after bargaining with the PSA and the other saying it would put it out of business unless it changed them immediately.

When our editorial was written, Luther Holcomb was acting chairman of the EEOC. Barron's asked him how he could expect a firm to follow conflicting orders from two federal agencies. He emphasized that PSA was an independent union. "If the AFL-CIO had been involved, we probably would have had the head of the AFL-CIO Civil Rights Division, in," he declared. He abruptly terminated the interview when asked why he didn't perform the same courtesy for an independent union.

(According to Don Slayman, Director of Civil Rights for the AFL-CIO, his organization had threatened to handle the matter through litigation unless the EEOC carried out its obligation to discuss discrimination with both a company and a union.)

The EEOC publicly humiliated the PSA and got it in bad with the Negroes who make up 35% of its membership, to say nothing of the rest of the members who saw the union contract ignored. At the outset, the Commission gave the impression that it would take care of the Negroes where the PSA had failed. Understandably, this split the union between blacks and whites. However, both soon learned of the perfidy of the EEOC.

After the agreement was completed with Newport News Ship, the Commission belatedly acknowledged its error in ignoring the union by making it a party to it. But when the PSA tried to take an active part in handling cases of alleged discrimination, it was balked by the EEOC. The former filed 83 complaints with the Commission over six months ago and has yet to hear anything on a single complaint.

Linwood Harris, the Negro co-manager of PSA, told Barron's, "We're left as the fall guy because the EEOC doesn't act."

Kenneth F. Holbert, EEOC Acting General Council, says the agency just hasn't had time to get around to handling the complaints but admits there is a legal limitation of 60 days for it to do so.

Understandably, PSA officials do not share Mr. Holcomb's enthusiasm over the benefits of EEOC's activities at Newport News Ship. Mr. Harris declares, "The good the EEOC has done is minute and not worth it because of the bad they've done."

PSA President Leonard Gauley says, "They've stirred up a hornet's nest that was completely unnecessary."

PSA Co-Manager Robert M. Bryant says, "the EEOC is a complete farce" and that it has brought about the end of an era for both the company and its employees.

One employee after another told us they'd never seen anything like it— that EEOC upset everyone.

Under such circumstances, it is not difficult to see why a union might concentrate on grievances involving a department made up largely of Negroes. And with workers in a state of turmoil incited by the EEOC, it is not hard to understand why a strike ensued.

We notice that the EEOC does not deny that Commissioner Samuel C. Jackson called for militancy in the community; we don't see how it can, since it was a speech at a public NAACP meeting. We also notice that EEOC does not deny that it sent representatives to knock on doors in Negro neighborhoods in Newport News to solicit complaints of job discrimination.

Commissioner Jackson also stirred up trouble by making false charges. In the aforementioned speech, he declared, "I have investigated discrimination complaints all over the nation, and never have I seen such massive discrimination in my life as at Newport News Shipbuilding & Dry Dock." This hardly tallies with a later EEOC conclusion that Newport News Ship was not guilty in a single instance of failing to give equal pay for equal work.

Heaping coals on the fire, exaggerations and false claims followed the false charges. Commissioner Jackson said the company's Apprentice School did not have a single Negro teacher out of nearly 500 instructors. The union subsequently pointed out, "At last count, we didn't have 500 students in the Apprentice School."

Mr. Jackson claimed that at least 5,000 Negroes (the total number of Negroes employed by the yard) would receive substantial raises as the result of the Commission's work.

On May 1, 1967, Secretary of Labor W. Willard Wirtz and Stephen N. Shulman, then EEOC Chairman, announced that 3,890 Negroes had been promoted at Newport News Ship because of federal action to insure equal employment practices. Both union and management say this figure is false, and they have told the government so. As noted in our editorial, the union threatened legal action to set the record straight.

According to both labor and management, the 3,000 merit increases were regular ones and at a volume established long before the existence of EEOC. A grand total of 155 employees received raises as a result of the agreement. In addition 250 Negroes were put on preferential lists for promotions when openings occur.

PSA Co-Manager Bryant told Barron's that any time the Secretary of Labor will claim 3,890 promotions under an agreement which actually produced 155, "I've got a lot of reservations about whether he should be the Secretary of Labor."

In the face of criticism from both management and labor, we note that Mr. Holcomb now claims the agreement produced 3,000 promotions rather than the 3,890 claimed by Messrs. Wirtz and Shulman and the 5,000 promised by Mr. Jackson.

EEOC also brought about a further deterioration of labor relations at Newport News Ship by forcing discrimination in favor of Negroes. No white employee may be promoted until the preferred promotion list of Negroes is exhausted unless the EEOC gives express permission. Moreover, during the year it took to draw up that list, EEOC did not allow the yard to make any permanent promotions. Many employees told Barron's that this alone seriously damaged employee morale.

The agreement further promotes reverse discrimination by stating that Negroes shall have the first opportunity to participate in training programs provided by the company. It assigns legal status for the selection of apprentices to civil rights organizations listed by the EEOC. In authorizing them to send "qualified applicants" to the Apprentice School, the EEOC, in effect, has established privileged groups of private employment agencies for Negroes.

The agreement also says that Negroes shall be promoted as rapidly as whites as shown by a sample of white promotions and that "consideration of the (Negro) employee's skill and ability are not germane to this section."

In view of the documentation presented here, it is almost incredible that Mr. Holcomb would say, "The Newport News agreement indicated significantly how sound governmental action taken in cooperation with interested parties can solve problems of employment discrimination and can do so without serious harm to the interest of employers and that in addition, benefits can result for white employees as well as for Negroes."

As noted, the EEOC action was not taken in cooperation with all interested parties—if one considers the union an interested party. According to PSA Co-Manager Bryant, the first word the union had of the completed agreement was in a national announcement on April 2, 1966. The PSA did not receive a copy of the agreement until two days after the announcement.

Mr. Holcomb's claim that there was no serious harm to the employer also is without substance. Donald A. Holden, President and Chairman of the Board of Newport News Ship, told Barron's that productivity went down as a result of the EEOC because people were upset. "I think it cost us in seven-figure kind of money in a year," he declared.

We fail to see how Mr. Holcomb finds benefits for white employees since, as noted, the EEOC is discriminating against them.

In conclusion we would like to call attention to an article in our issue of October 17, 1966. We mentioned that antipoverty and civil rights workers were campaigning to take over management of Greenbelt Consumer Services, Inc. One of the candidates of the insurgents for the board of Greenbelt was Timothy L. Jenkins. According to literature distributed by his sponsors, he was a Deputy to the EEOC and also "has held responsible positions in such groups . . . as the Federal Programs Section of the Student Non-Violent Coordinating Committee." While Mr. Jenkins no longer is with the EEOC, the records of its personnel office indicate he was serving as consultant to the chairman when the Commission was working on the Newport News case.

Appendix V: Reflections on the Newport News Agreement

by Alfred W. Blumrosen

Senator Fannin has raised some important questions concerning the agreement between the Equal Employment Opportunity Commission and the Newport News Shipbuilding and Dry Dock Company in the Congressional Record of Sept. 18, 1967, S. 13160-0- (daily ed.). This agreement, along with an explanation of its impact and significance was inserted in the Congressional Record by Senator Javits on Aug. 22, 1967, pp. S. 12001-07 (daily ed.). The agreement, which was negotiated by EEOC with the cooperation of the Departments of Justice, Labor, and Defense, resulted in major changes in the industrial relations system at the shipyard, eliminating the remnants of discriminatory patterns, and led to the promotion of some 3,000 Negro employees.

Senator Fannin suggests that the agreement is defective in three respects; (1) it was brought about by governmental "coercion," (2) the EEOC exceeded its authority under the Civil Rights Act of 1964 in negotiating certain provisions and (3) it would result in "reverse discrimination" by giving preferential treatment to Negroes. These are serious matters which deserve full consideration because of the important principle involved in the Newport News agreement.

This principle is that all concerned Federal agencies may join in negotiating with an employer or other respondent who is subject to federal law, an effective and comprehensive plan for the elimination of patterns and practices of discrimination; and may administer that plan and review compliance with it to assure that the promise of the laws against discrimination are carried out in the day to day life of the work place. This is what happened at Newport News. The importance of this principle cannot be underestimated. It is basic to the assumption that problems of discrimination can be solved through lawful processes. That assumption in turn is fundamental to the insistence on the maintenance of law and order.

The necessity for broad remedial programs such as that at Newport News is clear. If the government is confined to the remedying of individual cases of discrimination, the antidiscrimination laws will not work. Newport News is the symbol for governmental action to correct discriminatory employment practices throughout an entire establishment. The broad principle that the EEOC will seek to change entire systems, and not restrict itself to individual complainants cases, underlies the Newport News agreement.

This principle is both explicit and implicit in Title VII of the Civil Rights Act of 1964. Congress made the following points very clear in that statute:

(1) The Congress was concerned with the elimination of employment discrimination in individual situations (sec. 706).

(2) Congress was concerned with the elimination of patterns and practices of discrimination (sec. 707, 706(e)).

(3) The Congress desired appropriate coordination between various agencies of government involved in the elimination of discrimination. (sec. 706 (b)-(d) [state agencies], sec. 709 (d), 703 (b) [federal agencies], sec. 705 (g) (1), 705 (i), and 716 (c) [all public and private agencies]).

(4) Congress wished the details of the solution to the problems of discrimination to be worked out through negotiation and conciliation, if possible, rather than by litigation. (Section 706 (a) provides that if the Commission determines there is reasonable cause to believe a respondent has committed an unlawful employment practice, "the Commission shall endeavor to eliminate any such unlawful employment practice by informal methods of conference, conciliation and persuasion.")

(5) In reaching solutions to problems of discrimination, Congress envisioned that employers and other respondents would take "affirmative action" (sec. 706 (g) to effectuate the policies of the act).

It is therefore appropriate to deal with each of the issues raised by Senator Fannin.

1. *The "coercion" issue.* Senator Fannin suggests that the government "coerced" the agreement.

The Commission lacks coercive powers. EEOC cannot "order" anyone to do anything. It has no sanctions at its disposal. The Labor Department— Defense Department decision to suspend contracting with Newport News was neither disputed nor litigated. The power has been in existence for a number of years and has been recognized by the Congress. (See sec. 709 (d), which refers to the President's Committee on Equal Employment Opportunity, which had this power. The existence of the PCEEO or its successor is assumed in the cited section.) The private lawsuit which had been filed against Newport News had not come to trial. Each federal agency involved was carrying out its appointed function.

The Newport News Shipbuilding Company is the largest single employer facility in the state of Virginia. It is headed by highly competent management, and has been entrusted with the task of building a major part of the naval forces of the United States. Its counsel is an outstanding and distinguished attorney. The Company was not without resources to protect its interests against "overreaching" by the federal government. The Company demonstrated industrial statesmanship of the highest order, when it chose to solve its problems, rather than litigate concerning them.

The Peninsular Shipbuilders Association (not affiliated with the AFL-CIO) is represented by able and aggressive officers and counsel. Fully aware of the channels of recourse open to it, the Union chose to adopt the agreement rather than challenge it. It made this decision months after the agreement was executed. This too was industrial statesmanship.

Thus the suggestion of coercion appears to be without foundation. The doors of the federal courts were at all times open to both Company and Union to prevent overreaching by the government. Where competent and resourceful parties who are fully capable of exercising their rights preferred to settle the matter rather than litigate, there seems little room for the suggestion of coercion.

This disposes of the "coercion" issue, except for the suggestion that the agencies, EEOC, OFCC, DOD, and Justice, "ganged up" on the Shipyard. It is true that the activities of these agencies were coordinated; but this should be applauded, rather than condemned. There are serious problems of duplication of effort, of overlapping activity by various agencies in the Equal Opportunity field. These activities may have the effect of burdening respondents with repeated investigations by different agencies, and may lead to the uneconomical allocation of government resources. Coordination of various agency activities is desirable. In fact, had there not been coordination, it is quite possible that the agencies would be criticized for duplication of activity, wasting scarce government resources and imposing unnecessary burdens on employers and other respondents.

2. *The "excess of authority" issue.* This breaks down into a review of four aspects of the agreement: (a) the provision for the retention of an expert, (b) the provision for promotion of Negro employees who had been promoted at a slower rate than whites, (c) the provision for recruitment of apprentices, and (d) the waiver of the statute of limitations with respect to certain claims.

a. *The retention of an expert.* The agreement to retain an expert to review the rate and conditions of promotion of Negro employees was a major innovation in the field of race relations. Did the negotiation of a provision for such an expert, which provided that the parties would, within limits, be bound by his decisions exceed the authority of the Commission under Title VII?

First, under section 705 (g) (1) and (3), there is authority in the commission to utilize private agencies and individuals, which would include the "expert." Second, and far more important, Congress clearly intended that the difficult and complex problems of discrimination be resolved through conciliation. Conciliation presupposes the adoption of practical measures to solve problems of discrimination. The retention of the expert was such a practical solution. The alternatives to this solution were not inviting. They were either a time-consuming case-by-case investigation of thousands of employment records by government personnel or the conduct of such an investigation through the judicial processes of discovery and trial. Both of these alternatives would have plunged the employer, the government, and the charging parties into interminable proceedings which would have been costly, would have engendered hostility, would have taken extensive time of overcrowded federal courts. Such proceedings might well have exacerbated the dispute rather than resolved it.

The agreement followed many precedents in the field of labor-management relations in that the parties submitted their dispute to an outside expert acceptable to both. The expert selected, Case and Company, is a nationally known managment consulting firm which was suggested by the Company and found acceptable by the Commission. Case and Company brought a technical expertise to bear on their enormous problems at the shipyard. While it is unlikely that either the government or the Company agreed with all of the conclusions of Case and Company, both believed that their overall interests would be served by acquiescing in the conclusions reached by the expert.

Senator Fannin expresses concern that the Commission reserved the right to review the decisions of the expert. This reservation was essential. The Commission has been charged with the duty of enforcing Title VII prior to litigation and may not delegate that authority to a party not of its own choosing. Congress would have been critical, and properly so, of any such delegation. In fact, in most of the issues which arose during the administration of the agreement, the government and the Company accepted the conclusions of Case and Company. Where this was not possible, they negotiated a settlement of the issues. In retrospect, the use of the expert was one of the most satisfactory aspects of the agreement.

The language of the statute, the intention of Congress, the concept of conciliation, the experience in other areas of labor relations and the practicalities of the situation all combine to sustain the conclusion that the agreement to retain the expert to evaluate employment practices was appropriate under Title VII.

b. *The provision for promotion of Negro employees.* The Senator expresses concern with paragraph 4 of the agreement which provides a procedure for determination of whether Negro employees were promoted at a slower rate than white employees and remedies by way of promotion and preparation for promotion. The immensity of this undertaking is demonstrated by the fact that there are 5,000 Negro employees at the yard. To apply the Commission finding that Negroes were generally paid less than whites and promoted at a slower rate than whites was a monumental undertaking. If the procedure used had not been adopted, there might have been thousands of individual complaints, each going through a formal procedure. The procedure avoided this piece-meal approach in favor of a general systemwide review.

Once it was determined that Negro employees had been promoted at a

slower rate than whites, the provision for a remedy by way of either immediate or prospective promotion was obvious. There is clearly nothing "preferential" in this solution.

c. *The recruitment of apprentices.* The Shipyard conducts an apprentice
school, which is a four-year technical college. In its history, it had had six
Negro students at the time of the negotiation of the agreement. The student
body numbered nearly 500. The agreement provided for recruitment efforts
to increase the proportion of Negro students. In an area where Negroes make
up between twenty and twenty-five percent of the population and the labor
force, it was certainly appropriate for the shipyard to engage in "affirmative
action" in recruiting (see sec. 706(g)). Many employers which had engaged
in "affirmative action" had, in the experience of the Commission, hired only
a token few minority employees. It was important, therefore, to make clear
that the recruiting effort was not to be token. Thus the language expressive
of the long-range goal, suggesting that the "natural result" of the recruitment effort would be that the ratio of Negro to white apprentices would
approach that of Negroes and whites in the labor market area. In no sense
is this a quota. No court called upon to interpret it would call it a quota. No
one is entitled to an apprenticeship because of it. It is designed to make clear
what Congress expressed in the phrase "affirmative action" in section 706(g).
What is required is meaningful compliance with the statute, not tokenism.
This compliance will be measured by the extent of the performance, not the
language of the promise.

(d) *The waiver of the statute of limitations.* Senator Fannin was further
concerned with the agreement of the shipyard to waive the statute of limitations with respect to some individual cases which were not resolved at the
time of the conciliation agreement. This waiver provision was inserted for
highly practical reasons. The basic agreement had been hammered out in
several days of hard negotiation. It did not serve the interest of any of the
parties to delay the execution of the agreement for the additional time it
would take to resolve these remaining cases. The waiver of the statute makes
it feasible for the parties to execute the agreement with the understanding
that these other cases would be promptly disposed of. This is what in fact
happened.

Statutes of limitation are often waived by the parties when it is in their
interest to do so. In this case, the waiver facilitated the signing of the basic
agreement without further delay. It enabled the respondent and the government to take such additional time as was necessary to work out settlements
of these additional issues, without forcing the charging parties in those cases
to file law suits to protect their rights under Title VII.

Congress certainly did not intend that an employer who was cooperating
fully with the government should be unable to enter into agreements which
would extend the time for settlement of issues. If the respondent could not
waive the statute of limitation, then charging party would be forced to file
suit to protect his legal rights, even though it was clear that good faith nego-

tiations were proceeding toward a settlement which was likely to be satisfactory. This unnecessary litigation was certainly not desired by a Congress
which sought for solutions through conciliation. The statute must be read so
as to facilitate negotiation, not to encourage litigation. Since waivers provide
additional time for negotiation, they should be favored, not discouraged.
The provision in the Newport News agreement was aimed at supporting the
congressional policy in favor of a negotiated settlement in these cases.

3. *The "reverse discrimination" issue.* This is an important issue which
must be understood in the terms set by Senator Fannin. His conclusion is:

> That this "agreement" implemented in accordance with its terms would
> result in what might be termed 'reverse discrimination' to the disadvan-
> tage of all personnel except nonwhites singled out for preferential treat-
> ment.

This problem has several aspects.

a. *Remedying discrimination is not preferential treatment.* This is an
obvious fact which can be easily illustrated in other fields of law. If A and B
are both employees in a factory and the roof collapses, injuring A but not B,
due to the employers negligence, everyone would understand that A could
recover but B could not, because A was injured and B was not. No one
would say that A got preferential treatment over B because A recovered
either in tort or in Workmen's compensation payments. A was made whole
for the injury which the employer had caused. B, not having been injured,
received nothing. So too in the case of discrimination. The remedy runs in
favor of the minority employee because he has been injured. The administration of an appropriate remedy for him does not constitute "preferential treatment" at all. If an employer has been paying Negro employees less than
whites doing the same work, then he should raise the wages of the Negro
employees. The fact that white employees do not get raises at the same time
does not constitute "preferential treatment" of the Negroes. In fact, the argument that it does constitute preferential treatment is in effect, an argument that the white employees should continue to get more than Negroes for
doing the same work. But the phrase "preferential treatment" cannot be
used to support the claim of a white employee that he would be better off if
the employer continued to discriminate against minority group employees.
Title VII mandates the elimination of discriminatory treatment, and will not
permit its continuation under some other label. Remedying discrimination
does not constitute "preferential treatment."

During the period of administration of the agreement, there were constant promotions of both Negro and white employees. It was simply not the
case that only Negro employees were recruited as apprentices, promoted to
higher positions and to supervision. There was no "reverse discrimination."

b. *Sensitive administration required.* The parties faced many difficult
practical problems during the year after the signing of the agreement. These

problems were discussed extensively in both Washington and Newport News. From these meetings flowed adjustments and refinements which no one had anticipated during the negotiation of the agreement, which were necessary for its successful administration. It is possible that a rigid unthinking bureaucracy could have turned the agreement into an unworkable instrument. But this did take place. The administration of the agreement was sensitive to the practical needs of the parties, as the settlement of the promotion to supervisor question indicates. The proof of this lies in the affirmative results of the agreement.

Conclusion

Senator Fannin suggests several additional points. If they are each discussed, the document becomes unduly extended. If they are not, it may be challenged as failing to meet the issues. While I am prepared to deal with these other issues, my analysis will follow that used above.

The critics of the agreement also face a dilemma. Either the government was too "coercive" and achieved "too much" preferential treatment or the government bungled and accomplished nothing. The critics simply cannot have it both ways. I submit that the truth does not lie in either of these positions. The simple fact is that the agreement was successfully negotiated and administered to carry out the congressional purpose of eliminating employment discrimination, by agreement if possible, but by the force of law if necessary. The good faith of the Company was very important in the execution of the agreement, and I hope these discussions do not embarrass it unduly.

The government learned many things through its experience with Newport News. It learned that cooperation among agencies was possible; that a written agreement requiring far-reaching changes in an employer's industrial relations system was practical and would produce meaningful results. The Commission re-examined its procedures to assure that no question of inadequate consultation with labor organizations would arise in the future.

There is serious and deeply felt doubt in the land that the law is capable of coping with and resolving problems of discrimination. This doubt is expressed in the universities, the meeting halls, and, sometimes, on the streets. Newport News stands as the principal evidence that the law can solve these problems. The support for this proposition is worthy of our greatest effort.

Appendix VI: Congressional Record

(daily edition) Feb. 29, 1968, H 1536
Enforcement of Civil Rights Legislation

❖   ❖   ❖

MR. RYAN. Mr. Speaker, throughout America today public officials are echoing the call for law and order. But for all the talk about riots in the cities and crime in the streets, seldom is there a mention of a fundamental hypocrisy in law enforcement. Despite legal prohibitions against racial discrimination, discrimination persists without effective legal redress. America remains a white man's society where Negroes and Spanish-speaking Americans are short-changed. Until civil rights laws are vigorously enforced, black America can hardly be expected to have faith in white America.

In no area is this hypocrisy more apparent than in job discrimination. In no area is the right to equal treatment more clearly written into law and public policy. And in no area is the law less enforced.

In Newark, which exploded in riot last summer, construction projects will soon begin using Federal funds under the model cities program. The work force, constructing the buildings in full view of passersby, will be almost entirely white. Unemployed Negro residents, many of whom were driven by despair to the point of rioting last summer, will witness an almost all-white work force in jobs paying $6 and $8 an hour in their own neighborhood, knowing that these jobs are barred to them. The irony of public officials who call for law and order, but fail to uphold laws guaranteeing equal treatment is not lost on the ghetto.

❖   ❖   ❖

EXECUTIVE ORDER 11246

Executive Order 11246 was issued by President Johnson in September 1965. It is the latest in a series of orders dating back to 1941, which prohibit job discrimination by Federal contractors.

Unlike previous orders, 11246 covers not only employment directly related to the particular contract involved, but all employment in companies with United States Government contracts in excess of $10,000. In this way, the order is estimated to cover one job in three in the national economy, or between 20 and 25 million jobs out of 74.1 million jobs.

The language of Executive Order 11246 is unambiguous. It specifies that language shall be written into Federal contracts providing that:

The contractor will not discriminate against any employee or applicant for employment because of race, creed, color, or national origin. The contractor will take affirmative action to ensure that applicants are employed and that employees are treated during employment, without regard to their race, creed, color, or national origin.

The order also requires contractors to furnish the Government with a breakdown of racial employment data. Agency contract reviews are mandated, whether or not there have been specific complaints. And, unlike Title VII of the Civil Rights Act of 1964, the order contains a potent enforcement sanction—the withholding or cancellation of lucrative Government contracts. It provides that the Secretary of Labor or the appropriate contracting agency may—

Cancel, terminate, suspend or cause to be canceled, terminated, or suspended, any contract, or any portion or portions thereof, for failure of the contractor or subcontractor to comply with the nondiscrimination provisions of the contract.

If the administration took this order seriously, it could open new, formerly denied job opportunities to millions of Americans. Yet, the history of Executive Order 11246 is an inexcusable story of bureaucratic betrayal.

Since that order was issued in September 1965, not one contract has been canceled for noncompliance. Nor was a contract ever canceled under any of the predecessor orders.

Precious few contracts have ever been held up, even in cases of overt, documented discrimination. Companies, which have been cited for discrimination by the Equal Employment Opportunities Commission or State FEPCs or against whom the Department of Justice has brought action under Title VII of the Civil Rights Act of 1964, continue to benefit from Federal contracts in flat contravention of the order.

This leniency tells other companies, in effect, that they have nothing to fear from the order, that it is not to be taken seriously. Despite the good intentions of many equal opportunity officials, the complaint bureaucracy subverts the purposes of the order.

Under a system established in 1965, the principal enforcement body is the Office of Federal Contract Compliance—OFCC—in the Department of Labor. However, in practice, OFCC is merely a loose supervisory body, with a staff of only 12. Actual compliance enforcement is delegated to an equal opportunity program in each major Federal agency which contracts with the private sector.

This system subordinates an agency's compliance staff to officials who place the smooth flow of contracts above the promotion of job equality. The result is a dismal picture of mass tokenism. If a company can demonstrate anything remotely resembling "progress," it is usually "let off the hook." In the absence of firm support from higher officials, compliance officers are discouraged from energetic action, for their efforts will only be undermined. Where individual compliance officers here and there do make vigorous efforts to monitor contractors, they often do so at the peril of their own careers.

What has emerged instead of effective enforcement is a totally ineffective pattern of tokenism and voluntary compliance.

The so-called plans for progress program emerged in 1961 to enlist voluntary support of major companies which would declare themselves "equal opportunity employers" and pledge to recruit minority workers. More than one equal opportunity official has said that it is common knowledge that joining plans for progress enables a contractor to avoid close supervision under Executive Order 11246. In fact, plans for progress was sold to many contractors on precisely these grounds.

I do not mean to impugn the sincerity of every plans for progress employer. Plans for progress includes some genuinely progressive organizations. But it also includes companies against which the Department of Justice is proceeding, and other companies whose policies on equal employment have been deplorable.

Recent Equal Employment Opportunity Commission hearings in New York City established that out of 100 major companies, which voluntarily submitted information, the 46 which were signatories of plans for progress had minority employment records much worse than the 54 which were not. The Equal Employment Opportunities Commission report dated January 18, 1968, states:

While nonmembers had 1.2% Negroes in positions as officials and managers, Plans for Progress members had only 0.3% in these jobs.

Voluntary compliance is no substitute for enforcement. It is an easy way out, which tells minority job seekers and employers alike that the government is not serious.

On February 15, 1968, more than 2 years after Executive Order 11246 was issued, regulations pursuant to that order were proposed by the Office of Federal Contract Compliance. The Office of Federal Contract Compliance has been operating under regulations which apply to the previous order, which exempted certain categories of contracts and related to the President's Committee on Equal Opportunity. This is a sad indication of how seriously the administration takes its own order.

In the 2 years and 5 months since September 1965, when President Johnson issued the Executive order, the racial crisis has tragically deepened in large part because Negroes continue to be denied job opportunities. Recently the President announced, job opportunities in the business sector program for the hard-core unemployed, relying once again on the voluntary cooperation of the private sector, in effect cajoling industry to take minority trainees. Certainly substantial progress could be made by simply enforcing an order already on the books.

THE DOD CASE

I have said that the bureaucratic system which delegates contract compliance authority militates against effective enforcement. Let me describe, chapter and verse, the undermining and eventual dismemberment of the most effective Federal compliance program—that of the Department of Defense.

Approximately 80 percent of the dollar volume of Government contracts comes through the Department of Defense. About 20 million jobs are with companies which in one form or another do business with the Department of Defense. All of these jobs could be available on an equal opportunity basis.

For a little over a year the Department of Defense had a contract compliance program which took seriously Executive Order 11246. Beginning in October 1965, following the issuance of the order, separate Army, Navy, and Air Force compliance programs were centralized under the direction of a dedicated official named Girard Clark, with 94 men under him. The Department of Defense compliance program began reviews of all Defense contractors industry by industry. Corporations in a particular industry were reviewed at random. Where there seemed to be a pattern of job bias, employment patterns of the entire company were reviewed in depth. The company's senior officials were then told what steps were necessary in order to continue receiving defense contracts. In this way, unprecedented strides were made and employment barriers broken. In case after case, when corporations were confronted with a credible risk of loss of contract, they proved cooperative.

The BVD Co., for example, whose only link to the Defense Department was through the sale of articles to PX's and ship stores was informed that it could no longer do business with the Government until it took steps to desegregate plant facilities in the South—Pascagoula, Miss. Only after the company agreed to take the necessary action, did the Defense Department learn that it had in this way effected the first industrial desegregation in the State of Mississippi.

A few companies refused to open employment opportunities to Negroes, and they were barred from receiving further contracts. During the year in which the program was operating effectively, there were 40 top-level confrontations involving 35 companies. All but seven agreed to make the necessary changes in opening employment opportunities to Negroes.

The most spectacular and effective confrontation involved the Newport News Shipbuilding and Dry Dock Co.

The Newport News Shipyard, although a private company, depends almost exclusively upon Government contracts. In 1965, the NAACP filed complaints with EEOC, to the effect that Negro workers were barred from good jobs, paid lower wages for performing the same work, impeded from entering the company apprentice program, made to use segregated toilet and locker facilities, and other related complaints. The company initially refused conciliation. It was only after the Department of Defense and the Office of

Federal Contract Compliance threatened to refuse the Newport News Co. bids on four submarines that the company agreed to integrate its facilities and open job opportunities to Negroes on an equal basis with whites. According to Alfred Blumrosen, then Chief of the Department of Labor Conciliation Service, the Newport News case was "the only time during my stay in Government when Justice, DOD, OFCC, and EEOC worked together"—CONGRESSIONAL RECORD, August 22, 1967, S12007.

The Newport News success clearly proves that the Government has the power to open up jobs to Negroes, if it only has the will to use it.

By August 1966, when the Newport News conciliation agreement was signed, the Department of Defense compliance program was already on the way out. The program had incurred the wrath of both industry and many senior procurement officials. For example, a panic was created at the Department of Defense when sanctions were recommended against U.S. Steel for overt discrimination at the Fairfield works at Birmingham, Alabama. Although the compliance program director found that the charges were accurate, and that in no case was United States Steel the sole source of supply, top officials in the Department overruled the director of the compliance program and declined to take action.

Every time compliance officials are overruled in this way, industry is again served notice that it does not have to take the equal opportunity requirement very seriously. Every time an agency's compliance staff can be circumvented, the force of the order is undermined.

In February 1967, the DOD compliance program was reorganized out of existence. Gone was the centralized compliance office; compliance was put under the Defense Contract Administration Service, where it could no longer be an embarrassment. Actual contract supervision is now accomplished through regional procurement offices. There no longer exists an independent office within DOD which sees its task as the promotion of job equality. Compliance officers are now subordinate to procurement officers, who are much more inclined to put a premium on the maintenance of cordial relations with contractors.

The company reviews, which were an effective means of opening up job opportunities in an entire company, have been abolished. In short, the former Department of Defense compliance program was dismembered for being too effective.

In September 1967, five months after the effective DOD program was dismembered, officials of the new DOD program explicitly refused to cooperate with the supervisory Office of Federal Contract Compliance—OFCC. Specifically, they refused to inform OFCC in advance of compliance reviews, to provide OFCC with review summaries, or to notify OFCC when a defense contract officer had requested a review. DOD representatives said they regarded it "as an interference with their management prerogatives for OFCC to have any role whatsoever in the establishment of priorities, and in DOD determinations of contractor compliance."

This is a sorry contrast with the successful result of DOD–OFCC cooperation in the Newport News case a year earlier.

As an outrageous example of the failure of current DOD compliance policy, I cite the example of the Timken Roller Bearing Co., of Canton, Ohio. No less than five Government agencies have acknowledged that there is job discrimination at Timken. More than two years ago, complaints were raised that Negroes at Timken are kept in dead-end jobs, regardless of their seniority.

In the summer of 1966, complaints were filed with the EEOC and the Ohio Civil Rights Commision, both of which have since acknowledged that extensive discrimination is practiced by Timken.

The OFCC has publically charged Timken with refusal to cooperate— Wall Street Journal, November 1, 1966, page 1. The National Labor Relations Board has documented that Negroes are kept out of "white-only" job progression lines.

To this day, nearly two years after documented proof of deliberate and massive discrimination, the Timken Roller Bearing Co. continues to get government contracts.

Since the undermining of the Department of Defense program more than a year ago, a government mandate to open up millions of jobs has gone unused. A random examination of OFCC employment data on defense contractors shows hundreds of companies located in areas of Negro population concentrations, which have large payrolls and employ no Negroes whatsoever.

It should be stressed that a great many of these jobs involve skills which can be learned in apprenticeship training or on the job.

One company in New York employed over 1,000 workers throughout the State, and not one Negro. Another company in New York City employed 429 workers and no Negroes. A major airline had a payroll of 129 in New York, and no Negroes. Innumerable other companies employed Negroes, but only at unskilled or menial levels.

With many thousands of companies reporting employment data, it is inconceivable that the Department of Defense can even pretend it can fulfill its responsibility with a total compliance staff of 50. In the entire New England region there are only three DOD compliance reviewers.

9   A Survey of Remedies for Discrimination
   in the Union and on the Job

Racial, ethnic, and sex discrimination problems are now more central to industrial relations in a practical sense than ever before. This is a healthy development, though too long delayed. For the last quarter century government, labor, and management have made promises of equal opportunity. These promises were not implemented at the operational level. This period is ending as the law and the sense of public need are forcing reconsideration of industrial relations practices to root out discrimination. The history of pious platitudes of Plans for Progress, anguished affirmations of the AFL-CIO, and ringing policy statements from Congress and the President is giving way to the development of practical and enforceable remedies which will become part of the warp and woof of industrial life. Thus, for the first time, the technical problems of adjusting industrial relations are coming to the forefront, and the role of the technically competent person in labor and race relations is becoming more important. The purpose of this article is to deal with several of these practical problems of adjustment of industrial relations systems to eliminate invidious discrimination.

The federal and state legal regulations dealing with union and employer discrimination have reached the stage of maximum proliferation. The laws and their enforcement machinery include the following:

Law or Regulation	*Enforcement Mechanism*
State and local antidiscrimination statutes and ordinances	Administrative agencies—hearing and cease and desist order authority. State court review of agency action
National Labor Relations Act	National Labor Relations Board, Unfair Labor practice and decertification pro-

Law or Regulation	*Enforcement Mechanism*
	ceedings; review in federal courts of appeal; certiorari to U.S. Supreme Court
	Federal district courts open to suits for violation of Duty of Fair Representation
Civil Rights Act of 1964	Equal Employment Opportunity Commission: investigation; conciliation activity; reporting requirements
	Attorney General may sue in name of United States.
	Aggrieved parties may sue in federal court after using EEOC.
Executive order prohibiting discrimination in government contracts	Suspension of contract proceedings by Office of Federal Contract Compliance
	Suits to enforce "affirmative action" requirements
Fair Labor Standards Act: Equal Pay for Equal Work	Administrator, Department of Labor; suits in federal court
Bureau of Apprenticeship regulations	Bureau of Apprenticeship and Training; federal court review
Civil Rights Act of 1866	Direct suit in federal court
Fifth and Fourteenth Amendments to U.S. Constitution	Direct suit in federal court [1]

Professor Marshall's description of the racial discrimination problem,[2] and Professor Sovern's description of the legal system,[3] both written in 1965, remain generally valid. The major developments since these works have been written have been in efforts to bring the industrial relations systems into harmony with the requirements of the law. The task of translation of law into life, of moving, as it were, from law to

---

[1] See SOVERN, LEGAL RESTRAINTS ON RACIAL DISCRIMINATION IN EMPLOYMENT (1965). Since Prof. Sovern surveyed the law, there have been numerous important decisions under Title VII of the Civil Rights Act of 1964, two under the Civil Rights Act of 1866, Jones v. Alfred H. Mayer Co., 392 U.S. 409, N. 78 (1968) and Dobbins v. Local 212, IBEW 58 Lab. Cas. ¶9158 (S.D. Ohio 1958) F. Supp., and one under the Fourteenth Amendment, Ethridge v. Rhodes, 268 F. Supp. 83 (S.D. Ohio 1967).

[2] MARSHALL, THE NEGRO AND ORGANIZED LABOR (1965).

[3] Op. cit. supra, Note.

order, has been underway since 1965. But it is far from accomplished.

Employment discrimination will not be eradicated or heavily influenced by the passage of another federal statute or the creation of another administrative agency. We have all the regulatory machinery we need. We have identified the problems to which this machinery is to be addressed. We have been given the clearest possible policy mandate to end discrimination. Our need now is for workable solutions which change the face of the workplace, which translate law into the reality of human behavior, and which do so in the pragmatic and idealistic tradition, which has seen dramatic changes in the nature of industrial relations over the last half century.

I do not believe that, in the long run, the particular form of legal action will be too important. I think the substantive law and practical solutions will be substantially the same regardless of whether the issue is raised by individual suit under Title VII, a federal suit under Title VII, the invocation of other constitutional or statutory standards, or even the enforcement of executive orders requiring affirmative action. So I wish to focus on the substance of problems and solutions rather than on the form in which they are raised.

The following discussion assumes that illegal discrimination has been established, and that the remaining issue is one of designing an effective and appropriate remedy. Questions of "preferential treatment" and the like are not germane, for it is axiomatic that the victims of discrimination are entitled to a comprehensive, effective and immediate remedy.

I. Employer Discrimination—The Duty of Fair Recruitment[4]

The primary method by which employers discriminate against minorities outside of the south, is simply by not hiring them. Recruitment and hiring practices are established which have the effect of excluding blacks and other minorities from notice of job vacancies, and meaningful opportunities to obtain jobs. These practices range from word of mouth recruiting among employers, to preferences for friends and relatives, the use of walk-ins, advertising, and employment agencies which have traditionally produced white applicants. When these practices

---

[4] See ch. 6.

perpetuate segregated employment, they violate the Civil Rights Act of 1964. That act, I believe, imposes a "Duty of Fair Recruitment" which I have discussed extensively in chapter 6. The practical remedies for discriminatory recruitment include (a) changes in the sources from which applicants are drawn, to assure that the applicants will include minorities, (b) review and revision of hiring procedures to assure the hiring of minorities rather than paper compliance—of special importance as a remedy is the "affirmative action file" in which presumptively qualified minority applicants are listed and are hired when vacancies arise, unless the employer has an overriding reason to go outside the file—and (c) a reconsideration of the validity of those hiring standards which block minority participation in the labor force, such as educational requirements and testing programs.

II. Discrimination in Collective Bargaining Relations

The union's role in employment discrimination depends on the particular collective bargaining system of which it is a part, and on the internal history, structure and orientation of the union. Thus industrial unions have problems of discrimination in seniority systems because of the nature of their collective bargaining relationships, while construction unions and others which utilize hiring halls are enmeshed in questions of recruitment, referral, apprenticeship and membership because these issues are central to their mode of operation.

A. *Seniority Systems and Discrimination*[5]

Racial discrimination in collectively bargained seniority systems today is largely a present result of the practice of formal segregation of jobs in the South. The pattern of restricting minorities, mainly Negroes, to lower-paying, lower-skilled jobs also exists outside the South, but in less distinct manner. I think it is so clear that only the lawyers need argue about it that the present effects of past discrimination constitute present discrimination which must be remedied. The crucial issues involve the scope of remedies rather than the question of whether there

---

[5] See ch. 5.

is discrimination. On this remedial issue, there are four basic views:

(1) *Follow the white man.* Qualified Negroes can secure promotion into previous white jobs and seniority units after all white employees have received the benefits of the seniority system.

(2) *Freedom now.* Immediate displacement of all whites who can be said to be beneficiaries of discriminatory seniority systems—bumping. (This is more of a stalking horse for a less drastic position than a meaningful possibility.)

(3) *Promotion from within as rapidly as job openings and qualifications permit,* regardless of the form of the seniority system, until Negroes are no longer behind whites with lesser plant seniority.

I think some variation on this latter principle will become a part of the standard remedy in seniority discrimination cases. It has been ordered by at least two federal courts. In both the *Philip Morris* and *Crown Zellerbach* cases, the courts ordered an alteration of the seniority system to take account of the total relevant length of service of the Negro employees in their competition for previously white jobs. A collective bargaining agreement between the International Paper Company, the Paper Makers, and Paper Workers has adopted this approach.

(4) *Damages for present illegality.* If the principle of promotion from within is established, there will be financial losses suffered by Negroes who have to wait for vacancies, and by whites who may lose expectations because of Negro promotions. These financial losses may be extensive, and difficult to measure. Under these circumstances, and given the fact that the employer is also a wrongdoer in every discriminatory seniority system under collective bargaining, it is appropriate to impose financial liability on the employer to cover these costs. To alleviate the complex accounting problems which could arise, the courts and agencies may order development of and supervise the operation of an "equal opportunity fund" financed by the employer, which is designed to meet the costs of the ending of discrimination. This would be analogous to "automation funds" developed to cope with problems of technological change. I have developed this thesis more fully in chapter 5.

We have thus far considered the "length of service" component of seniority systems. But few systems overtly operate on the basis of length of service alone. There is usually a component in the seniority system of skill or ability or some other term which relates to the capability of the individual to learn or perform the job to which his length of service would presumptively entitle him. The exact relationship between length of service and ability is dependent on the collective bargaining relationship in particular cases. Whatever the relationship is, many minority employees will be at a disadvantage compared to white employees in the measurement of ability, because of patterns of discrimination either in employment or in education. If experience is used as a component for measuring skill or ability, then blacks will lose out to whites because only whites could have gained such experience in the time of overt discrimination, in which blacks were excluded from white jobs. The remedies here are threefold: (1) In comparing the ability factor, between whites and blacks, it is discriminatory to count experience gained when only whites could gain it. (2) Where at all possible, in remedying discrimination in seniority, carefully supervised probationary training periods should be provided for minorities who are entitled by length of service to upgrading. (3) The employer should be required to make upgrading training generally available to minority group employees so that when the time comes for them to exercise their newly acquired rights to promotion, they will be equipped to do so.

B. *Discrimination in Unions Which Operate Hiring Halls and/or Apprentice Programs*[6]

I believe that the questions of discrimination in the hiring hall situation will soon be resolved along the lines of the decisions in the *Asbestos Workers and Electrical Workers* cases, which rely on evidence of past discriminatory policies to conclude that otherwise ambiguous present action is discriminatory. Both of these cases involved findings that construction unions had discriminated in referral and admission-policies. The remedial problem issues are posed for us as follows:

1. Will these unions be required to recruit in the minority community? The district courts split on this. I think unions will be so required. They can do it and have done it successfully this year.

2. Will the unions be allowed unfettered discretion in administering

---

[6] See Ch. 7.

admission standards? If the administration produces substantial numbers of minorities, the answer is yes; otherwise the answer is no.

3. Will referral systems have to be modified to permit referral of minority persons ahead of present members and referees? It does seem clear that the union which has discriminated in the past must yield up, not only its restrictive membership system, but also preferences on job referrals to the white members based on experience gained at a time when Negroes were excluded. I believe that the practice of favoring resident active members of the local for referral may have to yield temporarily to the necessity of curing historic discrimination against Negroes. This is a complex matter requiring careful adjustment in particular cases.

4. Will the union have to yield control over the size of its membership? It would be realistic for unions which had excluded minorities to adopt a policy of admitting them until such time as it can no longer be said that the union is practicing racial exclusion. At that point, the basic union interest in keeping the size of the labor supply limited can be asserted without the involvement of the racial question. A union which does not adopt this policy must face the prospect of admitting both majority and mimority members in numbers it cannot control. The *Asbestos Workers* case is a forerunner of this development in that the court order required the union to submit a plan for the development of its membership in relation to projected needs of the trade.

III. Government Payments for Training Minorities

The latest direction of government in the antidiscrimination field is to pay companies and unions to train the unemployed. The problems of discrimination are, in this view, considered as part of a national manpower problem, to be dealt with by general manpower programs. Sometimes, this approach leads to the award of substantial training contracts to employers who have discriminated against minorities. Philip Morris was awarded a major training contract shortly after being found in violation of the Civil Rights Act by a federal court, and I have heard of a union or joint apprenticeship council receiving a training grant *during* its trial for violation of the Civil Rights Act.

I do not believe in vengeance and do believe in redemption, and do believe in a national manpower policy, but I hesitate to reward discriminators with Manpower Development and Training Act contracts unless those contracts are a part of a broad, carefully detailed and supervised companywide program of affirmative action. In the past, we had to rely on sanctions rather than rewards to secure socially acceptable behavior, because we did not have the resources to purchase it.[7] Today, in the affluent society, I suppose we can afford to purchase decent behavior to some extent. Yet, as we now know, our resources are limited, and I would prefer to see training contracts placed with good guys if they can be found, or at least with those seeking redemption.

Putting aside the above problems, I think it is important to measure the operation of these training programs, as they affect minority employment opportunities, by the test of the results. If these programs ameliorate the differences in minority and majority unemployment rates, and if this result cannot be achieved with less expense in other ways, then I will accept this approach with as good grace as I can muster. It is clear that the vast network of laws and agencies have not achieved the results which they were supposed to achieve. And it is true that, up to now, the law of enforcement approach has failed to solve the problems of discrimination in industrial relations. I attribute this to feeble enforcement of these laws, which, to an important degree, was the result of activities of labor and management who have resisted vigorous law enforcement.

Perhaps providing economic incentives to provide equal opportunity will help achieve what the law has been unable to compel. I have grave reservations as to whether any program which is not accompanied by vigorous law enforcement will succeed. I do not argue for vigorous law enforcement alone, but I believe it is a necessary condition for the success of any sophisticated program designed to improve the conditions of minorities in industrial relations. I am proud of the only major agreement I negotiated for the EEOC in the steel industry in Birmingham, which incorporated an MDTA training program as part of the settlement which opened previously white jobs to blacks. The MDTA training was to be considered by the employer in assessing whether an applicant for a position had the requisite ability under the seniority clause of the collective bargaining agreement. Thus the Negro employees could compete with whites in regard to the ability factor in

---

[7] BLACKSTONE, COMMENTARIES, vol. I, §2 (Sharswood, ed. 1904) at 54.

seniority for previously white jobs, even though only whites had prior experience on those jobs because of the historic exclusion of Negroes.

But I do not think there would have been *any* agreement in that case if the Negro employees had not complained to the EEOC under Title VII of the Civil Rights Act of 1964, if the EEOC had not found reasonable cause to believe the statute was violated, and if the complainants, through the NAACP, had not brought suit in the federal court. These factors enabled management to decide to solve, rather than perpetuate, the problems of discrimination in this establishment.

And so, I support the integration of manpower programs into the administration of antidiscrimination laws, and am prepared to view the antidiscrimination laws as a branch of national manpower policy. The role of the law is to shape the matrix in which the industrial relations community will resolve specific problems utilizing all of its understanding, skills, and programs.

A graduate of the University of Michigan, where he secured his bachelor of arts and doctor of jurisprudence degrees, Alfred Blumrosen began his practice of law in Detroit.

Since 1955 he has been a member of the faculty of Rutgers Law School, Newark, N.J., and a visiting professor at Louisiana State University and Howard University.

He has also served on the New Jersey Mediation Board, the Federal Mediation and Conciliation Service, the panel of arbitrators of the American Arbitration Service, and been a consultant to the New Jersey Civil Rights Commission, the Office of Equal Opportunity of the Department of Housing and Urban Development, and to the Office of Federal Contract Compliance of the Department of Labor.

Professor Blumrosen is the author of numerous articles on employment discrimination and labor relations and is coeditor of *Labor Relations and the Law*.

The text of this book was set in Caledonia Lino-type and printed by letterpress on Warren's # 1854 Regular Text manufactured by S. D. Warren Company, Boston, Mass. Composed, printed and bound by H. Wolff Book Manufacturing Company, Incorporated, New York, N. Y.